the glorious world of golf

Special Material. THE NEW Warranted Well Seasoned.

a ridge press book

the
glorious
world
of
golf

by
peter
dobereiner

special
photography
by
norman
snyder

amlyn · london · new york · sidney · toronto

Editor-in-Chief: Jerry Mason
Editor: Adolph Suehsdorf
Art Director: Albert Squillace
Project Art Director: Harry Brocke
Associate Editor: Moira Duggan
Associate Editor: Barbara Hoffbeck
Art Associate: Mark Liebergall
Art Associate: David Namias
Art Production: Doris Mullane
Picture Research: Marion Geisinger

Prepared and produced by The Ridge Press, Inc.
Published by
The Hamlyn Publishing Group Limited
London • New York • Sydney • Toronto
Hamlyn House, Feltham, Middlesex, England.
ISBN 0 600 33943 2
Printed and bound in Italy by Mondadori Editore, Verona.

For the golfing orphans, Jane and Ruth

contents

introduction 8

1 · the loneliest game 10

2 · how golf invented the scots 34

3 · action in america 66

4 · a universal passion 106

5 · secrets of the great courses 130

6 · of hickory and steel 150

7 · superstars 170

8 · the circuit 194

9 · royal and ancient … and antic 226

index 247

foreword

The Basset hound is a foolish dog and mine is a particularly stupid example of the breed. As I write she is crouched in the far corner of my study staring at me in suspicion with watery, bloodshot eyes. Already I can see by her furrowed brow that she thinks she has seen me before but can't quite place the face. When the moment of recognition dawns she will explode into violent activity and go tearing around the house knocking over small pieces of furniture in elephantine ecstasy and baying fit to wake the dead. A mile away across the valley the people in the village will know that I am home.

By now I have come to accept the experience of being snubbed by my own dog as an occupational hazard. In two weeks we will have another of these strained reunions. And so it will go on all year. The life of a professional golf writer seems to me in my blacker moments to be spent entirely in airport lounges listening to announcements to the effect that his flight has been delayed yet another five hours. I calculate that in one year I fly 70,000 miles, drive 20,000, and cover 10,000 miles by train. That's just getting to golf courses. Once there I walk a distance equivalent to hiking from New York to Waco, Texas, just watching other people play golf.

There is a truism in this business that the professional golf watcher never catches the action. I could write a volume on Great Moments in Golf I Have Missed. When Tommy Bolt hurled his wedge into the lake (well, one of the times anyway) I was two fairways away. When Arnold Palmer hit his shot-of-the-century at Royal Birkdale I was temporarily absent in the men's room. And at the time Brian Barnes was taking fifteen strokes on a par-3 in the French Open I was covering an amateur tournament in a different country.

With a game like golf that kind of thing is inevitable. Even so, I have seen many strange and wonderful events. And, perhaps even more rewarding, I have talked with many strange and wonderful people. In Portugal, respectfully seated at the feet of the Master, I have listened to Henry Cotton expound on the virtues of a dominant right hand in the golf stroke. In Florida I have dutifully recorded Lee Trevino's dissertation on the need for a dominant left hand. And in Melbourne I have sat with notebook agog as Peter Thomson demolished both theories with a sardonic laugh.

These, then, are my credentials for writing this book. I do not speak with the authority of a great player. What small facility I once had for the game has long since been lost in the turbulence of jet travel and the lack of playing opportunities. But I think I can truthfully claim that my enthusiasm for golf has not dimmed with overexposure.

Possibly I no longer thrill to a shot which pitches a yard past the flag, takes one bounce, and then screws back to the hole. The galleries go wild with delight, but now that I have analyzed the mechanics of such shots with a hundred different professionals my sense of wonder is attuned to subtler aspects of the game.

Although this book is not a history of golf, a certain proportion of it is devoted to the past because I feel this to be important. Let us take the analogy of a gourmet in a Chinese restaurant. Would he enjoy his egg more if he knew that it had been set aside specially for his delight a hundred years previously? I think he would. And I believe that those of us who play golf get a similarly enhanced pleasure from knowing something about the traditions and history of golf, and about some of the early exponents of the game, and about how the other half of the golfing world lives.

My life in golf has been a rewarding experience. My hope is that some of that pleasure will rub off onto anyone who may read this book. If it gives enjoyment in the reading, or if its afterglow heightens the enjoyment of playing the game, then it will have served its purpose.

April, 1973   Peter Dobereiner

1 · the loneliest game

What is golf? The question is easier asked than answered. Golf defies definition, although plenty of good men have tried. Arthur Balfour wrote, with the pomposity befitting a statesman: "A tolerable day, a tolerable green and a tolerable opponent supply—or ought to supply—all that any reasonably constituted human being should require in the way of entertainment."

On close examination that statement tells us more about politics than golf. Look at the care with which the words have been chosen to provide escape clauses. It might have been framed to resist attack by the militants of the Anti-Golf Party.

"Is the Prime Minister claiming golf to be the perfect form of entertainment?"

"No, sir! If the honorable gentleman will study my statement, he will notice the reference to 'reasonably constituted human beings.' I would not recommend golf to members of the Opposition."

Laughter, jeers, and cries of "Withdraw."

"Does the Prime Minister mean that for reasonably constituted human beings *like himself* golf is all the entertainment they ever require?"

"Again I would draw the honorable gentleman's attention to what I actually said. I have never suggested that in all circumstances. . . ."

And so on. Strip the qualifications from Balfour's definition and you are left with the insipid message that people who enjoy golf are occasionally happy to play. What profundity!

Bobby Jones, who wrote about golf almost as well as he played it, never attempted a definition. The nearest he came to encapsulating golf was in occasional reflective asides on aspects of the game, such as, "Golf, in my view, is the most rewarding of all games because it possesses a very definite value as a molder or developer of character. The golfer very soon is made to realize that his most immediate, and perhaps his most potent, adversary is himself." The

wisdom of this remark will quickly become obvious to anyone who takes up the game. It will do for a start.

Let us try a writer. A. A. Milne put it: "Golf is popular simply because it is the best game in the world at which to be bad." Now we are getting somewhere. Here is a bone on which we can chew, plus a meaty morsel of paradox. It is obviously true that in the army of golf the majority of players are humble private soldiers, the happy hackers, while the noncommissioned officers and the brass, the scratch golfers and lordly professionals, are serious fellows for whom golf provides more satisfaction than fun.

There comes a stage in the progress of a golfer which is the equivalent to winning his stripes. At this point he ceases to savor the good shots and starts instead to grieve over the bad ones. The hacker expects to hit bad shots. They are his natural stock-in-trade. Consequently, when he does fire off the rare winner, with the ball coming flush off the clubface and flying straight at the target, he experiences a glow of satisfaction which is positively sensual. He can savor the delicious memory of that one shot for a week.

For the good golfer such shots are normal. The ball flies straight(ish) and true(ish) most of the time. Some are better than others, but for him the exceptional emotion is disappointment. After a round, the scratch man kicks the door of his locker and curses the hooked drive into a pond which cost him a 6. The 24 handicapper comes in almost incandescent from the afterglow of that five-iron to the short hole which finished six feet from the flag. Never mind that he three-putted—that is beside the point.

How did the scratch man play that particular hole? "You mean the seventh? Oh, yes. Seven-iron and then my ten-footer lipped out. How they expect you to hole a putt on these damned greens, I don't know. I've told them a thousand times to lower the cutters to five thirty-seconds and cross-mow against the grain."

*Preceding pages: Blast! Golfer suits his action to
the word at Hilton Head, South Carolina.
For once, the violent banging of a club into the ground
may release trapped ball as well as emotions.*

12

Yes, the privates are the happy ones. Or are they? What wouldn't that hacker give to hit the 7th green with a seven-iron as a matter of routine. You name it—anything.

If the legend of Dr. Faustus were applied to golf we would quickly get to the truth about the game. The Devil offers a deal. In return for the deed to your house, your handicap comes down by four shots; exchange your bank balance for another four shots; throw in your wife and you can be scratch. . . . There would soon be a dramatic improvement in golfing standards—played by morose, divorced paupers. As with Wellington's army, every golfing private carries a field marshal's baton in his golf bag.

Perhaps the historian, Sir Walter Simpson, was nearer the truth with his bleak statement that "excessive golf dwarfs the intellect." Certainly, golf makes idiots of us all at times. However, let us take refuge in that word "excessive," since excess in anything is harmful. Simpson was writing in the context of match play and suggesting that it was prudent to bet on the dull-eyed fellow who did not have the wit or imagination to feel the destructive psychological pressures of golf.

There is a grain of truth in that idea. Certainly, many a golfer has been destroyed more by his own sensitivity than by the course or his opponent. But it is a matter of simple observation that the very best players are highly intelligent men who recognize the demons conjured up in their own imagination and face them squarely for what they are. The unimaginative clot with a sound method can make a good golfer, but it takes brains to make a great one.

You might think that the obvious place to find a satisfactory answer to our question, "What is golf?" could be found in the rules of the game. The laws are so complex that of the world's forty million players there are probably fewer than one hundred with a comprehensive knowledge of all the tangled legal ramifications. What other game comes to a complete halt while experienced professionals send for expert advice as to the correct procedure for them to follow? However, Rule 1, which is the nearest thing you can get to an official definition of golf, is relatively straightforward: "The game consists in playing a ball from the teeing ground into the hole by successive strokes in accordance with the rules. Penalty for breach of rule: Match play, loss of hole; stroke play, disqualification."

That flat statement, which has a certain elegance in its extremes of banality, does not get us far. It does raise the intriguing question of how you can possibly break this rule. In the preamble to the rules we are told: "Every word means what it says." That's clear enough.

There must be a reason for the rule, because it did not appear in the early codes of the game. At some time it became necessary for the legislators of the game to frame this law to the effect that the first rule of golf is that the game must be played according to the rules. And this is followed by a glorious rule giving a scale of penalties in cases where the lawmakers have not made any rules.

No wonder golfers are not too well versed in the rules. However, in the wider sense of our question, "What is golf?" the rules do supply one clue, albeit a false one. That first rule is headed "The Game." And one point on which all golfers can immediately agree is that, whatever else golf may be, it is not a game. How much simpler life would be if it were just a game, like tennis.

Anyone for golf? Off we go for a quick eighteen holes and then throw the clubs into a cupboard and forget them until the mood returns. It is all too rare for golf to hold its victims so lightly. For convenience we call it a game. It is supposed to be a game. But in reality, whatever else it may be, golf is not a game. The word "game" means a leisure activity performed for enjoyment in competition against an

HOLDING CLUB—CORRECT POSITION.

FIRST LESSONS IN GOLF.

BY CASPAR W. WHITNEY.

PROBABLY there is no game, unless it be court-tennis, that requires so complete a mastery of first principles and such faithful practice in its rudimentary strokes as golf. The elementary instruction of every game is of course most important, and its thorough adaptation by the pupil necessary

FRONT VIEW—BEGINNING OF THREE-QUARTER SWING.

FRONT VIEW—ENDING OF THREE-QUARTER SWING.

to the development of highest skill. In golf, however, as well as in tennis, one may never acquire consistent form if he has not started off properly. He may ride a bicycle, play lawn-tennis, baseball, box, and even fence in a duffer sort of way, yet make a fair showing and have good sport, but he cannot play golf until he has mastered the very first strokes. Herein lies the fascination of the game, which, while appearing so simple to the on-looker, becomes most difficult when he takes a club and makes his first attempt at driving off the tee.

It is not that there are so many intricate rules in golf, but the few must be mastered thoroughly, and it is well for the beginner to remember that one of England's champions declares it takes six months, playing three times a week, before one may be said to have acquired consistent form.

First of all let me say that no single chapter can give all the instruction necessary to cover the different strokes and situations arising in golf. This paper is intended solely for beginners, to whom I shall hope to give a few suggestions founded on sorrowful experience and a careful study of the game in its home. The illustrations of positions are from instantaneous photographs of Willie Dunn, son of the famous Willie Dunn deceased, contemporary of "old" Tom Morris, with whom he had many a golfing battle over Scotland's links. Dunn's form is said—by those who know—to be the very best, and we commend a study of the photographs to American golfers.

CHOOSING CLUBS.—The golfer of to-day uses more iron clubs than formerly, probably because of the substitution of gutta-percha for feather-stuffed leather balls, but more largely on account of the ingenuity of manufacturers, that has provided different-shaped heads for different "lies" of the ball. Then, too, experience has taught that certain situations require heavier and stiffer clubs for the best work. Really good clubs are hard to get, and the beginner will do well to trust their purchase to some one who is experienced. They must not be too heavy, else they overbalance the player, but

the shafts should be stiffish and of hickory, which is commonly used and the best. Orange wood and ash have been employed, but neither is so good as hickory. The heads of the wooden clubs should be of beech; other woods are harder, but it is not well to have it so, as the driving quality is lessened thereby. Remember, the more the face is laid back on all your clubs, the higher they will loft the ball. Straight-faced drivers and brassies drive farther and tend to more accurate play. Do not use extreme clubs of any kind; choose the one that experience has taught is the best for the play, and if you do your part properly the club will do the rest. There is somewhat of a fad among inexperienced players to buy, for large sums, clubs that professionals have used; but it is a futile extravagance; you may get just as good ones if you use judgment in their selection. The number of different clubs put on the market of late years is considerable, and new patents are constantly being taken out, but, as a matter of fact, seven are all any one needs, viz., driver, brassy, cleek, iron, lofter, mashie, putter.

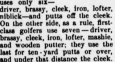

Willie Dunn uses only six—driver, brassy, cleek, iron, lofter, niblick—and putts off the cleek. On the other side, as a rule, first-class golfers use seven—driver, brassy, cleek, iron, lofter, mashie, and wooden putter; they use the last for ten-yard putts or over, and under that distance the cleek.

Driver.—Wooden club used off the tee, and thereafter whenever the lie is good enough. There are two kinds—straight-faced and bulgers; the latter, from the oval conformation of the head, are more difficult to handle, but, if you hit true, are better for straight driving. Beginners had best use straight-faced ones until they are absolutely certain of hitting where they aim. The bulger is only for the skilled player. Pick out a stiffish club, and execute the waggle to see how it feels in the hands—it should have a pronounced pliability down towards the head.

Brassy.—Wooden club, soled with iron, to be used where the lie of ball is not good enough for driver or the distance is less than full drive. It should be shorter and stiffer of shaft, and more laid back in face to raise the ball.

Cleek.—Iron club used for worse lie than brassy and shorter distance. Beginners are apt to use it for all driving, which is a mistake. If you cannot handle the regular driver (also a mistaken basis to start from, because you should persevere until you can manage it), have one made with shorter and stiffer handle. It is bad to begin your driving off iron. The cleek should be shorter than brassy,

FRONT VIEW—BEGINNING OF HIGH-LOFTING STROKE.

FRONT VIEW—FINISH OF HIGH-LOFTING STROKE.

you can use metal for short putts, and add a wooden one to your clubs for long ones.

HOLDING CLUB.—Do not grip the club tightly, nor yet loosely; the dividing line is narrow but distinct. You should feel the shaft with fingers and palm more firmly with left than right hand. Have the hands close together, the right in front of left; remember that every inch separating them means yards off the flight of ball. A loose grip argues uncertain driving; too tight with right hand, a tendency to slice the ball. Mr. Hutchinson and Willie Dunn advise both thumbs over the club, the left a trifle more so than right.

ADDRESSING THE BALL.—It would take a chapter alone to comment on the many different styles of addressing, and as it is not a matter of great importance it would be space wasted. There is altogether too much made of this incident to driving. A certain amount of it is good, but too much is—not precisely bad,

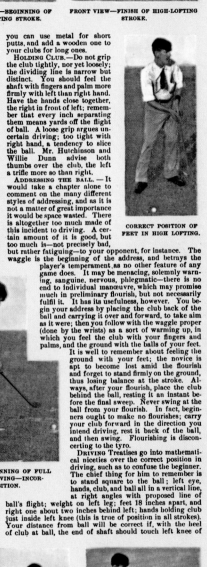

CORRECT POSITION OF FEET IN HIGH LOFTING.

but rather fatiguing—to your opponent, for instance. The waggle is the beginning of the address, and betrays the player's temperament as no other feature of any game does. It may be menacing, solemnly warning, sanguine, nervous, phlegmatic—there is no end to individual manœuvre, which may promise much in preliminary flourish, but not necessarily fulfil it. It has its usefulness, however. You begin your address by placing the club back of the ball and carrying it over and forward, to take aim as it were; then you follow with the waggle proper (done by the wrists) as a sort of warming up, in which you feel the club with your fingers and palms, and the ground with the balls of your feet.

It is well to remember about feeling the ground with your feet; the novice is apt to become lost amid the flourish and forget to stand firmly on the ground, thus losing balance at the stroke. Always, after your flourish, place the club behind the ball, resting it an instant before the final sweep. Never swing at the ball from your flourish. In fact, beginners ought to make no flourishes; carry your club forward in the direction you intend driving, rest it back of the ball, and then swing. Flourishing is disconcerting to the tyro.

DRIVING Treatises go into mathematical niceties over the correct position in driving, such as to confuse the beginner. The chief thing for him to remember is to stand square to the ball; left eye, hands, club, and ball all in at right angles with proposed line of ball's flight; weight on left leg; feet 18 inches apart, and right one about two inches behind left; hands holding club just inside left knee (this is true of position in all strokes). Your distance from ball will be correct if, with the heel of club at ball, the end of shaft should touch left knee of

FRONT VIEW—BEGINNING OF FULL SWING FOR DRIVING—CORRECT POSITION.

BACK VIEW—BEGINNING OF FULL SWING FOR DRIVING—INCORRECT POSITION.

and shaft stiffer. Choose thick heads, always remembering what is gained in loft is lost in distance. The blade is narrower than that of the lofter or iron; in fact, it has the straightest face next to putter.

Iron.—Shorter and stiffer shaft, and face more laid back than cleek. Is used for shorter distances than that club, and for playing out of long grass or what is called a bad lie. There are three kinds—driving, lofting, and heavy. Choose a medium one, with face not too straight nor too much laid back.

Mashie.—Compromise between iron and niblick, and has come to be used very generally now in place of the latter. Shorter and stiffer than iron, face laid farther back. Used for shorter strokes and for getting out of bunker, rut in road, long grass, or very bad lie. Beginners had better stick to iron, as the face of mashie, and especially of niblick, is so small as to require accuracy in hitting, though they pitch the ball dead.

Lofter.—Face most laid back of all the clubs. Used by experienced players with great skill in pitching ball dead on approach shot. Used largely for getting out of sand and over hazards; generally where it is desired to raise the ball in its flight.

Putter.—There has always been considerable controversy over the relative merits of the iron and wooden putter, and some of the old Scotch school have never become reconciled to the more modern metal. It is very generally conceded, however, by first-class players that wooden is best for long putts, and iron for short ones. The latter is a trifle laid back, and puts a drag on the ball, making it run off closer to the ground. When you become a veteran

FRONT VIEW—PUTTING. CORRECT POSITION.

FRONT VIEW—PUTTING. INCORRECT POSITION.

LOFTING A STIMIE.

THE WAGGLE.

FRONT VIEW—GETTING OUT OF A BUNKER.

players as he stands upright. Incidentally, remember, as distance for stroke decreases, have the ball nearer right toe.

The closer the feet the freer the swing, but if too close, the driving is apt to be weakened and inaccurate; with feet far apart, the player becomes stiffened, shortening the drive, though gaining great power. In the swing, bear in mind that as your club goes up so it will come down; slow up swing, relatively speaking, is a *sine qua non* of fine driving. Regard the left arm as part of the club, and keep it taut. The greatest amount of practice is necessary to allow arms to swing well away, and yet bring them down and in, for the club must be travelling in the intended flight of ball when brought down. Mr. Horace Hutchinson, whose Badminton volume is far and away the most complete, instructive, and interesting of anything published on the game, explains this point clearly thus: Take a spot on the ground, and then draw away your club. You will find the only way to extend the proposed line of flight, *backward*, is to straighten out the arms well; if you bend them, you find the head of club leaving the line. In the up swing, left arm should rest comfortably across chest, slightly bent at elbow; do not pause at top of swing; increase speed as you bring club downward, and get in your power when about 18 inches from the ball.

At the moment of hitting the ball you must be in precisely the same position as at the time of addressing it. This is the difficulty of golf, and can only be acquired by patient, persistent practice. There is no short-cut to golfing success. Remember to *sweep* away the ball, a sort of scythe motion; the beginner is likely to think only of hitting it; never jerk your club except in bunker or similar hazard. Do not tighten up when you strike the ball, nor try to knock it out of sight. Be easy, follow the ball with your club, and keep your feet on the ground. Hit fairly, clearly, firmly, not wildly.

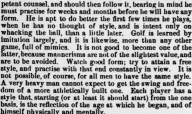

FRONT VIEW OF FEET FOR DRIVING—CORRECT POSITION.

Do not bother about too much detail at first. A beginner is likely to ask and be given no end of confusing and oftentimes worthless advice. He should seek competent counsel, and should then follow it, bearing in mind he must practise for weeks and months before he will have any form. He is apt to do better the first few times he plays, when he has no thought of style, and is intent only on whacking the ball, than a little later. Golf is learned by imitation largely, and it is likewise, more than any other game, full of mimics. It is not good to become one of the latter, because mannerisms are not of the slightest value, and are to be avoided. Watch good form; try to attain a free style, and practise with that end constantly in view. It is not possible, of course, for all men to have the same style. A very heavy man cannot expect to get the swing and freedom of a more athletically built one. Each player has a style that, starting (or at least it should start) from the one basis, is the reflection of the age at which he began, and of himself physically and mentally.

There is a great deal of buncombe about the waggle and style, the importance of both being greatly exaggerated. What the beginner need concern himself about is to get accuracy; keep the club travelling in the direction of the ball after the strike, and follow with the body; get the shoulders into the sweep, the entire body, in fact; bear weight on left leg at the address, transferring it to right on up swing, and again to the left as the ball is swept away. Let the lifting of knee and left heel on up swing be incidental to the swing, *i.e.*, you must not set out to do it—it will come in season. Stand steady, feeling the ground with your feet, keep direction of swing right, and the eye *always* on the ball. Above all, keep your mind on the business of the moment; think of what you are trying to do; beginners are inclined to fancy golf so simple as to require no special mental application. Never play weakly; remember the length of swing and not strength of sweep regulates carry of the ball. Use weaker clubs instead of making weaker effort. A full shot is the full swing: three-quarter shot, shoulders do not turn, work being done by arms, legs, and hips; half shot, use arms from elbow-joints only; quarter shot is chiefly made by wrists.

Concentrate your efforts on learning to get the swing (no matter whether you hit the ball or not at first, hitting is of small importance compared with get-

ting the swing properly), to drive straight; play out of a bad lie and loft out of a hole. When you can do these things in some degree of form you may call yourself a golfer. It is not enough to learn to drive. You must drive straight, that is important, else you get off the course, and lose considerably. This is where the value of accuracy makes itself apparent. Remember the injunction not to use the cleek for driving, and remember also, if you do, that the "divots" (sods) you cut out should be replaced at once. Practise with the driver until you master it—in fact, make it a point to take that club which puzzles you and work with it until you control it.

Most golf play is made up of driving, iron play, and putting, and of these driving is the most pleasing. Iron clubs are much the best for approaching the putting green, and you should endeavor always to lay your ball dead.

An approach shot is one within sixty yards of the green, and it is difficult play. Only your instructor can give you the practical instruction that is needed here. But bear in mind that in all iron shots you play off your right foot—*i. e.*, right foot in advance (whereas in driving left foot is in advance), weight on left leg—ball distant the length of

BACK VIEW—ENDING OF FULL SWING AFTER DRIVE—CORRECT POSITION.

FRONT VIEW—ENDING OF FULL SWING AFTER DRIVE—INCORRECT POSITION.

BEGINNING OF HALF IRON SHOT. CORRECT POSITION.

ENDING OF HALF IRON SHOT. CORRECT POSITION.

club to left knee, as in driving, and on a line that would run about midway between feet.

Putting is the least interesting and very important, though

BACK VIEW—BEGINNING OF FULL SWING FOR DRIVING—CORRECT POSITION.

FRONT VIEW—BEGINNING OF FULL SWING FOR DRIVING—INCORRECT POSITION.

many ignore, or rather slight it, because of the difficulty, which is greater than in driving. Many a game has been won on the green. Practise long and carefully, but be sure you have a well-balanced club. Hit smoothly without jerk. Putt with the wrists. Let the club work from them, in fact, as a pendulum. Assume a position from which you can best send the putter straight as it meets the ball. Stand open, half facing hole, weight slightly on left leg, right foot in advance, ball equal distance between feet. In short putts of three or four yards and less, rest right elbow on thigh; be sure of the *exact* spot on putter that will hit the ball; hold club with both hands equally, and always "be up"—*i. e.*, putt strong enough to reach the hole. It is better to pass it than not strong enough to reach it.

The pleasure of golf depends very considerably on the quality of ground. Your links must not be too easy, nor yet too difficult, and the carries (distances from tee over bunker) should not be too long, so that the medium driver may have a chance. There should be plenty of hazards, so arranged that every hole is guarded. In fact, for good golf a difficulty should be put in the way of every shot. Putting greens (and our American ones, generally speaking, are very poor) should be about thirty yards in diameter, and the hole ought to be moved when worn. Greens should be absolutely clear of obstruction and as smooth as possible. I mention this because so many that are planning home-made links seem to think the green should have its share of trials. There is tribulation enough on the green without increasing it by hazards. In building bunkers throw up the ground on the farther side, so the excavation becomes part of the hazard; the bunker should slant from the player (not straight-faced), and the bank be wide.

FRONT VIEW OF FEET FOR DRIVING—INCORRECT POSITION.

I follow with a few definitions in reply to the many letters received on the subject. *Links* is the course of holes—18 being the regulation, but 12 is the largest number on any links in America, though Shinnecock intends lengthening its 12 to 18. *Tee*—starting-point. *Caddie*—generally speaking, the boy that carries your clubs—on the other side, however, he is often counsellor and father-confessor. To *foozle* or *duff* a shot means to bungle it. *Topping*—not hitting well behind the ball. *Slicing*—bringing club down with a cut instead of squarely. *Heeling*—hitting ball with heel of club. *Toeing*—hitting with toe. *Fore* is called at the time of driving to warn players in front of you.

Two holes up means you are leading the opponent by two holes. *Dormie*—when you are leading your opponent by as many holes as there are left to play, so that were he to win all remaining, he could only tie you; for instance, if you were two-up and two to play.

Stimie is the situation where your opponent's ball is between yours and the hole, and more than 6 inches separating the two balls. You are obliged to loft over it; if the balls were within 6 inches of each other you could remove opponent's ball while you played.

He whose ball is behind always plays first.

Those on putting green are entitled to hole out before following ones play up to it.

Players in front are each entitled to second shot before following players tee off.

Do not talk while player is making his shot. Keep away 5 to 6 yards, and stand at side—never behind.

Never go on green while others are playing there. A four

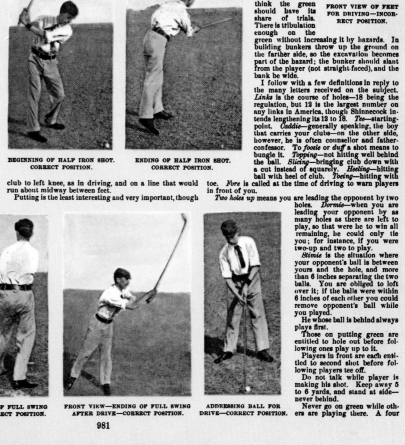

BACK VIEW—ENDING OF FULL SWING AFTER DRIVE—INCORRECT POSITION.

FRONT VIEW—ENDING OF FULL SWING AFTER DRIVE—CORRECT POSITION.

ADDRESSING BALL FOR DRIVE—CORRECT POSITION.

opponent. When Jones plays Smith at tennis this definition usually applies. They play against each other, enjoy the recreation, and eventually one of them wins.

But what happens when Jones and Smith go to golf? Jones plays against Jones, while simultaneously Smith does battle with Smith. Each man is involved in a struggle with himself, trying to discipline his muscles and control the seething anarchy in his mind. In golf, as Bobby Jones has shown us, every man is his own opponent and it hardly matters what his human adversary is doing. Nobody influences what happens to your ball except yourself. There are no high-kicking serves or cunning drop volleys to counter. The ball sits there quite still and, it seems at times, insolently mocks you. If you don't hit it properly it is no one's fault but your own. There are no excuses in golf, although man exercises his ingenuity to find them.

No matter how we may tell each other that we had a stinking bad lie or, as with the P. G. Wodehouse character, we were put off by the uproar of the butterflies in the next meadow, we know deep down that we fluffed it. Golfers are almost pathological

about cursing their luck. What they are really doing, of course, is trying to salvage the last shreds of their self-esteem. When all else fails—when the lie is palpably good and even the butterflies hold their racket for the moment—the golfer who misses the shot is forced to the ultimate desperation of blaming his failure on supernatural forces. Bad luck. Some people may even convince themselves for the moment that they are indeed the victims of malicious forces. But deep inside the golfer the dreadful truth, too shaming to admit even to oneself, registers on the subconscious.

"Whom do you think you are kidding?" asks Subconscious. "Mea culpa. It wasn't bad luck, but bad me. Idiot me. Stupid, uncoordinated me. How is it possible that a genuine half-wit, like that young assistant pro, can score almost as low as his I.Q., while an intelligent, strong, and virile fellow like me can't break a hundred, even playing Mulligans?" Conscious self says, "It will be better next time. I can do it." Subconscious self knows that it will be as bad as ever, for subconscious self is the saboteur who causes those shanks and feeble, half-topped drives.

17

Early fanaticism: in print—with Harper's *1894 instruction (preceding pages); in fun—Scotland's "Golf-Stream" (opposite above); in extremis—drawing by A. B. Frost (bottom); and in frustration—with a cruel lie (above).*

It is, then, in the murky regions of the psyche that the competitive element of golf is found. This is why golf is the loneliest game and why, once the conflict is joined, it grips with obsessional power. It may even explain the bittersweet story of the man who was bitten by the golfing bug early in life but could never really get the hang of the game. For forty years he played three times a week at his club without any distinction at all. Fate smiles occasionally on all of us and it is true that on several occasions this golfer played the first seventeen holes in quite respectable figures. Once, in his middle seventies on a calm summer evening, he needed a 4 at the last to equal par. This 18th was not long, only 380 yards, but it was an old-fashioned blind hole and reputedly a card wrecker. The drive was over the brow of a hill, and beyond this crest the fairway sloped sharply down to a pond on the left. If you drove too far right you found thick bushes. It was a tricky drive to be sure, absurdly tight, and by modern standards unfair. However, the club members took a perverse pride in their killer hole and nothing would persuade them to modify its terrors. Most people soon learned to play it as a par-5, popping a gentle iron to the top of the hill on the second shot, and then gingerly nudging another iron to a position from which a chip to the green might leave a single putt for the par.

This particular golfer would have no truck with such cowardly tactics. "Better to die like a man," he would announce, pulling the headcover off his driver, "than live like a chicken. It is only a drive and a pitch." His bravado was skin deep. Inwardly quaking, he automatically tightened his grip on the club, failed to complete his backswing in the belief that he was executing a compact, controlled stroke, and without fail, three times a week for forty years, he either flat-hooked into the pond or hit a high slice into the bushes. It is a matter of simple mathematics to calculate that he had played the hole something like six thousand times. He had never scored better than a 5.

The camera as Impressionist
conveys whirling, blurring,
imprecise mind of the golfer as he
attacks the enemy.

Now he faced that drive again, and not for a minute did he consider any other club than his driver. Anyway, at the age of seventy-five, he needed all the length he could get, especially as it had been raining for most of the week and there would not be much run on the ball. He carefully selected a choice spot to tee his ball and took his stance. As he strained every muscle in that premature lunge his right foot slipped slightly on the muddy tee. It was only a tiny skid, less than one inch, but vital. The effect was to throw the arc of his clubhead into a slightly different plane and to delay its impact momentarily. The differences were infinitesimal, but when you consider that the clubface is in contact with the ball for only half of a thousandth of a second, you can appreciate that the difference between a good shot and a bad one is a matter of fine adjustment.

The difference in this case was dramatic. The clubhead caught the ball exactly right, flush on the button, and square. The meaty "crack" of impact and that indescribable, sensuous tremor of the club told him that he had hit such a drive as he had never hit before. He held his follow-through position like a statue and perhaps, after forty years, we can forgive him this little vanity. No bullet from a rifle ever flew straighter nor, it seemed, faster as it pierced the air on a line directly above the center of the fairway. Nothing could prevent it from carrying clear to that flat area of fairway from which he would have a routine pitch for a simple 4, possibly a birdie. Nothing could prevent it? The ball hit a marker post planted on the brow of the hill. The impact was almost as loud as the blow from the club. The ball rebounded straight back with hardly diminished speed. It pitched, bounced twice, rolled onto the tee and came gently to rest against the leg of the prostrate (and dead) golfer. The expression on his face was quizzical. "Why?" he seemed to be asking. "Why?" They buried the ball with him.

That golfer, and we all know him, tells us

something about the game. It can be a lifelong crusade, and if such golfers do not always end in a figurative snowdrift clasping a banner with a strange device, at least Longfellow would understand the unswerving sense of purpose which directs their lives.

There are many other types of the genus golfer, not least the remarkable man who loves to hate the game. Of this variety there can be few more extreme examples than the business executive who, since happily he is still among us, must be identified only by his initials, R. G. He was a man of prodigious energy. The air positively tingled with static when R. G. was switched on, which was most of the time. He had little formal education, but a good mind and a flair for getting straight to the essentials of the most complicated problem. As a result of these gifts, his career (in magazine publishing) had been spectacular. Like most people with a quick brain, he was impatient with those who were slower to grasp an idea and he made little attempt to control his feelings.

Whether a quick temper is the result of high blood pressure, or the other way round, is a matter for doctors to argue. At all events, by the age of fifty-two R. G. had undergone two medical crises serious enough for him to be ordered to give up his fifty-a-day addiction to cigarettes and all forms of alcohol.

Human frailties—and the golfer certainly has his share—are source of most of the game's comedy. Here cartoons of Clare Briggs from the twenties.

20

Within another year the pace again caught up with him. This time the cardiac specialist issued an ultimatum: If R. G. continued to push himself at this pace it would be tantamount to suicide. It wasn't just a risk but a certainty. Retirement was his only chance. "Get out of the rat race and take it easy. You've made your packet. Relax and enjoy it."

R. G., who was still under light sedation, agreed. Encouraged by his success, the specialist, who rather fancied himself a psychiatrist, tossed out a suggestion: "Ever tried golf?" His reasoning was that a man who had led such an active life would certainly be unable to switch to a regime of tending his roses. He would need an interest, and what better release for tension could be found than the gentle physical activity of golf? A healthy open-air pursuit would safely absorb those restless energies. "Golf?" said R. G. "Never had time for that sort of nonsense." "I'll send you a book about it," said the specialist, "and when you're up and about, you might like to come out to my club. We've got quite a decent bunch of members and you can see how you like the idea of the game."

Next day a package arrived at R. G.'s bedside. It was a copy of Ben Hogan's *Modern Fundamentals of Golf* and the gardener who retrieved it from the hospital grounds said later that it had flown from R. G.'s window "as if fired from a howitzer."

The specialist might have taken warning from this incident. R. G.'s fury apparently had been aroused by the title. If golf was a sixteenth-century game, then its fundamentals could not be called modern, he said. And if, on the other hand, Hogan had meant the basic principles of a new golfing method he should have called his book *The Fundamentals of Modern Golf*. "That man's a sloppy thinker," said R. G.

The specialist was not deterred. Golf, he remained convinced, would be excellent therapy for his patient. Wisely, he made no attempt to defend Hogan. Ignoring the calumny on the most precise mind in golf, he went ahead and booked a lesson for R. G. with the club professional, a quiet lowland Scot with an uncanny ability to measure a golfer's potential at a glance. R. G. was an easy diagnosis. Handmade shoes meant money and the general air of the man was manic-obsessive. With the right encouragement he would be good for a new set of clubs every year, possibly two sets. "You've got the look of a golfer about you," he told R. G. as they walked to the teaching area. "Good hands and power in those legs." R. G. had a certain respect for technical experts, up to a point, and allowed himself to absorb two pieces of advice: that acquiring a correct grip was worth perseverance, even though it might feel unnatural at the beginning; and that unless you set yourself up properly it was impossible to hit the ball consistently.

That was enough instruction for R. G. "Let me hit one," he commanded. The pro put down a ball and R. G. carefully took his stance. What happened next was a parody of golf, a flashing, whirling, violent convulsion. The components of the swing—slow takeaway, transfer of weight to right foot, cocking of the wrists, return shift of weight, and smooth sweep of the clubhead through the ball—were compressed into a frenzied blur. The outcome, however, was all too clear. The ball, almost severed into two hemispheres,

*Evidence that golf should and can
be a visual experience with
examples from Bermuda's Mid-Ocean and (above)
Sugarbush Country Club, Vermont.*

scuttled about twenty yards. "Good God!" said R. G. "Give me another."

The pro put down a second ball and the process was repeated in exact manner, except that this time R. G.'s exclamation was uttered with a tone of less surprise and more acerbity. "Another."

The third attempt was identical. "Ball!"

The pro teed up another sacrificial victim. This lesson was beginning to work out expensively in murdered balls. "If you'd just . . ." "Shut up!" shouted R. G., decapitating another ball, "and give me another blasted pill."

There are, reflected the pro, two kinds of pupils: those who are willing and able to learn the game properly and those who are beyond redemption. R. G. was clearly of the second category. With these unteachables, all you could do was to make minor remedial adjustments to the contortions they called a swing in order that they could make some sort of contact. This time he positioned the ball opposite R. G.'s left heel. If that slashing attack returned the club to the same place there was just a chance. He had to do something. Judging by the vermilion flush rising from this character's collar, there was danger of losing a valuable customer for good.

This time, R. G.'s dervish onslaught ended with a crisp metallic click which golfers recognize as the sweetest note in the harmonic scale. The ball, first boring, then soaring, then seeming to hang in the sky, fell far down the fairway. "Got it," said R. G. "Didn't I say you were a natural?" said the pro.

This was the revelatory flash of magic every golfer experiences once, the moment when the virus gets into the bloodstream. In that second was born the most evil-tempered golfer in the history of the game. R. G. did have a certain facility for golf, and there are those who believe that if his temperament had been less volatile he could have been very good, indeed. However, the one golfing axiom which brooks no ex-

ceptions is that controlled golf and an uncontrolled temper can never coexist. Even when things were going well, R. G. was cantankerous and complained at every step. He played golf like a man drawing his own teeth.

In the long history of the game there has never been a flawless round. Bobby Jones perhaps came nearest to it; his 66 in qualifying for the 1926 British Open, at Sunningdale, near London, is often recalled as the closest approach to perfection, but even that exhibition of accuracy contained blemishes, at least by R. G.'s hair-trigger standards. Jones did not one-putt every green, for instance. For R. G., of course, a miss from 30 feet was enough to light the fuse. He fought it, but you could see that he had not fully regained his composure by the time he teed up at the next hole. That meant a stray drive and a fearsome oath, often compounded by a smashing of the club into the turf, or, as on one memorable occasion, the violent destruction of a tee box. Usually he managed to hold himself in until, still seething, he hit his second shot. That's when he popped his cork. His club-throwing technique was highly developed and he achieved huge distances. Once he threw his five-iron so far into the shrubbery that he could not find it. As always, once the safety valve had been opened, he was immediately contrite. "That's my favorite club," he moaned. "What am I going to do?" Any opponents who tried the classic reply, "Go back and throw another," were rewarded with a look of black hatred.

R. G. was good at hating. He found reason for dissatisfaction with his best shots, and never once in five years had he been known to show signs of pleasure or even satisfaction on the course. It couldn't go on. What with the complaining and explosions of fury the inevitable day came when, having put two balls and his four-wood out of bounds in quick succession, he had another seizure. They carried him in and made him comfortable on a bench in the locker room while the secretary telephoned the heart specialist. "This won't

Another cartoonist who loved golf was New York Herald-Tribune's H. T. Webster, whose favorite butt was Caspar Milquetoast, the timid soul.

*Head down in concentration
(at Wee Burn in Connecticut) and head
up in glorious fulfillment (at
Puerto Rico's spectacular El Conquistador).*

do," the doctor told R. G., after giving him an injection. "I'm sorry, old chap, I'm afraid you'll just have to give up golf." "What!" shouted R. G., fighting the sedative. "You made me stop smoking and you made me give up drink. Now golf. Dammit, it's the only pleasure I've got left."

So far, then, we have seen golf as a form of madness and an instrument of torture. Surely there is more to it than that. Cannot it also be good clean fun and healthy exercise, beneficial to the body and at the same time a civilizing influence on the character? Well, maybe. But when it comes to the *mens sana in corpore sano* syndrome, the muddled oafs and flanneled fools of the other popular games have the advantage.

Golf is not energetic enough for a muscular tonic. You have only to watch someone like Julius Boros playing golf to realize that for sweating off surplus poundage you would be better off with a furious game of dominoes. The proliferation of motorized buggies to transport the golfer between shots and carry the ice bucket, glasses, and martinis is to be deplored if only because they deny the golfer the conscience-saving excuse that golf is good for him. There is enough guilt on the course as it is, without losing the righteous glow which comes with physical exhaustion.

Golf takes many forms. In Ireland it can be miniaturized, played with only a wedge and putter, and with no hole longer than 75 yards. This pitch-and-putt version has its own separate administration and championships, and there are highly skilled players who have never played "the long game" in their lives.

In Japan it can be akin to archery, played

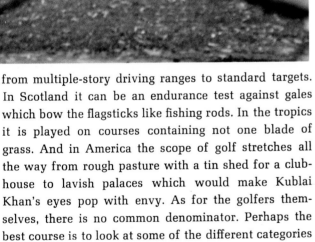

from multiple-story driving ranges to standard targets. In Scotland it can be an endurance test against gales which bow the flagsticks like fishing rods. In the tropics it is played on courses containing not one blade of grass. And in America the scope of golf stretches all the way from rough pasture with a tin shed for a clubhouse to lavish palaces which would make Kublai Khan's eyes pop with envy. As for the golfers themselves, there is no common denominator. Perhaps the best course is to look at some of the different categories of golfer.

One of the commoner types is the man with a virility complex, who sees the game as a trial of strength. He is a slugger and revels in outhitting rather than outscoring an opponent. For him the vital question is not "How many shots did you take?" but

"What club did you use?" On a short hole he will risk a double hernia getting up with a seven-iron and it does not matter if he lands in a bunker and takes three more to get down. His victory is in being pin high. You may be short with a five-iron, play a delicate run-up, and sink the putt for your par, but as far as he is concerned he has won a moral victory. There is no point in trying to deflate him by making remarks to the effect that it's not "How?" but "How many?" which counts in golf, because in his case it is not true. The only way is by beating him on his own terms, as in the following story in which only the names are fictitious.

In the annual knockout competition of a golfing society, the finalists who emerged were a bull-like creature we shall call King, a considerable player when things were going his way, and Peabody, a steady

Rain or shine, the putting ritual transcends meteorology—at New York's Leewood Golf Club and (right) under Minnesota's big skies at Bemidji.

player and a man of modest skills whose main strength was determination and a certain low cunning.

Peabody realized that his only chance was to attack King's muscular vanity, and to this end he had his pro make up a driver forty-six inches long, or four inches longer than normal. With this club Peabody practiced in secret for a week. The final was played on a course which began with a long-short hole, about 190 yards, and Peabody won the toss. His four-wood found the edge of the green and King was just through the back with a four-iron. They halved in threes and at the 420-yard 2nd Peabody played a three-wood and a four-wood, while King got up with a driver and a seven-iron. Another half, and King was beginning to swell up with self-satisfaction. In his terms he was slaughtering Peabody and the outcome was only a matter of time.

The 3rd hole was a monster, well over 500 yards, and the fairway was generously wide. Peabody teed up his ball, drew out his 46-inch driver, and removed its headcover prominently marked "2." It was the slowest swing you ever saw, as it must be with a

club like that. To King it looked like a lazy, halfhearted effort—which was exactly what Peabody intended him to think. "Just a gentle little brassie should do me," said Peabody as he watched the ball howl off down the fairway. King could hardly believe his eyes. He stepped grimly onto the tee with his driver and wound himself up for what was to be the biggest drive of his life. Measured strictly in terms of applied energy it might have been. But as we all know, distance is achieved not by hitting the ball harder, but better. And the violence of King's swing threw the clubhead off line. The ball zoomed away in a high slice, landing in the rough a 100 yards short of Peabody's ball. For all practical purposes the match ended there.

Peabody said nothing. Words were unnecessary, although many a lesser man would have been tempted to crow over his victim. He simply smiled a private smile, such as Delilah, scissors in hand, must have smiled after shearing Samson's locks.

He did not use the secret weapon again. For one thing, there was no other hole on the course

Satisfying shot to the green
(at Wee Burn) and frustrating search
for the ball (at Spyglass in
California) are all part of the game.

with a fairway wide enough to give him the necessary confidence. Anyway, it was superfluous. King, trying to hit harder and harder and harder, was all over the place. His timing had gone and his power was dissipated in a succession of half-tops and fluffs. By the end of the match Peabody was outhitting him, club for club, without any effort. It was a full month before King got his game going again.

Another subspecies known to country-club anthropologists is the Stylist. He can be recognized before he hits a shot. On the first tee you see him meticulously plaiting his fingers around the club. He coils to the top of his backswing and holds the position; his head turns to admire the straight line of left forearm and wrist and to check the angle of the clubface. This ritual is followed by a performance like a slide show of the various positions of the swing. Click! He slides his hips to the left. Click! He brings his hands to waist level with the right elbow tucked unnaturally close to his navel. Click! He makes an imaginary pass through an imaginary ball. Click! He stretches up to a classic follow-through position.

This routine may be followed half a dozen times before he is reassured that he has mastered every point in the latest magazine instructional article. The shot, when he eventually plays it, shows little resemblance to the slow-motion pantomime on the tee and the result seldom bears out the promise of the article or book which he has been reading ("Let Billy Casper show you how to knock ten strokes off your handicap"). And every time the Stylist hits a bad shot he remains rooted to the spot, performing a dumb show of the stroke he should have played.

It is not within the scope of this book (nor within the competence of the author, for that matter) to offer advice on how to play golf. But it is perhaps in order to suggest a method of clipping the Stylist, since the noble techniques of winning at golf go far beyond hitting the ball correctly.

The thing to do with a Stylist is to watch him closely for a few holes and deduce whom he is trying to copy. Stylists usually overdo it and will go as far as to ape the mannerisms of their hero. Thus, a Snead fantasy frequently includes the adoption of a straw hat. Now, having determined that your opponent believes himself to be a replica of Slamming Sam, you casually drop what the golfing gamesman calls a contra-suggestion. You might, for instance, say, "I can't help feeling that Doug Sanders has a point when he says that there is less room for error with a short backswing. I mean, it sounds logical."

That is a glaringly blatant specimen of contrasuggestion and with practice a skilled practitioner can refine the process to extremes of subtlety. One Stylist was completely thrown by a fractional raising of his opponent's eyebrow at a vital stage in the match. The tiniest grain of sand can grow into a fat pearl of doubt and confusion.

A rarer specimen, though a no less odious creature for that, is the Scorer. He cares nothing for style and takes no satisfaction in a well-struck shot. He normally can be identified by his hickory-shafted putter bound in several places with tape, and he usually is of Scottish descent. Often enough his clubs are a mongrel collection picked up over the years from the bargain barrel. Beware this man, for he is fireproof. He is immune to all forms of verbal gamesmanship and is in no way upset by being outdriven. You, with your natural flair for the game, boom your drives past him and produce a dazzling display of virtuoso shots. He doesn't even notice, let alone care. Where your shots come off the clubface with a report like a revolver shot, his go "plop." He has never hit the green of a par-5 hole with two shots in his life and, what is more, he has never tried. You annihilate him. And then you add up the scores at the end of the round and find he has beaten you by five shots. That should be lesson enough. Steer clear of him, for if you play with him often enough you are doomed to madness and despair.

These three basic categories of golfer, with numerous subspecies and hybrids, are, however, genuine golfers. The game is also peopled by those who do not so much play golf as play at golf.

There are social golfers for whom membership in an exclusive country club is a prop to an inferiority complex, or simply proof of their standing in the community. And there is a substantial category to whom golf is a business asset. There was a time when a bleached left hand was a badge of the professional; now it is just as likely to signify an insurance salesman, hustlers both.

Among these diverse types there is possibly one common characteristic, a universal capacity for self-deception. For some obscure reason, golfers of all standards, from the worst hacker to the mightiest professional, employ a defense mechanism which consists, to put it bluntly, of lying about their putting.

Is "lie" too strong a word? Let us examine a typical witness. A 2-handicap player goes round in 80 and explains to anyone he can trap in a corner of the locker room, "I couldn't buy a putt." In such circumstances most of us mutter some formal expression of condolence such as "rotten luck," and duck for safety. (It is one of the natural laws of golf that there is no more boring experience in life than listening to reports of other people's rounds, while, paradoxically, our own shot-by-shot accounts are spellbinding in their fascination.)

However, back to putting. If we can fight off the involuntary glazing of the eye and spontaneous twitching of the jaw muscles when our 2-handicap friend launches into his dreary recital of putting, we can crucify him on the cross of his own miserable conscience. We stand our ground, feign a look of lively interest, and say, "Trouble on the greens, eh? Tell me about it. How did it go on the first hole, for instance?" He may be taken aback by this unconventional response, but such is the vanity of golfers that he will certainly replay every shot for your benefit. Ignore all his guff about the diabolical luck when his drive kicked into the rough and the wedge slipped in his hand. Take note of the putts. Tot them up and confront him with the total: "I make that thirty-five putts altogether. You're *supposed* to take thirty-six. The truth is that you played like an idiot and now you're trying to blame your lamentable score on the greenkeeper. Know thyself. And stop this sickening mendacity; we don't care for brazen liars in this club." Now duck for safety.

There is no shame in putting badly. Miss a green with a nine-iron and you are a figure of ridicule; miss a four-footer and the world weeps with you. Nine times out of ten, the man who complains that he putted badly really means that he didn't hit the ball close enough to give himself the chance of a good putting round. To understand may be to forgive but, yes, the self-deception of the putting excuse is still a thumping great lie.

Finally, there are also a few rare characters who are not psychological cripples or charlatans or social climbers but are well-adjusted individuals who simply enjoy golf for what it is. Here we may enjoy a slightly conspiratorial liaison, because it so happens that you are just such a golfer. And, come to think of it, looking around at your circle of golfing acquaintances, you are the only one with a rational and adult attitude to the game. Isn't that so? What an extraordinary coincidence.

But all golfers, we must hope, experience at some time the combination of a glorious day, a beautiful course, the companionship of good friends, and an effective putting stroke which can make golf the second most satisfying activity known to mankind. In the end we must conclude that there are as many answers to the question "What is golf?" as there are golfers. Golf is as varied as life itself and, in the end, like life, golf is what we make it.

scots

t he explorer who sets out to find the source of golf soon discovers that his problem is not to grope his way through unmapped territories. The geography is all too familiar. He must choose among a tracery of streams, each marked, "Genuine Source of Golf." All these signs cannot be true, or can they? Perhaps they are all tributaries of equal importance. And what of the streams which bubble up out of the rocks? Are they springs, and therefore potential candidates for the honor of being called the genuine source? Or are they nothing more than extensions of the same tributary which has just gone underground for a while? The search then becomes a laborious effort to eliminate false sources.

The point of departure must be the earliest recorded mention of the word "golf." This occurs in the year 1457 in an Act of the Scottish Parliament under King James II, known as Fiery Face, which proved to be a prophetic nickname, since he was killed when a cannon he was inspecting blew up. His decree forbade the playing of golf: "the futeball and golfe be utterly cryed downe and not to be used." The reason for this harsh enactment was that Scotland was in a more or less permanent state of war against England and every able-bodied man was required to devote his spare time to archery practice for the protection of the realm. Clearly, men had been neglecting their military training for the more congenial pastimes of kicking footballs or hitting golf balls, both, incidentally, pursuits which retain the force of a national religion in Scotland to this day. So too does the ancient rivalry against England, but nowadays the traditional obsessions are neatly combined and battles against the old enemy are mainly confined to the football field.

The dereliction of duty of those early yeomen which so threatened the efficiency of the citizen army was not new. Some thirty-three years earlier a similar decree had been issued by the Scots Parliament, but in this case football only had been banned. Golf was not mentioned, so we can assume that in 1424 the game had not yet developed to a stage where it threatened the national security. We cannot, however, assume that it was not established in some form; indeed, it is highly unlikely that in a static medieval community, and one preoccupied with war and rebellion, any game could achieve widespread popularity over a relatively short period of time. The probability is, surely, that golf in some form was played in Scotland at least from the beginning of the fifteenth century.

Professor Douglas Young, who has written a history of St. Andrews, comes out with the bald, bold statement that golf was invented in Scotland soon after the founding of the University of St. Andrews (1414). However, his evidence in support of such a positive assertion is curiously flimsy for such a meticulous historian. We can admire the sight of a scholar crawling so far out on a limb, but perhaps it would be prudent to consider whether that precarious perch will bear the weight of our skepticism.

Until irrefutable proof is brought to light we must reserve judgment as to a specific birth date. In any case, is there a specific date to be found? The majority of historians prefer the view that one of the continental ball games was introduced into Scotland, probably by soldiers returning from European wars, and that the game gradually developed its essential golfing characteristics under local Scottish conditions. One persuasive theory is that the Scots troops, who were supporting their French allies against the British invaders, came home converts to the game of chole. A contemporary account describes how some Scottish officers were playing the game close to a river crossing near Bauge, when they caught sight of the standards of an English party advancing for a surprise attack. The Scots troops formed up and knocked the stuffing out of the English—one of the few reverses for England since Agincourt. That would date the importation in 1421. The origin of chole can be traced back for a fur-

36

ther three hundred years at least, so here is a possible parent of truly respectable antiquity.

Once again, however, we must scrutinize the theory for probability and common sense and, alas, it does not pass the test. Chole, a game indigenous to Belgium and northern France, has a superficial resemblance to golf. Chole clubs have iron heads resembling those of golf clubs and the game is played with a ball made of wood (as all early golf balls were). But there the similarity ends.

The basic conception of chole is entirely alien to golf. In chole, having chosen a distant target such as a barn door, one team hits the ball toward the goal while the opponents, or decholeurs, try to frustrate the process by hitting the ball back into difficult places. If chole was played by Scottish soldiers in France (as seems likely), and was brought home to Scotland by them (which is possible but conjectural), it must have undergone such a fundamental transformation as to constitute a new game altogether.

Another favored candidate as the progenitor of golf is the Dutch game of *Kolven*, especially since it is played with an instrument called a *Kolf.* Language offers other seductive clues in the Dutch expression, *"Stuit mij!"* meaning "It stops me," which therefore corresponds in sound and sense with the golfer's "stymie." And then there is the warning cry of *"Vooor,"* which fits "Fore" so neatly. There are more seemingly uncanny similarities between golfing expressions and Dutch equivalents. Unfortunately, as Robert Browning, the author of *A History of Golf,* points out with crushing logic, there is a simple explanation. "Kolf" and "golf" sound the same because they have the same origin in the German word, *Kolbe,* meaning club. The words, then, exist quite independently of the games to which they are applied.

That is all very well, but it fails to explain why the word "golf" was not established in the language before the coming of the game. Surely, people would have called any type of club a golf. However, this line of inquiry is sterile. For whatever similarities there may be in the language of golf and kolven, the games themselves are poles apart. Kolven was played with a large ball on a paved court, or on ice, and has no affinity with the national game of Scotland beyond being a club-and-ball pastime. And if we are going to round up all the club-and-ball games as suspects for our paternity suit, there is no limit to the possibilities. What about the French game of *jeu de mail,* which was played in England as pall-mall? One of London's noblest streets is named after it, but it was played with mallets and so, although it may have sired croquet, we can acquit it of responsibility for golf.

What about another French game, *jeu de paume,* which was played, as its name implies, with the palm of the hand, but with a leather ball stuffed with feathers just like the later golf balls? The feather ball, however, did not come into golf until the seventeenth century and, anyway, the ancient Romans had been making balls this way centuries previously. Possibly jeu de paume was the forerunner of tennis, fives, or handball, but we must dismiss it from the golf inquiries. *Crosse,* an ancient French game, was played with a curved stick or club and that is about as much as we know about it, so crosse too must be released from the case for lack of evidence.

If we follow up every ball-and-club game, the quest will be endless. We know such games were played by the early Greeks, and that the Romans amused themselves with one called *paganica.* And such games probably go back much further than that; it is the most natural action in the world, having picked up a stick, to hit something with it.

Obviously, our search for golf's origins has taken us too far. We must retrace our steps and this time see what we can do to define golf more specifically. If golf is taken to be a cross-country club-and-ball game with the ultimate object of putting the ball *into a*

hole, the search is immensely simplified. In that case the claims of Scotland to be the birthplace of golf are enormously strengthened.

In *The Royal and Ancient Game of Golf,* Garden Smith writes rather petulantly: "The poor Scots are denied the possibility of having a game of their own evolved by themselves, in accordance with their own ideas and temperament and suited to their country and climate. How the importation idea arose it is impossible to conceive. The evidence is all against it, but writers on golf have nearly all followed it like sheep."

That little outburst is hardly justified, but even Smith does concede that golf was influenced by the continental games as, of course, it must have been. The close alliance between Scotland and France, with the natural interchange of ideas and people, could not have failed to make its mark on golf. When the first modified rules of golf came to be written they bore such similarities to the rules of *jeu de mail,* almost word for word in places, as to be beyond coincidence.

Having conceded these two debts to the continent, Smith goes on: "There seems to be no reason for doubting that, in all its essential particulars, golf is a purely Scottish product. Apart from the available evidence, literary and pictorial, which is all against a Dutch or other continental origin, the game is characteristically Scottish. It is not Celtic. There are Celts in Scotland, but when we talk of a typical Scot we do not mean a Celt. Golf is certainly not a Celtic game and is, indeed, entirely foreign to the Celtic temperament, which delights in faster and rougher games, such as shinty or football. But anything more typical of the slow, canny, yet strong and resourceful Scottish character than golf is not to be found in the whole range of Scottish institutions. Golf, in fact, in its conception and essence, is the very epitome of the elements which have given the Scottish character its strength and individuality. It is the game of the patient, self-reliant man, prepared to meet whatever fortune may befall him. As the early Scot found life a hard battle, with good and evil fortune mixed capriciously, and only to be won by patience and steadfastness in adverse circumstances, so in his game he sought to reproduce the greater struggle for the smaller stake. He was in no mind to make the game easier or less trying, but rather sought to increase its natural difficulties, recognizing even in his recrea-

Chole as played in France in 1497 (above).
Paintings by Esaias Van de Velde (top l.), Adriaen Van de Velde (top r.), and Aert Van der Neer depict variations of the Dutch game kolven.

tion, that the harder the struggle, the greater was the joy of mastery."

What wonderful nonsense, all the more nonsensical for that parody of the Scottish character. Slow, canny, strong, patient, resourceful, and steadfast —these are Scottish qualities of the music-hall cliché. They are the characteristics you might cite as circumstantial evidence that the Scots invented an activity like tossing the caber, but they hardly support the theory that the Scots invented golf.

Let us play Smith at his own game and look at those Scottish institutions which reflect that national character according to Smith. We can formulate a persuasive thesis. The architecture fits. It is, above all, stolid. Even the humblest cottage is built with the ponderous simplicity of a stanchion for a bridge, not surprising since the Scots are a race of engineers. No frills, nothing so frivolous as decoration is added. Function is all. The Scottish literary tradition rests almost exclusively on the reputation of novelists whose works are as worthy and nourishing and exciting as haggis. They have produced one poet in a thousand years, and on most people's teams of all-time greats he would not get farther than the substitutes' bench. As for philosophy, the only Scottish contender in the heavyweight division is John Knox, and all he had was a ponderous left hand: "Whatever you are doing, stop it." The Scots, according to the Smith school of thought, excel at the technical pursuits. If you want your appendix removed, or a harbor spanned, or a ship designed, or your books balanced, or an enemy machine-gun post wiped out, you cannot do better than look in the appropriate section of the Yellow Pages under "Mac."

But in the realm of ideas and imagination, on Smith's blueprint of the typical Scot, you would be advised to look to another race, possibly one of those Johnny-come-lately Celts. If the Scots are really so dour, it hardly supports the theory that they invented golf, in the sense of having given birth in a flash of creative inspiration to that paradoxical, diabolically subtle, almost poetical notion of combining the *Donner und Blitz* element of power play with the gossamer delicacy of holing out? Now there's a frivolous embellishment if ever there was one.

Anthropology is a dangerous game. It may be true, in a general sense, that every race is the child of its geology and climate. It does not follow that the Scottish character is all gale-swept granite. People are individuals, and despite Smith's implications to the contrary, a Scot could easily have invented golf, just as a Scot could have written *Hamlet* or composed *The Messiah*.

On the other hand, the probability is that nobody invented golf. Picture for a moment what life was like on the east coast of Scotland at the beginning of the fifteenth century. St. Andrews was a compact fortress town with mean and narrow streets which in those days did duty as drains, rubbish dumps, and sewers. Life was hard. Most of the men clawed a precarious living from the sea or the land, and every arable inch was closely cultivated. The only place to go for recreation was the strip of sand dunes alongside the beach. This sour land could not be cultivated, and all that grew there were hardy whin bushes and a fine turf where sheep grazed. The area performed the function of park, backyard, and social club for the people of St. Andrews. The women brought their washing and draped it over the whins to dry. This was the place for the Sunday walk. Men played football and took their dogs onto the dunes to catch rabbits, and it was here that the compulsory archery practice was held. (Absentees were fined and the money used to buy drink for the regular attenders, a splendid example of the common sense which runs so strongly through the Scottish judicial processes.)

If any form of outdoor game was to be played, this was the only place to go. If some returning soldier did interest his friends in chole or kolven,

41

they would have to go out to the links. Of if a traveler came with the news of some native sport played with clubs and ball, possibly from Ireland, the story would be the same. As we have seen, at that time there was nothing original about club-and-ball games. We may presume, at all events, that at some stage a band of pioneers advanced on the links armed with clubs and balls, either at St. Andrews itself or some place like it along this stretch of coastline.

Now, how should they proceed? The lie of the land would dictate their route. They would naturally follow the smooth valleys between the dunes, skirting such obstructions as the archery range and the washing. But what should they aim at? On this bleak landscape, with no trees or convenient church doors to play to, the only natural landmarks which would stand out clearly would be rabbit holes. It might have been planned beforehand to use a hole as a target, but the probability is that it all happened by fortuitous accident. The peculiar nature of the links surely dictated the form of golf. It might have been an act of individual inspiration, but that theory looks, on the face of it, unlikely. A Scot might have invented golf; more probably Scotland invented golf.

It is a point of academic interest only, except in one particular. The administrators of golf are concerned, and rightly so, with preserving the game as nearly as possible in its original form, and if the rabbit was indeed the original greenkeeper, then the hole into which we frustrated golfers try to aim our putts in this twentieth century ought, for the sake of tradition if nothing else, to be rather more generous in diameter than four and a quarter inches. Many people believe that there is a disproportionate emphasis on putting in the modern game. They claim that the balance of golf has swung too much in favor of the specialist putter and that a six-inch hole would restore the importance of shot-making. They have logic on their side, and, if the rabbit-hole theory is true, they have an ally in tradition.

In this 17th-century painting of chole players by the Flemish artist Paul Bril, door at left serves as target. Note length of the clubs, size of the ball.

That argument must be pleaded at another time in another place. For the moment we must return to medieval Scotland and to fact rather than fancy. And the fact is that, whatever its genesis, golf captured the public imagination so strongly that eventually it threatened national security. Men neglected their archery for the new sport. And in spite of the decrees outlawing the game—or possibly because of the added spice of illegality—golf flourished.

At the beginning of the new century, a treaty of perpetual peace was signed between England and Scotland. The optimism of this document may not have been entirely justified by subsequent events, but by and large the heat was off. It was no longer necessary to keep armies in readiness for war and the way was open for golf to develop and spread.

Shall we shed a tear for the men who made bows and arrows and who now, in these peaceful times, found themselves in a falling market? Not at all. One reason for the spread of golf was that the game inherited a ready-made industry to service it. The bowyers and fletchers were craftsmen wise in the properties of native woods and skilled in the arts of turning and balancing shafts and forging iron. A man who could shape the arrow for a longbow or a crossbow's bolt had at hand the tools and skills to make golf clubs. Who better than a bowyer to know about the flex and torsion of a blackthorn bough, or the security to be found in a rawhide grip?

They turned naturally to clubmaking as a profitable sideline and golf's debt to archery has never been properly appreciated and acknowledged. If golf had relied on the rude agricultural implements used for kolven the game would surely never have achieved such popularity. By later standards, when clubmaking became a highly developed art, the early clubs may have seemed crude but at least they proved effective.

For something like two hundred years after that first proclamation outlawing golf the game

44

THE PENNY MAGAZINE

OF THE

Society for the Diffusion of Useful Knowledge.

181.]   PUBLISHED EVERY SATURDAY.   [JANUARY 31, 1835.

THE GAME OF SHINTY

[Game of Shinty.]

In the Highlands of Scotland it is customary for persons to amuse themselves, in the winter season, with a game which they call "shinty." This sport has a considerable resemblance to that which is denominated "hurling" in England, and which Strutt describes under that name. The shinty is played with a small hard ball, which is generally made of wood, and each player is furnished with a curved stick somewhat resembling that which is used by golf players. The object of each party of players is to send the ball beyond a given boundary on either side; and the skill of the game consists in striking the ball to the greatest distance towards the adversaries' boundary, or in manœuvring to keep it in advance of the opposing side. Large parties assemble during the Christmas holidays, one parish sometimes making a match against another. In the struggles between the contending players many hard blows are given, and frequently a shin is broken, or by a rarer chance some more serious accident may occur. The writer witnessed a match, in which one of the players, having gained possession of the ball, contrived to run a mile with it in his hand, pursued by both his own and the adverse party until he reached the appointed limit, when his victory was admitted. Many of the Highland farmers join with eagerness in the sport, and the laird frequently encourages by his presence this amusement of his labourers and tenants.

Summer kolven—in winter it was played on ice—from Flemish Book of Hours of 1530. Stained glass window (r.) of Gloucester cathedral is earliest pictorial evidence (mid-14th century) of golf in England. (Detail, upper r.)

was an informal affair. There were no codified rules, although no doubt there were conventions on how the game should be played, probably varying from one community to another. (This is another reason for doubting whether the distinction of having invented golf can ever be ascribed to an individual. The game had been evolving for three hundred years before it achieved anything like a standardized form.) There were no set "courses" as we know them today; you simply played over whatever suitable ground happened to be available, cutting holes where necessary with a pocket knife.

The game went through vicissitudes, at times being repressed by decrees forbidding it on Sundays, sometimes being encouraged by royal patronage. Most of the Scottish kings were golfers and poor Mary Queen of Scots was accused of callously playing golf immediately after the murder of her husband. For the keen student of the history of golf it is a fascinating period, with a wealth of documented evidence, but the next significant change did not occur until the early part of the seventeenth century with the introduction of the feather ball, or "featherie."

At its best, the featherie must have represented a considerable improvement on the earlier balls of turned boxwood. Its irregular surface pattern would have given it far better flight characteristics. Distance records are unreliable because one can never be quite sure what the conditions were like at the time but, taking a cautious average from contemporary accounts, it is clear that a good player could drive a featherie 200 yards. And in 1836, a French schoolmaster at St. Andrews, on a frosty Old Course and with a gentle following wind, hit a measured drive of 361 yards. In wet weather the featherie was not nearly so effective since it absorbed water and became heavy and soggy. And, of course, one injudicious blow with the sharp edge of an iron club was liable to split the cover and disembowel this expensive missile.

The featherie was made by the same process employed by the Romans. A cover of untanned bull's hide was stitched, leaving a small aperture so that it could then be turned inside out, with the raised seams inside, and stuffed with boiled feathers—traditionally, enough to fill a top hat. The aperture was then stitched shut and the ball pounded into shape. As the feathers dried they expanded to make a hard, resilient ball, ready for painting. It was a skilled operation to make a featherie and a craftsman was doing well if he turned out half a dozen a day.

Compared with the earlier boxwood balls, the featheries were prohibitively expensive, costing twelve times as much, and this inflationary move was reflected in a social change in the game. Golf became a luxury, and although the Scots managed to keep the classless tradition of the game alive, the situation was very different in the game's missionary fields. The golf which spread to England early in the seventeenth century, largely through the enthusiasm of her Scottish-born king, James I, was most definitely a game for the nobility. The idea of golf as a pursuit of the well-born and wealthy proved to be enduring and damaging to the development of the game. Even today, three hundred years later, when the talk at the pit face among coal miners is just as likely to concern how they scored in the monthly medal competition, the notion persists in some quarters that golf is a game of the privileged minority. In England, local authorities of a socialist bias still refuse to consider the provision of municipal golf courses on the grounds that public money should not be spent on amenities for "toffs."

If the featherie must take initial responsibility for this state of affairs, it also advanced the game considerably. The improvements arose not only through the superior properties of the ball itself, but because of the new challenge it offered to the clubmaker. Whereas a club which had to withstand constant impact with unyielding wooden balls had of necessity to

be of sturdy construction, the featherie presented opportunities for refinement. From this time the craft of clubmaking developed into an art.

The oldest surviving clubs date from the seventeenth century and provide some evidence of what golf was like in the early days. The set consists of six woods and two irons, which confirms the theory of the historical development of golf. Probably in the very beginning golf was played with a single wooden club. Then variations were introduced to deal with specific situations. One such would be the baffing spoon. The original play club (later called the driver) would have served its purpose well enough when the ball was teed up on a pinch of sand. But the straight-faced play club would have been ineffective from a tight fairway lie. Hence, the introduction of a club with

an angled face and the technique of baffing, or bouncing the clubhead into the turf just behind the ball to make it rise. From that point we may surmise the introduction of further variations, such as the long spoon and the holing-out club, or putter. The seventeenth-century set marks the transitional period when iron clubs were becoming popular and the proliferation of woods began to decline. It gives an impression of size and crudeness. Each is about six inches longer than the equivalent club of today. The heads are deeper and more heavily weighted. In every case the face is slightly concave, presumably in an attempt to impart control. This hollowing of the face, combined with the name "spoon," may give us a clue to the method of using the clubs. The inference is that the ball was spooned, with a scooping action, which would tally with the club's

"The Sabbath Breakers" by J. L. Dollman portrays the dire result of Edinburgh town council's ban of 1592 on "ony pastymes or gammis within or without the toun upon the Sabboth day, sic as Gof." Fine: 40 shillings.

general dimensions. Anything in the nature of a "hit" would be impossible with implements of this weight and size. Restoration golfers would most certainly have had to "wait for it" as those great, weighted heads built up a ponderous speed on the periphery of their wide arc. These clubs would need to be swung with a lazy, sweeping action, probably embellished by a dipping or scooping motion in the contact zone. As to the outcome of the shot, we can only apply our modern knowledge of aerodynamics and insist that the balls must have been roughened in some way to produce an approximately true flight path. In constant play any ball, whether of boxwood or bullhide with feather interior, would become scuffed, and we do know that the tradi-

tion arose of the need for golf balls to "mature."

We should not assume that, simply because the equipment was crude by modern standards, it was many times less effective. As soon as authenticated records appear we find surprisingly good results being recorded. The laws of dynamics have not changed over the ages and the distance a ball may be struck was governed in the seventeenth century by the same forces that govern it today: the size, density, and resilience of the ball combined with the mass and speed of the clubhead. The resilience of the ball would have been inferior, but if it were smaller and heavier than today's artificially regulated examples the overall difference might well have been small.

The other fundamental change, the use of the steel shaft, does not make the slightest difference in the speed of the clubhead. It is vastly more convenient, and it makes the task of swinging a club somewhat easier, but a modern set of irons could be fitted with wooden shafts without altering their performance in the slightest degree. So, if we assume that these early golfers mastered a technique of extracting the maximum theoretical performance from their clubs —and the continued popularity of the game suggests at the very least that golf for them was a highly satisfying pastime—we must suppose that they hit a proportion of shots which were good by any yardstick. Of necessity, it would be low-trajectory golf, since their equipment simply would not produce the high-soaring modern shot. But on hard, unwatered linksland a low shot which pitches and runs is often the most effective, especially in windy conditions.

We may, in summary, rest assured that this early golf was, at its highest levels, considerably more refined than the popular notion of bumbling the ball along the ground in hundred-yard stages. At the same time, looking at those hollowed faces with the knowledge that even the finest of contemporary professionals does not strike every shot exactly off the "meat," we must accept that the perfect shot was a somewhat rarer occurrence in the seventeenth century than it is today. They must have had plenty of foozles

Trendy sportswear for the links as favored by the younger set of 17th-century Holland and gentlemen golfers of Scotland at the beginning of the nineteenth century.

in every round. No wonder they drank such prodigious quantities of alcohol afterwards.

Incidentally, although the use of numbers to distinguish clubs may be appropriate to this computer age, golf surely has been impoverished by the loss of those wonderful Scottish names for clubs. Dull of soul is he who feels no difference between a five-iron and, as it once was called, a mashie. The driver retains its name, although of comparatively recent origin (being the successor to the play club). The wedge (much more recent) continues to resist attempts to submerge its individuality in the No. 10. And the putter defies the passion for numerology, which is only proper since of all the clubs it is the most personal—indeed, in temperament the most human. There would be little satisfaction in breaking a No. 11 across your knee, and the love-hate relationship most golfers enjoy with their putters could scarcely survive the substitution of an anonymous number. But the brassie and spoon are disappearing from the language of golf while cleek, baffie, mashie, and niblick have already vanished.

For tournament professionals golf has become a science rather than an art and for them numbered clubs may be appropriate. But club golfers who play the game for pleasure, and for whom aesthetic considerations are half the charm of the game, would surely get satisfaction from a revival of those wonderful names. Those soulless businessmen who mass-produce matched sets and are concerned with balance sheets rather than traditions, say that numbers are necessary because there are not enough names to go round. What they overlook, because it suits their pockets, is that the average golfer does not need fourteen clubs and is quite incapable of benefiting from such a range.

In the hands of a powerful pro a four-iron will hit the ball 15 yards farther than a five-iron. For a handicap golfer this differential comes down to 10 yards. However, the average amateur is not con-sistent enough to exploit that small difference. His well-hit five-iron goes farther than his indifferent four-iron shot. For him—and he represents well over ninety percent of the world's golfers—a set of irons graduated according to the modern scale, that is, a three, four and a half, six, seven and a half, and nine, would adequately cater to his needs. In other words, cleek, mashie, mid-iron, mashie-niblick, and niblick. Add a driver, brassie, and spoon with lofts equivalent to one-wood, two-and-a-half-wood, and four-wood, plus a sand iron, wedge, and putter, and he has a set of eleven clubs, which is two more than Harry Vardon needed to win his six Open Championships.

Quite apart from the considerable financial saving such a set would represent and the added pleasure the player would find in his named clubs, the game itself might well become more enjoyable by bringing back the need to "invent" half-shots, cut-ups, and the "feel" strokes. Golf's appeal lies in the combination of power and artistry. In this brutal golfing age anything which tends to emphasize the artistry is to be encouraged. However, we dupes allow ourselves to be persuaded that fourteen clubs constitute a "set," and that unless we are equipped like Jack Nicklaus we cannot hope to play like him. The premise is as absurd as the aspiration.

After the formation of proper clubs, a process that began around 1740, the next significant development in golf was the standardization of courses and rules. This was the period when golf ceased to be a happy-go-luck activity and formality entered into the game. Nowadays golfers who travel around the country-side like to tell each other, "What a place this would be to build a golf course." In those early days that thought was enough. If you had clubs and balls to hand you played wherever you found a piece of suitable country. In Scotland the golfing grounds were of necessity the common lands, but when we read of royal personages playing golf in the royal park at Greenwich,

Early styles of golf. Drawing probably uses some artistic license but the meticulous painting gives historical weight to the larger-hole protagonists.

it does not mean a golf course was there.

The earliest references to stroke play date from this era in the middle of the eighteenth century, as does the earliest surviving code of rules. It is interesting to note that our ancestors managed to get along on thirteen brief laws, compared with the present proliferation of forty-one, many of them divided into numerous subclauses, definitions, appendices, and instructions on etiquette.

Although the game was in a fairly advanced state of development, there still was no such thing as a formalized golf course as we know it today. At one of the earliest links, for instance, at Leith, near Edinburgh, the game was played over five holes measuring 414, 461, 426, 495, and 435 yards. If these distances are adjusted for the equipment of the day, they are the equivalent of about 600 yards for each hole, good three-shotters for the best players. Here again we have direct evidence to refute the modern view that putting is half of golf. Nowadays, on a par-72 course, the first-class golfer is allowed a "ration" of two putts a hole, thirty-six in all. The ratio of shots through the green to putts in the days when Leith was a five-hole course must have been nearer two to one. A round at Leith probably consisted of three circuits, so there could be no basis for comparison with the golfers of, say,

Perth, whose course had six holes, or Montrose, which had twenty-five.

In any case, stroke-play golf with card and pencil had not yet become popular. Golf was mainly man-to-man encounters, blood-and-guts matches with all the interest of private wagers and the interplay of personality. Those of the generation reared on a diet of almost unrelieved match play tend to regard it as the "real" golf, and find stroke play insipid stuff by comparison. In this respect at least we must concede that the traditionalists are right. One of the regrettable trends of modern times is the decline of match play, following the pervasive example of the professional tournaments with their necessary emphasis on scores.

Whether or not the first golf was played at St. Andrews, the city of Edinburgh must be given credit for forming the first club. In 1744 a group of "honorable gentlemen golfers" petitioned the city fathers to provide a silver club for open competition among the golfing community. The trophy was duly provided and the championship announced by proclamation and tuck of drum. Twenty years later the Honourable Company of Edinburgh Golfers was formally constituted as a club, although it had no clubhouse, nor indeed did it own the golfing grounds at Leith. Nevertheless, minute books were kept of the club's activities

St. Andrews was (and is) golf's Mecca. Preceding pages: 1850 Grand Match, painted by Charles Lee, is a group portrait; girl serving ginger beer symbolizes the 15th, or Ginger Beer, hole. Above: Old Tom Morris on first tee, 1895.

and from such records we can get an accurate picture of the golfing way of life of those days.

Let us take a typical Saturday in, say, 1780, when the club tradition was well established, and follow the movements of a prosperous merchant. The only paid official of the club was a boy whose job was to call on every member and inquire if he proposed to dine with the club on Saturday. Having given due notice of his intention to be present at dinner (cost: one shilling) the merchant would dress in his scarlet club uniform with crested buttons, and call for his carriage to take him to his appointment on the links. There he would meet his prearranged opponent, possibly a surgeon or an officer from the castle garrison, and their regular caddies. These caddies, probably reeking and fuddled from their ale-house excesses of the previous night, would take their owners' clubs in a bundle under their arms and play could begin. Undoubtedly it would be a match, and after pinching up

a small pyramid of loose sand, the golfers would tee their balls and strike off with their play clubs.

The sight of these two splendid creatures in their finery would certainly attract a gallery of casual strollers, and the caddies would be kept busy clearing picnic parties and dog-walkers from the path of the match. By all accounts the caddies would not be too particular about the language they employed in their control of the public. For all their faults, the caddies were fiercely partisan and jealously protected the rights of their masters. The tradition among caddies of knowing how to milk a fat tip is as old as golf itself. On one occasion, when a spectator was crowding the hole so closely that he impeded the player's stroke, the caddie grabbed the onlooker by the back of the neck and thrust his nose into the hole with the words: "There now! You can see the ball's in the hole right enough."

After the game the serious business of

Lining it up: Formidable professional partnership of Allan Robertson (bending) and Tom Morris in a match at St. Andrews, 1849, and a daintier scene of the ladies of Westward Ho!, Devon.

Those were the days, before the First World War, when
life was leisurely—at Baltusrol, New Jersey,
(above) and at St. Andrews (top r.)—and Walter
Travis (opposite) was a power in golf.

the club would begin. The golfers would change into their dining uniforms, possibly blue or gray coats with black facings and gilt buttons, and repair to a private room in a local tavern for dinner, presided over by the Captain (an office automatically assumed by the winner of the club championship). It was customary for members to provide food from their own estates, and these golfers did themselves well. Club minutes recall feasts of a round of beef stewed in hock, haunch of venison, saddle of mutton, reindeer's tongue, pigeon pie, and sheep's-head pasty. The Royal Aberdeen club accounts show an average consumption in excess of three bottles of liquor per man at their dinners, and Tobias Smollett writes of the club golfer customarily

retiring with a gallon of claret in his belly. The business of the club was transacted during the meal. A member who had been observed playing golf out of uniform might be fined half a dozen bottles of rum or Highland whisky. And then the wagers would be recorded. This ritual was the normal method of organizing matches for the following week. One member might challenge another to a match for a gallon of whisky and the details would duly be recorded in the book. At the same time, from reference to the previous week's entries, settlement would be demanded for that day's results. Since booze in some form was the common currency of golf wagers and payment was exacted at dinner, we can imagine that late in the

Golf began to change, with players like young Walter Hagen breaking through and equipment improving from the featherie (opposite, top) to the gutties (dark ball and starred ball below it), and early rubber-cores, including 1899 Haskell (top r.).

evening some imprudent challenges were made. Never mind. It was an age of high conviviality and good fellowship; golf was not the solemn affair it later became. And the morrow was a day of rest.

Two fortuitous events combined to shape the future course of the game. First, the golfers of St. Andrews achieved the reputation of being the pacesetters and unofficial authorities on the game, largely as the result of what the historian, Dr. Young, describes as a tourist promotion stunt. The Society of St. Andrews golfers put up a trophy in the form of a silver club for open competition. The success of this contest established St. Andrews as the premier golfing town, and when, in 1764, the Society changed its course from twelve holes to eighteen, other clubs followed suit. Hence, eighteen holes became the "correct" number for a full course.

New courses naturally were built to the St. Andrews pattern. Previously, the St. Andrews golfers had twelve holes, playing eleven going out and then retracing their steps and playing eleven holes home, over the same fairways in reverse direction. A "round" was thus twenty-two holes. Then the Society decided to turn the first four holes into two and the round was thereby reduced to eighteen.

Other clubs did not follow the famous St. Andrews practice of shared fairways and greens, because this was essentially dictated by the narrow strip of duneland available. In any case, greens—in the sense of large areas of carefully prepared turf—were unknown. The practice was to tee up your ball within a club's length of the hole just completed. If putting was not so important in those eighteenth-century days, it must have been an even more tiresome process than it is on today's superbly groomed carpets.

The first reference to golf in America was the formation of the South Carolina Golf Club at Charleston, around 1786. The Scottish transplant did not long survive on the alien soil of the New World,

however, and another hundred years passed before the game was reintroduced to the United States, this time to stay. By then, it had made considerable progress. The Society of St. Andrews golfers was dignified by William IV (1830-37) with the title of "Royal and Ancient" and the era of championships had begun, first the Amateur and then the Open, which began as a thirty-six hole professional tournament for a championship belt. Even more significantly, perhaps, in the mid-1800s was another happy accident, the invention of the gutta-percha ball, or guttie. A professor at St. Andrews University, so the legend goes, received a statue of Vishnu which had been packed in gutta-percha for protection. This rubber-like substance is tapped from a tree and turns hard on exposure to the air. The professor, a keen golfer, idly rolled a piece of it into a ball. (It must have been heated to reach this degree of malleability, but let us not spoil a harmless legend for the sake of a technical detail.) He wondered whether golf could be played with his gutta-percha ball, tried it out, and failed to achieve anything better than bumbling shots along the ground. It takes more than a minor setback to deter a true Scot inspired by the vision of saving a few pence, however. He persevered and in time, as the gutta-percha ball became scuffed by the battering of the clubhead, it began to fly. The reason, as we now know, is that a golf ball obtains lift from its dimples. It is an aerodynamic necessity to have an irregular surface; a perfectly smooth ball has no lift. And so, after more trial and error, the guttie came to golf. At first, its surface irregularities were hammered by hand, but later the guttie was produced in molds and many novel surface designs were tried to produce better performance, such as an imitation of a feather ball's stitched seam, a bramble pattern, and a lattice formation.

The guttie had several advantages. It was cheap, and when it became misshapen or chipped, it could be plunged into hot water and remolded. There was some resistance to the new ball, especially from the professionals whose ballmaking activities were a profitable sideline. Their opposition could not long hold up progress, for progress this certainly was. The cost of golf, after the initial capital expense of clubs, was now reasonable again, and the game was ready for its second era of expansion.

The British empire was serviced by expatriates, many of them Scots, and golf followed the flag. Clubs were formed in imperial outposts. And it was reintroduced into the U.S. in 1888. This time the game clicked. Although the guttie ball lasted for only sixty years, this was perhaps the most important period in the history of golf. For between 1850 and 1900 golf became truly international. The beachheads were established from which golf was to enslave the world.

Another effect of the guttie was that the clubmakers again had to make adjustments for this stone-like ball. Wooden clubs designed for use with the featherie could not be expected to withstand the impact shock of the unyielding guttie. At first they tried facing the clubs with patches of leather, which served to absorb some of the initial shock but also reduced the effectiveness of the shot, especially in bad weather. They then turned to new hardwoods for the clubheads, and the design of the heads themselves evolved by stages from the graceful banana shapes of the traditional design into the rounder forms which, with variations, are used today.

Most writers who review the history of golf tend to see the development of the game in terms of eras and, indeed, in this chapter an attempt has been made to isolate the significant changes which altered the course of the game and guided its destiny. The difficulty is to determine which were the decisive influences. For instance, there comes a point when golf in America ceased to be an offshoot of a foreign game and flowered in a uniquely American way. The child began to dominate the parent.

Obviously, it was a developing process over a period of twenty years or so, and the problem is to fix a date for the era. Should it be from the first major American contribution to golf (Walter Travis's victory in the 1904 Amateur Championship at Sandwich)? Or should it be from the time when American golfers were established beyond argument as leaders of the world (Walter Hagen's 1922 Open triumph)? Since the game has so often been shaped by changes in equipment, as we have seen, perhaps the date of another and far-reaching technical development is an appropriate moment to select as heralding the coming era of American domination.

In 1901, a Cleveland chemist, Coburn Haskell, invented a method of making golf balls by winding rubber thread under tension around a central core. Others had tried to use rubber for golf balls, and a composition ball, made to a secret formula which certainly used rubber, had enjoyed limited success; the "puttie" as it was called, might have developed into a popular substitute for the guttie, but Haskell's ball was so obviously superior that it quickly ousted all rivals. This invention, America's first significant contribution to golf, followed the formation seven years previously of the United States Golf Association. Incidentally, the Royal and Ancient Golf Club of St. Andrews, although the acknowledged authority for golf and its rules, was not invested with the management of the Open and Amateur Championships until 1919, so, in this respect at least, the R. and A. is junior to the USGA.

Within the space of eighteen years, Walter Travis beat the British in their Amateur Championship, Francis Ouimet beat the best of the overseas challengers to win the U.S. Open, and Walter Hagen recorded the first of a long succession of American victories in the British Open Championship. The game which had started as an informal knock-about on the sandy turf of a Scottish fishing town four hundred and fifty years previously was now full grown and under new management.

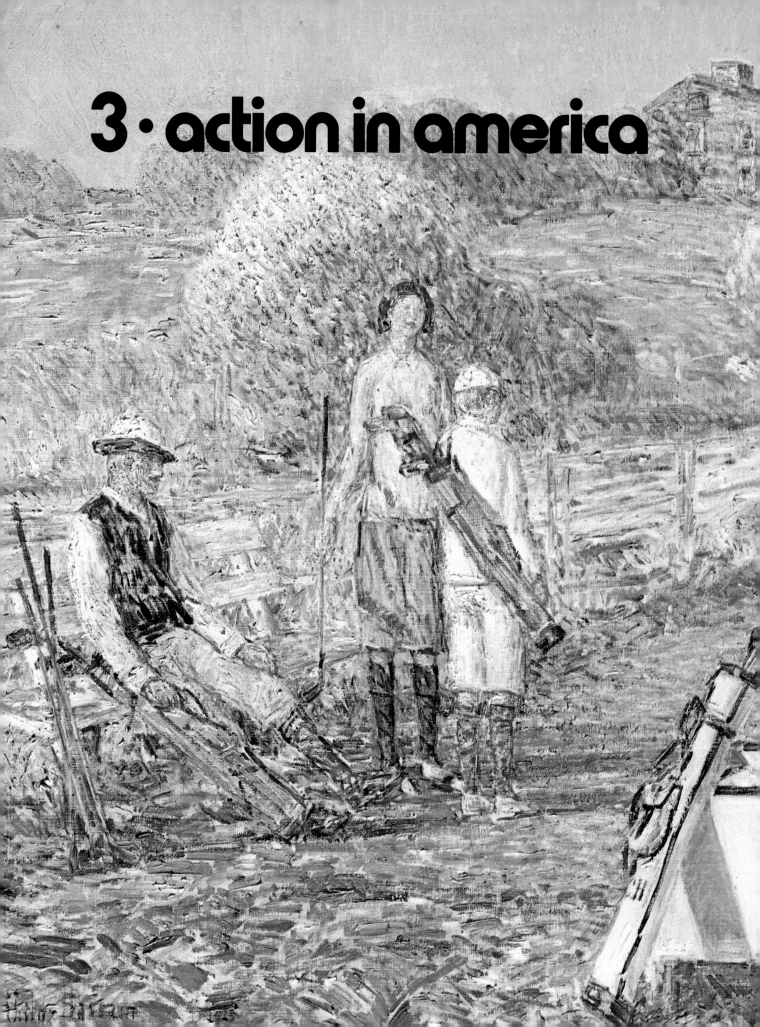

3 · action in america

erhaps the most teasing problem facing the historian of American golf is to determine how and where and when the game first came to be played in the United States. The question, however, is of purely academic interest, because although there are a number of references to golf dating from the middle of the seventeenth century, it is equally clear that the game did not survive at that time.

Of that first introduction of golf to America we know very little, and there is even some doubt whether those earliest references applied to the Scottish game at all. The evidence suggests that the Dutch game of kolven was played by the settlers of New Netherlands and it was probably this game, not golf, which earned the displeasure of the magistrates at Fort Orange in 1657. Once again, as in Scotland, the first evidence of a golfing game is found in official attempts to outlaw the pastime.

A number of tantalizing references to golf between 1779 and 1812 have survived. What are we to make of an advertisement, for instance, which appeared in *Rivington's Royal Gazette* in New York on April 21, 1779?

TO THE GOLF PLAYERS
The Season for this pleasant and healthful
Exercise now advancing, Gentlemen may be furnished
with excellent CLUBS and the veritable Caledonian
BALLS, by enquiring at the Printers.

This notice had nothing to do with kolven. Since Rivington was an importer and merchant, as well as printer, he may have shipped in some equipment for Scottish officers and found himself with some surplus clubs and balls on his hands.

The Savannah (Georgia) Golf Club today proudly displays a framed invitation of 1811 which reads:

GOLF CLUB BALL
The Honor of Miss Eliza Johnston's company
is requested to a Ball to be given by the Members
of the Golf Club of this city, at the Exchange,
on Tuesday evening the 13th instant,
at 7 o'clock.

Here we have proof of the existence of a golf club, but no golf relics have survived from those days, and no references have been discovered to prove that the members actually played Caledonian golf. Perhaps they did. If not, we are left with the charming theory that the good people of Savannah had copied the social aspect of Scottish clubs, with their emphasis on dining and conviviality, and simply adopted the word "Golf" as a title. Possibly the members consumed their regulation gallons of claret and sides of beef without bothering themselves with the tedious ritual of hacking a ball around the countryside.

Subsequently, the records make it clear that both golf and kolven were established as distinctly separate sports, with clubs devoted to each game, by the end of the eighteenth century. If South Carolina and Georgia were indeed the early strongholds of golf, it is interesting to note that when the game was reintroduced a hundred years later these areas again flourished as golfing centers.

Golf disappeared from public record with the war against Great Britain in 1812, and the next significant development took place in 1887, when a Scot, Robert Lockhart, imported half a dozen clubs and a quantity of guttie balls. His friend John Reid of Yonkers was intrigued by Lockhart's stories of golf and decided to try the game for himself. Reid interested some friends and they had a three-hole course laid out in a meadow near Reid's home. Was this the first American golf club?

Let us pause and consider the social scene. By the time golf returned to America the nation had

Preceding pages: Childe Hassam's "Mixed Foursome,"
painted in 1923, shows first tee of
the Maidstone club on Long Island. Father, at left,
may have hooked one out-of-bounds.

changed greatly. The political union had been accompanied by an ethnic fusion. Whereas the first American golf had been played by transplanted Europeans, the second golfing invasion was made on a country whose people saw themselves as citizens of a new nation. Instead of a country fragmented into colonies of exiles, America was now inhabited by Americans. So we cannot say that golf was introduced to America when Lockhart and Scottish-born merchants began to amuse themselves by hitting golf balls around a New York meadow, but we can assert with confidence that golf had truly arrived in America when John Reid and his native-born friends took up the game.

In fact, a group of Scots who formed the Oakhurst Golf Club in West Virginia have a stronger claim to the honor of being the first of the modern American golfers by a year or so, but the Yonkers players deserve most of the missionary credit. Reid and his friends formed themselves into The St. Andrews Golf Club at Yonkers-on-Hudson in 1888, and when they moved four years later to an apple orchard, with six holes, the club became known as "the Apple-Tree Gang."

The sportswriter, O. B. Keeler, who was best known as the traveling companion and biographer of Bobby Jones, wrote that the Apple-Tree Gang laid out their lunch behind the 6th green, where bar service was dispensed from a wicker-covered demijohn of whisky. By tradition, the holes at the Merion Golf Club near Philadelphia, one of the earliest clubs in the country, are marked not by flags, but by sticks topped with wicker baskets. No one knows the origin of the baskets of Merion, but it is possible that they hark back to the Apple-Tree Gang. After all, it would be quite logical for the Yonkers players to impale their empty bottles on sticks to mark the holes. And what could be more natural than for the founding fathers of Merion to follow suit? Stranger things happened in those formative years, when no one knew exactly how to set about this odd game. (The British historian, Robert Browning, reveals that when the Shinnecock Hills Golf Club laid out its course on Long Island, a visitor criticized its lack of apple trees which, he felt, were an essential feature of the game.)

An extraordinary native version of golf could have developed in the United States if the model offered by the St. Louis *Globe-Democrat* of February 24, 1889, had ever gained favor. As described in a syndicated article by a special correspondent, golf was "a popular Scottish pastime which affords lots of excitement." A subhead explained further that "No dude can play it because brawn and vigor are essential qualities. The players have servants and sometimes run many miles—spectators in the way."

The article, in part, read as follows:

"Given a strong pair of lungs, firm muscles upon the legs and a healthy desire to emulate others in physical exercise, a man may become a golf player. Without these he had better stay out of the sport, for no man who cannot run several miles without stopping can make any kind of a respectable appearance in the game.

"In addition to the fact that it appeals to men of athletic development, it is also by the nature of the game itself, a most aristocratic exercise; for no man can play at golf who has not a servant at command to assist him. The truth is that the servant is as essential to the success of the game as the player himself. Perhaps the best description of the game, which would certainly be unique in a republic, may be given in the words of one of the most expert players in this vicinity, Mr. Alexander D. MacFarlane.

" 'To play golf properly we need a very large expanse of uncultivated soil, which is not too much broken up by hills. . . . Having selected a field, the first thing necessary is to dig a small hole perhaps one foot or two feet deep and about four inches in diameter. Beginning with this hole, a circle is devised that in-

cludes substantially the whole of the links. About once in 500 yards of this circle a hole is dug corresponding to the one I have just described. The design is to make as large a circle as possible, with holes at about the same distance apart.

" 'The game then may be played, with two or four persons. If by four, two of them must be upon the same side. There are eleven implements of the game, most important of which is the ball. This is made of gutta-percha and is painted white. It weighs about two ounces and is just small enough to fit comfortably into the holes dug in the ground. Still it should not be so large that it cannot be taken out with ease. The other ten implements are the tools of the players. They are of

various shapes as may be inferred from the names of the implements. The spoon, for instance, is a rough approximation to what we generally understand as a spoon and is designed to lift the ball out of holes, or sinks, in the ground. The club, of course, is simply an instrument with which to bat the ball. The same practically applies to the driving putter. All these implements of the game are designed to fit into the various situations in which the player may find himself.

" 'At the beginning of play each player places his ball at the edge of a hole which has been designated as a starting point. When the word has been given to start, he bats his ball as accurately as possible toward the next hole, which may be, as I have said,

Earliest photo (1888) of golf in America is of St. Andrews club's pasture course (top l.) before move to the orchard (l.) which gave members the "Apple-Tree Gang" nickname. Above: Course construction when horsepower meant horses.

Growing boom of golf was reflected in 1901 advertising and in some ludicrous attempts (opposite) to explain the game to newspaper readers of America in 1889.

either 100 or 500 yards distant. As soon as it is started in the air he runs forward in the direction which the ball has taken and his servant, who is called a "caddy" runs after him with all the other nine tools in his arms. If the player is expert or lucky, he bats his ball so that it falls within a few feet or inches, even, of the next hole in the circle. His purpose is to put the ball into that next hole, spoon it out and drive it forward to the next further one before his opponent can accomplish the same end. The province of the "caddy" in the game is to follow his master as closely as possible, generally at a dead run, and be ready to hand him whichever implement of the game the master calls for, as the play may demand. For instance, the ball may fall in such a way that it is lodged an inch or two above the ground, having fallen in thick grass. The player rushing up to it would naturally call upon his "caddy" for a baffing spoon and, having received it from the hands of his servant, he would bat the ball with the spoon in the direction of the next hole.

"'You can see that in this the "caddy" really gets about as much exercise out of the sport as his master, and he must be so familiar with the tools of the game that he can hand out the right implement at any moment when it is called for. If a player has succeeded in throwing or pushing his ball into a hole, his opponent must wait until he has succeeded in spooning it out before he begins to play. Obedience to this rule obviates any dispute as to the order in which a man's points are to be made. For if I have my ball in a hole and my opponent has his within an inch or two of it, he must wait before he plays until I have gotten my ball clear of it and thrown it towards the next hole. Following this general plan the players go entirely about the circle, and, as you may see, in a large field it may involve a run of several miles. If I should throw my ball beyond the hole at which I must next enter, I am obliged to knock it back until it shall enter the desired place and be carefully spooned out again. While I am doing

72

Waiting for the Word

Scoring at a Hole

Player and Assistant

Playing Well Together

Where the Spoon Is Handy

*The American tradition was born—with resort golf at
Long Beach and the palatial standard set by
Stanford White's 1892 design for first U.S. clubhouse,
at the Shinnecock Hills Country Club.*

74

this my opponent may by a lucky play get his ball within the proper limit and thus gain some distance on me.' "

What a pity that America did not respond to the idea of such a healthy sport! It is interesting to speculate how this special correspondent managed to get quite such a garbled picture of golf. Clearly he had never seen the game played; perhaps the most charitable explanation is that the article arose from a chance meeting in a bar with Mr. Alexander D. MacFarlane, and that they both made a night of it.

The glorious absurdity of the MacFarlane version will be appreciated by anyone with the slightest acquaintance with golf. At the same time, it must be admitted, the formative years of American golf did involve some eccentricities hardly less credible than the fantasies of Mr. MacFarlane and his amanuensis.

In a situation of snowballing popularity for a game about which few Americans had any real knowledge, there was ample scope for scoundrels. Two men who did much to misdirect those first halting footsteps of American golf are worthy of mention. According to American golf writer Charles Price, one of the villains was Tom Bendelow, who worked as a compositor on a New York newspaper.

Bendelow was a Scot and although Americans had great difficulty understanding his accent, they assumed he knew what he was talking about. Actually, his knowledge of golf was of the sketchiest, but he realized that he was ahead of the market. He talked himself into a job as an architectural consultant. Price's description cannot be improved: "Bendelow's methods were simple, to say the least. As an appropriate spot he would mark the first tee with a stake. Then he would pace off a hundred yards and stake off that spot with a simple cross bunker. Then he would march another hundred yards and mark this location for a mound that was to be built in the shape of a chocolate drop. Then he would walk another hundred yards, more or less, and mark the location for a green. All of Bendelow's

greens assumed one of two shapes: perfectly round or perfectly square. None of the greens was protected by hazards, most of them were indistinguishably flat, and all of them had to be ploughed under within a few years because, as anyone with a smattering of agronomy could see, they were nothing more than weed nurseries."

Bendelow could lay out a course in one day, for a $25 fee, and he managed to perpetrate more than six hundred monstrosities.

The other notable rascal of the day was of a very different breed. Charles Blair Macdonald was a big man in every way. He had a large physique and a large voice, a large personality, and a large opinion of himself. Unlike most Americans, he had a thorough knowledge of golf from his years as a student at St. Andrews University and he was a considerable player. Who better than Macdonald, then, to ensure that championship golf in America was organized on a sound basis? That, at any rate, was Macdonald's opinion when he failed to win an invitational tournament over thirty-six holes of stroke play organized by the Newport Golf Club. Macdonald roared his objections, including the complaint that it was absurd to consider a stroke-play competition as an amateur championship. Nobody knew what was correct. Later the St. Andrews Club organized a match-play tournament. Again Macdonald was beaten, albeit in the final and in the aftermath of an injudicious bottle of champagne over lunch. And again Macdonald ranted that this was not a proper championship, his main argument resting on the fact that he had not won it. At least the farcical situation resulting from Macdonald's bull-like personality prompted remedial action. A group of prominent golfing businessmen got together and invited a number of representatives of leading clubs—including Macdonald himself—to form an association to conduct the amateur and open championships. Thus the United States Golf Association was born and with it the first official amateur championship.

This time the result stood, which was pos-

The golfing manner when the century was young—
including a hot day in Vermont (top l.) and a hot drive
from pro Alex Pirie (above). Although long
skirts were lovely, they hampered women's swings.

sibly less a reflection of the authority of the new body than of the fact that the winner was Macdonald. The man who had twice proved that he had the force of personality to upset the golfing applecart now turned his massive powers to the defense of the golfing establishment. With the maverick safely yoked, the path of progress was clear. As to the standard of American golf in these early years, some indication can be gleaned from Macdonald's figures of 89 and 100 in that first, abortive championship. In the first round, at least, he was sober enough and that was the leading score.

In the ten years between 1890 and 1900 American golf blossomed from one scrubby pasture course to more than a thousand. The standard of golf was of the novice variety for the most part, and if most of the courses, such as those of the Bendelow variety, were little more than good fields spoiled, there was one exception. The course built at Chicago at this time set a high standard and established a level of quality from which later architects were to take their soundings. It was designed by Charles Blair Macdonald.

For thirty years or so after the rise of the Apple-Tree Gang, the game spread through only one stratum of society. It was a rich man's sport and a snobbish one. New clubs were formed and immigrant Scottish professionals were engaged to teach the new game and supervise the construction of courses. The first municipal course was opened (in Boston) in 1890, and American technical ingenuity produced the rubber-core ball. But as far as the broad mass of the population was concerned, golf was a foreign fad for the nobs. On a competitive level, Walter Travis's victory in the British Amateur Championship in 1904 was a false dawn. Overseas players and foreign-born residents continued to monopolize the major competitions. Even the famous victory of the American amateur, Francis Ouimet, in

79

The genus Caddie was the butt of much satirical fun
in popular prints around 1900. In reality
the caddie worked too hard and for too little reward
to be able to appreciate the jokes.

beating the English champions Harry Vardon and Ted Ray in the U.S. Open of 1913, failed to capture public imagination. The newspapers made little of it, reflecting the general indifference to the game. Any impetus which might have been given to golf by Ouimet's triumph was stifled by the onset of World War I. For a time, America was to be preoccupied with more serious events.

      With the armistice came a vast change. The Roaring Twenties produced a mood of national euphoria. America put up the shutters to the outside world, rolled back the carpet, and had a ball. This was the time when golf boomed. Many people see the game's expansion as a natural extension of the fun-loving atmosphere of jazz, flappers, and a national appetite for recreation. The real reason is possibly more prosaic. Rather than being swept in on a river of bootleg booze, golf owed its expansion to economics and the growth of the motor industry. People were making money and the cheap and reliable automobile was widely available. It was a period when sportsmen became national heroes and the golf professional in his turn benefited from the trend. American players dominated the championships, America dominated the game. Golf shed the last trap-

pings of Scottish influence and became a national game.

      By 1931 there were two hundred and eighty-three flourishing public courses and golf was established as a sport for everyman. Tournament golf had progressed to purses of $10,000, and—although it was still a minority sport in terms of spectators—golf news was beginning to be accepted and looked for on the sports pages by the great newspaper-reading public.

      The quality of the courses built to cater to the expanding game was a significant factor in the rise of American golf. The new school of golf architecture no longer looked to the links of Ayrshire and Fife for inspiration. Architects, adopting an analytical approach to the problem, produced designs suited to the terrain. They built fine, tightly bunkered courses which forced the golfer to plan his tactical approach and to execute shots of great accuracy. Of course, such requirements also obtained on the Scottish links, but there they were mainly imposed by the ever-present wind. The American architects built strategy into the topography of their courses.

      As a result, the thirties and forties saw a subtle revolution in golfing technique. Harry Vardon

81

Dress fashions for golf reflected everyday clothing. Usually, the only special item for golf was a pair of walking boots with tackety studs hammered into the soles.

had popularized the conception of good style, but his golf was mainly a matter of improvisation; playing into a blasting forty-mile-per-hour wind, he used a swing quite different from that for a similar shot in still air. American players had a different set of problems. Most of the time wind was not a hazard. On the other hand, they had to meet a higher standard of accuracy.

A new breed of technicians—Ben Hogan, Byron Nelson, Sam Snead—sought basically to hit the ball just as Vardon did, but they achieved their aim with minor variations on the same repeating, grooved swing. Their example inspired a craze for analysis, technical instruction, and aids to the perfect swing. Hardly a part of the human anatomy escaped recognition as the "key" to good golf. Amateurs were awash in a flood of literature exhorting them to move their left thumbs a quarter of an inch around the shaft, or to concentrate on digging in the big toe of the right foot on impact. Much good it did them.

But for the masters, the standard of golf was raised to an unprecedented level of excellence. Seeing these Americans swing on visits to windswept St. Andrews, knowing Scots shook their heads and prophesied that the Yanks would be blown off the course. Two generations of American golfers have proved them wrong. Perhaps a whole winter of gales would ruin a grooved American swing, but on short visits American golfers do not have time to succumb to wind-cheating methods. Their style has stood the challenge year after year in the British Open and proved the efficiency of the American way of golf.

The triumphs of American professionals after World War II, not to mention the enthusiasm of a golfing president in the White House, encouraged another period of expansion.

At this time an ex-Coast Guardsman named Arnold Palmer asked Mark McCormack if he would manage his affairs as a professional golfer. McCormack, who had played on his college golf team and was just setting out on a law career, agreed. There was no formal contract, and at the outset McCormack limited himself to setting up exhibition matches. With Palmer freed of administrative details and able to concentrate singlemindedly on his game, his career, which had begun with high promise, quickly prospered to a degree which made him the most astonishing phenomenon in modern sport. Palmer's success had repercussions in every corner of the world. There is no profit in pursuing the chicken-and-egg question of whether McCormack made Palmer, or Palmer made McCormack. Their contributions were complementary.

In the early days of Palmer's career each victory, and every headline extolling the excitement his swashbuckling golf generated, gave McCormack another negotiating lever. He was soon in the driver's seat and dictating terms. Everybody wanted Palmer, and McCormack was calling the price. The squeals of anguish from the smoke-filled rooms reverberated across the land, and if McCormack won few friends in the process, he earned a grudging respect. As Palmer became a national figure, McCormack spread his activities beyond conventional golf contracts. He proved that the Palmer name could sell anything from dry cleaning to real estate. Palmer's commercial involvements grew into a million-dollar enterprise. Nobody doubted that McCormack was good for Palmer; but the question many people asked was whether McCormack was good for golf.

In the sense of performing altruistic acts, McCormack himself probably would not claim to have heaped benefits on the game. However, in the broader sense, no single man has done more for golf. Everyone whose living is dependent on golf has benefited from his influence. In 1941, the pro golf tour was worth less than $200,000 a year in prize money. During the time Palmer was the biggest attraction in golf the purse rose to $5 million. When McCormack negotiates for one of his clients—who have included Gary Player and Jack

The social status of golf is reflected in the opulence of the Glen Cove, New York, club, but by the twenties the broader appeal of the game was being celebrated, and propagated, in the songs of the day.

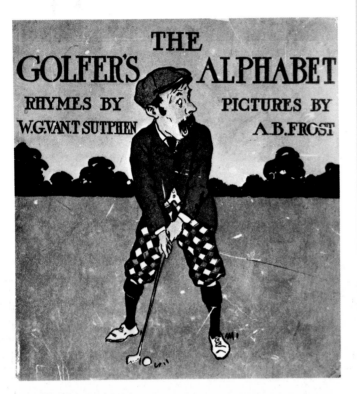

THE
GOLFER'S ALPHABET
RHYMES BY
W.G.VAN.T SUTPHEN
PICTURES BY
A.B.FROST

D is the Duffer, the Drive
    that he cuts,
And the Something he says when he
    misses short putts.

M is that Moment of
    agony keen
When it's one for the Match
    on the very last green.

R is the Rub that may lay
    us up dead,
Or leave us in sand buried
    over the head.

G is the Game we expected
   to play,
But which didn't come off on
   the tournament day.

J is the Jerk that would
   drive in a pile,
But the ball, as you see,
   wears a cynical
   smile.

N is the Niblick, retriever
   of blunders,
And now and again it accomplishes
   wonders.

O is the Odd that we play
   for the tin,—
Peculiar indeed that it
   doesn't get in.

X is the X-pletive
   sometimes employed.
For a golfer is human, and
   easily annoyed.

Z is for Zero, the sign of
   despair.
"Awa' wi' your gowf! we
   will play it nae mair."

THE NEW BOOK OF GOLF

EDITED BY HORACE G. HUTCHINSON

Nicklaus—he negotiates incidentally for every professional. The contracts he signs inevitably raise the rates
for all. All professional golfers have been swept along
in McCormack's slipstream to a new standard of living.

There have, of course, been many contributing factors to the growth of professional golf. Television has had enormous impact, both in popularizing
the sport and in propagating it as the result of specially
filmed competitions and general enlargement of purses.
Golf was expanding, anyway, in the warm sun of the
affluent society, and the pressures of inflation tended
to push the prize funds upward. But the process was
certainly accelerated by Palmer's golf and personality,
and by his manager's acute exploitation of them.

If critics must still ask what McCormack

has done for golf, there are two major achievements for
which he must be given a share of the credit. He was
instrumental in reviving the flagging reputation of the
British Open Championship by his policy of encouraging his players to attain international status. Today
no championship in the world attracts a stronger field
than the Open and by that token, at least, it is not only
the oldest but the greatest of the Big Four grand-slam
events. McCormack's part in the creation of the Piccadilly World Match Championship was even more direct. It was his baby, and at first was seen as something
of a McCormack benefit. Over the years, however, it has
grown in stature and now ranks highly in international
esteem. Invitations to compete in the eight-man field
are eagerly sought and the winner counts his success

*Timeless drawings by A. B. Frost (preceding pages) and
period knicknacks, including Bobby Jones statuette and McCoy golf
recorder (opposite), found market among
golfers—such as wealthy mandarins of the game (above).*

Americans triumphed at Brookline in 1913.
Francis Ouimet (above), with caddie Eddie Lowery, on
his way to U. S. Open eclipse of Britain's
mighty Ted Ray (opposite, on left) and Harry Vardon.

high among his achievements.

The spread of golf has been accompanied by wide social repercussions. Although the game belongs to the masses as a major spectator sport and is played at every level of class and income—by ten million people in the U.S. alone—it has retained the aura of a gentlemanly activity.

In some ways golf's status has been elevated. The club professional, for instance, ranks in the community with the doctor and other professional men, whereas twenty years ago he was regarded on the level of a skilled artisan. The big-name tournament player walks with kings, and no one raises an eyebrow when he is invited to dine with the President. As for the young caddie who shows an aptitude for the game, he no longer aspires to an assistantship sweeping out the shop, but is induced to enter college on a generous scholarship. Golf remains a prestige game and the manufacturer who wants to stress the quality of his product uses a golfing association in his advertising. And it is undoubtedly true that golf does convey the image of style, good breeding, and a healthy out-of-doors feeling exuding the tang of pine needles and masculinity.

Alas the picture is illusory. The Madison Avenue idea that the golfer is a man for whom only the best is good enough and who, furthermore, makes it big with the dollies is sheer fiction (at least as far as his powers of discretion are concerned). In reality, once a man takes a golf club in hand he becomes a gullible idiot. For proof you have only to watch him on the course. The president of a large company, whose daily decisions affect the lives and well-being of thousands, escapes into a fantasy world in which he is a super-Nicklaus, judging by the shots he attempts. The cautious banker turns into a reckless gambler, going for the hundred-to-one chance of threading a three-iron through a two-foot gap in the woods. And after the game, still bereft of all their normal faculties, they read advertisements in the golfing press claiming that this glove will

put yards on their drive or that a different brand of clubs will save them six shots a round.

It has been worked out that if all the claims in golfing advertisements were true, and a player equipped himself with the full range of magical new socks, gloves, clubs, balls, tees, shoes, and practice aids available to him, he would not only play to scratch within ten days, but the total promised extra yardage would have him driving the ball half a mile. And yet the captains of industry with speed slots and sweet spots dancing before their eyes, slide purposefully to the pro's shop and figuratively beg: "Please sell me the Brooklyn Bridge."

Despite this suspension of elementary common sense, the golf courses of the world have become extensions of business offices. Millions of dollars worth of business are transacted on golf courses every week. We can only hope that these golfing businessmen retain their professional acumen while conducting their *al fresco* discussions, even though on the golfing level they may have abandoned themselves to cuckooland. If golf adds a little oil to the cogs of domestic commerce, it supplies a positive gusher to the world of international business. It is the common ground on which the captains of industry can instantly find rapport.

In the bad old days, a visiting buyer might be feted around the night clubs and possibly introduced to the redhead in the front row of the chorus. Nowadays he is more likely to be taken out to the country club and partnered with the company's public-relations officer, who has been appointed to the job solely for his ability to get around in par or better after six martinis.

The value that corporations put on golf for purposes of good will was never more clearly demonstrated than in the Alcan tournament. The company allotted a vast budget for its promotion, which involved the co-sponsorship of qualifying tournaments in different parts of the world, culminating in a "Golfer of the Year" tournament with the richest first prize in golf.

*More than anything else, the expanding car industry
was responsible for the mushrooming
popularity of golf, a popularity reflected in the
decoration of articles of everyday use.*

The usual motives of commercial sponsorship were secondary in this case. The company was not particularly concerned about newspaper publicity or TV coverage, nor was the income from admissions an important factor in its budget calculations.

The format for the competition, involving total scores at the different qualifying events, was so complicated that it required lengthy calculations to keep track of a player's progress. The formula could have been simplified to make it readily understandable to the man in the street, and therefore more interesting, but here again the sponsors were noticeably unconcerned. Their prime motive was directly to influence business associates and potential customers. The outlay of millions of dollars was primarily for the benefit of a relatively few people, on one occasion no more than could be comfortably accommodated in the Gleneagles Hotel for the tournament at St. Andrews. Specially favored guests were allocated in the preliminary pro-am events. To an outsider one of the mysteries of these promotions was the arbitrary classification of guests according to their importance. For instance, a small customer would be given complimentary tickets to the tournament, another man would get, in addition, an invitation to the banquet, while the mighty moguls of aluminum would get a favored draw in the pro-am and a lavish trip to an overseas tournament.

You might expect human nature to react against such discrimination. A man would surely reason: "I may be only a small customer today but in a few years I could be the biggest aluminum consumer in the country. So where do these people get off handing me a gate ticket and a box lunch, while my rival is being put up in the best hotel in town and paired with Billy Casper in the pro-am?"

Most of us would surely bridle at such a slight and switch our business to a rival supplier. Not, apparently, so. During the five years of the Alcan tournaments, there was never a hint of acrimony on that

Golf becomes fashion conscious—or fashion becomes golf conscious. Either way, the Flapper Era was a swinging scene and the game was established in the American way of life.

JUNE 16, 1921

Life

PRICE 15 CENTS

Golf Number

The Wearing of the Green

5¢ a copy
10 Cents in Canada
July 21, 1923

Collier's

THE NATIONAL WEEKLY

Edna Crompton

In this issue:
They Call It Ruin by Richard Washburn Child

score. The sponsors were confident in their psychology that a man who had been omitted from the VIP list would react by striving harder than ever to win his way into favor by increasing his business the following year. We have seen that golf can cause rational people to behave in an irrational manner, but this probably was the first example of exploitation of golf's obsessive qualities in the cause of business.

More commonly, commerce uses golf for its associations. Alcohol and tobacco have to live down a continual assault from medicine and morality, and one of the ways this is achieved is by association with the healthy image of golf. The British Professional Golf cir-

cuit is mainly supported by cigarette and alcohol sponsors. American sponsorship has taken a different course. The vast dimensions of the nation have created a situation which makes it necessary for communities to advertise their importance. The resort town which shouts the loudest gets the tourist. If it is true that community spirit is stronger in America than anywhere else, it is also true that nowhere is community spirit so important to the economics of a city. As a result golf administrators all over the world look with envy and wonder at the American pro golf circuit, which is sustained by a gigantic voluntary effort. The message of a promotion like the Piccadilly World match-play championship is that

*The making of a legend—Ben Hogan indicates
a round of 10 under par in Chicago in 1942 and eleven
years later, after winning the British Open,
receives a national hero's welcome on Broadway.*

by association the great athletic heroes of golf endorse Piccadilly cigarettes.

The message of the Cleveland Open, on the other hand, is that Cleveland is a place with everything going for it, including Jack and Gary and Arnie. Cleveland's desire for publicity is helped by the fact that the only chance local golfers have to see the stars is to promote their own tournament. The country is so big that the golfing caravan can pass their way but once a year, and then only if the inducements are big enough. All these factors conspire to produce a goad which pricks the Clevelander in his two most sensitive areas: his billfold and his local pride. The result is a huge volunteer response. Armies of committees work from one year's end to the next to prove that anything Los Angeles can do Cleveland can do better. Los Angeles tries even harder, and so professional golf rides forward on a wave of local rivalry and volunteer effort.

Ed Carter, a professional administrator with responsibility for a number of tournaments, once costed a golf promotion on the assumption that prevailing rates would be paid for labor and equipment. It came to half a million dollars. Obviously, without voluntary labor from the business community, there could be no golf circuit at all.

Just look at the logistics of a tournament. First, a golf club must relinquish its course and premises for at least a week. Certain facilities—grandstands, tentage, and scoreboards—have to be provided. Players and officials need transport; up to two hundred cars and drivers must be made available. A complicated system of communications must be established to relay hole-by-hole scores to headquarters and back to the scoreboards. To accomplish all this, the tournament requires at least twenty skilled men to marshal the crowds at each hole, another hundred to operate the scoring and communications systems, a hundred or so to attend to such diverse activities as manning car parks, operating turnstiles, and organizing facilities within the club-

house. It is easy to see that even $500,000 would not go far if all the people had to be paid, especially for the many hours of preparatory work during the year before the event.

Imagine the reaction if anyone were so foolhardy as to walk into a British golf club, pick a member at random, and pose the question: "Would you like to serve on a tournament committee for a year, meeting for two hours every week, contribute the services of your office, equipment, and staff to the tournament, take a page advertisement in the program at an exorbitant rate, buy a uniform, and then take a week of your annual holiday to spend sitting in a tent relaying scores on a telephone?" The reply would be an explosion of indignant refusal, yet this is what happens all the time in America, and people fight for the privilege of volunteering.

With communities anxious to pour more and more cash and work into golf, the PGA's biggest problem is to select the richest plums. And all the while there is a rich fallout to charities. Unfortunately, there are times when some golfers lose sight of the source of their bounty. To the tournament player, of course, golf is a job and one week is much like the next. The point is that each week is the culmination of twelve months' hard work for the locals, and to them it is very special indeed. Hence, an unguarded comment about the quality of the course or a harsh word with a marshal may be a triviality to the golfer, but it is a blow to the victims. The PGA tries to indoctrinate its tournament recruits, but occasionally the lesson is forgotten. The golf circuit is a real-life example of a goose which lays golden eggs —a very good reason for taking great care not to ruffle its feathers.

If the volunteer worker is the backbone of American pro golf, the paying customer who buys his ticket at the gate is a very different proposition. Generally speaking, the golf spectator is less exuberant than the fan at the football or baseball match. Even so, he

Golf becomes a truly international sport. Gary Player and Neil Coles (top) in Piccadilly tournament, Wentworth, England, 1966, and Mark McCormack, man who guides the careers of golfing globe-trotters.

can get pretty involved; he has that great American birthright giving the man who has paid his dollar the right to express his opinion.

In Australia the sports fan does not admit that he goes to a match to support his team. He says he is a "barracker" for his team, meaning that he goes to jeer rather than cheer. The British like to consider themselves impartial, always excepting the oafish tradition of association football, and applaud skill no matter who displays it. That tradition is perhaps best seen at Wimbledon, where an outright winner is greeted with immediate applause. If the point is won by default, because of the opponent's misplay, there is a moment of silence in consideration for the victim before the ap-

lause begins for the winning of the point. Anyone who clapped immediately would be frowned out of the courts as a bounder. It is all very admirable in theory, but rather bloodless. It denies the essence of sport. Impartiality has no place in sport, which is cops-and-robbers in adult form. Certainly the enemy can be applauded, but this gesture should denote grudging admiration rather than lavish praise. Sport is partial. To become truly involved the spectator must associate with one side or one man and truly rejoice in his successes and grieve for his misfortunes.

This honest involvement is an American characteristic and explains the phenomenon of "Arnie's Army." Rooting for Palmer naturally involves seeing

Golf develops into a major spectator sport. Arnold Palmer sinks winning putt for 1964 Masters and (above) shares hero-worshipping with the man who was to topple him from the golfing pinnacle, Jack Nicklaus.

all other golfers as enemies, and if this explains the booing of Jack Nicklaus in the early days of his career, it does not necessarily excuse it. Eventually, the PGA took some of the heat out of golf watching by forbidding the carrying of banners on the course. Even so, the American golf watcher remains the loudest cheerer and the most fervent groaner in the world. In Britain it is possible with a little practice to interpret the course of a golf match by the noise of the gallery. The quality of the applause for a 20-foot putt to save a half is quite different from the reaction to a winning 20-footer. And if the putts miss (in silence, naturally), there are different reactions again for the tap-ins. In America, cheer interpretation is much more difficult. An explosion of glee on the other side of a hill may mean that Don January has holed out from a bunker, or simply that Palmer has made a joke on the tee. There was a time when an agonized groan could mean that Palmer had missed a putt or that Nicklaus had holed one.

At least, the reactions are genuine. When the late Tony Lema was engaged to play an exhibition round in Copenhagen, the organizers were so concerned to make him feel properly appreciated that they hired a large crowd of bemused spectators at $15 a head.

There was no shortage of curious spectators for Walter Hagen's exhibition match in Palestine (as it was then), but his opening drive, one of the best he had ever hit, was greeted by silence. His opponent hit a very poor effort which hopped feebly forward and received tumultuous applause. The explanation was that the spectators, completely unaccustomed to golf and having no idea what was supposed to happen, did not see Hagen's ball depart and having no clue where it had gone did not know if his shot was good or bad.

Golf is one of the few games where the fan has to follow the action on foot, and the logistics of moving several thousand people around a four-mile course are complex. There are two principal methods of handling a golf crowd. For bigger events the usual

practice is to fence off the fairways and permit a free-for-all behind the ropes. The other method, and a vastly superior one where the circumstances permit, is to let galleries follow the golfers up the fairways under the supervision of marshals and stewards.

In both cases the fan will get more pleasure from his watching if he spends a moment or two in preliminary preparation. If the fairways are fenced and the crowds are dense, the best plan is to use the leapfrog technique. You take up your position behind a tee to give yourself the best possible view of the drives. After the players have hit their tee shots you resolutely ignore all temptations to see the second shots and march purposefully to the green and take up station directly behind the flag. In this way you have avoided the scramble of the herd and are in prime position to watch the putting. Once the players have holed out you allow the mob to dash to the next tee while you walk in dignified comfort to the place on the ropes where you judge the tee shots will finish. By this method you get a good view of every other shot, your progress unimpeded and your temper tranquil.

Compare that experience with the sweaty frustration of joining the stampede and trying your tiptoe best to watch every stroke. Watching golf can be more tiring than playing the game because of the infighting and standing about, shifting your weight from foot to foot. A brisk walk is positively refreshing in comparison to the scramble among the infantry of Arnie's Army, and the deplorable slowness of modern professional golf makes it preferable at times to follow one match for a hole and then leapfrog to the match in front. By this method you can get a sight of twenty-seven players by the time you reach the turn and pause for your well-earned beer. At that point you can decide whether to continue moving up through the field, or whether to wait and pick up one of the threesomes you have already seen.

Another variation is more suited to those

101

Vast resources of cash and equipment—
including effects mike and cherry-picker camera
hoist seen here—are deployed
to bring golf to the television screen.

enlightened fans who hold the opinion that life has
no more tedious sight to offer than a pro golfer spending two minutes missing a 6-foot putt. After all, if a
man has a one-iron shot over a ravine there is an infinite variety of possibilities as to the outcome. With
that putt there are only two results—hit or miss—and
the reaction of the crowd should indicate what happened. Confirmation, if needed, can usually be obtained by one of those eager beavers who run between
shots in order to get into position for every moment of
action. These flying advance scouts from the main
body of troops are usually accurate witnesses to a
simple question such as, "Did Casper hole that putt?"
However, be warned never to trust any on-course
intelligence reports of a more advanced nature. If the
scout adds that Casper is now four under and needs
only to par the last two holes for victory, treat the
information with suspicion. It is nearly always wrong.
You cannot guarantee that the scout is mistaken, of
course, so the best method is to regard him as you
would a clock which has just struck thirteen or the
man who announced, "Every statement I make is a
lie." Assume that this present statement is incorrect
until it is confirmed (and, whisper it softly, there are
times when a scoreboard on the course is not much
more reliable than the gallery grapevine).

     If you are at a tournament where you
are privileged to walk on the fairways, certain adjustments can be made in the leapfrog method. The advantage now is that you have the privilege of inspecting the lie of the ball. Golf watching immediately takes
on a new dimension. No matter how well prepared a
golf course may be, every player will get a bad (or
difficult) lie on the fairway on an average of once in
three shots. Having seen his lie, you are in a much
better position to appreciate his shot. Furthermore,
having inspected the lie of the ball, you also have had
the opportunity to visualize the shot the player must
face, and this is very different from the problem you

*Cameramen and commentators are positioned to relay
action on the small screen. Golf is seen
on even smaller screens by spectators jostling for
vantage points with their periscopes.*

have perceived from behind the ropes.

(Try this experiment the next time you play golf. When you come to a place where you have a good broadside view of a distant fairway, pause and watch the golfers playing their shots. Imagine what club you would select for the approach shot you are watching in the distance. To you, from your side view, it looks an even seven-iron. File away that judgment in your mind and bring it out when you reach that same fairway. What looked like an easy seven has suddenly become a full three-iron shot, preferably with a shade of draw to hold it up against the slope of the green. Golf is an easy game from outside the ropes.)

There is, in addition, one specific golfing bonus from allowing spectators to follow on the fairways. When the crowd is behind ropes or fences it must of necessity walk through the rough. That is, it starts off as rough. Very quickly, however, the rough is trampled flat and the player who sprays his drives is not penalized. At times some players take advantage of the crowd's depredations and aim deliberately to areas which would normally be high rough, knowing that they are sure of a playable lie. Nowadays it is increasingly rare to allow galleries onto the fairways, owing to the vast increase in crowds, the requirements of TV cameras to get unrestricted shots of the play, and the well-publicized (though not always disinterested) criticism of players. It is a pity, because for the true golf fan fairway watching is the only way to see the game. Unfortunately, whenever crowds are allowed onto fairways, there are always a few people who disrupt the system, either through bad manners or ignorance or sheer enthusiasm. It is here that effective marshaling is vital and all too often it fails.

Crowd control is a tricky business but doing it well is mostly a matter of good manners and common sense. The first requirement is to win the confidence of the mob. The worst mistake any marshal can make, and unfortunately it is the commonest, is to create a situation in which he, representing authority, commands obedience to arbitrary instructions. You, sir, are a reasonable man and as cooperative as anyone, but if a red-faced marshal yells at you, "Get back on the left, you people," at the same time thrusting a bamboo staff across your stomach, your reaction, having paid your hard-earned dollar to watch the golf, is to snap the bamboo across your knee and edge farther forward. We understand, sir, and forgive you. We applaud you for your spirit and sturdy independence. We all move farther forward. And we find ourselves in a situation where Arnold Palmer hands us his clubs and says, "You play my shot. You're standing closer to the ball." So we all laugh sheepishly and push back a yard or so.

The trouble is that the marshal tends to see the crowd as an entity, as a flock of sheep to be manipulated. But although we do display a herd instinct in some ways, we are all individuals and determined to maneuver into the best positions. If the marshal adopts a hectoring attitude, he becomes our enemy and we naturally feel free to outwit him the best we can. However, there is a way, and that is for the marshal to win us over. Instead of yelling, "Hold it right there," he can simply suggest, "If we make a circle here, we all can see." Immediately we are all on the same side and, with a certain amount of common sense, an orderly and disciplined gallery can watch in comfort and good humor. In short, golf watchers can be led but not driven. It is a lesson few marshals ever master completely.

This problem of crowd control is perhaps more acute in Britain and mainland Europe than in America, but that is no reason why golf administrators should ignore it. If more attention were paid to crowd-managing techniques perhaps more tournaments could permit the galleries onto the fairways, and that would benefit everyone. But the attitude has been fostered that the golf spectator is a necessary evil, to be tolerated as long as he behaves himself, on the grounds that first priority must be given to the golf and the golfers. Quite right. Nobody would suggest that spectator facilities should be developed to the detriment of the golf; but that is no reason why the paying fan should not receive every possible consideration.

Today we hear more and more frequently of golf fans who say they prefer to watch a tournament on television. TV has done extremely well in popularizing golf and educating the public about it. For instant analysis of the golf swing, the techniques developed by TV—stop-action, slow-motion replay, and split-screen shots showing a golfer making his stroke from two angles simultaneously—are superb. Backed by a knowing commentator, TV golf is a valuable tutor.

At the same time it must be said that TV golf is a vastly inferior substitute for the real thing. At the present state of technical development, with static cameras covering a few selected holes, TV shows part of the game and gives only a sketchy impression of that part.

Looking sideways at a distant fairway, shots may seem easy. Very seldom can the camera convey the problem from the golfer's standpoint. And the nature of the game forces the TV producer to focus on the longueurs of the putting ritual. Here again the game is diminished because the camera's-eye view flattens the contours of the green and makes every putt appear level. The worst by-product of this situation is that the viewer sitting at home is indoctrinated with the fallacious idea that in order to miss a 4-foot putt it is necessary first to remove one's glove, inspect the putt from every point in the compass, pick up imaginary grains of sand from the line, and indulge in a lengthy practice session away from the ball in order, presumably, to invent a method of striking it. In fact, you can miss that putt (or indeed hole it) just as certainly if you step straight up to it and give the ball a tap. All over in a few seconds. Honestly, it's true. You can.

To be fair—as if that were much of a virtue in this context—much of the tedium on the green is caused by the knowledge that the time has to be filled somehow. If the players putted out briskly they would only have an even longer wait on the next tee while the players in front moved out of range. (There are also those who believe that there is a law of diminishing returns on the green and that there comes a point, after a certain period of reconnaissance, when the longer a golfer delays the moment of striking the less likely he is to hole out.)

The administrators of golf are concerned with speeding up tournament golf because of the bad example to club players. At a time when the building of new courses is lagging far behind public demand, it is unfortunate that existing courses are clogged by four-balls taking up to six hours for eighteen holes. There was a time when a day's golf meant a full round in the morning, another eighteen after lunch, and then nine holes of fun golf, using perhaps one club only, in the evening. Imagine trying to do that on a modern course. The pros do a good job for the club game, but inadvertently by their example they are also spoiling it. As things are going, the need for some rule on time may become acute. All manner of suggestions have been made, and possibly the chess players' practice of "starting the opponent's clock" may suggest a helpful convention, if not a firm rule, which golf clubs could adopt. For example, once a man has reached his ball, he would be required to play the shot within, say, 30 seconds, and on the green, having replaced his ball after marking, he would be permitted perhaps no more than 15 seconds.

Such drastic measures could be avoided, however, if the members of the golfing public stopped thinking of themselves as tournament-playing pros and let themselves be drawn—by the simple pleasures of the game—back into the righteous path of speedy golf as the Scots gave it to us.

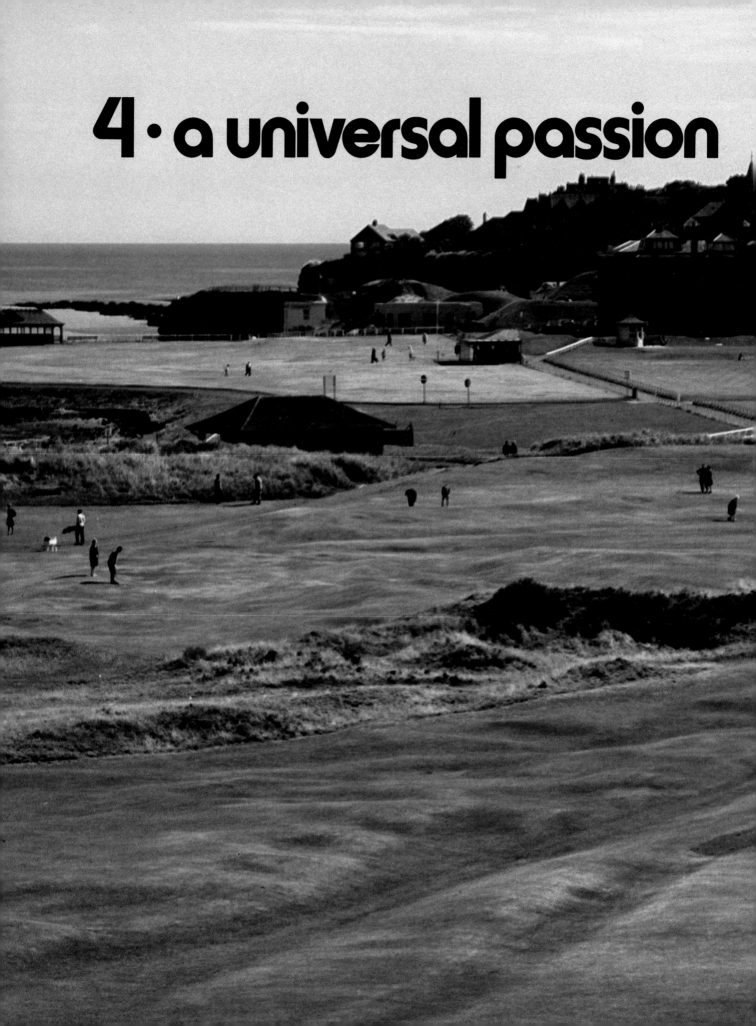

4 · a universal passion

For a Victorian gentleman, the highest estate to which any human being could aspire was that of the Victorian gentleman. In the heyday of British imperialism, therefore, when God was a middle-class Englishman, it was a Christian duty to bring enlightenment to the world and to convert everyone into replicas of Victorian gentlemen. Civilization meant, simply, the English way of life. It naturally followed that those sons of the shires took with them to the far posts of Empire not only their commercial acumen and missionary zeal, but also the household gods of their society. The holds of the P. & O. liners were packed with tennis racquets, cricket bats, golf clubs, port decanters, dinner jackets, and hunting kits. And on arrival in some tropical fever swamp, the Englishman's first concern was to arrange his surroundings so that he might, with a little imagination and a lot of gin, believe himself never to have left Surrey. In short order he built a club, drained enough swamp to lay out tennis courts, cricket pitch, or golf course, and the wives held musical evenings every Wednesday. There were many corners of foreign jungles which were forever Weybridge.

As social changes rearranged the quality of life back in England, these colonial outposts remained faithful to a vision of a vanished England—snobbish and pathetic parodies of a bygone age. But they made their imprint on the overseas countries, particularly in the field of our special concern.

You may think that these golf courses were built for the wrong reasons and for the wrong people. But in time, as intended, the indigenous populations did become close copies of Englishmen in their adoption of these weird pursuits. And very often the pupils became more enthusiastic and more skillful than the masters. In India, especially, the ball boys and caddies who were recruited to service the Anglo-Saxon games progressed to become professionals. They did not have to reach very high standards to shine by

comparison with the sahibs. In the English code it is bad form to practice a game; it is only permissible to excel at games by virtue of a natural gift.

Golf clubs were established in India, the Far East, Australia, Canada, and Europe long before the end of the nineteenth century, and very strange courses they were, compared to the Scottish seaside courses on which they were supposedly modeled.

The other force which motivated the building of golf courses all over the world was the nature of the game itself. Golf has often been likened to an infection which gets into the bloodstream and cannot be eradicated. What is more, as we have seen, golf addiction can produce hallucinations, irrational behavior, and an insatiable craving. Whatever you like to call it, the obsessional nature of golf has manifested itself in some strange places.

In appearance, the oddest courses born of this addiction are those which have been built in deserts. Golf requires water, either natural rain or piped, to produce its full glory. The golfer relishes greenness. Phrases such as "lush turf" and "velvet greens" have an emotive force synonymous with excellence. No wonder many golfers believe that Ireland offers the finest golf courses in the world. Certainly they are the greenest, which is hardly surprising in a country where housewives habitually peep out of their cottage windows and observe that it is a beautiful day for hanging the washing out to rinse.

Whereas rain in Ireland is so commonplace that it is not even mentioned (a steady drizzle is greeted as "a nice soft day"), in some places it is so rare that for practical purposes it does not happen at all. The idea of pouring this precious commodity onto the ground to encourage grass to grow is so farfetched as to be out of the question. A favorite cartoon in the Middle East shows a prospector sinking a trial bore and replying to the inquiry, "Any luck?" with, "No, I keep on striking oil."

Preceding pages: St. Andrews, spiritual home of "the Anticient and healthfull Exercise of the Golf" and today capital of an empire embracing some fifty-five golfing nations.

Desert golf courses are literally "watered" with oil; instead of greens they have "browns," areas of leveled sand compacted with crude oil. At least one of the major professional tournaments on the African circuit is played on a course with browns, and there are many golf courses which cannot boast a single blade of grass. Hell, we tell ourselves, that is just not golf. But this is a highly prejudiced reaction. Basically, golf is a cross-country game ending with putting into a small hole, and grass as such is not necessary in any way to the golfer's progress. The club makes contact with the ball, which thereupon departs. Subsequently the club may gouge a divot of bleeding turf, but that of itself is of no consequence. The effect is exactly the same if, instead of a grassy divot, the club plows up a handful of dry grit.

Indeed, playing off hard-packed sand may improve the game because it requires a more accurate technique. Christy O'Connor, the great Irish golfer, is generally acknowledged to be one of the finest strikers of a golf ball of his generation and a genuinely natural player. While it may be true that he never had a formal lesson, it is absurd to suggest that he was born with his swing. He learned his golf by trial and error, and the place where he learned was on the hard-packed sands of Dublin Bay. He learned to strike the ball accurately because that was the only way that worked. A slight mis-hit off grass may produce a satisfactory result as the club slices through the soft turf. The same shot from sand goes nowhere.

In the same way, the professionals of the Far East who play on hard, bare courses much of the time, have evolved a short-game technique which is uncanny in its accuracy. Where the western professional squeezes the ball into the turf with his wedge, the easterner flicks the ball cleanly off the unyielding surface. All in all, then, that part of golf which we call "through the green" can be every bit as satisfying when it is played "through the brown."

But what of putting? Surely you cannot putt as well on an oily patch of sand as you can on a well-tended grass surface? In fact, once you have adjusted to the difference in pace, putting on browns is considerably more consistent. Any irregularity is obvious to the naked eye. No matter how closely the golfer studies his line on a green he cannot see the worm casts and spike marks below the surface of the grass. What is more, on a green there is often the problem of nap, or grain, and he must try to guess how his ball will be deflected by the direction in which the grass lies. The usual practice after putting on browns is to drag a doormat over the surface to smooth the irregularities you have created. So everyone gets a pristine surface for his putt.

In one major respect, however, the "brown" golfers are truly underprivileged. If we hold the view that half of golf is the aesthetic experience—being surrounded by beautiful countryside—then the desert version is only half a game.

Not so mountain golf. Mountains offer an unusual and spectacular terrain. While the purist may scoff, mountain golf is an exhilarating experience every golfer should sample if he can. For a start, there is Capilano, which perches dramatically on a mountain in the Canadian Rockies overlooking Vancouver. Although its elevation frequently provides the eerie experience of playing above the clouds, it does not qualify as a true mountain course since it is built on a gentle escarpment. The fairways slope rather than plunge, and the player who walks the course does not risk a coronary. In the same way, Crans-sur-Sierre is set so high in the Swiss Alps that the ball flies prodigious distances in the rarefied air. (When the Swiss Open is played here the pros get up at a par-5 hole with a drive and a nine-iron.) Again, the slopes underfoot are gentle. Both courses are worthy of a pilgrimage, as is Banff for the majesty of its surroundings; but for real mountain golf we must go to a course like Semmering,

in Austria. This is set in picture-postcard country of isolated farmsteads high among the peaks, with cow-bells tinkling in the Alpine meadows. Here the golfer must have calf muscles like steel hawsers. A wayward drive can literally travel a mile, bouncing down, down, down into the misty valleys. You drive blind over brows, slice violently in an attempt to hold up your ball on a wicked sideslope, and take extravagant care not to overshoot a green which may be sited on the brink of a ravine. It is trick-shot golf and one of the tricks the visitor soon discovers is that it is advisable to use the clouds as points of aim. Nowhere is this more necessary than on one short hole which is a sheer drop.

You inch nervously to the front of the tee, fighting vertigo, and there, directly below, is a tiny shelf of a green set into the side of the plunging mountain. Miss that green and the ball will bounce down into oblivion. It seems that you could spit onto that green, but that diagnosis is not too helpful since it is impossible to translate into a golf shot. Should you tee up the ball and simply flip it over the end of the tee with a putter and let gravity take care of the rest? In fact, surprising as it may seem, it is all too easy to be short here. No matter how unlikely it may appear looking down from above, the ball will stop and lodge on that fierce gradient. The trick is to pick a convenient cloud in line with

Variations on the theme of golf—oceanic
at Castle Harbour, Bermuda (above); mountainous, at
Crans-sur-Sierre, Switzerland
(opposite, top); pastoral at Acquasanta, Rome.

the flag, take a firm command of your nervous qualms and hit a full wedge out over the precipice. The ball, plummeting vertically, splats into the turf and buries itself up to the waist for one of the most unusual and satisfying experiences golf has to offer.

Any writer who attempts to describe American golf courses simply sets himself up as an Aunt Sally to be knocked down. Even the blandest generalization is overwhelmed by the weight of the exceptions which prove it false. Many visitors remark that wind is not as important a factor in the U.S. as elsewhere. True enough, as far as it goes. But formulate that observation as a dogmatic statement—"generally speaking, American golf is played in still air or gentle breezes"—and the writer leaves himself wide open to a flurry of counterpunches. Golfers on both seaboards snarl at such ignorance, and the sand-blasted enthusiasts of West Texas, glaring from behind the motorcyclist's goggles they are obliged to wear, drawl, "The wind in Texas is the strongest in the world." From the wreckage of the argument we are left with the conclusion that in some places the wind is strong some of the time and in others it isn't some of the time. The thought is not worth expressing.

What then of the widely held view that American greens are watered to a spongy consistency which turns the game into outdoor darts, with every approach shot plugging where it lands? Again, the half-truth is matched by the half-lie. On the evidence of the great championships, you could as well claim that American greens are the fastest in the world.

The fact is that there is no such thing as the American golf course. In the North, courses are closed for the winter and in the South some are closed for the summer. On a continent which spreads from the Arctic to the tropics, every type of course is to be found. The American course is as diverse as the American golfer.

Having established that *the American golf*

course does not exist, and having therefore disarmed criticism in advance, it is perhaps possible to isolate one common type of course and identify some of its typical features. This is what we might call the middle course—the middle-class, middle-income, country-club course found through the central states—which represents a sizable proportion of American golf. The visiting Briton is immediately struck by certain basic differences between the American golf course and the British, the chief one being that American golfers value comfort and luxury and are willing and able to pay for it. Many British club members have incomes which do not amount to $2,000 a year, and they fight to keep the cost of golf as low as possible. The annual dues at some of the "best" clubs around London, where demand so far exceeds supply that most clubs have two-year waiting lists for membership, averages about $100. Needless to say, very few British clubs offer anything like the clubhouse accommodations and facilities found in American counterparts. The British tradition is for a functional, if not downright spartan, clubhouse—a place to change, have a drink after the game, and perhaps enjoy a light meal. The clubhouse exists to service the needs of golf. Social activities at these clubs are limited. When a British golfer finds a companionable party raising the rafters in his club, he knows a visiting golf society is playing that day. Indeed, there is a breed of golfer—and quite numerous he is—known as a "car-park member," who rarely enters the club at all.

The American club, by contrast, is much more of a family affair. The club probably will offer tennis, swimming, and indoor game rooms as well as golf. The members will see their club as a community center. Private rooms will be hired for family celebrations and wedding receptions, and it is by no means exceptional for members to be required to spend $2,000 a year in the club. It also is not unusual for members to assume their share of the club's indebtedness by purchasing debentures when they join, which gives

With protective goggles and a touch of
fanaticism golf flourishes in the most inhospitable
surroundings—even among the sand dunes of
the Namid Desert of South-West Africa at Walvis Bay.

everyone a real sense of participation in, and obligation to, the club.

A Briton entering an American country club, providing he survives the tidal wave of hospitality, will notice certain differences about the course. Mainly they will be points of emphasis. Fairways on the whole will be wider, and the rough, such as it is, seems short both in length and in menace. (He may revise the latter view when he discovers the tough texture of the grass.) He may also form the opinion that the architect has rather overdone the number of trees, sand bunkers, water hazards, and the size of the greens. The effect is that these courses encourage the golfer to swing

without undue inhibition in the knowledge that the scale of punishments for a wild stroke is a fair one. The golf course will give him what he deserves. In Britain and Ireland, as a broad generalization, the golfer tends to be inhibited by the course with its narrower fairways, penal rough, and daunting feeling that quite a good shot may be punished severely. If anyone cares to draw conclusions as to whether conditioning by these two types of courses accounts for the performance gap between the leading professionals of the two countries, he is at liberty to do so. Most American pros approach the game more aggressively than most Britons.

It might be inferred from all this that at

113

championship level the British courses are tougher tests of golf, and this conclusion might be justified if championships were played on courses in their everyday condition. This, as we all know, is not the case. A year of preparation goes into transforming the landscape for the U.S. Open. In country-club trim, a course like Merion is, with the exception of the last four holes, not unduly difficult compared with, say, Carnoustie. But by the time fertilizer by the ton has been lavished upon it to encourage the rough, and the rough has been allowed to grow into the fairways, it is a totally different proposition, especially with the greens dehydrated to the USGA's sadistic specifications.

At the highest championship level there is little difference between the standards of the shotmaking test set by the examiners whether the event is played at Pinehurst, St. Andrews, or Royal Melbourne. The critical factor is the great unknown, the weather. Since the R. and A. insists on holding the British Open on seaside courses, it is practically guaranteed that at some stage in their championship the weather will make a decisive and generally unpleasant intervention.

Golf on marvelous courses in spectacular settings is now tourist bait the world over. Spain, Portugal, and—somewhat belatedly—Italy are encouraging golf and golfers. France was slow to appreciate the drawing power of golf, possibly because she is so rich in tourist attractions of other kinds. On the other hand, Yugoslavia has embarked on an ambitious program to cultivate golf—for itself as well as for its visitors. The Yugoslavs are undertaking to build fifty courses and are adopting golf as a native game.

Island paradises—from Bermuda to the Caribbean, and from Hawaii to Fiji in the Pacific—are attracting tourists with a new breed of golf course. Once a bulldozer has cleared the fairways and the surface of coral rock has been prepared, the seedling grasses need only a plentiful supply of water to create what is virtually an instant course. For the visitor these

"The finest meeting of land and sea in the world"—the Monterey Peninsula's golfing treasury has no equal to Pebble Beach, whose 9th hole often effects a meeting between golf ball and sea.

lush playgrounds offer a novel experience. If he misses a fairway he must reconcile himself to a lost ball, because any attempt to penetrate the thick jungle of undergrowth is doomed. He will seldom recover his ball and may do himself some injury in the search. On some of the beautiful Bahamian courses a local rule permits a player to drop another ball on the fairway opposite the point where his shot entered the tangle of vegetation, under penalty of a stroke, of course, and the professional's shop does a healthy trade in packs of cheap pick-ups.

Just as English colonists introduced golf to the British Empire, so in a similar situation Americans introduced golf to Japan. The forces of occupation after World War II built courses for the troops' recreation and soon the Japanese took to the new game, just as they adopted baseball. If we in the West consider ourselves to be slightly unhinged in our enthusiasm for golf, it is nothing to the reaction of the Japanese. They

took up the game with almost religious fervor which quickly proved an embarrassment to this small, highly populated, industrial country. With such intense competition for land from agriculture, housing, and industry, golf was possibly not the most appropriate game for a new national mania. A chess boom they could have handled, or even an epidemic of pole squatting. However, golf was not to be denied, never mind if it did need some two hundred acres of precious land for every course.

Thanks to an economic miracle there was no shortage of wealthy patrons and enough courses have been built to accommodate some four million golfers. Unfortunately that still leaves another four million golfers (some authorities claim six million) with nowhere to play. You might think that in such a situation the hordes of frustrated would-be golfers would become discouraged, sell their clubs, and take up another hobby. Any such conjecture misjudges the appeal

Clubhouse styles vary from that of Shinnecock Hills, where the American tradition of spacious luxury was established, to Byzantine architecture of the Medinah Country Club in Illinois (above).

Gracious golf in the South: The incomparable
Augusta National club with two water-threatened
short holes, the 16th (above) and the
12th, and a tastefully understated Georgian clubhouse.

of golf and the nature of the Japanese. They insist on playing. The solution to this intractable problem was to build driving ranges, if such an outcome can be dignified by the word solution.

There are no fewer than three hundred ranges in Tokyo alone, all of them thriving. They vary in size and scope from small halls with a net at the far wall and mats for half a dozen players, to a building the size of a department store with three tiers of driving bays, where the scale of charges varies as in a theater, with ground floor stalls most expensive. All the ranges prosper. Day or night they are crowded by enthusiastic golfers. Office workers devote their lunch breaks to hitting buckets of balls. Many of these embryo golfers will never have the opportunity to play on a real course; they will never know the satisfaction of hitting a golf ball off crisp green turf, of exploding from sand, or rolling a putt across a velvet lawn. Heather,

bracken, gorse, and tufted grass will never cleave to their nine-irons and no tree will stymie their approaches. Not knowing golf's agonies they cannot really know its joys, but they do not seem to mind.

Even scoring, which we luckier golfers hold to be central to the game, does not concern them. One would imagine, with such an involvement in range golf, that a new game would evolve with standardized targets and a regulated scoring system, a variety of golfing archery, if you like. But no. For the Japanese range golfers the hitting of a ball seems a sufficient end in itself.

For those Japanese who can afford to join a club or patronize a municipal course, the game is superficially far removed from the Scottish prototype. It offers nothing similar to the spartan granite clubhouses of Fife with their wasteland courses of bleak dunes and arthritic trees stunted and bowed by

Opposite: Sunningdale, England (top), and Ireland's
Portmarnock—where wind gauge in the bar helps members decide
whether it would be more prudent to remain indoors.
Above: Rugged country of Long Reef, Sydney, Australia.

*Majestic and magical golf of Ireland: Royal
Portrush in the north (opposite) and, with four-legged
mower-fertilizers, Lucan, near Dublin
(top). Above: Castletroy, Limerick, with adjacent confessional.*

Golf-mad Japan—with multi-tier driving ranges, women caddies, bilingual markers, and parasols all contributing to the distinction of the modern tee ritual.

the prevailing gales. Where a Scottish architect naturally tends to produce a prison-cell-block of a clubhouse and the American tends to the gin-palace school of design, the Japanese draftman's plans come out as temples. The visiting westerner is made to feel that he should remove his shoes and speak in a respectful whisper in a Japanese clubhouse. The idea that a building should be merely functional is as repugnant to a good Japanese architect as that it should be tarted up with gewgaws and gimmickry.

That tradition extends to the course itself. There are many American courses where trees and shrubs are planted with extreme care to achieve continuity of flowering and aesthetic effect, but the Japanese see their golf courses as gardens, Japanese gardens, of course, with trim beds of chrysanthemums bordering the tees, trees painstakingly cultured into satisfying shapes, and crystal-clear water hazards floored with hand-picked stones and stocked with ornamental fish and flowering plants. It is positive pleasure to slice into a Japanese pond.

All this requires an army of maintenance staff, and when labor charges are added to the prohibitive cost of the land, Japanese golf becomes an extremely expensive occupation. A man must be rich, or have a generous expense account, to consider joining a club and in some cases he must satisfy stringent social requirements. At some clubs a potential member has to be entered at birth, as at an exclusive school, or inherit his membership—and his proportionate share of the debentures. He will have to pay large annual dues plus, in some cases, additional green fees for every round he plays.

To the Japanese it is worth every yen, especially if he is in business. In the world of commerce, nothing carries more status points than membership in a golf club. It stamps the Japanese businessman as a fellow of substance and, at the same time, helps him professionally by putting him on a man-to-

124

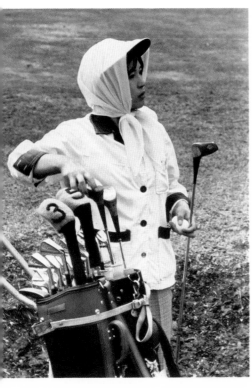

Morocco, where royal patronage
(that's the king's private entrance to the course
from his palace) has started a golf boom
which extends even to the bazaars of Marrakesh.

man footing with the leaders of industry. If martinis at the 19th are the lubricant of American industry, clubhouse green tea serves the same purpose in Japan.

The exotic trimmings of Japanese clubhouses and courses are only a veneer. When the Japanese golfer takes club in hand he may be attended by a teen-age girl caddie, whose burden is increased by a bag of sand and grass seed to dress the scars on the precious turf, but inside he is the same as any other golfer. A thousand years of unique culture may have produced a race with little in common with western man, but down among those primitive instincts and emotions that are stirred by golf all men are equal in their struggle to attain a goal which is so clearly within their grasp and yet remains elusive. Golf unites all men in universal frustration.

One other custom separates the Japanese golfer and that is the tradition of gambling. The high rollers are almost unknown in Japan, where no matter how wealthy a man may be his stake on that Sunday morning four-ball will be purely notional. At one wealthy club the tradition has grown of playing for a bar of chocolate, and some token on this order is the common currency. Like his compatriot on the driving range, the Japanese player holds golf to be a sufficient end in itself and winning its own reward.

Golf mania in Japan is fired by extensive coverage in the papers. Hardly a day passes when golf is not presented in some form on television. The professionals have a strong tournament program and the best Japanese pros can hold their own against anyone. There is no question that the Japanese are second only to the Americans in the ranks of international golf.

The Japanese experience is repeated in a somewhat modified version in Taiwan. Here again the American allies popularized golf and the local population took up the game in some numbers. Possibly the clearest indication of the growing strength of Chinese golfers was seen in the British Open Championship at Royal Birkdale in 1971, when Lu Liang Huan chased Lee Trevino all the way home and came within two strokes of creating the biggest upset in modern golf.

On the continent of Africa golf is mainly the preserve of the white population in the old colonial tradition, although some notable exceptions are beginning to emerge with the changing political situation of the newly independent nations. The game came to Egypt as a legacy of British rule, but has long since been absorbed into the national life, albeit as a rich man's game. In Morocco the enthusiasm of the golfing King Hassan has given enormous stimulus to the game. The first major international golf event in Morocco was interrupted by a bloody battle when revolutionaries invaded the links and tried to overthrow the loyal government. The king survived the attempted coup and so, in consequence, did the game of golf.

Africa maintains two professional golf circuits, one in the Republic of South Africa and the other among the newly independent nations to the north. In South Africa golf is strictly segregated—like all other aspects of life. Blacks and Cape Coloreds who have an opportunity to play the game at all are restricted to their own courses which are very inferior affairs, indeed.

One way or another, golf has spread to almost every corner of the world, from tropical deserts to the glaciers of Iceland. But perhaps the strangest manifestation of the game's resilience in a hostile environment occurred in 1943, in the middle of World War II. In Britain at that time golf balls were unobtainable, and many courses were taken over to grow food. A few fortunates continued to play intermittently, with a pathological concern not to lose a precious, scarred veteran of a ball such as today would be discarded from anyone's practice bag. Special local rules were approved to permit players to replace balls moved by enemy action (many courses still retain bomb craters as legacies of this period), or to lift and drop clear of unexploded bombs.

If you feel that golf could hardly survive even worse conditions than this you would be wrong. There was one course where the penalty for being out of bounds was not the loss of a stroke or the loss of a ball but quite possibly the loss of life! Pat Ward-Thomas, who later became golf correspondent of *The Manchester Guardian,* was shot down on a bombing raid over Germany and imprisoned in Stalag Luft 3, the main camp for air-crew officers. Soon after his arrival, a hickory-shafted ladies' mashie turned up in the camp and its discovery caused great excitement. How such an unlikely implement came to be in a POW camp in the middle of the forest of Sagan nobody knew. Or cared. Immediately the history of the golf ball was reenacted in miniature. The prisoners' first ball was made by winding string around a wooden core and covering it with cloth. Then someone found some shreds of rubber and, just like Sandy Herd with the coming of the Haskell rubber-core ball, he spread-eagled the field with his jerry-built missile. Some tried to remain faithful to their string gutties, but progress would not be denied. The rubber-bound ball, covered with medical sticking plaster, had come to stay. The technique was further refined by cutting up rubber-soled shoes and producing leather-covered balls which conformed exactly to the specifications of the Royal and Ancient Golf Club: 1.62 inches in diameter and 1.62 ounces in weight.

As the golf craze grew, the prisoners turned their attention to clubmaking. Shafts were whittled by penknife and heads cast from melted stovepipes in molds made of soap. The course evolved gradually, again following the pattern of the original medieval process, with the first games being played haphazardly between the huts. In time, as the home-made equipment proliferated and more prisoners began to play, the course became formalized, nine holes with "browns" of packed sand, bunkers, and contoured approaches. Eventually parcels from home brought real clubs and proper balls, and golf at Stalag Luft 3 caught up with the twentieth century. Tuition was organized for learners, exhibitions were arranged by the hotshot players, and a championship was held.

The severest penalty in the history of golf faced the man who played a loose shot. Anyone stepping over the rail which marked the inner perimeter was likely to be shot by the guards. In time the Germans came to adopt an attitude of uneasy tolerance and a white coat was issued to be worn as a mark of good faith that the wearer was simply retrieving a golf ball and not trying to escape. It was ironic that the Germans should have watched these harmless golfing activities with such mistrust. For under their noses one of the most daring escapes of the war was being engineered, via a tunnel dug under cover of a wooden vaulting horse. The Germans barely gave the vaulters a second look.

With the spread of golf across the globe, there was only one more frontier for golf to conquer and that was outer space. And so, in due course, it happened. On a mission to the surface of the moon astronaut Alan Shepard astonished his earthly TV audience while performing official EVA, or extra-vehicular activity. The prospect of weightless golf proved altogether too tempting for him. He had a six-iron head fitted to his moon pick and smuggled a golf ball aboard his spacecraft. The encumbrance of a space suit did not do much for his swing—indeed, you could say his first attempt was an air-shot, except that there is no air on the moon. Before the lunar dust had settled he took another swipe and gave a cry of satisfaction as the ball flew off under the effortless restraint of only one-sixth of the earth's gravity. For distance, Shepard's 900-yard drive humbles the boasts of every long-ball hitter to date. Those of us who could not be dragged within a mile of a space capsule can envy him that one supreme chance for one-upmanship.

5 · secrets of the great

courses

ne of the attractions of golf, some would even say its main charm, is that it is nearly always played in beautiful surroundings. There are some unattractive courses, generally unnecessarily so, since almost any open area can be transformed by imaginative use of trees. Golf can be a dreary experience if the course is little more than an open field in the middle of a heavily developed area. Trudging up and down parallel fairways at such places we miss the feeling of remoteness and being "away from it all" which should be part of the game. Golf after all is a form of escapism and it helps if we really can escape from the sight and sound and consciousness of our everyday worlds.

Out of sight, out of mind is a precept which green committees should keep constantly in mind. And if, therefore, a member's course happens to border the grounds of an ugly factory, he should lose no time in agitating for a screen of trees to be planted along that boundary. Never mind if it makes a fairway rather too narrow for comfort, or that he will not live to enjoy the full benefit of the improvement. His children will appreciate his foresight, and if in the meantime he has to take an iron off the tee to keep his ball in play, he can enjoy the masochistic delights of recalling his part in creating a "monster."

From the aesthetics of golf we can now turn to the golfing requirements of individual holes. This subject illustrates, but fails to explain, one idiosyncrasy common to the majority of golf-club members, namely, that nearly everyone believes his course a good one. Perhaps it is the result of natural community pride, and probably there is an element of self-deception as well. After all, no one would care to admit that anything about his golf was bad. Members like to think of their courses as being difficult but fair. Visitors are constantly being asked to agree that this is a "pretty good course," or that such is a particularly fine hole. And we visitors, with the politeness which is the obli-

gation of the guest, always agree. Yet if the proud member is taxed with the question, "Why do you say this is a good course?" or, "Why do you consider this a good hole?" the answer, as often as not, suggests quite the opposite. "We had a bunch of pros down here last summer for an exhibition and not one of them made par at that fourteenth." Such a statement merely implies that there is something wrong with the 14th. The difficulty is that no two golfers agree on what constitutes "good" or "bad" in golf courses. These are emotive words and hardly appropriate to the subject, but since they are the common coinage of golf discussions, let us by all means continue to use them after having first agreed what they mean.

At once we must discard the convention of visualizing a golf shot in terms of a line. It is all very well to stand on a tee and mentally plot a shot: "I will hit my drive from here to there, and then I will play my second from there to the green." That process involves two lines which, alas, all too often prove illusory. You set yourself up to aim, say, 4 yards left of a fairway bunker. How often does the shot follow that ideal path? Even if you are the world's straightest driver, your drives will deviate somewhat either side of the target. Actually, most of us can delete that comfortable word "somewhat" and substitute something like "considerably." The architect must think of us all. So he forgets about lines and works in angles. For the sake of discussion, let us take ten degrees, which is a pretty thin slice of pie but a generous enough angle for golfers. The architect may consider that a golfer with a driver in his hand should be able to hit his shots within five degrees either side of the perfect line. He can now draw a ten-degree arc on his plan and any area outside that arc is fair game for punishment in the form of light rough. He may now superimpose another arc, say twenty degrees, although in practice that would be highly benevolent, and the land outside this second arc may be severely punitive, with heavy rough,

*Preceding pages: Pebble Beach's famous
7th hole whose 120 yards across the tip of peninsula
may require a wedge or anything up to
a wood, depending upon the mood of the weather.*

132

trees, water, or boundary fences. All this may seem pretty basic, and so it is in relation to the drive, but when we come to consider the second shot, the principle of working in angles becomes more important.

The architect now starts from the area where a decent but not outstandingly long drive will come to rest. This time, on a two-shot hole, his ten-degree arc will govern the size of the green. Naturally, the greater the distance the bigger the target must be in order to cover the ten degrees of the arc. And it is here, in the second shot, that we can generally make a judgment as to whether we are playing a "bad" hole. Certainly, if we have hit a good drive and then have less than five degrees of leeway either side of the perfect second shot, we are entitled to feel that the hole is not entirely fair. Don't forget that for a first-class player it ought to be normal, not the exception, to hit the green in regulation figures under good conditions. Right. We golfers now have what amounts to a bill of rights. As long as we hit the ball far enough off the tee and within that ten-degree arc, we should expect to avoid trouble. In practice, almost every golf hole affords a much larger area of trouble-free fairway.

This is where the cunning of the architect comes into play. Very often he will provide the wide-open spaces, but if he is a good architect he will have made sure that the ten-degree principle operates. He will have contoured the hole in such a manner that the second shot must be played from a certain area on the fairway. And if you are outside that optimum area, you may have a perfect lie and be able to see the green, but you won't have a ten-degree arc to play through.

An entire book could be devoted to the subject of putting greens. And remarkably dull it would be: informative, but boring. In many instances the greens are the most distinctive mark of the architect, his signature if you like. Robert Trent Jones, the fashionable and successful (and, at times, superbly

skillful) American architect, is noted for the size and eccentric shaping of his greens. (He is also notable for one of the most elegant responses to criticism in the history of golf. His short 4th hole over a pond at Baltusrol, New Jersey, is justly famous, but at first it was felt by the club to be unfairly difficult. Jones was summoned for a consultation. On the tee he scanned the scene across the pond and listened patiently while the shortcomings of the hole were explained to him. Then he took a club, dropped a ball, and holed his tee shot! Words were unnecessary.)

In the opinion of some golfing "graphologists," the Jones signature became excessively flowery in his later courses. These things are a matter of taste. But we can assert that very pronounced contouring of a green is unfair practice and often a tacit admission by the architect that he has failed to provide sufficient interest and challenge from tee to green. Plunging gradients on a green are an abomination and a defiance of the essence of golf, which is power allied to subtlety. The green is one area of the course where the architect must leave his work (and reputation) in the hands of other people. Having shaped it, and provided adequate drainage and irrigation, he departs. Now the greenkeeping staff takes over and it can quickly ruin the job. Standards of greenkeeping vary widely from course to course, and the condition of a green is much more important than its conformation. A good head greenkeeper is a treasure beyond price. Once a club has found such a man the committee should not hesitate to use blackmail, bribery, or the procurement of beautiful women to retain him.

As with the game itself, Americans, having learned course design from foreigners, have now become preeminent in the field. Traditionalists claim that new American courses are artificial—and that may be literally true in some cases. But is that so bad? Given the unpromising material with which the architects have to work, flat acres of scrub or wooded

133

wasteland, the result must be artificial if it is to succeed as a golf course. Of course, an undulating green layout with trees and manmade lakes is incongruous in a flat desert, but it is hardly out of place. The wonder is that it is there at all. Given a large enough budget and a blend of imagination and technique, a golf course can be built anywhere. And to call the result "artificial" is as absurd as criticizing the Taj Mahal for not being a mud hut.

The first requirement of a golf hole is that it be playable, which sounds so obvious as to be not worth mentioning. Remember, though, that golfers of every caliber, from the lordly pro down to the novice, must be able to play the hole. So if the architect provides a 170-yard carry across water from the tee, he will have made a hole which is unplayable for a segment of the golfing community, even though it may pro-

duce the simplest of challenges for stronger players. The 16th hole at Merion is a case in point. The second shot here is over a quarry and long enough to put the green out of range for some players even if they lay up to the very brink of hell. The solution which has been provided—and it can hardly be described as satisfactory—is a "ladies' aid," a detour of mown fairway around the quarry, turning the hole into a rather uninspiring par-6.

Those who practice the black arts of golf-course architecture are well versed in trickery and they know the occult powers water possesses. Water creates a neurosis in golfers. The very thought of this harmless fluid robs them of their normal powers of rational thought, turns their legs to jelly, and produces a palsy of the upper limbs, in much the same way as other liquid affects them at the 19th hole. Architects

For green, read brown: Oiled sand is the putting surface on the grounds of Morro Castle, Puerto Rico. Opposite: Example of the penal school of sandtrapping, 15th hole at National Golf Links, Long Island.

134

use these occult properties of water to telling advantage. The commonest method, and by far the most effective, is to present the golfer with an oblique view of the water hazard, so that he may be playing across the corner of a lake. That is to say, instead of confronting the player with a direct shot over water, the architect offers him a series of options, playing on the golfer's fears and greed in the hope that he will be of two minds when he hits the ball. And, as we all know, indecision is the most destructive attitude in golf. How many times have we cursed a bad shot when in fact we were never really sure what shot we were trying to play?

So we look out across the water and try to calculate distances (itself a difficult process over water) and decide how much of the corner we can safely cut. Nongolfers are incapable of understanding our problem. They argue that since a player is looking at the ball when he hits it, he cannot see the water and this should be a case of "out of sight, out of mind." What blissful ignorance! Those of us who try to play the game know that we cannot entirely dismiss the water from our thoughts, no matter how hard we concentrate on the process of swinging. The germinal fear directs our muscles. No matter how hard we try, unless we are very good players indeed, we involuntarily steer the shot away from the water, and this is why we seldom make really flush contact with the ball when there is water to be negotiated.

Experience reassures us that we hit our drives, say, 200 yards. Experience of a more bitter nature further tells us that when there is water about we make a mess of the shot. The temptation to look up prematurely to allay our anxieties all too often ruins the shot and simply confirms our secret fears. An architect does not need a fearsome expanse of water to play havoc with a golfer's subconscious. A narrow stream is enough if it is employed with cunning.

Again, the best holes are those which avoid a direct confrontation; instead of the stream running square across the fairway, it is much more effective if it crosses at a diagonal. This immediately sets up a conflict in the golfer's mind. Should he try to carry the stream at its nearest point? What if he tops the shot? No, perhaps it would be safer to play down the side where the water is farthest from him. Here, however, the fairway is tapering to a point and the longer the shot the more accurate it must be.

The 17th at Carnoustie is one of the more notorious finishing holes in championship golf. Here the Barry Burn winds to and fro across the fairway, effectively turning the hole into three islands. For the burn not only crosses the fairway but in strategic places it runs alongside as well. When the wind blows, as it frequently does with great force on Scotland's east coast, it is one of the truly intimidating challenges in golf. This hole has been the scene of many dramatic turns of fortune, but what was perhaps the biggest potential reverse proved an anticlimax.

In the Open Championship of 1968, the fourth round eventually resolved itself into a two-man struggle between Gary Player and Jack Nicklaus. After driving out of bounds at the 6th, Nicklaus seemed to have put himself out of the hunt, but by the time they reached the 17th tee there were only two shots in it to Player's advantage. Those two long final holes at Carnoustie are endowed with enough trouble to furnish an entire golf course, with the burn snaking all over, knee-high rough, out-of-bounds, and lavish acres of sand traps. A two-shot lead with two to play is not enough insurance to silence your jangling nerves at any time, but at Carnoustie it means less than ever. This was just the situation to inspire Nicklaus to throw off his natural caution and let rip. His drive at the 17th was awesome in its power. Seldom before can a golf ball have been struck harder. That drive cleared everything, contemptuously flying the dreaded burn and coming to rest less than 100 yards from the green.

The Improved Ladies' Tee

Special Golf-Links for Short-Sighted Players

Player, who is no slouch himself when it comes to driving, also hit a good one, just short of the last twist in the burn. He had a long-iron shot to the green, while Nicklaus had a three-quarter pitch with his wedge. Club for club, then, it was odds-on for a Nicklaus eagle against a regular birdie for Player. If Nicklaus could get back a stroke here he had every chance of catching Player on the 18th, because with his extra power he could hit the green with an iron, while Player would need two good woods. Probably these thoughts were running through Nicklaus's mind as he addressed himself to that short pitch. At all events it was not a very good one. By his standards it was downright sloppy. The shot came up short, leaving him a long putt from the front of the green. Both men made fours and now, with his two-shot lead intact, Player was able to take an iron off the 18th tee and play the hole for a safe and winning 5.

This incident illustrates another element which is necessary, or desirable at the least, in a golf hole: It should combine a potential for disaster with an equal potential for reward. And the two should be closely associated. In other words, the golfer with the skill and nerve to gamble for the reward—by cutting off the corner of a dogleg, for instance—should be exposed to the severest penalties if he fails.

One of the most famous holes in the world, and deservedly so, is the 16th at Cypress Point, California, which combines all the elements required for golfing excellence. It is spectacularly beautiful and is probably the most photographed hole in the world. By the yardstick that a great hole attacks the golfer even before he takes a club from the bag, this one has few equals. Most handicap players are beaten by this one before they play it. Stepping onto that tee, with the ocean crashing against the rocks below and the sea lions honking derision, the golfer is a tumult of emotions. Fear, awe, admiration, and indecision fight for supremacy. The hole is obviously playable; there is an easy, though cowardly, inland route by which the fainthearted may approach that daunting green set on a promontory. But there is also the prospect (unless the wind is especially unfavorable) of hitting over the inlet straight at the flag. It will have to be a good

Golf has been a staple source of fun for
Punch, *the British magazine, and these two examples were reprinted in New York in anthology* Mr. Punch on the Links *in 1929.*

one, but if it succeeds the golfer can bask in the glorious memory of the moment for the rest of his life. Nowhere is he offered the chance of a richer prize or a more enormous failure. It is quite possible to stand on that tee and hit ball after ball into the Pacific, and many a man has done so. On the other hand, Bing Crosby can look back and reflect that his life has not been in vain, even if he discounted all the triumphs of his career, simply on the grounds that he once made a hole-in-one here.

Another rule-of-thumb measurement for a good hole is that it should inspire the power of total recall, even if played years before, and then only once. This 16th is certainly unforgettable, although the memory is challenged by numerous other examples from the treasure house of golf of the Monterey peninsula.

A common weakness on many holes is to site the most difficult hazards in places where they will catch only the worst shots. If a golfer duck-hooks his tee shot and squirts the ball only 150 yards, and wildly

off line in the bargain, he will have provided his own punishment in most cases. The green will be out of range for him, anyway, and it is rather rubbing his nose in it if his ball is tangled in deep rough as well.

Many courses have too much rough, especially some of the seaside links in the British Isles. For the indifferent player, golf on such courses can be misery. Every wayward shot finishes in thickly tangled grass from which—if you can find the ball at all—you have no other course but to chip back to the fairway. The purpose of golf, after all, is to provide enjoyment for all, good and bad player alike, and a hole which can only be tackled by a superior golfer is a bad hole.

There are, however, bad holes and bad holes. There is no excuse for the unplayable hole, but a case can be made for certain categories of bad hole. In fact, when we speak of bad holes it might be said that every course should have at least one. One weakness of the Augusta National course is that it lacks a rank bad hole. That apparently contradictory statement

139

Hazardous golf: The golfer must run a gauntlet of sand on the 6th at Seminole in Florida, which Ben Hogan called the best par-4 in the world. Beware water at the Williamsburg Inn course in Virginia.

needs clarifying, and for further enlightenment we must now change our viewpoint. Instead of looking at courses from the architect's standpoint, think in terms of the golfer. For the man who plays the game, golf holes can be divided into four categories: the hole which looks easy and is easy; the hole which looks easy but is difficult; the hole which looks and is difficult; and the hole which looks difficult and is easy.

For our purposes of providing a "bad" hole for every course, we must go to the first category and seek a pushover hole, one that plays as easily as it looks. It can take many forms, possibly a short par-3 with a generous green, or a 300-yarder with a wide fairway and no trouble to speak of. Essentialiy, it is a hole where our firing arc has given us a much wider margin for error than usual and which makes no great demands on length. It is, then, what we tend to dismiss in our lofty way as "a nothing hole." And that is exactly how the architect wants us to think of it; indeed, that we should not think about it at all. Here at last is a hole where we can just tee up and let fly, where par is a matter of routine. Coming in the middle of a good course which has taxed our powers of concentration it is a relief to arrive at a hole with no niggling worries about bunkers or trees, and where all we have to think about is hitting the ball. There is no catch in it. The hole is a pushover and we move on with that deliciously smug feeling of having got the game licked.

This momentary euphoria is exactly what the architect planned to induce. And if he is a good architect—which is to say an evil, conniving genius— he will follow his nothing hole with an example from the second category: a hole which looks easy but is difficult. The poor deluded golfer, still glowing with arrogance from his success at the previous hole, will hit off with the same abandon. And then the trap is sprung. The most elegant victory an architect can contrive is to produce a situation where the golfer comes to grief with a good shot. Life offers few more superbly ludicrous sights than that of a good golfer hitting a full-blooded drive exactly as he intended and then watching his ball rattle into trees or plop into a lake.

How can such supreme idiocy be contrived? One method—and it is really a clumsy confidence trick—is to offset the tee at an angle. The golfer, like any other human, is about ninety percent sheep and if he is accustomed to playing from tees which are built in the direction of the target area, he becomes conditioned to setting up his stance square to the tee. Ninety-nine times out of a hundred that stance is also square to the fairway. Now, with the tee offset five degrees, confusion is created in his subconscious. The pattern of lines caused by the mower does not, for once, correspond with the direction of his shot. He may hit his usual shot in relation to the tee and drive straight off the fairway. More likely he will make an unconscious adjustment in his swing to compensate for the novel situation and hit across the ball.

The championship tee of the 8th hole at Royal Birkdale is lined up on the right rough, and that is exactly where many shots finish. This technique, one feels, borders on unfair practice, almost on the level of using blind holes and placing bunkers out of the golfer's sight.

The deception should be, and can be, more subtle. In the best cases it involves optical illusions. Every feature of the hole should be clearly in view, which is the architectural equivalent of the conjurer showing he has nothing up his sleeve. The illusionists make use of several natural peculiarities. An unbroken expanse of land, or water, with no bunkers or other landmarks to provide focusing references, always looks longer than the reality, especially if there is a slight brow, so the golfer cannot actually see the distant surface of the fairway. A hazard at 240 yards will appear to be well out of range. A depression in the ground has the reverse effect, and this is especially useful for playing havoc with a golfer facing a long

second shot to the green. The eye's depth perception is deceived by the hidden ground and the player can be tricked into under-clubbing, sometimes by as much as three clubs. It does not help to *know* that the green is 190 yards away. If it *looks* to be 150 yards the human mechanism will react to the visual evidence. Even if the golfer selects the right club, he will spare the shot, without any conscious intention of doing so, and come up short.

The other main optical illusion is created by a change of levels. Playing from an elevated tee everything looks nearer than it is, and the golfer from his commanding position overlooking the scenery feels stronger. Perhaps we can call this the Empire State Syndrome. If anyone doubts that it exists, it can easily be checked by a single experiment. Go onto the roof of a tall building and imagine yourself hitting a good drive, a real Sunday Special. Judge where this drive would finish. Now go down and pace off the length of that imaginary drive. It may surprise you to find that you have allowed yourself to believe that you could hit the first half-mile drive in history.

Hitting to an elevated green is equally confusing. Looking upward, the golfer feels insignificant and intimidated. It looks farther than it is. For architects, however, this particular illusion can be self-

141

In pragmatic approach to course design,
Bobby Jones plots what must be the most strategic
golf course in the world, during
building of Augusta National in 1932.

defeating, because although the golfer may be conned into taking one club too much, he is likely to lose distance through trying to hit the ball too hard. So he may end up pin high after all, although he may be wide of the green.

These, then, are the main tricks of the architect, employed with infinite variety and often unconsciously, for they are all tricks of nature rather than man. Many notable examples of golfing psychological warfare are accidents of nature, especially on the featureless, duneland courses of Scotland.

The last two categories of hole are largely self-explanatory. The hole which looks difficult and requires no explanation; it's too obvious a type. The commonest form of hole which looks difficult but in fact is easy has a tremendous hazard to strike terror into the heart of the golfer, but is so sited that it does not come into play for practical purposes. Although

it is physically irrelevant its presence impinges itself on the subconscious with damaging effect. A good example occurs on an otherwise undistinguished course near London. It is a short hole of 150 yards or so, so length is no problem, and the green is both expansive in size and benign by nature. However, directly in front of the tee there yawns an abyss, actually a disused quarry. Peering into its dark interior overgrown with brambles, you get the feeling that the golfer who ventured down those precipitous banks would be fortunate to emerge again, let alone play a successful recovery shot from that tangle of shrubbery. The quarry measures only about 100 yards across, so it should not come into the reckoning at all. Yet it exerts such a baleful influence on the fainthearted that in their anxiety to see the ball safely over the trouble, they look up too quickly—and top their shots into its ravening maw.

The sign to quicken the blood of any golfer and the realization (r.) which tests the strongest nerves, as the player drives the 12th over a wilderness of hidden bunkers.

142

One rather neglected element in modern golf architecture is the short par-4. These days the emphasis is on length, and yardage is too often taken as the criterion of greatness. Members speak with awe of holes nearly 600 yards long, but in truth these are often the dullest part of golf, particularly for better players. Frequently, the second shot calls for nothing more than forward motion. Just move it ahead and it makes very little difference whether this object is achieved by topping a driver along the ground or hitting a crisp three-iron.

The very expression "par-5" strikes a forbidding chord and the golfer flexes his muscles to meet the challenge to his virility. In fact, if we are thinking in terms of par, as we should be, most par-5s are the simplest holes on the course. A birdie can often be achieved with two indifferent shots and one good one, and the hole yields a par to three mis-hits. The standard of stroke-making needed for par-5s is lower than for any other type of hole, provided—and the qualification is all-important—that we are content to settle for a 5. What happens more often is that we approach these long holes with a vague ambition to get up in 2, although we would be hard put to defend that aim with rational argument. We try to hit that little bit harder, miss the drive, and then seek a miracle of recovery with subsequent shots.

Long par-4s are a much more testing proposition. These, too, lose their challenge if those of us who cannot make the distance accept that fact with grace and play them as three-shotters, taking advantage of our handicap strokes. Vanity, which shares with fear the doubtful distinction of being the golfer's worst enemy, all too often undoes us again. But the short par-4, of 300 yards or less, is well within everyone's range and offers scope for the architect to display his cunning. The best examples, employing the principles we have already discussed, should offer a good chance for a 3 to the player who can match his bold-

ness with accuracy, but threatens him with a 6, or a 7, if he falters. The 9th on the Old Course at St. Andrews is an example, all the more extraordinary because at first sight it might qualify as one of our "nothing" holes. It is flat and wide and the green is not sculptured in any way, simply a prepared area of putting turf on the fairway. The hole is almost drivable and yet the second shot, the shortest of pitches most of the time, has been the undoing of many a fine player.

Another Scottish course, Turnberry, has a beauty, the 13th, and here the problem is quite different. After a good drive you have to pitch to a plateau green, an island elevated just high enough to play optical tricks and affect judgment of distance.

Possibly the most important convention of course architecture, so common that we rather take it for granted, is the dogleg. There are courses, mostly laid out by unqualified men working with restricted areas, which consist largely of dead-straight holes. Trudging up and down these drab fairways, often laid out in parallel, like sardines in a can, is the nearest experience to boredom golf has to offer. The pity of it is that often such unimaginative layout is unnecessary. A change of direction in the middle of a fairway makes all the difference in the world. The game is transformed in that a player must decide whether to gamble on cutting corners and risking trouble for the chance of a shorter second shot. And if the hole is bordered by trees there is the added bonus of changing vistas as you progress up the fairway. There is no excuse for dullness on a golf course when variety can be achieved so easily.

A fine example of ingenious use of the dogleg is seen at the east course of the Royal Melbourne Golf Club, whose two courses on the famous Melbourne sand belt must rank with the finest championship courses of the world. Here the boundary of the club's property is a straight fence imposing the necessity of a chain of straight holes. The architect solved this problem by planting stands of trees along the boundary, so that the tee shots are directed away from the fence. The result is a sequence of interesting holes and playing them one is not conscious of the out-of-bounds at all.

The deliberate use of out-of-bounds as hazards seems to many people to be a sign of weakness. Occasionally, it cannot be helped. St. Andrews and Troon, for instance, are bordered by railway lines which have the respectability of history to commend them. But another British championship course, Royal Liverpool at Hoylake, is confined in places by artificial out-of-bounds, mere trenches cut in turf banks, and this is surely a practice to be discouraged. After all, if we are going to stoop to these strategies, golf might as well be played over a flat field with the fairways marked out like a football pitch.

Most, though not all, architects agree that golf holes should be as natural as possible and fit into the landscape with as little disturbance as possible. The skill of the architect comes in the siting of trees and greens in such a way as to combine a golfing challenge with a natural setting. Nature is the real architect: Man simply makes a few minimal adjustments.

In fact, in these days of earthmoving machinery it matters little where a course happens to be built. The decisive factors are geology and climate. A wet and temperate climate is best—or, what amounts to the same thing, a temperate climate plus a good irrigation system. As to geology, the finest subsoil for golf is sand, or gravel, with good natural drainage. It supports fine-bladed grasses and the conifers—larch, spruce, and pines—which are a feature of so many excellent courses.

Seaside golf is highly regarded in Britain because of the springy turf; the only way you can get a bad lie on it is by the misfortune of landing in someone else's divot scrape. St. Andrews, Muirfield, Carnoustie, Troon, Old Prestwick, Royal Birkdale, Sand-

wich, Royal Lytham and St. Anne's, Sunningdale, Walton Heath, and Westward Ho! all are built on sand, inland in some cases. Mostly they remain much as they were left by the receding tide ages ago, ridged and fissured by the sea, and now simply grown over with the most perfect turf you can imagine. The golf on these linksland courses can be a severe trial to a man who subscribes to the view that punishment should be the sanction for error. Play St. Andrews or Sandwich in a dry spell, when there is bone in the ground, and a perfectly hit drive to the center of the fairway can kick capriciously into the rough. This sort of experience is supposed to test a golfer's character. In the main it provides an impromptu display of his vocabulary.

There are exceptions. Muirfield, although undoubtedly by the sea, is a fair course if a difficult one, and by and large the golfer gets the due reward for his shots. As it is prepared for the Open Championship, such as when Jack Nicklaus failed with the third trick of his grand-slam attempt in 1972, it is tight and the greens are fast and hard. And if Nicklaus ever reflects on the part luck played in that Open it will concern the unbelievable good luck the winner, Lee Trevino, enjoyed in his last two rounds. By Trevino's own reckoning, he saved himself at least six strokes by hitting the flagstick with over-bold recoveries, holing out twice. When the fates are favoring one man to that degree it is impossible to prevail against him.

In America there are no links courses in the true sense of the expression. But there are sand courses, and none finer than Pine Valley, New Jersey. It is slightly specialized in its appeal, but given the ability to make 175-yard carries off the tee, Pine Valley's claim to be the best course in the world—a claim made on its behalf by enthusiastic visitors, rather than by the club itself—is not so preposterous. Some prefer to label it the most difficult course in the world, but this is a judgment which must be flavored according to the ability of the golfer. On his first visit Arnold

Tony Jacklin, playing alongside the railway at Royal Lytham and St. Anne's on way to his 1969 Open Championship, exhibits characteristic leg action. Below: The Windmill, Wimbledon, and the "Maiden" at Sandwich.

How nature can deceive the eye: Two examples of distorted depth-perception which makes clubbing difficult—over.Royal Portrush's undulating wilds and at an elevated tee at Hermitage, Ireland.

Palmer beat par, for instance, and thereby won a large enough bet to buy an engagement ring and elope. The hazards are forbidding, but there is no law compelling a man to put his ball into a vast, unraked bunker or into the stands of pine bordering the fairways. It is a magnificent golf course, and a majestic one, which is something rather different, and it is all because of sand. Next time you curse the stuff as you flail away in a bunker, pause in your sweaty labors and reflect that those dastardly grains of crushed silica are the golfer's best friend. You may have to reflect rather hard, but it is true.

We have been discussing the golf architect's job solely in terms of strategic responsibilities, or what we might call the visionary side of his work. This is where he needs a special form of insight; indeed, in some cases genius would not be too extravagant a word. Most of us imagine we could lay out a golf course, and sometimes, when we come across a grassy promontory by an ocean bay and say "What a golf hole that would make," we might even be right. Only a fool could fail to recognize the obvious. But the architect may have to fight his way through thicket or gaze out over a flat wilderness of sandy scrub. That is when he needs his visionary powers to plot the course of the bulldozers. He also needs technical skills to cope with a multiplicity of problems of drainage, watering, and the cultivation of turf. But we need not concern ourselves here with the plumbing.

Our concern is to try and understand how the architect is plotting our downfall as golfers, so that perhaps we can foil him, or at least appreciate in retrospect the mastery of the man who has brought us to despair. We have examined the theory. Now let us browse over a few notable courses and see how the precepts of great architecture have been translated into practice. Where better to start than Augusta National, the beautiful and exacting monument to the greatest golfer of all time. Bobby Jones built Augusta with Dr.

Alistair Mackenzie, one of the supreme masters of his craft, who was also responsible for Royal Melbourne. Between them they produced a course which fulfills nearly all the qualifications. If one had to find a criticism of Augusta, it would be that it is too good. The concentration is too concentrated. The golfer who hopes to beat par has to apply himself singlemindedly on every shot. There is no let-up. If it had a "nothing hole" to provide a change of pace and break the player's concentration, it might be even more difficult.

Augusta is a good example of the strategic type of course, as opposed to the penal variety which depends for its difficulties on savage length and harsh penalties. The fairways of Augusta are as wide as you could wish, in the main, and the greens are large. For a good player par is not an exceptionally difficult target, easier than on most championship courses. The problems begin with ambitions to improve on par. It is not enough to hit the fairway with the drive. In order to set up a birdie chance the drive must be positioned with great accuracy and only then can an approach be made with any reasonable expectations of finishing near the hole, and on the preferred side of the hole. Just where the optimum areas on the fairway will be depends, of course, on the position of the hole. At Augusta, more so than on any other championship course, the siting of the pins must be taken into account while setting up for the drive. For the handicap golfer, with some concessions in length from the forward tees, Augusta is not unduly severe, although those fast and undulating greens frequently require three putts from the edge.

There is another important quality to Augusta which owes nothing to the architect or the physical layout of the course. Any golf course which has a long history of great events acquires a patina of awe. Only the dullest of golfers can fail to be affected by the realization that here Gene Sarazen had his famous double eagle and there is the pond in which

Ben Hogan's hopes were drowned.

At St. Andrews the ghosts of the mighty are even more populous and there is the added feeling, whether historically justified or not, that here is where it all began. It would be no exaggeration to say that many golfers approach St. Andrews with the reverence of pilgrims and that their games suffer accordingly. Many a fine player has thus been disappointed by his first experience on the Old Course, but nearly all of them grow to like the links over subsequent visits and are inspired by its historical vibrations. To contemporary eyes, it is hopelessly old-fashioned, with its vast double greens accommodating two holes, and its myriad bunkers, mostly with individual names and frequently hidden from view. For all that, the unprejudiced golfer who accepts St. Andrews for what it is, without bemoaning its unfairness or quaking at its reputation, can plot a route between the spattered pot bunkers just big enough, in Bernard Darwin's phrase, to hold an angry man and his mashie.

In the Open Championship of 1970, Tony Jacklin almost committed the sacrilege of taking St. Andrews apart. In the first round, playing late in the day, he was out in 29 and started back in the same birdie mood. Was the unthinkable about to happen, was the Old Course about to be humbled? A storm broke with savage fury, the round was suspended, and when Jacklin resumed in the gray dawn next morning, the spell was broken. At that time it was easy to believe that the flashing lightning and growling heavens were an act of supernatural intervention.

The caliber of a golf course must always be a personal assessment in some measure, depending on the degree of importance which the golfer puts on different features. Those of us who play purely for pleasure—if we took the trouble to analyze the sources of our enjoyment—would probably agree on the following priorities: (1) scenic beauty, (2) quality of turf and greens—which depends on the nature of the soil, (3)

strategic layout of the holes, (4) incidental facilities, such as the quality of the clubhouse.

On that formula, Irish golf demands at least a footnote in any review of courses. This small country contains more superb courses than any area of comparable size. To explain the special appeal of Irish golf we must return to an original thought that half the appeal of the game is "getting away from it all." Ballybunion, Portmarnock, Lahinch, and Portrush are rugged links. Inland there is Killarney, ringed by purple mountains and set at the side of vast lakes. The setting is almost too beautiful, especially when the air carries the opiate scent of peat smoke.

If these are the jewels of Irish golf there are also many semiprecious stones, indifferent courses, and downright bad ones. But to continue the metaphor, Irish golf is unpolished. The stones have not been faceted and tricked up with the frills of modernity. The golfer gets the feeling that this is how golf used to be—and how it ought to be. Remote and primitive on a tee at Ballybunion, with the Atlantic crashing below and the wind stinging his face, the golfer can imagine that the world we call civilization does not exist.

And, what's more, for the moment the courses are not overrun by visiting hordes and infected by golf's most stultifying disease, the obligatory five-hour tourist round. No matter how well God and the architect may have done their work, the pleasure of the game must ultimately come from within the golfer. The Mountains of Mourne may sweep down to the sea; the ball may sit up as prettily as you could wish on the fine grass; and the shot may be as inviting as you ever dreamed. All these are as nothing if you have to wait five minutes on every shot while a four-ball in front blithely disregards all the canons of golfing etiquette and the natural laws of good manners. The final element in golf-course architecture, then, is the golfer himself, the player who respects the course and who allows others to take pleasure from it.

6 · of hickory and steel

america is for winners. The idea that all men are born free and equal may be honored in constitutional theory, but in practical terms it is to many people a thoroughly spurious notion. Whether or not every American child starts from the same mark, he is quickly involved in a competitive society which measures success in terms of outdoing others. To neutral outsiders it sometimes seems this emphasis on success, which has created the richest nation on earth, is unduly hard on losers. It was an American who said, "Nobody remembers who came in second." It may be a sentimental reaction, or even socialistic, but that remark seems to call for the response, "What a pity." Losers, after all, are essential to winners.

While society rewards its winners with wealth and respect, the nation, clinging to the ideal of equality, makes no official recognition of success. Arnold Palmer may be invited to dine at the White House, but if he had been born in a different country we can imagine that such an invitation would include a tap on the shoulder and the command, "Arise, Sir Arnold." One exception to this official disdain of honors is New York City's splendid practice of the ticker-tape parade. Such a parade, with marching bands and cheering crowds, took place in the summer of 1930.

The triumphant hero was a stocky young Georgian, Robert Tyre Jones, who had just returned from winning the British Open and the Amateur Championships. These days such a "double" would perhaps not be quite such a remarkable achievement. It takes no flight of fancy to imagine the golf coach at some university finding a young Jack Nicklaus with the potential to do it. But in 1930 the situation was very different. Jones had proved himself the outstanding golfer of his era. He had won the U.S. Amateur title four times and taken three national Open titles, and on two previous occasions he had beaten the best British professionals, which at that time meant the best in the world, for the Open Championship.

The gulf between professional and amateur was not so wide in those days as it now is. The British amateurs, Roger Wethered and Cyril Tolley, were fine players and quite capable of beating anyone, especially over the short sprint of an eighteen-hole match in the Amateur Championship. That year it was played over the Old Course at St. Andrews, where on an earlier visit Jones had torn up his card in disgust and further signaled his opinion of the place by teeing up his ball and deliberately driving it into the sea. Over the years Jones came to respect and love the Old Course. He wrote: "Truly, if I had to select one course upon which to play the match of my life, I should have selected the Old Course." As it happened, this is exactly the ordeal he faced in 1930, for after narrowly surviving the preliminaries he came up against Tolley in a semifinal round.

It was to prove one of the great matches of all time. To read Jones' account of "the completely brutal ferocity of that man-to-man contest" is to bring home how insipid stroke-play golf is compared to a good match. This is not the place for hole-by-hole detail. Suffice to say that Tolley squared the match at the 16th, and then occurred the incident which provokes argument to this day. Jones' second to the notorious road hole hit a spectator. The question is whether it would otherwise have carried onto the road, which surely would have cost him the match. If's and but's do not count in golf. Jones halved the hole and the next. And he won the 19th to take the match. "It was the kind of match," he said, "in which each player plays himself so completely out that at the end the only feeling to which he is sensitive is one of utter exhaustion."

A measure of luck is necessary for any champion, and if the spectator at the 17th had indeed provided a stroke of fortune for Jones, it was nothing compared to the chance that this match took place in the afternoon. If it had been played in the morning and

Preceding pages: Re-creation of nineteenth-century clubmaker's workshop includes P. R. Wilson driver (c. 1875) in vise, long spoon by McEwan (c. 1840) at left on bench, and, beside it, Spalding driver (c. 1898).

152

Jones had been required to play another match the same day, he must surely have been beaten. As it was, he had a night's sleep in which to recover his strength and restore his competitive fires. And the title, after a final against Wethered, was his. The first quadrant of the Grand Slam was successfully achieved.

The Open Championship followed at Hoylake on the flat and uninspiring links course of the Royal Liverpool golf club. In the last round Jones was in contention, and for the first time that week he played the opening holes in respectable figures. He felt that a reasonable score probably would be good enough to win the title.

Then, at the 480-yard 8th, he took a 7 in what he described as "the most reasonable manner possible." Every golfer has suffered the experience of running up a big score without playing a bad shot and that is just what happened. A good drive was followed by a solid spoon shot which just missed the left edge of the green. The ball lay on the fairway some 20 yards from the hole with no intervening obstacles other than a brow. Jones had to get his ball up the slope and then stop it quickly on the green, which fell away quite steeply. Anxious not to run too far past the hole on the fast downslope, he chipped short by a foot or so and the ball did not make the green. He chipped again, still conscious of the danger that the ball could roll well past the hole—and left it ten feet short. His putt went a foot past and then he hurried the tap-in and missed it.

That body blow knocked all tactical thoughts from Jones' head. It was, he said, no longer a case of attacking or defending. His only idea was to go on hitting the ball as best he could and get the round finished. And that he did. Another stroke of luck came when a wayward drive rebounded kindly from a steward's head. Jones finished in orderly fashion and with no real threat from the opposition. Two tricks of the Grand Slam were his after the hardest championship of his life. He had earned his ticker-tape welcome.

The U.S. Open that year was played at Interlachen, Minneapolis, and began on the hottest day Jones could remember. (He was so saturated with perspiration at the end of the round that his tightly knotted tie had to be cut free with a knife.) The golf, at least, was not quite so feverish. Jones had a five-stroke lead after three rounds and for a player of his caliber such a margin was enough to cushion him against the inevitable faltering of the last round. Macdonald Smith's brave challenge was, as it had been at Hoylake, not quite strong enough. Three tricks.

At this point we may perhaps pause for a moment of idle conjecture. Let us make some fairly sweeping assumptions and put ourselves in Jones' position at this period. Here we are, the finest player in the world, poised on the brink of the greatest challenge that golf has to offer, the Grand Slam. What would we have done? Most of us, surely, would have taken a short rest and then launched into an intensive program of preparation for the final ahead. Jones did nothing of the kind and this illustrates more clearly than anything the remarkable qualities of the man. He was a real amateur in the sense that he played golf for fun. For the moment he had played enough and went home, back to his law office to work, and to play an occasional social game with his friends at East Lake, Atlanta. Jones was not exactly complacent about his prospects in the U.S. Amateur Championship (he never undertook any major golf event lightly or with any other intention than of winning it), but he realized that over 36 holes of match play he could expect to beat the best that amateur golf could offer in opposition.

The championship was held at Merion. The highly strung Jones was assailed by doubts and fears during the week, but these arose mainly from the tension of the situation rather than from the quality of the opposition. Each round was a triumphal progress and the final a formality. The Grand Slam was his, sealing the greatest golfing career of all time. In seven years

he had won thirteen major championships and finished second six times. It is possible that the record of thirteen championships will be surpassed and that another Grand Slam, in its modern form, will be achieved. However, it is inconceivable that anyone will do it in the Jones style, as a weekend amateur who often put his clubs away for months at a time. During his fourteen years of competitive golf, Jones studied for examinations and took honors degrees in law, English, and engineering. He also worked at his legal practice. For him golf was a diversion and when he completed the Grand Slam he retired.

Although he had withdrawn from the lists, Jones' contributions to golf were by no means over. With his friend Clifford Roberts he constructed the Augusta National, incorporating many of the ideas he formulated from playing championship courses and creating what is probably the finest inland course in the world. And here he instituted an annual tournament for his friends, which grew into the Masters, one of the elements of the modern Grand Slam. He died in 1971 of a wasting spinal disease which had kept him a cripple since middle age. The records may fade, but

Bob Jones' memorial in the azaleas and towering Georgia pines of Augusta will surely endure as long as golf is played.

Although Jones played with hickory-shafted clubs, in almost every other respect he could be classified among the moderns. He was certainly a modern player in style and outlook. On that basis we would have to consider Harry Vardon as the first of the moderns, even though he played mainly with hickory shafts and the guttie ball. Incidentally, in one respect Vardon was uncompromisingly old-fashioned, even though he could well be called the father of modern golf. He refused to have anything to do with the method of attaching a shaft to the head of a driver by gluing it into a socket bored into the neck, which had become universal practice during his early career. He insisted that the old way was best, that is to say, a tapered shaft glued to a similarly tapered neck and firmly bound with twine for the entire length of this splice, or "scare." Vardon maintained that a scared driver was a better union of shaft and head, and consequently gave him better control of his drives. Perhaps it did. Or perhaps it was a case of wishful thinking, a

Above: Wood-faced irons to cushion shock of stonelike guttie balls (l.), and early nineteenth-century master woods.
Opposite: Developing ideas, including rubber-faced pitching club (l.) and first metal shaft, 1914 (r.).

common habit among golfers at all levels. It does not matter, because the result was the same. When it comes to a golfer and his clubs, faith is more important than fact. The man who believes his driver to be perfect, makes it so. And conversely, believing a club to be "wrong," particularly putters, makes the most scientifically perfect implement useless.

In those days of handmade clubs, a golfer might swing two hundred mashies before he found one with the right feel. Those were the days of mysticism. Legends say that these early masters had such sensitive touch that the sets they laboriously collected were later found by modern scientific measurement to be perfectly "matched." In fact, such sets, like those of Bobby Jones, were found to vary widely in swing weight from club to club. Whether this is due to fallibility in Jones' touch or to shortcomings in the swing-weight system is an open question.

Nowadays Vardon is remembered mainly for giving his name to the commonest method of gripping the club, with the little finger of the right hand overlapping the left forefinger. The Vardon grip is, by almost universal consent, the correct grip. In fact, Vardon did not invent the method at all. It had been used by other players; Vardon's place in the story was to make it popular. He was for years the finest player in

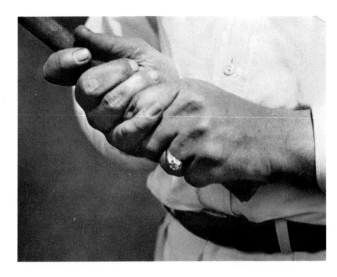

the world, and as such it was natural for golfers to copy everything about his method. Actually, Vardon did employ a unique grip on occasions. When faced with a short chip shot and anxious not to drag the ball to the left by having the right hand overpower the stroke, he sometimes overlapped the last two fingers of his right hand. This kept the left hand in control of the stroke and the clubface square to the target.

The real contribution to golf of this Channel Islander, who won the British Open six times and the U.S. Open once, was the standard he set in method. Before Vardon, golf was a power game. Players clenched their clubs with two-fisted grips and with the right hand well under the shaft. They spread their feet wide apart to anchor their tackety boots firmly to the earth, and they whacked into that little ball. Style as we know it today meant nothing. Golfers used whatever method seemed appropriate and no one thought the worse of him for unorthodoxy. Many players stood very open to allow themselves an uninhibited bash.

Golf at this time was played in two distinct phases. A player used distance clubs for getting into the vicinity of the target and then accuracy clubs to play to the green. The function of the wooden clubs was to move the ball forward as far as possible in the hope that it would not stray off line too far for a shot to the green. It is easy to imagine the impact of Vardon's arrival on the golfers of the day. The brawny giants who made the earth shake with the fury of their striking were joined by the slight figure of the self-

Great amateurs: Britain's Cyril Tolley (opposite), and Bobby Jones (above l.) talking to the man who founded U.S. Amateur Championship and won inaugural event, Charles Macdonald. Small photo shows Jones' classic grip.

159

The Immortal Bobby, winner of his third U.S.
Open at Winged Foot; Jones playing during first leg of his
Grand Slam, the 1930 British Amateur
Championship at St. Andrews, and with hero's escort.

taught professional who stood lightly to the ball, like a soldier "at ease," and gripped the club gently in the fingers. With a deceptively smooth and rhythmic swing following through to a well-balanced pose facing the target, he whisked the ball past the musclemen and straight up the *middle* of the fairway. What a revelation! Vardon may not have been the first to try combining distance with accuracy, but he was the first to succeed. He did not hope to "get up" with his brassie; he expected to hit the ball near the hole—and he did so. By experiment Vardon also discovered how to control his shots without sacrificing length. The exacting new standards he brought to golf could not be denied. You could not slug it out in this company.

It was necessary to study Vardon and

copy him. From him, then, came the idea that style was important, that percentage golf paid off, and that practice and dedication were essential for the golfer who hoped to compete at this game of accuracy allied with power. The new golf had arrived and Harry Vardon was its high priest. He made several visits to the United States and was in great demand for exhibitions. Golfers flocked to watch him, hoping to discover the secret of his method.

Another legend grew about Vardon's accuracy. It was said that when he played two rounds on the same day, so great was his precision that in the afternoon round he would hit the ball out of his morning divots. Extravagant nonsense, of course, but the fact that such a story gained general currency tells us

161

Broadway hailed the conqueror (in second car)
after he won the British Amateur and Open
Championships in 1930. Above: Jones, with wife Mary
behind him, at City Hall with Mayor Jimmy Walker.

Position for the Drive *Three-Quarter Stroke* *At the Top of the Swing*

something about the reputation of this taciturn man. Another story—this one with the virtue of authenticity —tells how Vardon, being engaged to hit golf shots in the sports department of a large store, relieved the boredom of this sterile exercise by aiming at the valve of the fire-sprinkler system. He hit it so regularly that the manager feared his store would be flooded and begged Vardon to stop.

It is impossible to think of Vardon without recalling two golfers whose names were linked with his: J. H. Taylor and James Braid. Taylor was a West Countryman who grew up on the breezy links of Westward Ho! in Devon and developed the wide, sweeping style so often associated with seaside golfers. J. H. was quick-witted and quick-tempered at times. He was a small bird-like man in contrast to James Braid, a large man in every sense. If Vardon was an artist, and the term is perhaps not too fanciful, then

Taylor and Braid were superb craftsmen. In Braid's case this was literally true, for he began life in his native Scotland as a joiner. He moved to England as a clubmaker and soon won a reputation as a fine golfer and a man of extraordinary personal qualities. We can see from contemporary accounts and early photographs that both Taylor and Braid modified their styles and their grips over the years, and there can be no doubt that it was Vardon's example which prompted the changes. Among them these three players dominated British golf before World War I. The newspapers christened them, somewhat ponderously, the Great Triumvirate. Between 1891 and 1914 they won sixteen championships, and Taylor was the major inspiration in organizing the Professional Golfers' Association.

Vardon transformed golf and Taylor contributed to the improvement of the professional's lot. Braid's place in the history of the game is secure for

Golf instruction of 1892, which may explain
the tradition of drowning one's disappointments in strong
drink. Opposite: Engraving by W. Dendy Sadler,
"A Winter Evening"—dreaming of spring, no doubt.

162

the thrilling eloquence of his play and the style of the man himself. Few professionals have been so well loved as the tall Scot. As professional at Walton Heath he was in great demand as a playing companion by visiting politicians. In such company a man who listened politely and hardly spoke a word would indeed be popular.

On his visits to America Vardon traveled with Ted Ray, a stolid and powerful professional of the old school, who hit the ball prodigious distances. Ray was never the equal of the Triumvirs, although he did win one Open and tied (with Vardon and Francis Ouimet) for the U.S. Open one year. He was, however, a congenial companion, and for American spectators it must have been particularly instructive

to watch Vardon and Ray together. Between them they epitomized the two extremes of golf, the rapier and the broadsword, or the artist and the artisan. A contrast in styles makes for added interest in a golf match, as in any sporting encounter, and doubtless this element was one of the reasons why Vardon liked to have Ray with him.

Before the period of the Great Triumvirate, that is to say, through the turn of the century, there had been many fine professionals, although in the matter of the development of golf, no one of them was particularly more significant than the other. Old Tom Morris and his son, Young Tom, whose bearded faces figure prominently in so many golfing prints in the world's clubhouses, made the Open Championship

'Twas ever thus—the craftsmen made the
equipment and then the crafty men of the advertising
world set out to beguile the customers
with seductive promises and bargains in the public prints.

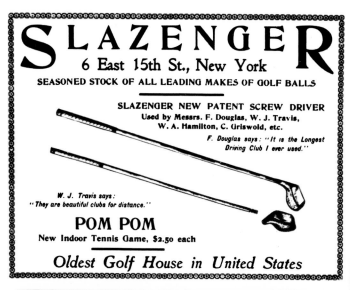
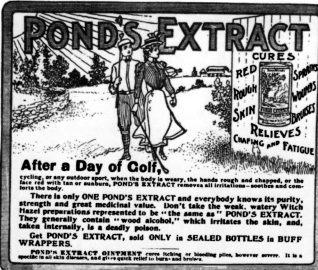

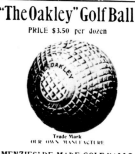
165

something of a family affair in its early years.

By all accounts, including the judgment of Tom Senior, who may have been prejudiced, Young Tom was the more accomplished player. In the mythology of golf he certainly commands the greater attention, since he died before reaching his prime. His wife died in childbirth while Tom was away from St. Andrews playing golf, and his father kept the news from him until they were returning home. Young Tom fell into a deep melancholy and shortly afterward followed his wife to the grave. We do not know how good a player Young Tom was. The reports are sketchy and the scores tell us little, since Scottish coastal golf is so greatly affected by the weather. Young Tom won his third championship belt, ancestor of the silver jug which is now the Open trophy, with a two-round score of 149 in 1870. Since he won it three times in succession, it became his personal property. We may be tempted to draw exaggerated conclusions from the fact that ten years previously the winning score had been twenty-five strokes higher, an average of twelve shots a round worse. However, as visitors to Scotland will know, it is quite possible for conditions to vary by as much as ten strokes a round. All we can say, then, is that the Morrises were the best players around during their day.

These days the professional golfer is inclined to see his predecessors as servile creatures. Yet in terms of social advancement the nineteenth century was a period of considerable progress. The first professionals were caddies who were capable of playing when the occasion arose. Gentlemen golfers were warned not to tip their caddies generously since these rascals would certainly dissipate their money on drink. For their own good, caddies had to be kept firmly in their place. As late as 1900 the golf historian Horace Hutchinson wrote: "The professional, as we are now chiefly acquainted with him, is a 'feckless,' reckless, creature. In the golfing season in Scotland he makes his money all the day, and spends it all the night. His sole loves are golf and whisky. He works at odd times—job work or time work—in the shops; but he only does it when reduced to an extremity. If he were but ordinarily thrifty, he could lay by in the autumn sufficient to carry him on through the season of his discontent, when no golf is. He can lightly earn seven and sixpence a day by playing two rounds of golf; or, if he does not get an engagement, three and sixpence a day by carrying clubs. These are about the fees paid at St. Andrews and Musselburgh, Scotland, which are the great manufactories of the professionals who go forth to many links as green-keepers. . . . In the medal weeks

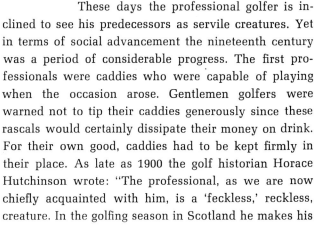

When British golf was supreme. Left to right: James Braid, J. H. Taylor, Ted Ray, and Harry Vardon, who among them won 17 British Opens and two U.S. Opens. Braid, Taylor, and Vardon were known as the Great Triumvirate.

they pick up a little more, and an extra shilling or two comes into their pockets from bets. . . . They often sell with great advantage clubs to young players, who fondly imagine magical properties to dwell in the wand itself, rather than in the hands of the sorcerers who wield it. Occasionally they combine with golf-playing more general branches of industry, which they pursue in a spasmodic fashion. Thus, when we asked of one of them whether a brother professional had no other trade than that of golf, he replied, 'Ou, aye! he has that—he breaks stanes.'

"Improvidence in the hours of plenty often brings him to very sore straits. But now that so many more openings are occurring for green-keepers, in the increase in the number of links all over England, we may hope to see these further inducements developing better habits in the professional class."

As we can see from Hutchinson's remarks, the respected and responsible job was that of green-keeper. Yet within a space of fifty years, and in a period when the rigid stratification of society was notably stable, the golf professional evolved to a position of respect and affection. By modern standards he was still, for the most part, a paid retainer of the club and far from achieving equal standing with the members. However, the relationship had changed greatly. His station in life was now more like that of a sergeant major vis-à-vis the officers, or of a head gamekeeper on a large estate. He was a man from whom a gentleman could properly seek advice and tuition. He was the master of his shop and a skilled craftsman. He made and repaired clubs, taught members the techniques of the game, and was much in demand to join them for a round—of golf, that is, not drinks. After the match the pro retired to his shop while the members repaired to the club bar and no one thought anything amiss in that arrangement, least of all the professional himself, who seems to have been content with his lot. Some of today's professionals remember these "good old days,"

regret their passing, and rather resent the emancipation of the profession, since it places on them the burdens of competing socially as well as athletically.

For many of today's senior golfers the professional's shop was where it all began. In those days of hickory-shafted clubs, the shop was a magical place, smelling of tallow, tanned twine, and varnish. In the middle of the clutter was the pro, usually an amiable Scot in tweed plus fours, who made and mended the wonderful adult toys. A boy, if he was lucky, might be privileged to help the great man with small jobs.

Boys, who are great ones for breaking things, have a special respect for people who are skilled at repairs and there is something in youth's nature which associates manual skills with wisdom. The pro was therefore a great man, indeed. In fact, many of them were remarkable men by any standards. Educationalists insist that team games are great character builders. Life, however, is not a team game and to that extent a better case might be made for golf. It teaches a boy self-control, independence, the value of perseverance, and humility. And since golf is a game at which it is so easy to cheat, and so pointless to do so, it places a high premium on honesty. It is a matter of common experience that the golf professional is nearly always a man of sterling character. There are remarkably few bad hats in golf and in this respect those of us who play the game are fortunate.

A few professionals in early times supplemented their club incomes with competitive golf. Pro golf got away to a modest start; formal tournaments were modest in size and numbers. There were only eight entrants for the first Open. Competition golf mainly took the form of challenge matches, and exciting affairs they were, all the more tense for the fact that the golfers were playing for their own money. Willie Park of Musselburgh, a tidy golfer who did not hit the ball very far but was a demon putter, had a standing challenge in the golfing press to play any man for £50 a side, winner take all, and frequently the stakes (worth something like twenty times that today) were higher. Park's motto, "the man who can putt is a match for anyone," was disproved in a famous series of matches with Vardon, but on balance he did well enough.

These challenge matches created enormous public interest and did much to popularize golf, although they brought little direct benefit to the profession. Money circulated, but little was put into the game from outside sources. Cheap golf thus became traditional in Britain, and especially in Scotland. As the national game—or one of them; Scots play every game they adopt with religious fervor—golf was regarded as something of a birthright. Many courses in Scotland, including St. Andrews itself, are owned by the local authorities and golf is provided as a municipal amenity, like water. As a result, even today, the cost of playing a round on a Scottish championship course is less than any self-respecting American visitor would tip his caddie. This accounts for the high proportion of Scottish boys and girls who become very good players at an early age, and it has also resulted in golf being a classless game in Scotland. Much the same situation exists in Ireland.

The historical importance of inexpensive golf in Scotland is that it produced a large number of players of professional standard and skilled clubmakers who could not earn a living in their own country. When golf became the rage in America, there existed a pool of experienced professionals all too anxious to emigrate to the new world. The small village of Carnoustie, which even today is barely more than a one-street town, sent more than a hundred professionals to America to spread the word of golf and put the game on a secure footing.

One such emigrant was given a typically Scottish send-off before departing for South America. He made his farewells and staggered into the night.

When he awoke at dawn from the stupor into which he had fallen, he decided that the first thing he must do was to build a home in this new country. Bemused, he picked out a site before he realized where he was. That hole on the Carnoustie links is known as South America to this day. The story had a happy ending. The emigrant actually built his South American home and lived there for the rest of his life.

While the public has benefited enormously from Scotland's tradition of inexpensive golf, in one respect Scotland has suffered. It is a matter of keen national disappointment that no home-based player has won the Open since the days when the championship was a modest, virtually local competition. Scots *have* won it. Braid took the title five times, but only after he had settled in England. Tommy Armour won the Open in 1931, but by that time he was a naturalized American. Sandy Herd's triumph was muted in his native Scotland by the fact that he had gone to live and work in England.

For some reason which is seated deep within the patriotic breast, there is a special Scotch prejudice against Scots who settle in England. They are known contemptuously as "Anglos." There is a considerable body of Scottish opinion which holds that those guilty of such an act of betrayal as to move to a country where they can earn a living should not be eligible to represent Scotland on international teams.

Can it be that this atavistic prejudice contributes to the phenomenon that, while Scotland produces a large number of very good young players, they do not develop to world class? It may be that the subconscious knowledge that he will almost certainly have to go "abroad" to earn a livelihood, and so attract the odium of the Anglo label, is a disincentive to the young Scottish professional. It is, in other words, more important for him to be true to Scotland than to his own potential. Better a second-grade golfer and a first-class Scot than the other way around.

7 · superstars

9 olf's modern era began in 1929, with the perfecting of the tubular steel shaft. As far as playing the game was concerned, it simplified matters considerably, since the golfer no longer had to contend with the problem of torque (the twisting of the shaft during the swing), which made hickory-shafted golf such an exercise in manual control. Straight-grained hickory shafts had many qualities suited to golf. They were strong, flexible, could be shaved to achieve perfect balance, and imparted a lively "feel" to the shot which has never been satisfactorily reproduced by steel, aluminum, or—though it comes close—fiberglass.

The disadvantage of hickory was that it had insufficient resistance to twisting. Under the forces exerted in the golf swing, with the clubhead acting as a lever, this torque action could twist the face "open" at impact. The trick of hickory golf was to time the shot so that the moment of striking coincided with the face in the square position. It was this need for control and timing which made the swings of Vardon and Jones so smooth and graceful. For a player with a short backswing and a powerful action, such as Doug Sanders, hickory golf would be a frustrating activity, since the clubface would always be twisting open at impact. The tubular form of the steel shaft almost eliminated torque and permitted the introduction of hitting at the ball, rather than swinging. Timing still was vital, but now the criterion was to achieve impact at the fastest point in the stroke, with the hands controlling the squareness of the clubface, rather than waiting for the clubhead to square itself, which was the hickory player's problem.

Some golfers made the transition more easily than others. Jones never hit the ball with his old mastery once he took to steel, although it should be remembered that he had long since retired from competitive play. No doubt if he had still been fired by his early spirit and applied his great intellect and golfmanship seriously to the problem, he would quickly have discovered the tricks of the new technique. Some players went on using much hand action in their swings and are remembered for virtuoso shotmaking.

As a generalization, however, the steel shaft and the graduated matched set of irons robbed the game of much of its artistry. The need to contrive different shots for different situations largely disappeared. Today's professionals are much more concerned with using one standard stroke for each of their great variety of clubs. The old school carried many fewer clubs and varied the stroke. If you asked Vardon how far he hit his mashie you received a very dusty answer. It depended entirely on how he played it. Ask Jack Nicklaus the same question about his five-iron and he will tell you to within three yards. It is dangerous to be too dogmatic on this subject because it is not a matter of absolutes. Some modern players do vary their strokes considerably according to conditions. Lee Trevino comes to mind as an example. But, generally, hickory golf was a game of manipulation and inspiration; steel golf is a game of precision and calculation.

With the coming of steel, although not necessarily because of it, golf became a truly international sport. America continued to dominate the game, but other countries, notably Australia and South Africa, began to produce players of world stature. Possibly the most significant figure in this period of transition was Walter Hagen. This brash young man with the patent-leather hair style and flamboyant clothes began his golfing career as a figure of fun. The older pros, brought up in the dour Scottish tradition, did not have much time for this flashy braggart, who announced that he was going to annihilate them and then attempted to make good his boasts with the wildest swing they'd ever seen. However, there was more to Hagen than mouth. He worked hard and, although he never eliminated the exciting possibility of a really dreadful shot, he hit more brilliant ones than anyone else. The brash-

Preceding pages: The greatest? Certainly the most effective golfer of all time with his combination of power, accuracy, competitive spirit, and golfing sense—Jack Nicklaus, here playing in the 1972 Jackie Gleason tournament.

ness matured into confidence in his own superior ability and pretty soon he was cleaning up on the American tournament scene.

Hagen was shrewd enough to understand that the galleries liked their heroes larger than life, and so he stressed his natural tendencies. The clothes became flashier, the bold shots were stage-managed with much pacing about and changing of clubs to make them appear more difficult, and the locker-room psychological warfare ("Who's going to be second?") was ruthlessly continued. Off course, he lived like a millionaire playboy, and a heavily publicized one at that. In comparison with his brother professionals, brought up in the virtues of modesty and self-effacement, Hagen seemed a prince. By behaving as if he could not be beaten, Hagen eventually reached the stage where his opponents began to half-believe he was invincible. The Hagen legend was probably worth two strokes a round to him and each success made the next one that much easier. Of course, Hagen cashed in. That, after all, was the point of the exercise. He toured the world, playing tournaments and challenge matches and giving exhibitions, often in the company of Joe Kirkwood, the trick-shot artist.

What, you may ask, was the significance of a traveling showman who financed his high living with displays of golfing skill? The answer is indirect. Hagen set an example for his brother professionals, an extravagant one, perhaps, but in his style Hagen showed them the possibilities of professional golf. In Britain, for example, the pros were changing their clothes in the caddie sheds and touching their caps to the members—while Hagen hobnobbed with the Prince of Wales, danced until all hours at fashionable night spots, and mixed easily in high society. It did not concern him that as a professional he was not allowed into the clubhouse. His clubhouse was the best hotel in town, far beyond the means of most of the members, and he walked directly to the first tee from the most opulent limousine in the car park. And because he was Hagen, the great champion, the public accepted him as an original character and loved him for it.

In a rather different category at this time was Henry Cotton, a dedicated and remote English pro. Cotton did not conform either. He was, for a start, a gentleman and had been educated at a good public school. Unlike Hagen, Cotton knew the social rules and knew all too well that by becoming a pro he was déclassé. Cotton refused to play the conventions of that snobbish game. He, too, stayed at the Ritz and his chauffeur-driven Rolls-Royce was his clubhouse. While the pros went off to the caddie shed to eat their cheese sandwiches and the members repaired to the club for Lancashire hot pot, Cotton had his man produce a Fortnum & Mason hamper from the Rolls and picnicked on caviar and champagne. The popping of the cork was largely symbolic, for the highly strung Cotton could take only the lightest refreshment during the tension of a tournament, but it sounded the opening shot of a social revolution.

The barriers of social prejudice could not withstand such an elegant assault. Between them, Hagen and Cotton opened the clubhouse doors and gradually the golf professional was accepted on terms of equality by the members.

In the United States, where it is not a crime to be born poor provided you do not stay that way, the period following the retirement of Jones brought two golfers to full maturity. It is true that a young Italian felt it prudent to Anglicize his name from Saraceni to Sarazen, but thereafter his only obstacles were the regular hazards of any golfing career.

Gene Sarazen brought more to golf than an outstanding gift for the game. Blessed with a lively and progressive intellect he advanced the techniques of golf in one notable manner. At this time the all-purpose club for high pitches around the green and for bunker play was the broad-faced niblick. This club, with its thin, almost circular face, had a cutting edge like an ax, and in the hands of a skilled player was a spectacular instrument. A player could open the face and cut up the ball with an almost vertical trajectory to clear an obstacle, or hood the face and hit a low, punched shot into the wind. While it was a most versatile club when the shot succeeded, it had vast potential for disaster. Unless the stroke was perfectly executed the result could be damaging. Hit the ball a fraction thin and that sharp cutting edge sent it skimming yards past the target—and probably cut the cover in the bargain. Hit the shot fat and the clubface dug into the turf and resulted in the feeblest of duffs. In bunkers, where the technique was to skim the blade under the ball, an error either way left the ball in the sand.

Sarazen felt that this club was altogether too chancy. In the tension of tournament golf a club was needed which could be relied upon to get the ball out of sand every time, even if the execution was not perfect. He experimented by welding a flange onto the bottom of the club, shaping it in such a way that when he hit down with it, the clubhead did not dig farther into the sand but was instead deflected upward. So the family of wedges was started, later evolving into specialized clubs for sand and pitching purposes. Players such as Billy Casper and Gary Player have achieved such mastery of the wedges that it is unthinkable they could do better with any other form of club.

Yet in one way it is a pity that Sarazen's new club enjoyed such success, for it tended to discredit the old spade niblick entirely. Certainly the wedge is more reliable and gives the player a welcome margin for error. But there are some things the wedge cannot do, even in the hands of a master, which are possible with the niblick. All of us have been faced at times with a fluffy lie on a downslope with the prospect of having to carry a bunker and trying to stop the ball quickly on a fast and sloping green. In this situation the pro lays open his sand wedge and tries to play a delicate, lazy-looking shot. But that flange, so useful in sand, is now a hindrance and unless the stroke is perfect the clubhead may bounce into the ball and ruin the shot. The thin-bladed niblick could be skimmed smartly under the ball, which popped into the air, floated down to the green, landed softly as a cat, and braked hard with backspin. Such a club does not fit the so-called "matched" set. It would appear to be an odd-man out. All the same, there is a good case for its revival—just as there is for the jigger, the useful club for short run-ups. Certainly our stereotyped attitude toward clubs could profitably be reexamined.

Along with Sarazen, we must consider the career of Byron Nelson, or at any rate one season in that career. In 1945 Nelson, a quiet Texan, won eighteen official PGA tournaments, eleven of them in succession. His season's stroke average was 68.33. They say that nobody remembers who came second, but it is worth a footnote to Nelson's year that he finished as runner-up seven times, and that his worst performance of the season was ninth. His winnings, incidentally, amounted to $52,500, and it is possibly worth remarking that if anyone could reproduce that record today he would win rather more than $700,000.

Some people have argued, rather ungenerously, that since this was wartime Nelson did not have much opposition. Perhaps there were not many great players among the opposition, although with Ben Hogan and Sam Snead in the line-up, no tournament was a pushover. Nelson's real achievement, however, was not the winning but the manner of winning. A stroke average of 68.33 brooks no argument. For consistency there has never been anything like it, before or since. This was the only year Nelson devoted fully to tournament play. Until then he had been mainly a club pro, and afterward, having won the U.S. Open, Masters, and PGA championships, and with his ambitions sated by records, he eased into semiretirement.

There have been many judgments of Nel-

175

Gene Sarazen (l.), in one sense the first of
the modern breed of professional. He brought a lively
intelligence and deeply analytical approach to
the game and pioneered the use of broad-soled wedges.

Golf's first showman, the dandy Walter Hagen,
who talked a great game of golf and who most of the
time matched his words with his deeds on the
course. Opposite: With Californian star Helen Lawson.

son's golf by his contemporaries, and the consensus is that during 1945, when he played almost as if in a trance, his iron play, in particular the confidence with which he worked and finessed the ball up to the flag, was his greatest strength. A dissenting minority holds the view that his supremacy lay in his driving. He always hit his approach shots from the right place and was naturally more successful with them than his rivals. The evidence of Nelson himself can be called to support both sides. Nelson rather dismisses his driving, modestly conceding only that it was very consistent at that time. This may be taken to mean he felt his approach work was the more telling part of his game. On the other hand, it also could mean that he paid little attention to it because he did not need to, and therefore took it for granted. His retirement, prompted no doubt by a temperament which did not relish the nervous tensions of tournament golf, cut off a career which might have reached any heights. As it was, he packed into that one year enough successes to sustain most players for twenty years or more.

The idea has grown that Nelson's year of triumph was a phenomenon which defies explanation. He himself has given some weight to that theory by admitting to being superstitious and saying that perhaps this period was a particularly propitious one for him. Every golfer has at times enjoyed the experience of knowing with utter certainty that the long putt he is about to strike is going to fall into the cup. Such moments of enlightenment occasionally accompany other types of shots. In Nelson's case, there is another and more prosaic factor. Before that season began he carefully analyzed the weaknesses in his game. He objectively researched the areas of his golf where strokes could be saved and made a number of adjustments to his play, such as altering his technique for short chip shots. He also made a slight but fundamental change in his swing, getting into a more upright plane with his feet positioned closer to the ball.

176

This upright style, sometimes glibly called the American swing, may have been the key to his successes. Every individual has what may be called an optimum arc, a swing plane which suits him best. It is obviously a personal trait, which is why the search for the perfect, "universal" swing is such a forlorn cause. Lee Trevino clearly performs best with a flat, sweeping swing, while Jack Nicklaus is better with an upright style. The trouble with most of us golfers is that we try to model ourselves on (or allow ourselves to be taught) styles which may not be suitable to our personal idiosyncrasies. Perhaps Byron Nelson found his best swing plane in the spring of 1945 and the rest just followed naturally.

So-called style, or good form, has bedeviled modern golf and we do not have to look far for the culprit. Ben Hogan, the singleminded perfectionist, made himself into the finest striker of a golf ball the world has ever known. He came nearer than anyone to perfecting golf. Unwittingly he became the model for millions of golfers who argued with simple logic that since Hogan's results were best, Hogan's methods must be best. So they were—for Hogan. And that's where the logic broke down. Manifestly we are not all Hogans, and it is futile to pretend we are. What worked for Hogan may be absurd for a short, fat executive of advancing years whose muscles are conditioned for the chairbound life. When we see someone like the 6-foot 5-inch George Archer play golf we are not surprised that his swing is not like Hogan's. Obviously it could not be. What is less obvious, but equally true, is that the golfer who is an exact physical match for Hogan in his prime may be totally unsuited to Hogan's method of swinging a golf club. There is much in Hogan's golf and life, of course, which the aspiring young golfer can usefully copy. His dedication, his perseverance, and his courage are models for all. But as to method, the young player would be wise to follow Hogan only as far as the great man's own start-

The typical Haig—cool, calm, and collecting
British Open trophy in Sandwich, 1928, while his golfing friend,
Edward, Prince of Wales, listens deferentially
behind him. After all, on the course Hagen was King.

ing point—and that is to go out and discover by long experiment and painstaking practice what works best for him. What he has to develop is a swing that delivers the clubhead to the ball at speed, square to the line of flight, along the line of flight, and at the appropriate angle of attack (that is to say, not scooping or digging). Any eccentricity of swing is permissible provided that the four ·golden rules of impact are consistently achieved. The trouble with unorthodox methods is that, while they work well for a time, they often put such physical strains on a golfer that his swing does not endure. The method that works for most people is the so-called classical style exemplified by the swing of

Sam Snead and which has served him for more than forty years.

It is interesting to observe the new generation of young professionals and try to isolate common points of style which might then be defined as "the modern swing." There is only one common denominator and even that is not entirely universal. It arises from the basic difference between pro and amateur golf. The amateur wants to score as low as possible while the pro is concerned not to produce a high score. It is, of course, a matter of emphasis rather than dogma, but the difference is there.

In the last analysis it does not matter if

Two international stars—Henry Cotton
of England, three times Open champion, and (opposite on
right) South Africa's Bobby Locke, who won five
Opens and was probably finest putter in history of golf.

an amateur takes an 80. All he hurts is his ego. But for the pro, an 80 can mean that he does not eat that week. If he can average par for a season he will live well; indeed, in some years such an average would make him the leading moneywinner. As a result, his thinking about the golf swing is directed toward the elimination of error. Control is everything. Most amateurs—and the old-time pros as well—play with a loosely hinging wrist action at the top of the backswing. It is a powerful technique, since the clubhead describes a full arc, but it requires immaculate timing to deliver the club-face to the ball in exactly the right place at exactly the maximum clubhead speed. In the new golf as played by the pros, such an action is characterized as "floppy at the top," and they work to achieve a controlled firmness of the wrists at the top of the backswing. Of course, if they left it at that their arcs would be shortened and they would lose distance. So they work—and it really is work in the sense of physical athleticism—to increase the body turn. They coil the spring that much tighter.

If an amateur golfer is interested in reducing his handicap there is much he can learn by watching, say, Jack Nicklaus, provided he is prepared to be honest with himself. Imagine a typical situation. A 15-handicap player watching television sees Nicklaus, in knee-high rough, take out his seven-iron and smash the ball onto a green 180 yards away. The commentator explodes with ecstasy, as if this were a miracle rather than an everyday occurrence. Then a slow-motion replay is shown with an expert pointing out, "Notice the way Jack keeps his head absolutely still during the stroke." If our 15-handicap friend tries to emulate Nicklaus in that situation he is headed straight for the osteopath's couch and bitter disillusionment. But there is a useful lesson to be learned, provided the amateur is prepared to deal in realities rather than fantasy. The question the amateur golfer must ask himself is: "What would Nicklaus do now, *if*

he had a swing like mine?"

Now we can pick Nicklaus's golfing brain. Now the amateur, if he has been watching sensibly, has Nicklaus at his side nominating the shot. And the answer is obvious: Take a wedge, pick a spot on the fairway, and very deliberately pitch the ball out sideways to the safety of the mown surface. Then you can play an ordinary approach. Sure, you may drop a shot. But at worst you are home with a 5 instead of a certain 8. And, who knows, you might sink a putt and save your par. Even with all his skill, Nicklaus seldom aims directly at the flag. He plays the percentages and goes for the center of the green. And he is Jack Nicklaus. Where do you get off, with your 15-handicap swing, firing away at the pin? The one important lesson the club golfer can learn from watching the pros is to play within the limits of his ability. The pro goes for the shot he knows he can produce. All too often the amateur gambles on what he recognizes (if he stops to think about it) must be the shot of a lifetime for him.

Hogan's distinguished record did not adequately reflect the clear superiority of his golf. This is partly explained by the loss of what should have been some of his most productive years, and partly by the premature onset of putting troubles. As is well known, Hogan suffered multiple fractures when he threw himself across his wife to save her as their car smashed into a bus. That seemed to end the most polished golfing talent the world had ever seen, but Hogan confounded his doctors by torturing his broken body back to golfing fitness, and claiming once more his place at the peak of American golf. Anyone, however, who plays golf with the intensity of a Hogan, a man to whom every shot was a matter of vital importance, must be liable sooner or later to what we callously call the yips, or twitch. This is a nervous complaint or, more accurately, a symptom of a nervous condition. Its effect is to short-circuit the lines of communication between the brain and the hands, thus bringing about a break-

Postwar swingers. Standing (l. to r.): Henry Picard, Martin Pose, Jimmy Hines, Horton Smith, Gene Sarazen, Lawson Little, Jimmy Thomson, Sam Snead; front: Ben Hogan, Byron Nelson, Jimmy Demaret, Dick Metz, Craig Wood, Paul Runyan, Clayton Heafner.

down in free will. The brain commands the hands to take the putter back slowly, but there is no response. Eventually the message gets through in the form of a desperate SOS and the hands respond with an uncontrolled jerk. The yips are caused by tension, and it is only in the heat of a tournament that they occur.

Sufferers will try anything to cure this condition, but changing grips or putters, or trying to exorcise the spell on the practice green, is useless. The one possible way to a cure is to induce a relaxed frame of mind, but since golfers may spend twenty years on the circuit without conquering their nervous tension, this is easier said than done.

The only practical palliative is for the golfer to immobilize the affected muscles. Usually the yips start with the smaller muscles of the fingers, those normally employed for delicate work. In that case, control can be regained—albeit at the expense of some

degree of touch—by locking the hands on the club and putting with an arm action. If the arms are also affected they can be locked, clamped firmly against the side, and the putter moved by a swaying motion of the hips. This may not be a particularly effective method of holing out, but at least it gives the twitcher a chance to regain a measure of confidence.

It is one thing to tell an ordinary club golfer with the yips that salvation lies in taking his golf, and perhaps himself, less seriously. But such a cure was not open to Hogan. At his level golf is serious by definition. Unless the player gives the game total concentration it loses its point. Hence, one of the saddest sights in modern golf was the last competitive appearances of Ben Hogan. The command with which he struck the ball from tee to green was nullified by his sweating agony as he stood locked over a putt. Eventually, by a huge effort of will, he broke the paralysis

with a convulsion which might send the ball 20 feet past its target. Those people who urged Hogan to return to big-time golf on the grounds that he still hit the ball better than anyone did not realize the ordeal they were asking him to endure. To Hogan there was no satisfaction in giving what amounted to exhibitions of stroke play. He did not have to prove anything. Golf has always been two games. At one of them Hogan was unrivaled. At the other, the game within a game, he could no longer compete. And since these games cannot be separated, he called it a day.

No one could ever accuse Bobby Locke of being a slave to style or to any golfing orthodoxy. In many ways Locke was the opposite of Hogan. It is impossible to describe his swing without making it sound like a parody, which in truth it was. The American public was astonished at the sight of this young South African, whose naturally cheerful personality was

rigorously subdued on the course behind a solemn expression as unchanging as a mask; he had the stately air of an archbishop conducting a funeral. He set himself as if to hit the ball forty-five degrees to the right of the target, and he took the club back with an action which was more of a pirouette than a backswing. From here he swung down and delivered what appeared to be a rather dainty flick at the ball, following through to another pirouette. The ball flew off in the direction you would expect from such an exaggeratedly closed stance and many were the suppressed smiles as Old Muffin Face's ball flew toward the right-hand rough.

Then, in keeping with his ecclesiastical demeanor, the miracle occurred. As the ball reached the height of its trajectory, it went into a left turn and homed back to the fairway. Every shot was the same controlled draw. Even the short irons started out right of the flag and, as if under remote-control guidance,

Three women champions—Glenna Collett Vare, national champion six times; Patty Berg, national and Open champion; and one of the greatest sportswomen America (or anywhere else) has produced—Babe Didrikson Zaharias.

plummeted back on target. If the galleries found Locke's highly personal method amusing, there was very little laughter among his fellow professionals. This guy was picking up fat checks week after week and taking the bread out of their mouths.

Locke's right-to-left style was not suited to all conditions and courses. Most modern professionals prefer to move the ball the other way, with a slight fade. The higher trajectory of the fade and increased braking effect on landing give the golfer greater control, since his shots are less likely to run on into trouble. Locke, however, had two other assets. From tee to green his philosophy was unadventurous in the extreme. He played well within himself and his drive nearly always finished twenty yards short of his fellow competitor's ball (although he could belt it out with the best of them when he wanted). Most of the time he was content simply to move the ball modestly or safely forward. But once on the green he had a decided edge because he was by general consent the finest putter of his day.

He had an unvarying routine with an old hickory-shafted blade putter. This began with a close examination of the line, even down to what appeared to be a distasteful examination of the hole itself, like a head waiter examining a bowl of soup which has been the subject of a complaint. People used to joke that Locke was reassuring himself that the hole was big enough to receive his ball, but the explanation was less fanciful. Brought up on the nappy greens of South Africa, he had naturally fallen into the habit of inspecting the rim of the cup to confirm the direction of the nap. And Locke was nothing if not a creature of habit. After this leisurely reconnaissance he became decidedly brisk. He took his stance, made two quick practice putts, shuffled an inch or so forward, and hit the putt with a rhythmic, wristy stroke which found the cup in an astonishingly high proportion of cases.

But hit or miss, his deadpan expression

never changed and here was Locke's second great asset. Temperamentally and emotionally the man was fireproof, or so it seemed. He suffered from nervous tension of course. Everyone does. But by self-discipline he trained himself never to show by the flicker of an eyebrow how he was feeling. Just how much this self-control helped him to suppress his natural jitters we do not know, but what is beyond dispute is that by seeming never to lose his cool, the other players believed him to be nerveless. And that in itself, as in the case of Walter Hagen, was a considerable advantage to Locke.

Locke was the first major figure to be produced by what we might call the emergent golfing nations. The breach in Anglo-American domination of the game was quickly widened by more great players from different nations. Along came Roberto de Vicenzo of Argentina, a superb striker and proof that this serious new game need not be solemn or lose its qualities as a sport, despite the arrival of the businessman pro. Peter Thomson of Australia has never received his due recognition as a player and influential administrator, either in America or, strangely enough, in his own country. Yet his contribution to the advancement of golf and the improvement in conditions of the profession, not to mention his contribution to the record books, is unsurpassed. His reputation in America suffered because he is an uncompromising enthusiast for old-fashioned natural golf. He believes that golf should remain a game of inspiration, unraked bunkers, and improvised shot-making. He even approves of the element of chance, the lucky or unlucky bounce, and so it is perhaps natural that his views were received coolly in a country where the tendency is to take luck out of golf as much as possible. However, his lack of recognition in Australia is less easy to understand, especially as sport in his country is almost a national religion.

New Zealand has produced Bob Charles, the only left-hander to achieve international status. That fact is difficult to explain in the light of the pro-

The agony and the payoff for Gary Player,
the small South African whose dedication elevated him to
the front ranks of the golfing giants. Bottom:
With his wife after another of his championship triumphs.

portion of lefties occurring in nature. If golf is compared with, say, tennis, the dearth of left-handers is astonishing and the only explanation is that young golfers are encouraged to play the wrong way round. A left-handed boy is advised to persevere with right-handed clubs on the grounds that in golf the left hand should dominate the swing. This doctrine that golf is a left-handed game, which can easily be proved false, must have done incomparable harm to many thousands of players who would have been better and happier as southpaws.

In the sixties, golf became a truly international game. Nothing proved this more completely than the emergence of the so-called Big Three (echoes of the Great Triumvirate) in the person of two Americans, Arnold Palmer and Jack Nicklaus, and a South African, Gary Player. If their manager, Mark McCormack, had

sat down and worked out the theoretical specifications for a national sporting idol he would have come up with a blueprint for an Arnold Palmer. Appearance: rough-hewn good looks and the air of a boy who is up to devilment; a face that is quick to smile and which clearly reflects its owner's moods. Physical assets: the build of a good middleweight; big hands; long, tapering back; strong, stocky legs—the perfect conformation for hitting a golf ball. Personality: tough, aggressive, and self-centered, but with an easy-going and responsive veneer and a taste for the dramatic. It is little wonder that once Palmer began to win he attracted a huge personal following, both for his golf and his personality.

Palmer's swing is no classic. On the back-swing he tends to throw the club out of its plane, so that coming down he has to fight to bring the clubhead

Admiration and elation: Popular Charles Sifford,
whose dexterity with a golf club is matched only by his
skill at cigar chomping, and (opposite) Billy Casper
hailing one that dropped for him in the 1971 PGA Championship.

Gallery favorites: Lee Trevino signs, Ben Hogan
swings, and Sam Snead does his unorthodox
thing on the green. His sidewinder putting works—for him.
Right: Palmer, Nicklaus, and Trevino at World Series.

into the "slot." This compensating action gives him his characteristic high finish with a "twiddly bit" at the end, and when his timing is slightly off, as it must be with everyone at times, his bad shots are likely to be wilder than the mis-hits of more conventional swingers. However, Palmer's greatest asset is a combination of a gambling instinct (or optimism or foolhardiness) which makes him attempt dramatic recoveries from trouble, and his physical strength, which so frequently makes these attempts successful.

The ordinary spectator cannot relate to a Ben Hogan, because his brand of flawless golf is entirely outside the ordinary run of country-club golf. Not so Palmer. He gets himself into places which are all too familiar to the Sunday morning four-ball. The difference is that Palmer extricates himself with his score unscathed. The spectator can admire Hogan in a cool, objective sense, but he can bleed with Palmer and rejoice with him at the happy ending. If Harry Vardon changed the method of golf, Palmer more than any man changed the manner of the game. His deeds on the course turned golf into a major spectator sport and a multimillion-dollar business.

The case of Gary Player was quite different. As a youth he would not have fitted anyone's blueprint for a sporting hero. He was small and frail, and his golf, both in the way he gripped the club and the way he swung it, suggested he would be better advised to take up a different career. But circumstances of background and physique combined to produce in

Player a classic Napoleon complex. He believed in Gary Player. And with the thoroughness of a true fanatic he set out methodically to prove the adage of the song that "anything you can do I can do better." If he was too small and weak, he would make himself big and strong. If his grip and swing were unsound, he would change them and make them the best in the business. Player's campaign of self-improvement was the most punishing body-building regime any golfer has ever undertaken. He practiced longer than anyone else. He favored diets of nuts and fresh fruits. The zeal which he lavished on his body reached cranky proportions. At one time he wore black outfits "to absorb the strength of the sun," and he pursued every health fad on the market. And he did not neglect his mind. Those around him may have thought his attitude of "my strength is as the strength of ten because my heart is pure" was sanctimonious, but in total the mystical amalgam of nuts, fingertip pushups, and divine inspiration has worked.

He became a great golfer, as good as anyone around, and pound for pound better than any of them. In the process, the overcoming of handicaps became habit-forming. As a major figure in world golf, with nothing left to prove, Player still has to prove himself to himself every time he plays. With no obstacles to overcome he must invent imaginary ones. Hence, his outbursts against the condition of courses, or the "hook" which he claims is plaguing his game. If he can raise a demon for his combative spirit to wrestle and overthrow, he is a magnificent golfer. Have him 7 down against Tony Lema with 18 holes to play in the Piccadilly match-play tournament, and he produces the most remarkable golf of his career. It is not enough for Player to beat his colleagues. If the whole world is against him, as it seemed to him in the beginning, then Player has an opponent worthy of his mettle.

Jack Nicklaus, too, faced more than the golfer's traditional enemy, par, when he came into the pro game. He had to fight a legend. Nicklaus, a prodigy as a young amateur who had almost snatched the U.S. Open championship from the cream of professional golf, was always going to be one of the greats. Nobody doubted that fact for a moment after watching the big teen-ager belt out a drive. The trouble was that there can only be one rooster on top of the haystack and that perch belonged to Palmer. If Nicklaus was to become champion he would have to depose the darling of the golf world.

That did not worry the two golfers unduly. Such, after all, is the way of sport. But for the hero-worshipping public Nicklaus was the iconoclast who threatened to smash their idol. At that time Nicklaus thought of nothing but golf. Issues such as personal appearance and public relations did not help him hit a golf ball and so were no concern to him. In time he grew to appreciate that they did, indeed, affect both his golf and his income, but as a youngster subtleties of this kind entirely escaped him. He was frankly fat and his crew-cut hair accentuated a quality that people quickly associated with arrogance. In fact, Nicklaus has his share of the arrogance essential to a champion, but in his case it is more an honest realization of his capabilities. In the British Open of 1971, against Doug Sanders, when Nicklaus peeled off his sweater and drove through the last green 385 yards away, it looked like an act of arrogance. In reality, it was an example of his rather conservative nature. He was playing safe. He knew objectively that in those conditions he could have reached his target with a three-wood, but he cautiously took his driver to make sure.

In the same way his deeds and public utterances were often misconstrued when he first became a professional, especially at that time when many people were all too eager to see him in a bad light. The Palmer-oriented galleries booed him shamelessly and nothing that Nicklaus has achieved in golf is more becoming than his dignified behavior during that trying period of his career. If he suffered privately he kept it to himself and gradually his golf won him due respect. In fact, the booing was probably counterproductive in total effect, because although it may have upset Nicklaus it certainly embarrassed Palmer and probably upset him more.

What makes Nicklaus the greatest golfer of his generation? He does not strike the ball with anything like the consistency of Hogan. His short game and putting are probably below the standard of the average tournament professional, and his golfing outlook is possibly too conservative. The answer, of course, is power, but it would be a gross oversimplification to see Nicklaus as just a slugger. Many of his triumphs, after all, have been achieved on short courses where there is no great premium on length. The key to his success is power through the full range of clubs. It is obvious, except in the case of oddities like Britain's Tommy Horton, that a golfer is more accurate with an eight-iron than he is with a four. If we categorize the long irons, one to four, as being mainly distance clubs and the others, five to nine, as predominately accuracy clubs, then we can see that Nicklaus is often playing for accuracy while his opponents are more concerned with distance. He may take a one-iron off the tee and seemingly throw away the advantage of his power. But then, when he and his opponent are both roughly in the same part of the fairway, Nicklaus can hit a six-iron while the rest need fours. And if the circumstances are propitious, as on that day at St. Andrews, he can let out his driver and give himself an even greater advantage with his second shot.

There are, it is true, some golfers who can hit the ball as far as Nicklaus, club for club, but they are the true sluggers who hit flat out. Nicklaus gets his distance while playing well within his physical powers and he therefore has the edge in accuracy. In the record books Nicklaus has already proved himself the most formidable player of all. (He cannot be compared with Bobby Jones because of the vast difference in their circumstances. No matter how many championships Nicklaus wins he can never usurp Jones' standing as the greatest of them all. Better, yes, but greatness involves more than scoring and the manner of Jones' triumphs cannot be approached.)

If we are mainly concerned with significant contributions to golf the superficial view of Nicklaus is as the first of the great method players. He pioneered the system of pacing out courses and charting distance. However, that is a mere matter of mathematics, and the natural product of his logical mind. Indeed, many people would argue that the habit of measuring every shot diminished golf in that it robbed the game of an element of judgment and, perhaps more important, added a time-consuming ritual to a game which had already become intolerably slow. Since it is inevitable that club players will copy the acknowledged masters of the game, pacing and other tedious pro habits have become a commonplace (and pointless) exercise for lesser golfers, and a round of four-ball play has come to mean a five-hour marathon (instead of the old norm, about three and a quarter hours).

No, we can hardly heap laurels on Nicklaus for his part in this retrograde tendency. His contribution is more like that of Harry Vardon in setting a new standard of play. It is almost a cliché among tournament players to pass remarks to the effect, "When Jack is on form the rest of us are playing for second place." They cannot hope to live with him at his best. However, the younger players coming into the game are not daunted by Nicklaus, simply because it is the nature of youthful ambition to set no limits to their potential. For them Nicklaus represents the standard which they must attain and surpass. Just as Roger Bannister's four-minute mile released a psychological block in athletics and ushered in an era of unprecedented speed, so the standards of Nicklaus have opened the way for a generation of super-golfers.

193

8 · the circuit

much in the manner of the British postage stamp, which has no word to label the country of origin, so in golf it is not the British Open but simply the Open Championship. This is not affectation. When the event began it was the only one, so there was no reason to distinguish it. However, to avoid confusion we will refer to it as the British Open and risk the wrath of pedants.

It all began casually enough when the Prestwick Club was formed. The idea of a general golf tournament was kicked around in committee for several years. At last, in 1860, they got around to playing it, with eight invited players competing for a handsome red morocco belt mounted with silver plaques. They played 36 holes in one day, three rounds of Prestwick's 12-hole links, and it is interesting to recall in the light of today's turgid, five-hour rounds that those first Open contestants did not hit off until after lunch. It was four years before the idea of prize money arose, and even then it was limited to £5 for the runner-up, £3 for third, and £2 for fourth. The tradition that glory was more important than financial reward, which was later to bring the Open into low repute, was thus established from the start.

In the first eight years the original field of eight was augmented by additional players from time to time (they had fourteen entries one year), and the stout figure of Prestwick's home pro, the splendidly bearded Tom Morris, was adorned by the championship belt four times. In 1868 the fans had to start referring to him as Old Tom because his seventeen-year-old son, Young Tom Morris, burst upon the golfing scene and swept the board with an unprecedented score of 154. He won it the next two years in succession and so, according to the rules, the belt became his property. That set a problem for the host club and a year elapsed before it succeeded in finding a satisfactory solution. The outcome was that Prestwick joined forces with St. Andrews and the Honourable Company of Edinburgh Golfers and subscribed for the present cup, on condition that the championship be held at each of the three clubs in turn. Thus the foundation of the modern Open was laid, although at that time it inspired vastly less interest than the club championships. Rather, it was a novelty tournament for the servants of the game. It was not until 1892 that the championship was extended to 72 holes, or four rounds of the standardized 18-hole course.

By now the Open had begun to accumulate a respectable fallout of the anecdote and legend from which tradition is formed. Modern promoters try all manner of tricks to buy instant tradition, but there is no shortcut to the real thing. The golfer who registers for an Open Championship at St. Andrews cannot fail to be affected by the history of the event; a newly sponsored tournament, even though it is over the same course for the same, or bigger, purses cannot provoke the same response.

One of the incidents which helped build the awesome tradition of the Open was the experience of David Ayton at St. Andrews in 1885. Ayton came to the 17th five shots ahead of the field in the last round, and when he hit two good shots to the throat of the green everyone believed it was all over. He ran up his approach shot rather gently—after all, he could afford a conservative 6 if need be—but the ball rolled back down the slope of the green and stopped in front of the bunker. We can now imagine him telling himself that the one thing he must guard against is the ignominy of topping the ball feebly into the sand. He played boldly, a shade too boldly, and the ball rolled over the far brow of the green down onto the road. Four. We do not know how he felt as he addressed that first recovery shot from the road. But when his ball failed to make the green it is a safe bet that the panic of desperation guided his second attempt. He got it up off the road all right—and into a bunker. Having lost two shots on that road he didn't want to return there and

*Preceding pages: The most beautiful, and most
exasperating, par-3 in the world—240 yards across the
bay for the 16th at Cypress Point,
California. Bing Crosby had a hole-in-one here.*

196

his first bunker shot was indecisive. The ball stayed in the sand. Seven. It was still there after his next sweating attempt. Eight. Out it came on the third try, and two putts gave him an 11. He lost the Open by two strokes and golfers began referring to the 17th as "the dreaded road hole." The legend had begun, spread from golfer to golfer by word of mouth and doubtless embellished in each retelling.

With the rise of the Great Triumvirate of J. H. Taylor, James Braid, and Harry Vardon, the Open became more or less the private preserve of these three around the turn of the century. And, as if it were not painful enough for Scottish pride to have a couple of Englishmen beating them at their own game, the Open was now extended to England on a rota system which brought it to Hoylake, near Liverpool, and Sandwich on the south coast. By modern standards both courses seem hopelessly old-fashioned, and they are now off the Open championships rota because of their inadequate amenities. In many ways it is unfortunate that big golfing events today have to be staged at clubs chosen for such extraneous reasons as parking space rather than golfing excellence. In these cases, however, we need not regret their absence too deeply.

When Harry Vardon won a record sixth Open at Prestwick in 1914, an era came to an end. The war put the Open into abeyance for six years and when it was resumed a new breed of golfer came to the fore, mainly from across the Atlantic. The first was an expatriate Scot, Jock Hutchison, but he was followed by native-born Walter Hagen, Jim Barnes, Gene Sarazen, Denny Shute (also an ex-Scot), Tommy Armour, and the amateur Bobby Jones. Armour was a remarkable character. As an amateur he played for Great Britain's Walker Cup team and then, having been decorated for bravery in the war, he emigrated to America, became a naturalized citizen, and represented the USA in Ryder Cup play. At the end of his distinguished playing career he won a new reputation as a teacher of golf.

These were lean days for the British home professionals, but highly significant ones in the history of golf. As we have seen, Jones completed his Grand Slam and Hagen laid the foundations for modern tournament golf. These two men were responsible for two of the famous single shots in the history of golf, both on the same day. It was the last round of the 1926 Open at Royal Lytham and St. Anne's, and Jones, playing with the leader Al Watrous, started two shots behind. By the 17th they were level, and Watrous hit a good drive up the fairway, leaving him a clear sight of the green on this slightly doglegged hole. Jones, usually the straightest of drivers, for once pulled his tee shot. He not only missed the fairway on the wrong side—he could not even see the green over a wilderness of scrub and bushes—but his ball lay on a sandy scrape. Today the spot is a formal fairway bunker, but in those days it was no more than a barren area of rough sand. Jones took his mashie and played a superb shot, taking the ball cleanly off the top of the sand. It drifted slightly in the crosswind, as Jones had intended, and finished inside Watrous' ball on the green. Watrous, thoroughly unnerved by this master stroke, three-putted and Jones made his 4. The site of that knockout shot is today marked by a commemorative bronze plaque.

Jones, having safely disposed of his main challenger, was in the clubhouse watching the remaining players finish. The only possible threat lay with Hagen, and even that was a million-to-one chance. If Hagen could get down in two on the long par-4 last hole he could tie with Jones. Hagen hit a good drive which left him about 150 yards from the green. He asked his scorer to go forward and hold the flagstick. The official, after an incredulous pause, advanced just short of the green and stopped. Hagen had to walk forward and shout: "I want you to hold the flag." The gallery roared with delight. There are witnesses who swear that if the flag had been left in the hole Hagen's shot would have hit it and possibly dropped in. As it happened the ball pitched dead on line, hopped over the hole and ran through the green. Jones told Hagen later: "I turned my back on you, Walter, because a guy with that much confidence would be fool lucky enough to make it."

Some years later, in 1947, a similar situation arose at Hoylake. The Irishman Fred Daly was in the club not daring to watch as the great American amateur Frank Stranahan came to the last needing a 2 to upset the apple cart. Like Hagen, he hit a fine drive and left himself 150 yards from the green. He walked all the way to the hole before rolling up his sleeves and hitting a perfect shot. The ball pitched dead on line and rolled straight at the flag. With the roar of the crowd rising to a frenzy, the ball died just six inches short of the cup.

It was not until 1934, with the emergence of Henry Cotton, that British golf began to produce a succession of domestic champions. Cynical observers have commented that this period of British domination in the Open coincides with the period of extreme isolationism in America and that the political stay-at-home mood extended to professional golfers. The charge has little substance. Cotton's opening 67 at Sandwich gave him a good lead, and when he followed with a 65, the lowest round in the history of the championship, he had the field at his mercy. The weather turned foul for the third round and Cotton's 72 was good enough to keep him well clear. He had such a lead, in fact, that a severe attack of stomach cramps and a last round of 79 was still good enough for a five-shot victory. Regardless of the opposition, this was irresistible golf.

And three years later no one could criticize the quality of the field over the toughest course on the rota, Carnoustie on the west coast of Scotland. The American Ryder Cup team had just inflicted a crushing defeat on the British and was present in force for the Open. Gene Sarazen and Tony Manero missed the cut, but that still left Walter Hagen, Sam Snead, Byron Nelson, Horton Smith, Ed Dudley, Henry Picard, Denny Shute, Ralph Guldahl, and Johnny Revolta in the shake-up. As if it was not enough that Carnoustie should be intrinsically the most testing championship course, the weather took a hand, as it does so often on Scottish links. The last round was played in a lashing rainstorm. Everyone was soaked to the skin and any possibility of keeping grips dry was out of the question. Cotton always maintained that his 71 in those conditions was the best round of his career.

Another of the celebrated single strokes in the history of the Open was played by Harry Bradshaw at Sandwich in 1950. In retrospect, it now seems clear that the shot should not have been played at all. In the second round Bradshaw pushed his drive into the rough and when he found his ball he saw it lay inside half of a broken beer bottle. Nowadays, of course, any pro in a similar predicament would sit down on his bag and wait for a referee to come and give him his due privilege of dropping the ball clear without penalty. In those days, however, there were no experts on hand to give rulings. The happy-go-lucky Bradshaw, brought up on the principle of playing the ball wherever it might lie, never for a moment considered an alternative. He took his venerable wedge, closed his eyes to protect them from flying glass, and smashed at the bottle. The ball moved twenty yards or so. The incident, nevertheless, unnerved him and the strokes he lost on this hole possibly cost him the title. He tied with the South African Bobby Locke and was decisively beaten in the play-off. Many a golfer would carry the scars of such an incident to his grave. Not Bradshaw, who says of it: "I am only proud to have earned a play-off with a grand champion like Bobby Locke."

The event did leave its mark, however.

The British Amateur Championship of 1896 at Sandwich.
Freddy Tait (far r.), who was later killed as
lieutenant of Black Watch during Boer War, played dashing golf
to suit his nature and beat Harold Hilton in the final.

Today any visitor who enjoys the privilege of playing with Bradshaw over his beloved Portmarnock course, near Dublin—and he remains the finest chipper (with that same wedge) and putter in the world—will notice that the only thing which ruffles his genial temperament is litter on the course. He is forever darting off into the rough to retrieve any small scrap of discarded paper and stuff it into his pocket. Bradshaw's misfortune did at least introduce a worthy champion in Locke, who was destined to win three more Opens with his curiously looped swing, superb putting touch, and the best-controlled nerves in the game.

Open championships do not always fall to the best golfer in the field—luck and the vagaries of current form are too uncertain for that—but they nearly always produce a deserving winner. Of modern British professionals, no man has conducted himself with a greater awareness of his obligations to the game and its public than Max Faulkner. He likes to give the crowd its money's worth, hence the colorful costumes which earned him the nickname of "the Knicker Man" in America. And he is always anxious to put something back into the game which has provided his living, whether it is giving exhibitions for charity or helping young players. So his victory at Portrush in 1951, the first time the Open had been played on Irish soil, gave general satisfaction.

A justice of a different and more poignant quality was to follow two years later at Carnoustie. There can never be any generally accepted outcome to the arguments of who is, or was, the best golfer of all time. Most judges, however, would probably bestow a triple award—that the *greatest* golfer, less for his achievements than the manner of his successes, was Bobby Jones; that Jack Nicklaus for his record, his all-around talents, and the scale of his game is the *finest* golfer; but that for the sheer perfection of striking and consistency (through the green) Ben Hogan was the *best player*.

Here we make a distinction between *golfer,* which incorporates a multitude of personal qualities, and *player* in the narrower sense of striking the ball. Hogan, like Vardon before him, set an entirely new standard in perfection of striking a golf ball. After his tragic accident and torturous recovery, Hogan was persuaded that his crown would never be complete without the jewel of a British Open. So in 1953, having taken the Masters and U.S. Open, he arrived in Scotland, bent on the classic triple. Fittingly for a golfer of his caliber, the Open was at Carnoustie. No worthier test could be devised. The championship itself was not particularly exciting. Drama in golf is bred of mistakes and Hogan gave an almost flawless exhibition of ac-

curate stroke play. His putting, never much more than adequate and later to become a private cross, was unexceptional, but he still won by four shots and a record aggregate. He returned home to a ticker-tape welcome. If his name on the Open Championship trophy confirmed his reputation, it also enhanced the championship itself. For over a hundred years every golfer with any pretensions to greatness has won that old claret jug. Without the name of Ben Hogan engraved on it, the cup would surely be incomplete.

The young Australian Peter Thomson now stepped from the wings and took the center of the Open stage. Three victories in succession and then, at intervals, two more threatened Vardon's record of six

201

A water-logged Henry Cotton, winner of the Open at Carnoustie, 1937, after what he described as the round of his life. Above: Fifth Open championship for Peter Thomson, at Royal Birkdale in 1965.

championships and firmly established Thomson among the greats. If his reputation must be qualified, as a small-ball player preeminent on fast links courses, this was a matter of his own choosing. As a golfer Thomson's career has been hampered by a high intelligence and firmly held opinions; prejudices might not be too strong a word in some cases. In addition, he reproached himself for playing a frivolous game while the world fought and starved. And when he did rationalize his life and accepted that his contribution to society was a valuable one, he nevertheless refused to sublimate his personal prejudices in a singleminded assault on golfing fame and wealth. A manager would have been mad with frustration at Thomson's refusal to exploit his own talents. As noted earlier, he did not like the big ball or the modern style of watered courses. As a result his American appearances were strictly limited, and because he did not like American courses and the trend to target golf, the legend grew that he was anti-American. However, on the fast links of Britain he was supreme. The traditionalist in him responded to the challenge of running up approaches to the hard greens, and this type of golf particularly suited his game, which is based on touch, instinct, and improvisation.

The Thomson era coincided with a decline in the standing of the Open, not that this in any way detracts from his achievements. The championship organization was sketchy and old-fashioned and the prize money poor. The Open had failed to keep pace with the developments in golf and few American players felt it worthwhile to make the trip.

All that began to change with the rise of Arnold Palmer. His name was selling clubs in Britain and the manufacturer, Dunlop, wanted him to be seen by the home fans. Besides, like Hogan, Palmer was hungry to prove himself a true champion. His victory in 1961 at Royal Birkdale, and even more dramatically at Troon the following year, restored the prestige of the Open and probably contributed to a new dyna-

mism within the R. and A. No longer was it enough for the Open to be the oldest championship in golf. A gentlemanly revolution within the R. and A. brought a determination that the Open must become the best championship in every way. Many people within golf would claim that during the following ten years most of those worthy aims were achieved.

The roll of American Open champions is itself a potted history of the competition. The first National Open, celebrating the inauguration of the USGA in 1894, was a match-play event, and in the final Willie Dunn beat Willie Campbell and won $150. Those names, like their successors Rawlins, Foulis, Herd, Anderson, and Auchterlonie, have about them the salty tang of the Scottish fishing villages of their origins. Some of the same names occur in the early records of the British Open—Dunn, Campbell, Herd, Anderson, and Auchterlonie, all well-known Scottish golfing families. The U.S. Open was largely an annual gathering of the immigrant clansmen of the next generation.

One family, the Carnoustie Smiths, was represented by three brothers, Willie, Alex, and Macdonald. The last was generally judged to be the most accomplished, although he was the only one not to win a title. However, the outstanding player of this era was Willie Anderson, who took the Open four times. Like Young Tom Morris, he died at an early age (thirty-two), leaving to conjecture what further honors might have been his. The only golfers with any chance of breaking the Scottish-American monopoly were visiting pros from Britain, such as Harry Vardon, who managed the considerable feat of missing a two-inch putt on the last green of the Chicago Club, in Wheaton, Illinois, but won by two strokes.

The one pitfall in reading American social history into the names of Open winners is Johnny McDermott, who might be assumed to have been another immigrant. In fact, McDermott was American-born and obsessed with the ambition to prove that

203

home-bred golfers could play as well, and better, than the foreigners. In 1910 he finished in a tie with two of the Carnoustie Smiths, Alex and Macdonald, but could only beat one of them in the play-off. McDermott was involved in another play-off the following year (against Mike Brady and the Englishman George Sargent), and this time he came through to end the British supremacy. He won again in 1912, just to emphasize the close of the era. But was it really ended? The next year, 1913, the formidable pair of Harry Vardon and Ted Ray, the colossus of British golf and the reigning Open champion, were entered for the National Open at the Country Club in Brookline, Massachusetts. McDermott, the wiry bantamweight with the peppery temperament, was generally regarded as America's best bet to give the invaders a run for their money. But a flashy young braggart from Rochester, with slicked-down hair and an outrageously colorful outfit, showed up to register his entry and announce that he had come to help lick the British. Everyone laughed. Who was this brash kid, anyway? Hagen? Never heard of him. For that matter, nobody had heard of a certain twenty-year-old clerk who had been persuaded to file his entry by a USGA official. The organizers were so anxious to make a show of the Open that they were even encouraging unknown amateurs to have a go. When the name of Francis Ouimet began to appear among the leaders, few people knew how to pronounce it (Wee-met). As expected, Vardon and Ray dominated the qualifying rounds, but both Ouimet and Hagen managed to survive.

In the championship proper, McDermott's game was off and at the halfway stage Vardon led by two shots over Ray. It was, it seemed, the old story. Who was left to mount a challenge? No one of consequence. The local amateur with the funny name was still in sight and so—barely—was that kid Hagen. But golf galleries knew that hot rounds by unknowns meant very little. When it came to the pressures of the closing stages it was the hard men who held on. So even when

Ryder Cup at Royal Birkdale, 1965, with Arnold Palmer (l.) and Don January. Invincible on this occasion, the Americans returned to the same course four years later. That match resulted in a historic tie.

What the Ryder Cup means to Britain: Thousands turned
out in 1965 to watch Dave Marr (above on left) and
Arnold Palmer, and (r.) a slightly pensive foursome
in Tony Lema, Gene Littler, Don January, and Billy Casper.

Ouimet caught Vardon at the end of the third round, it was a cause for congratulations but hardly for hope.

In the last round Vardon, whose putting was always vulnerable, could make nothing of the sodden greens and was around in 79 for a total of 304. Ray tied, and the best possibility for a challenge seemed to lie with Hagen, who picked up four shots on par in three holes, and could conceivably join the leaders if he played out steadily. Hagen attempted a grandstand finish with a spectacular fairway wood, topped the ball feebly, and bowed out of the championship, to return presumably to the oblivion whence he had come. Predictably, the inexperienced Ouimet was making a hash of his last round in accordance with the honored conventions of precocious youth. He was out in 43 and

needed to improve on that performance by eight strokes coming home to catch Vardon and Ray. On that rain-soaked course and by the way he was playing, his chances seemed slim, indeed. Ouimet himself was not daunted. This shy, quiet young man had a plan. He calculated that if he could birdie the two short holes and get par figures on the others he could do it. Like all such plans on the golf course, it went wrong. He got his first 2 by chipping into the hole, but at the next short hole he had to sink a 9-footer to save par. The second birdie would have to be found elsewhere. It came on the 17th, after a string of pars helped erode the Britishers' lead. He made a 20-foot downhill putt, which was blessed with a certain degree of luck, and assured himself a tie with a 5-footer on the last. He had

done it, although a good many spectators did not see his triumph because they had gone home, believing his cause to be hopeless. The uproar among the three thousand who remained was unprecedented in the decorous history of the Country Club and this euphoric moment was not time for realistic thoughts about the play-off. Ouimet still had to meet Vardon and Ray.

It was expected that the youngster would suffer a reaction and collapse in the decisive encounter. In the morning Ouimet hit a few practice shots on the 18th fairway (which would disqualify him under to-day's rules), and then joined his opponents on the first tee. So far events had gone like the plot for a story in a boys' magazine, and a magazine sponsored by the League of Purity at that. Ouimet, the humble lad whose

lips had never been sullied by tobacco, alcohol, or pro-fanity, had matched the foreign invaders at their own game. Purity and innocence must surely triumph in this coming denouement. Now, however, the story line deflected into farce. Ouimet's ten-year-old caddie, Eddie Lowery, handed him the driver with the stirring advice, "Be sure and keep your eye on the ball, Francis."

All his life Ouimet remained modest and unassuming and never lost the air of a quiet country boy. But like many another quiet country boy, he was nobody's mug even at the age of twenty. He was a fine player and exceptionally composed on the course no matter how bleak the situation. In terms of pressure, Vardon and Ray, with everything to lose and nothing to gain, were at a disadvantage. Ray put himself out of

In love with success: Gary Player admires the PGA trophy at Newton Square, Pennsylvania, 1962, and Tony Jacklin is escorted by the Lancashire police after his Open victory at Lytham in 1969.

the reckoning as the play-off reached the critical stage. Vardon drove into a bunker at the 17th as Ouimet stroked in an 18-footer for a birdie. If anyone broke, it was Vardon, with a 6 at the last, while Ouimet made the coolest of 4s to complete the most famous victory in golf's long history.

Some American golf historians, such as the admirable Charles Price, are undecided about the impact on American golf of Ouimet's triumph, pointing out that it was to be many years before the ascendancy of American golf was reflected in results. Obviously, it did not make the American pros better players over-

night. The immediate and overwhelming effect was psychological. Proof had been given in the most dramatic possible manner that the native game could go it alone. McDermott and Ouimet had provided a glimpse of a new Jerusalem, an all-American capital of the golfing world. And that is exactly what happened. In suceeding years the Anglo-Scottish domination of the National Open gave way to foreign-sounding names like Dutra, Manero, Guldahl, Boros, and Venturi. These were the second and third generations of Americans to whom Italy, Poland, and Hungary were just places on the map. Oddly enough, the more the list of competi-

tors for the Open read like a roll call at the United Nations, the more American it became. It is still very much a domestic championship. While there may be thirty different nationalities represented in a British Open championship, it would be unusual to have ten nationalities in a U.S. Open field. As long as this remains the case, and there is no good reason why it should, the National Open cannot be regarded as an unofficial world championship. In many other respects, however, its preeminence is secure. In the matter of organization and the preparation of courses, the USGA sets the standards which the rest of the world tries—

and in most cases fails by a wide margin—to follow.

The Masters is undoubtedly one of the modern classics, accepted as an essential trick for the Grand Slam, and yet it has no official status. Technically it is a club invitational tournament. The factor which gives the Masters its unique status can be expressed in one word: continuity. All the elements of the tournament's success owe something to the fact that it is held at the same time of year on the same course with the same officials. It would be absurd to suggest that mistakes and snags do not occur at Augusta, but continuity of organization means that the

211

Engrossed crowds watch the agonies of the short 16th during the 1971 Masters at Augusta. If and when the players safely carry the water, they face ordeal of trying to hole out on the fast, two-tier green.

Color in the galleries—including modesty
carried to Victorian lengths with a knitted cover for
periscope. This, then, is California, land of the
beautiful people, and the 1972 U.S. Open at Pebble Beach.

212

same mistake is not allowed to happen twice.

An efficient organization is not of itself enough to make a great tournament. For that you need a strong field and a course good enough to ensure a worthy winner every time. As for the course, the seeds were planted a hundred years before Bobby Jones and his friends bought the site in 1930, because this was an old tree and shrub nursery. So the Augusta National was blessed with instant maturity in the stands of great Georgia pine and the wealth of decorative shrubs. Over the years the club has built permanent crowd facilities, such as grandstands and refreshment huts with their inevitable corollaries, and camouflaged them to blend as unobtrusively as possible into the landscape. Continuity provides that bonus. Augusta does not need flapping canvas to mount the Masters and so avoids the circus feeling of most golf promotions. The atmosphere of the Masters is more that of a garden party.

We have discussed the quality of the course in an earlier chapter. Small changes are made from time to time to keep it up to the highest championship standard as golf equipment and techniques improve. For example, when Jack Nicklaus began to flout the authority of a fairway bunker by carrying it with the contemptuous power of his drive, the bunker was moved 20 yards farther from the tee. As for the quality of the field, Bobby Jones' reputation gave the first invitations the power of a royal command, and in due course there evolved a codified system by which golfers qualified for an invitation.

With organization, the course, and the field, the Masters needed one more ingredient to achieve international stature. It was only a matter of time before the missing ingredient—a tradition of greatness—began to accrue to the new tournament. In its second year, the Masters produced the most famous single shot in the history of American golf. Craig Wood was in with a total of 282 and looking safe enough when

Gene Sarazen addressed his four-wood to the ball for a 220-yard approach to the par-5 15th. He needed to clip three shots off par on those testing last four holes to tie Wood's score and he appeared a good bet to pick up one of them as his approach shot bored straight at the flag. The ball carried the water, pitched, rolled, and dropped into the hole for a double eagle, or albatross in the British idiom. With that one masterly shot, Sarazen had made up his three shots and he matched par over the remaining holes for a tie. He won the play-off easily and the legend of the Masters was born.

Wood's turn came six years later, but meanwhile, in 1937, Byron Nelson had his dramatic day. He seemed to be coasting home in the wake of the front-running Ralph Guldahl. At the short 12th Guldahl had a 5 and he dropped another shot to par at the next hole. Nelson had a birdie and an eagle on these same two holes, picking up six strokes in the process, and won by two shots.

Nelson made more Masters history in 1942, when he had to play off after a tie with the redoubtable Ben Hogan. It began to look ominous when Hogan went three shots ahead over the opening five holes. Over the next eleven holes Hogan was rock steady and one under par, but Nelson, in an inspired burst, caught him nonetheless and had a two-shot lead as they teed up for the 17th. Hogan got back one stroke but Nelson hung on for a single-shot triumph.

Hogan again got the worst of a play-off, against Sam Snead in 1954, the year after his second victory. In all, Hogan was runner-up four times, a remarkable record of consistency, second only to that of four-time winner Arnold Palmer.

Jack Nicklaus won his first Masters in 1963 at the age of twenty-three. The wind was high and so were the scores, but two years later conditions were perfect and Nicklaus produced one of the great tournament performances of modern golf. His score

Like a matador poised for the kill—Lee Trevino plumb-lines his putter during 1971 Westchester Classic while the aficionados await moment of truth. This time truth turned sour—he missed the cut.

of 271 was unprecedented—it is usually ten shots higher. (His own winning aggregates on other occasions were 288 and 286.)

Although the story of a great tournament must necessarily be mainly about winners, there is a place for losers and surely none is more poignant than Roberto de Vicenzo in 1968. The popular Argentinian is one of the purest strikers of a ball that golf has seen. Only Snead has won more tournaments, a statistic which must be subject to ratification, since de Vicenzo himself is not sure of his record after twenty years of globe-trotting. He is content to let other people concern themselves with details of that sort. And it was just such a happy-go-lucky attitude which was his undoing at Augusta. In the last round an audience of thousands (plus millions of TV watchers) saw him tie with Bob Goalby. But his playing partner inadvertently marked him down for a 4 on a hole where he had taken 3. De Vicenzo signed his card after a perfunctory glance at the total (which was correct). However, golfers are not responsible for returning a correct total; their duty is to sign for the scores at the eighteen individual holes, and under the rules of golf de Vicenzo had attested to that spurious 4 and it had to stand. So Goalby was the winner and a most unlucky one at that. Through no fault of his own he was widely regarded as having won by default, the champion by a technicality. De Vicenzo was overwhelmed by public sympathy and stole every headline. Winning the Masters is usually a springboard for a fortune in endorsements, exhibitions, and advertising. Goalby, although he had undoubtedly won, was not seen as the winner. He wanted a special dispensation to allow de Vicenzo's score to be adjusted, so that they could play off and give him the chance to prove himself the unchallenged Masters winner. Unfortunately, the rules forbid such incidents to be resolved in accordance with the dictates of common sense and natural justice. A marker's error and an idiotically inflexible law made this a hollow victory for Goalby. But the next year, as was to be expected on past Masters form, a small enclosure was erected behind the 18th green where an official carefully checked every card with competitors before they were permitted to add their signatures. In accordance with the Masters tradition the same mistake was not to be allowed to happen twice.

The Professional Golfers' Association Championship is the fourth of the classics and it must be said that for some years it held this elevated status under false pretenses. The original championship, instituted in 1916, was a match-play event. In man-to-man golf the quality of the course is of secondary importance, since it is the same for both players and, given the usual element of chance in an eighteen-hole match, the better player will win. The interplay of personality becomes a factor, as does the opponent's performance.

In stroke-play events the purpose is to set an examination, and in order to produce a worthy winner there must be a worthy course. It should test the player's skills with every club and every variety of shot. In stroke play a golfer must ignore what his playing partner is doing (unless they are both challenging over the closing holes), while in match play a man's tactics will be dictated by his opponent's fortunes. The better player will (or should) win whether they are playing a good course or a bad one.

An obvious example of how tactics are dictated by the progress of a match would be when an opponent hits a superb, or lucky, approach shot right by the flag, especially to a tightly guarded green. Instead of aiming for the center of the green, which would be the usual practice in a stroke-play competition, the player must now suppress his golfing instincts, ignore the dangers, and go for the flag himself.

Again, if a man finds himself four down with six holes to play there is no point in playing conservative golf. He has to gamble. At a tight hole, where he would normally use an iron off the tee (and

217

Master of the expansive gesture, Trevino hurls his cap into the Royal Birkdale gallery after sinking the putt that won him the 1971 Open championship, by a shot from the Formosan Lu Liang Huan.

which is exactly what his opponent will be doing), he must decide whether to risk the driver and win a possible advantage. Nearly every professional announces before a match that he intends to "play the course" and forget about what his opponent is doing. Yet nearly always those brave words have to be eaten before the match is over. The circumstances of the match force him to revise his game plan.

The roll of winners in the match-play era shows that the best man did indeed win. Walter Hagen, whose bursting confidence gave him the equivalent of a two-up start against most opponents, won four times in a row; Gene Sarazen took three titles; and the names of Sam Snead, Ben Hogan, and Byron Nelson all appear more than once on the winners' roll.

In 1958, under pressure from television, which cannot cope with match-play golf, the championship format changed to four rounds of stroke play. It thus became indistinguishable from any of the other tour events, especially as it was frequently played on courses which could not be considered of championship standard, either in their intrinsic layout or their preparation.

For a time the importance of the PGA championship lay mainly in the fact that the winner was exempted for life from prequalifying for all PGA-sponsored events. It was thus a valuable title to win, but as a golfing accomplishment it really meant very little more than any other bread-and-butter tournament. The old tradition withered and the only new tradition which developed was the unwelcome superstition that the victor would not win another tournament. This notion arose from the experience of players such as Bobby Nichols, Dave Marr, Al Geiberger, and Don January, who all had prolonged spells in the doldrums after becoming PGA champion. Then, after the revolution within the PGA, which resulted in the formation of an autonomous Tournament Players' Division, the fortunes of the championship began to

Rivals as a partnership—Lee Trevino and Jack Nicklaus confer on the line of a putt during the World Cup at Palm Beach, 1971. So what went wrong (above)? Nothing serious. Despite this setback the Americans won the cup.

revive. The improvement stemmed from the appointment of Joe Dey, a former director of USGA, as commissioner. All Dey's instincts and experience insisted that a championship must be played on tough courses, prepared so that only outstanding players could come through. It would obviously take a few years for his policy to burnish the championship's reputation.

Fifty years ago the Amateur Championships of Britain and the United States ranked as classics, and were indeed elements in Bobby Jones' Grand Slam. In those days there was little incentive for a gifted young amateur to turn professional. John Ball, the great Hoylake golfer, competed in the Amateur for fifty years, winning it eight times, and since he also won an Open, he was in his prime clearly a match for any pro. The standard in the first Amateur Championships was probably higher than in the first Opens. Although this trend was reversed, and decisively so, as the years went by, we have the evidence of Bobby Jones that as late as 1930 it was just as difficult to win an Amateur as an Open. As pro golf became more lucrative, however, the Amateur championships declined in importance, since the best young players were being skimmed off every year. In America the Amateur Championship was changed to stroke play in 1965, in step with the fashion, and to a large extent it became an initiation test for embryo professionals. In 1973 the U.S. Amateur reverted to a match-play championship.

The true amateur (in the sense of a weekend golfer who plays for fun) can hardly hope to compete against the young tigers from college golf teams who are almost full-time players and come to the championship hardened to the rigors of tournament play. The same kind of thing, in a modified degree, is happening to the British Amateur, although it is not so apparent, since Britain offers no golf scholarships. As in most things, British golf takes its lead from the States—the good ideas normally take ten years to cross the Atlantic, the bad ideas ten seconds—and it is

Palmer's unique style: The high flourish (actually the result of a correction during the swing required by an unorthodox take-away), and naked emotions are his trademarks. Here, the Westchester Classic, 1971.

221

only a matter of time until the British Amateur becomes the steepest nursery slope before graduation to professionalism.

With the huge expansion of golf in the postwar years, a subtle evolutionary process began to divide it into virtually two different games. On the one hand, we have golf as a recreational activity, grown to an enormous degree but still basically the same as always. On the other hand, there is professional golf, which year by year becomes further removed from the amateur or country-club variety. Once the two worlds of golf were inextricably linked; the pros were a part of the clubs and deeply involved with them, and the game they played was not so different from that of the more skilled members.

Today, with a handful of exceptions, amateur golf cannot begin to compete with tournament professionalism. The gulf in playing standards is vast and growing. Superficially, it is not easy to detect the extent of the difference. After all, there are plenty of amateurs who regularly return scores at their home clubs which compare favorably enough with the scores on the pro tour. But a 72 in the club championship cannot be compared with a 72 in, say, the Westchester Classic, because the circumstances are so widely different. And to understand that difference we must examine something of the structure of the pro tour. How, for instance, does a likely young amateur become a tournament professional?

The days are long gone when all he needed was a bag of clubs, a good swing, and unlimited ambition. Modern golf is an expensive business. It costs about $500 a week on tour, and to play forty tournaments requires an outlay of $20,000. So you finance the second tournament from your first week's winnings? Oh, no, the PGA won't allow that. You have to prove that you can afford to play the circuit before you are allowed onto it. But, says the rookie, if I had $20,000 I would not *need* to turn pro. I haven't got it. Then, says

The victory salute as Palmer wins the 1971 Westchester. This picture really needs scoring for massed chorus of delirious fans roaring appreciation. For personal popularity Palmer is winner every time he plays.

the PGA, find it. In the majority of cases, the youngster has to start off with a backer and it is here that his troubles are likely to begin. There are philanthropists who are prepared to give a young golfer a start in life without seeking any return on their money. However, in life there are few genuine fairy godmothers. Sponsors are mostly businessmen who are looking for a profit. And they know rather more about the intricacies of drawing up contracts than golfers do.

As a result, many players discover that they have signed away their lives. At least one recruit to the circuit finished with nothing, although he won $65,000 in his first season, simply because he had not read the small print in his sponsor contract. Another player won $100,000 three years in a row—most of it unfortunately for the sponsor who had him tied up in a legal stranglehold.

Let us assume that the young player has solved the cash situation, possibly by putting himself in the hands of a reputable manager. Now he has to submit his golf to close official scrutiny. It is now that he comes up against that agonizing prefix "pre"—in the first instance, a prequalifying school. This is a regional preliminary tournament to determine which players are suitable candidates for the PGA's qualifying school. It is the first mesh of the grading system which ensures that only golfers of outstanding skills join the tour. If our lad safely passes this test he may enter the qualifying school at PGA headquarters.

The term "PGA school" is somewhat misleading since the element of instruction is small. And while the candidates are given a certain amount of lecture-room advice on professionalism—how to deport themselves on the course, how to talk to the press, how much to pay caddies—the one thing they are not taught is how to play golf. They know that already. Teaching golf is part of the PGA's function, but this is conducted through its club-professional members. Pros receive advice on how to teach others and what to teach others,

but by the time the embryo tournament player is ready to go to the PGA school he must be a player of very considerable skill. The PGA will not undertake to teach him to achieve pro caliber. For many school candidates, how to play and how to compete are lessons learned during their years on college golf teams. University golfers get the benefit of four years or so of intensive coaching, as well as considerable experience of competitive pressure in college team matches, major amateur tournaments, and possibly as members of international teams.

The main function of the school is to provide an examination of playing ability in the form of a six-round, stroke-play tournament. The results are decided by the number of places available on tour. If six players have dropped out of the circuit, the leading six candidates will be chosen as replacements. The successful ones are given probationary cards as members of the Tournament Players' Division, and these TPD cards are their passports to fame and fortune. Like passports, they simply allow the bearers to proceed to the next stage. In their case it is a PGA tournament or, more precisely, the prequalifying round of a tournament, usually known as Heartbreak Monday.

There may be two hundred golfers taking part, and because of exemptions and invitations, there may be only six vacancies in the field for a particular tournament. It has often been remarked that a golfer has to play better to get into a tournament than to win it. That may be true. Certainly the pressures are much more intense.

Let us assume that our boy manages to get one of those six places. He is now "in," one of perhaps one hundred and forty-four golfers with a chance to win some real money. It is still only a chance. First, he has to play well enough in the first two rounds to survive the cut. Now, and only now, can he hope to cover his expenses or, just possibly, make a profit on the week's $500 outlay. Failure at any point means going back to the previous stage. Miss that cut and you are back to prequalifying the following Monday. And possibly the next. And if you do not show progress the PGA may withdraw your precious TPD card in the annual review. No wonder most recruits drop out.

Some make it to the level where they can live on their winnings—but no higher. A tiny proportion—and it is much smaller than the opulence the official money lists suggest—becomes wealthy from playing golf.

To the sporting public pro golf is about winning tournaments. To the pros themselves, however, the purpose is to win money. That means it is far better to finish in the first twenty or so week after week than to bring off one flashy victory and do nothing for the rest of the season. For many pros winning is not the name of the game at all. They do not want to win. The winner must endure special pressures, and make speeches and submit to being lionized. That is all very well for those who like it, but many pros are not temperamentally suited to the limelight. They prefer the comparative calm of the second echelon and the motto: Play steady, eat regular. Year after year they pick up official winnings of $50,000–$70,000, which is not spectacular once they have deducted their expenses, since it costs everyone the same amount, according to life style, to play the tour. But it should be remembered that official winnings are by no means the same as total income. Every tour player has contracts with equipment and clothing manufacturers. They all pick up useful supplements from pro-ams and exhibition matches. There is no formula for computing how much a pro can earn in "unofficial" money, but a conservative estimate in most cases would be to double the figure for official winnings.

Among the stars the official money is the least part of their income. More than one golfer has signed his name to a million-dollar contract. For such men the act of airily donating a winning check to charity is an expansive gesture but under modern tax structures not a particularly generous one.

On the surface the pro tour is friendly, easygoing, and relaxed. Basically it is as tough a rat race as modern life has to offer. The amateur who picks up his newspaper and remarks that he could shoot better golf than those guys on tour should pause and consider the prospects very carefully indeed before he attempts to put that boast to the test. It is not just a different game. It is not a game at all.

That being the case, it is hardly appropriate for us club golfers to try to model ourselves on the professionals. Perhaps it is inevitable that we should watch Jack Nicklaus and then attempt to copy him; all the same, it is ridiculous. While there may be very good reasons for Nicklaus to pace out his shots to the green, or to spend two minutes sizing up a putt, it does not follow that we lesser players will obtain the slightest benefit from such practices. We will continue to do so, of course, and by aping professional golf we will continue to obscure the gulf which divides us from the pros. Logically we ought to accept the fact that we are participating in an utterly different activity.

If we could swallow our pride and absorb that distinction, we might begin to search for solutions for our problems. Try as he might, the 22-handicapper will not get down to 20 by copying Arnold Palmer's swing. He has a good chance of making a dramatic improvement if he deliberately swings three times as slowly as Palmer. And if at the same time he goes through the card before his round and writes "par-5" against every hole longer than 400 yards—and adjusts his game accordingly—his scores will immediately improve. Alas, human nature does not work like that. Self-deception is altogether too powerful for us to concede that those guys are playing a different game. We will struggle on, grotesque parodies of our heroes. It will cost us dearly in side bets and drinks—but that serves us right for being such blinkered dupes.

9 · royal and ancient . . .

and antic

When it came to filling out his entry form for the British Open of 1965, Walter Danecki had a brief crisis of conscience. He had to state whether he was an amateur or a professional, and that was a difficult decision for forty-three-year-old Walter, a mail sorter from Milwaukee who played weekend golf on a municipal course and who proposed to take a holiday in Britain. He also proposed to play in the Open. This was straightforward enough: Walter's amateur status was unstained. As he later explained, he did not charge if he gave a lesson. On the other hand, Walter believed he could beat Arnold Palmer and, what's more, he was determined to win the Open. "I wanted the crock of gold, so my conscience made me write down 'professional,' " he said.

Walter had made inquiries about joining the PGA and had been put off the idea because of the stipulation of a five-year apprenticeship. "What I'll do is win one of the big ones," he told himself, "and then they'll have to let me in." Boy, would his friends be impressed when he came home with the trophy. And if perchance some unforeseen catastrophe beyond his control should rob him of his triumph, putting him in second place, say, or even third, then the whole venture would be his little secret. Nobody at home need ever know. So, true to the spirit of the rules of amateurism governing "professional intent," Walter filed his entry as a pro, and the R. and A., which at that time did not scrutinize credentials very closely, accepted it.

Walter was drawn to play the prequalifying rounds at Hillside, just over the fence from the Birkdale championship course. Hillside is generally reckoned to be a few shots easier than Birkdale. Against the par of 70, Walter and his playing partner reckoned that two 75s would be good enough to qualify. Walter went round in 108. Officials of the R. and A. thought that Walter would quietly fold his tent and creep away after this debacle. They arranged for a substitute to play the second round with his partner.

Next morning Walter presented himself on the tee, not a whit abashed. "I don't like to quit. I like to golf and that's what I came to do," he said. This time he had a considerable gallery in attendance. He started with two 7s and an 8 and then settled down with two solid bogey 5s. Then a 7 and a 9 were followed by two more 5s to put him out in 58. Perhaps that total unnerved him, because he started back 9, 6, 10 before he got it going again for an inward half of 55. Round in 113, or 43 over par, to make a two-round aggregate of 221. He missed qualifying by just 70 strokes. But the indomitable Walter wasn't making any excuses. Far from it. "I want to say that your small ball is right for this sort of course," he said. "If I had been playing our bigger ball I would have been all over the place."

God bless you, Walter. The world would be a poorer place without people like you. Happily, golf is full of Walters. No game is as rich in human eccentricity as golf, and its foibles are carefully recorded in The Golfer's Handbook. This work, which is published in Glasgow every year, is basically devoted to golfing records and useful information, but the best of it is a section headed "Interesting Facts, Feats and Extraordinary Occurrences in the Game." There follows a great number of subdivisions under such headings as "Spectators interfering with balls," and "Balls in strange places." The entries, which cover more than a hundred pages of fine print, are presented in deadpan, almost telegraphic fashion, although occasionally the editors reveal a flash of personal opinion. For instance, under "Freak Matches," there is an item reading, "In United States competitions with nondescript hazards, such as suspended barrels to be played through and gates played around, are frequently held"—and here one can detect a pursing of the puritanical lips—"to provide what are supposed to be amusing variations of the game."

For the most part this section is a casebook of golf lunacy. Here an eminent violinist plays a

Simplicity of golf when the century was young—just an easily carried bag of a few clubs, bramble-pattern rubber-core ball, and the prospect of forty-five holes of golf in a day.

match attired in a suit of armour. "He was beaten by 2 and 1" the item adds, which we cannot help feeling served him right. A millionaire travels between shots by helicopter and another rare spirit plays a round by divebombing a course in a light airplane and hurling golf balls at the greens. He completed eighteen holes in 29 shots. Golfers challenge archers, javelin throwers, racquets players, and flyfishermen and hardly a day passes, it seems, without somebody attempting a speed round or a cross-country marathon.

The editors reserve their greatest enthusiasm for disasters. The lady who required 166 strokes at a short hole gets a fat entry, and fatal accidents on the course are recorded in morbid detail. The carnage caused to fish, birds, and animals by golf balls gets a separate section. But aficionados of these golfing curios were dismayed by recent editorial pruning of the section "Hit by ball—distance of rebound." In earlier editions this was a rich treasury of tasteless trivia. The record was held by an unnamed South African caddie who, on September 28, 1913, was struck just above the right temple by a ball driven by Edward Sladwick. The rebound was measured at 75 yards. This shattered the record. See here, the longest rebound in the book is Barton, playing at Machrie, beaned a caddie named John McNiven. Out came the tape measure to record a rebound of 42 yards, 2 feet, 10 inches. We can imagine the excitement as Mr. Barton and his friends consulted *The Golfer's Handbook.* "We did it! It's a new world record. See here, the longest rebound in the book is thirty-four yards, set up way back in August, 1908, at Blairgowrie at the ninth hole." How transient are such moments of triumph. Just twenty-seven days later the title went to Mr. Sladwick. Still, Barton retains the British native record.

It is now useless to consult the *Handbook* if you should have the good fortune to catch a caddie flush on the forehead. The records have been withdrawn. You will be all right if you step into a bunker and sink waist deep. You will find such deeds in an appropriate section, but you are doomed to disappointment. On July 11, 1931, at Rose Bay, New South Wales, Mr. D. J. Bayley MacArthur did the same thing, only he sank to the armpits. If your ball impales itself on a hatpin without dislodging the hat, or pierces a spectator's topper, or lodges in a donkey's ear, or drops down a chimney into a pot of Irish stew bubbling on the hearth, you may make it among similar examples. But rebounds are out.

As for freakish scoring, you will have to do something really spectacular to qualify. It's no good starting off 1, 2, 3, 4, 5, 6, for instance, because it has been done already. If your opponent holes out with his tee shot you should not delude yourself with the heady thought that it would be quite unprecedented to do an ace yourself and halve the hole. It has happened before. Several times. Almost commonplace. What about a hole in one at successive holes? Sorry, it's been done: in 1971 during a PGA tournament in the British circuit. John Hudson, making a rare tournament appearance as a break from his duties as a club pro, holed out at a short hole at Norwich golf club. The next hole, played from an elevated tee and partly blind from a stand of trees, measures 311 yards. Hudson cracked one with his driver, although most of the field was playing discreetly short because of the tightness of the approach to the greens, and holed out.

For sheer luck it would be hard to surpass the experience of the golfer who sliced his drive at Prestwick's first hole. The ball flew out-of-bounds, hit the railway line, and rebounded into play. He sliced his approach shot. Again it carried the O.B. fence, again it hit the railway line, and this time it rebounded onto the green and rolled into the hole. Fair enough, but a similar incident had an unhappy sequel at Los Angeles in 1950. Bob Geared sliced his tee shot at the 425-yard second hole and his ball bounced on the road and landed in a passing truck. The driver tossed the ball back by the green and it went into the hole. The committee heartlessly ruled that he should have played another ball off the tee under the O.B. rule.

Not every curious incident finds its way into the *Handbook.* Possibly because they do not have a subsection for "Sexual Deviants on the Links" the editors missed, for instance, the Effingham affair. A foursome of lady members was playing on the exclusive suburban course at Effingham, near London. They were putting out when a man wearing a bowler hat and nothing else sprang from the bushes. Undaunted, the lady captain demanded sternly, "Are you a member?" and receiving no satisfactory reply—it would hardly have done to offend, say, an influential committee chairman—dispatched the intruder with a sharp blow from her eight-iron. All golfers will understand why she did not risk damaging her putter on such an unyielding target.

In the normal course of events sex has very little association with golf. That statement may provoke boisterous laughter in ten thousand clubhouses, and I quite understand. Every club has its scandals from time to time, but this is essentially *après-golf* and has no direct connection with the game. On the course men and women tend to avoid each other's company, no matter what they may do later. The golf is the thing at the time. Among the professionals a few, such as Walter Hagen, could cast an appraising eye over the galleries and chat up a dolly while playing an important match. But, generally, the pros keep their minds on the game. What they do later is their business and no lurid revelations will be made here.

In one part of the world sex and golf do coexist. The wealthy mandarin golfers of Taiwan have evolved a local custom which may surprise visitors. When two western businessmen were invited to join two merchants for a round, they were only too glad and readily agreed to play for "the usual stakes," thinking this would mean a $5 nassau or something of that

order. They won, rather easily, and accepted an invitation to play again the next day on the same terms. They won again and the Chinese said they would send the winnings round to their hotel. That evening the businessmen were duly paged and found in the hotel lobby fourteen giggling girls who announced that they had come to give the golfers their bath. Somehow it is difficult to imagine the practice spreading.

Women generally have been the second-class citizens of golf. Although there is abundant evidence of their interest in the game, they were less than welcome in many clubs for many years. Only in the United States, even today, have women golfers won equality. There are a few men-only clubs in America and some lesser examples of discrimination can be discovered, but generally speaking American women golfers have achieved a freedom that is the envy of their overseas sisters. If they occasionally feel slighted, they might reflect on the situation elsewhere. In Australia, for example, the woman golfer is even denied her womanhood. Oh, she can join a golf club right enough if she is prepared to accept the condescending label of "associate." That is the word which marks her cramped and relatively inferior quarters in the clubhouse. And that is how she is called by the men—"I got held up at the ninth by a couple of associates"—as if she were a different species of lesser being. At that, she may be in a happier situation than her English counterpart who is dignified by the title "lady"—and by not much more in some clubs. Emancipation is spreading slowly in Britain but the process is fiercely resisted in certain bastions of male reaction where women are suffered, and themselves suffer.

In extreme instances, women are permitted to play the course, provided they stand meekly to the side of the fairway (preferably getting right out of sight) and allow any male match to go through with unimpeded progress, and provided they change their shoes in the car park and on no account attempt to set

Compare cartoonist Frank Reynolds' study of
"An Actor" in his 1933 series "Finishes of the Famous"
with the photograph of Arnold Palmer on
page 220—a case of life imitating art?

The Finishes of the Famous

A Politician

A Novelist

An Actor

A Scientist

A Welfare Worker

A Painter

A General

A Footballer

A Film-Star

foot in the clubhouse. The more usual restrictions consist of a kind of golfing purdah with the women confined to their own cramped quarters, forbidden to play at certain times, and subject to rigid rules of how they may dress. Some clubs maintain ludicrous regulations such as forbidding women to use a certain flight of steps in front of the club. Restrictions on the times when women may play are still fairly general. Most men see women's golf as a slightly frivolous, and miniaturized, version of their own game. And every golf club which permits women members can provide examples to support that smug theory. At the same time the theory is false. As in life, so in golf: Women are different. Mostly they play for different reasons. Psychiatrists are not notably reticent when it comes to talking rubbish, but none has yet suggested that women's golf involves an urge to display their virility. Women have no need to flex their muscles in public, and so from the very outset their basic reasons for playing golf are different. The appeal of the game lies in what it provides them—release from the domestic scene, companionship, fulfillment of the competitive instinct, and a congenial way of filling the waiting hours while husbands are at work. If that sounds patronizing, it is not meant to be. Once women become addicted to golf and set their minds seriously to it, they become highly proficient at the game.

Making due allowances for the disparity in horsepower, it is probably fair to say that the best women golfers achieve a higher level of skill at golf than the best men. At the professional level, and here we are talking mainly but not exclusively about the American women's golf circuit, the players at the strongest end of the scale are just about the equal of the shortest hitters on the men's tour.

But once the drives have been struck, the effective difference becomes progressively less marked through the range of clubs. A good woman player can use her four-wood to match the shot of a man playing the same distance with his four-iron. And once we get into the area of "touch shots" around the green, the women stars are not just the equals of the men but possibly their superiors. Where women golfers are at a disadvantage is in the controlled application of explosive power—as in bunkers and heavy rough—but they normally avoid such situations better than men because of greater accuracy.

Such a judgment must be generalized. It cannot be stressed too strongly that the distance a golf ball may be hit is governed less by sheer strength than by the speed of the clubhead. And clubhead speed can be generated by timing and technique in the hands of a physically frail woman, provided—and it is a proviso which is almost universally misunderstood, or ignored—that the weight of the club is reduced. It can be safely asserted with a mass of scientific proof that women's golf is grotesquely handicapped by the use of clubs which are totally unsuitable in weight. For confirmation we have only to watch women at golf. Control of the club is clearly essential. Yet when you see women playing golf it is obvious that very early in the stroke the club is swinging the women rather than the other way round. Clubmakers do employ women advisers, but they are famous players and as such exceptional. If women's golf is to be liberated, the battle must be waged on a much broader front than the area of male prejudice among club committees. They must get into the factories and insist on rational research and development. Burn your bras if you must, dear woman golfer (although *that* is probably the last garment for a golfer to discard), but for true liberation cast off the shackle of those 13-ounce drivers.

The search for improved performance on the golf course—and it should be made clear that we now are off the subject of sex—has strained the ingenuity of man to the limits of absurdity. Both the R. and A. and the USGA maintain black museums of illegal clubs which have been submitted by hopeful inventors.

Nearly all are designed on fallacious scientific theory. Most of them are weirdly contorted—the clubs, that is—and grossly violate the rule that clubs must conform to conventional shapes. It was in that spirit that the R. and A. banned the center-shafted Schenectady putter after the Australian-born American, Walter Travis, won the 1904 Amateur Championship at Sandwich with a putting display that was positively inhuman in its accuracy. Possibly there was an element of pique behind the decision since Travis, a man of waspish disposition, took no pains to conceal his animosity after being shabbily treated by the pompous officials. It was nearly fifty years before the center-shafted putter received official blessing.

The USGA was on rather firmer ground with its first decision concerning the form and make of golf clubs. In the inaugural U.S. Amateur Championship, won by the mighty Charles Macdonald, one of the competitors had a novel idea. Richard Peters insisted on putting with a billiard cue and was duly disqualified.

Many golfers have had the same idea since then and have tried to devise a putting method which uses the billiard-cue principle. It is, after all, the easiest way, some might even say the only way, of directing a ball at a target with any degree of certainty. One solution to the problem of getting the hole, the ball, and the eyes in a direct line was the shuffleboard putter. This came in a variety of forms, the favorite being a cylindrical head on a long shaft, up to eight feet in some cases. The technique was to place the clubhead on the turf behind the ball, take aim along that barrel of a shaft, and shove. It worked only too well, if not quite so effectively as a billiard cue, and the authorities duly ruled it out of court. Apart from offending against tradition, the shuffleboard putter could be indicted under Rule 19, which requires that "the ball must be fairly struck at with the head of the club and must not be pushed, scraped, or spooned."

The legal position was rather more moot

232

when the croquet putter came into fashion. The club conformed to the center-shafted specifications, and the stroke itself, swung between the legs with the player facing the hole, did not offend against Rule 19. Many golfers, especially those whose nerves had become worn to shreds through years of putting tension, found a new lease on golfing life through the croquet method. Sam Snead, the most notable exponent among the professionals, has achieved some success with croquet putting. Although it helped some golfers, croquet putting was not a superior method, per se. No great championship successes were achieved by the croquet brigade, nor were any putting records broken. It was different but demonstrably not better. The croquet putter did not give its user an unfair advantage. All it did was to permit some golfers to compete on level terms again with conventional putters.

So, you may ask, why not leave well enough alone? The argument was persuasive—and advanced with great force and forensic skill at the time —but in the end the powers of tradition prevailed and croquet putting was banned. That is to say, rules were introduced forbidding a golfer to stand astride the line of his putt, and the specification of putter was altered to forbid the shaft to be sunk into the putter head exactly perpendicular. Sam Snead neatly got around the new regulations by facing the hole, as usual, but positioning himself beside the ball, instead of behind it. He

The American women's team of 1930, the year which saw the first unofficial match against Great Britain (later to become the biennial encounter for the Curtis Cup). Glenna Collett Vare is standing second from right.

called it his sidewinder style and found it no less
effective than the old croquet method. Most of the other
erstwhile croquet putters simply reverted to the conventional style. Although the authorities took a particularly ponderous steamhammer to crack this inconsequential nut, they were surely right to ban croquet
putting. It most certainly was not golf. Above the
tedious legal wrangling there remained the feeling that
croquet putters were not playing the game as we had
come to know it. The governing bodies are often criticized, and with justice, for their pettifogging legalistic
attitudes, but in most cases they are motivated by a
genuine desire to preserve the original forms of the
game. Their instincts are sound, as they proved when
they brought in the fourteen-club rule. Professionals
were sponsored by manufacturers on the basis of the
number of clubs they carried (or, to be accurate, their
long-suffering caddies had to carry). Absurdity was
achieved when pros had thirty clubs in the bag and
the idea was spreading through the ranks of club players that such a complement of ironmongery was
"necessary." Some believe that the maximum limit
could well be lowered further to eleven or ten.

Weird and wonderful clubs by no means
exhaust the inventive genius of golfers. Patent offices
are stacked with designs for devices to make golfers
play better. Enormous contraptions fitted with pulleys
and clanking cogs have been built to educate a golfer's
muscles to perform a geometrically perfect swing
There is even a design for a pivoted tee from which the
ball will be dispatched with magically induced extra
energy.

The ball has not been neglected. Every
possible variety of filling for the inner core has been
tried, including porridge, with subsequent claims of
almost supernatural qualities. Alas for us golfers, the
main thrust of inventive energy in the field of golf
equipment has been directed toward marketing and
advertising. Very little valid scientific research has

World premier women's championship, the U.S. Women's
Open—here at Winged Foot, 1972. Lower pictures show a few
of the stars of the distaff circuit; left to right:
Althea Gibson Darben, Betsy Rawls, Kathy Cornelius, Judy Rankin.

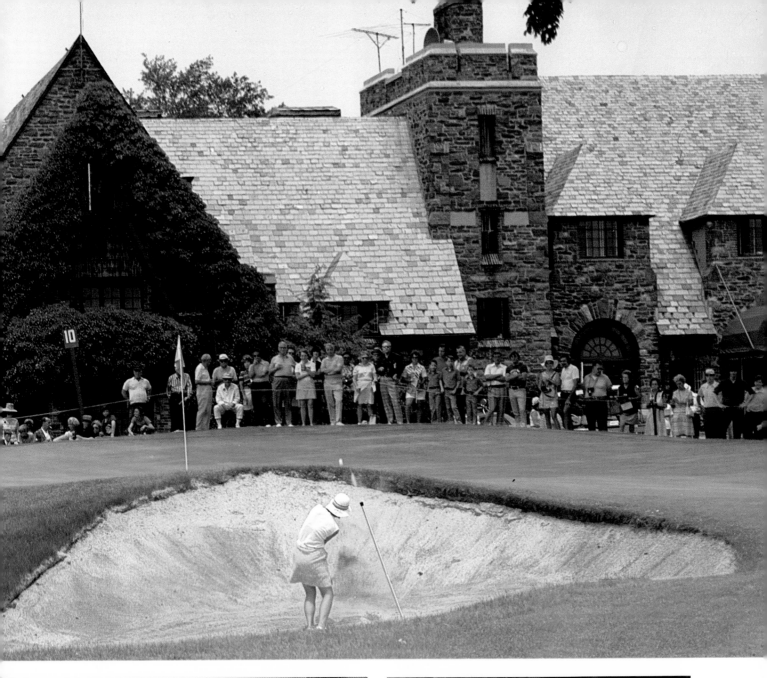

gone into golf. Those studies which have been under-taken suggest, indeed prove in some cases, that many of the accepted theories about the properties of golf clubs are scientifically unsound. Yet the makers continue in their old ways, preferring to employ a copy-writer who can turn out effective scientific mumbo jumbo for their ads, rather than put a scientist to work to improve the product. It is all very sad, knowing that technical improvements could be made in our equipment, but at the same time it must be admitted that

the most important quality a club can possess is the faith of the man who swings it.

The Irish professional Jimmy Kinsella hammered a second shaft inside the shaft of his driver. Scientifically, the idea is absurd. As Bobby Jones wisely observed, the shaft simply connects the hands with the clubhead and of itself imparts nothing to the shot. Of course it doesn't. It is nothing but dead weight. Yet because Kinsella believes in his double-shafted driver it works for him in the same way that Roberto de Vi-

cenzo can play well only with a ball marked with a "4." A surprising number of golfers are victims of such superstitions. Some have lucky colors. Others perform odd rituals like kissing their putters before every putt. (Bobby Locke actually slept with his, but that was more to ensure that no one stole the precious wand than to keep it in a good mood.) Nearly every tournament pro likes to follow a set routine, which seems sensible enough until you realize that these preliminaries often include such irrational details as insisting on putting on the left shoe first. It is all harmless enough most of the time, but if circumstances arise to upset the *idée fixe,* then the golfer can be undone. If that lucky sweater is lost so is the player.

Occasionally superstitions produce ludicrous situations, as in a mixed-foursome competition some years ago. A woman had got into the habit of teeing her ball right up against the tee marker, within three inches of it. The habit began as an aid to break her tendency to an exaggerated in-to-out swing. The

Cartoonist Charles Saxon's view of golf. The comedy is not greatly exaggerated—such incidents are not unknown on the course, although usually the salvage operation is to recover prosaic item such as car keys.

arrangement made her swing along the line of the shot, and it got so that she had to have the tee marker right by the ball whenever she used her driver. This time, aware of the crowd watching and playing with a famous partner, she was naturally nervous, and she missed the ball completely. So the next shot had to be played by her partner. That tee marker would have been disturbing enough to any golfer, but in this case it was worse because he was left-handed. All he could do was make a token pass which counted technically as another air shot so that she could have another go. The woman made contact on her second attempt but it was not much of a shot.

No golf club is complete without a re-production of a portrait showing an early golfer in his splendid uniform of scarlet jacket. In our enlightened way we tend to find the thought of a uniform for golf slightly amusing. "Fancy getting yourself up in an out-fit like that to play golf" we tell each other, without realizing that we ourselves are hardly less given to

peacock finery on the links. Those old golfers in-herited the tradition of uniforms from the archery societies whose colorful coats performed the same valuable function as the red jackets which modern hunters are encouraged to wear. They identified the wearers and saved them from being shot at and did likewise for golfers. Even today on one London munci-pal course in a deer park, the patrons have to wear red shirts or sweaters.

However, the impulse to dress up, and thereby make leisure activities more enjoyable, is a basic human instinct. The only special article of dress we actually need for playing golf is a pair of studded shoes, and even then a player who is properly balanced does not require anything like the full set of destruc-tive studs of a modern golf shoe. (The studding pattern of golf shoes is one area which has been neglected by researchers. Yet if the teachers of golf are to be be-lieved, a right shoe with studs only under the ball of the foot and the inside of the sole ought to ensure

Preceding pages: Results of human ingenuity to simplify golf, all illegal and often misguided, include toothed water-mashie, streamlined driver (bottom), and putter with aiming device. Above: Contentious 6/100th difference, British and American balls.

240

correct leg action. And any arrangement which reduced the number of studs would be a boon to greenkeepers. In a four-day tournament over a million studs pierce the surface of greens and make putting difficult in the closing stages.)

Yet we sheeplike creatures wear special clothing for our game, and what is more we allow ourselves to be persuaded that the trademark on a golf shirt affects our game. Today's golfer believes that by buying clubs with Arnold Palmer's name stamped on them he is purchasing some degree of his skill. The assumptions in this subconscious train of thought are too foolish to enumerate, but the effect is a powerful marketing force. In the same way, but even more absurdly, Billy Casper shirts, Lee Trevino hats, and Gary Player slacks are jujus to us sophisticated golfers. Protest as we may to the contrary, the idea of reserving special clothes for golf proves that at best we are sheep following the flock and at worst we are superstitious sheep who imagine that we are turning ourselves into tigers.

When there is no advantage to be found in clothing or equipment, there is always the leverage inherent in a judiciously offered bet. The tradition of having a little "interest" on the side must be nearly as old as golf itself; in moderation a little flutter is harmless enough. As to what constitutes "little," this depends. The safe rule is never to gamble for more than you can afford to lose without flinching. As soon as a golfer goes in over his head he can be quite sure that his game will suffer. The hustlers know this and use their knowledge to advantage. And there are more than a few unscrupulous characters about, mainly operating resort courses, who are all too anxious to take the unsuspecting golfer for his roll.

The usual American convention is the nassau, which means three bets: one on the first nine holes, one on the second nine, and one on the match. A $10 nassau thus involves a total liability of $30. In addition, there is the four-ball system of corners, $10 a corner on the match. Here the novice should establish clearly what is meant. Usage varies. Sometimes a $10 corner is taken to mean that each of the two losers pays $10 to both winners. Sometimes it is taken to involve a total liability of $10 from the losing side to be shared by the winning pair. More correctly, this is a bet of $10 a side, but it is good to be sure of the liability before the match starts. For match play there is the extra complication of the press bet. That is, when one player (or pair) falls two holes behind he can "press," start a new match on the remaining holes for half the stake (as well as continuing the main bet, of course). Further complications arise over byes. When a match is finished, say by four and three, the remaining three holes can be played as a separate match, or bye. Thus it is possible to get a complexity of bets going at once, with the match and its bye, the first press and its bye, and the second press and its bye, and so on. Few golfers have the mental agility to keep track of all these transactions and the safe rule is to note all the scores and bets on the card for a grand reckoning at the end. But what sounds like a straightforward $10 match can easily involve $100 changing hands, so it is wise to be wary.

On the subject of hustling, even greater caution is required. Hustlers usually operate singly, although they occasionally hunt in pairs. A golfer on vacation is the favorite quarry and the operation normally begins with an affable invitation for a game with a small stake. The object is to assess the quality of the opposition and to let the vacationer win. This is a process known as salting the pigeon and produces an obligation for a return match. This the vacationer is usually all too happy to provide. He may be allowed to win again, for a bit more interest. He is being set up, and once the psychological moment arrives there follows some casual remark such as, "I had a good night at the tables and I might as well lose it to you as give it all back to the roulette wheel. Shall we raise the ante?" It is at this point that the wise vacationer suddenly develops a chronic attack of rheumatism.

The madness of golfers takes two general forms. There are the idiosyncrasies the player brings with him when he takes up the game; the irrational examples we have been discussing fall mostly into that category. Then there is the rather more insidious form of disorder which comes from long exposure to the mind-bending game itself.

For instance, take the singular experiment of the three golf balls and the effect it had on its victims. At the time when the USGA and the R. and A. were pondering the possibility of a uniform golf ball for all the world, a number of examples of the suggested compromise ball fell into the hands of an evil newspaper golf correspondent.* In the interests of the golfing public he took himself off to try out some of the new-size balls. After hitting several shots he began to think he was losing his reason. Being a Machiavellian fellow, he thought that rather then send himself mad it would be vastly preferable to inflict this fate on the members of his club. He knew that, given a uniform shot, the small, British-size ball 1.62 inches in diameter would go farther than the 1.68-inch American ball and that the medium-sized compromise ball of 1.66 inches would perform somewhere between the two extremes. And this is exactly what happened, in accordance with the immutable laws of dynamics.

However, when he collected up all the balls and threw them down in haphazard fashion, there were instances when he could not distinguish which balls were which. When that happened, and he did not know the size of the ball he was hitting, the results changed. There was no pattern to the shots. Some of the big balls went just as far as the small ones, and vice versa. The middle-size balls' behavior was similarly capricious. The cynic will say that the explanation was simple: He was a lousy golfer who couldn't hit a con-

sistent shot and, as a matter of fact, the cynic would be right. But why, in that case, did the small ball go farther in the first experiment? A number of club members were summoned, some of them players of no mean skill. Just to make sure, the pro was included among the guinea pigs. The same thing happened. When they did not know which ball was which, the golfers performed much the same with every shot. Some went farther than others but the outcome was entirely random without any relationship between distance and the size of the ball. Yet when they tried again, this time being told which ball was which, the results conformed almost exactly with expectations. Disregarding obvious mis-hits, the small ball outdistanced the 1.66, and the big ball came last. (The exception to that norm was the pro who, knowing the ball sizes, hit the big one consistently farther than the other two sizes. He explained that since he always played the big ball—as required by the British PGA—he had developed a technique which was especially suited to it.) The effect on the ordinary players can be imagined. Believing for years that their small ball gave them 15 yards extra on their drives, they now had proof that notwithstanding the laws of nature they played just as well with the 1.66 or the 1.68. In fact, the size of the ball had the same significance for practical purpose as the number 4 painted on Roberto de Vicenzo's ball.

Even more traumatic experiences await the golfer. Nongolfers are frequently puzzled by the extraordinary rituals which pros perform as they face up to a 3-foot putt. "Why is he going through that song and dance over that tiddler? Why I could knock it in with one hand."

And so he could, once or twice, or maybe ten times. Then he would miss one and his troubles would start. For the pro the importance of the occasion makes the difference. Apart from that, golfers acquire a personal case history of disaster which can affect them almost as strongly as a physical jog on the elbow

* The author.

242

at the critical moment. Imagine the residual damage caused by Walter Hagen's experience of twitching a putt out-of-bounds, which itself may have been the result of past disasters.

Brian Barnes, the British Ryder Cup player, was in contention for the French Open at Saint-Cloud in 1968 and was going well when he came to the 8th hole in the second round. It is a par-3, and a short one at that, with no special difficulties. Barnes bunkered his tee shot and his recovery left him a long putt. Still smarting at his poor recovery, Barnes proved again the old saying that an angry man never hit a good shot. His approach putt was 3 feet short and with that old red curtain coming up over his eyes he lipped out the 3-footer. He raked at the ball and missed and by now he was lost. He patted the ball to and fro and by the time it dropped, what with penalty strokes for hitting a moving ball and standing astride his line, his playing partners reckoned him to be down in 15. Not surprisingly Barnes made a hurried exit from the scene. Who can tell what scars that experience left on his subconscious long after the incident was forgotten?

Tommy Armour was just one golfer who allowed his stubbornness to get the better of him. The week after he won the U.S. Open he was feeling that he could make the ball do anything he liked. He came to the 17th hole of the Shawnee Open and decided that the best way to play was to hit a long draw off the tee. The difference between a draw and a hook is, all too often, the out-of-bounds fence and that's just what happened. Armour was determined to play that draw shot and fired away off the tee, only to see ball after ball soar over the fence. His card was marked with a 21 for the hole, but afterward Armour disputed the figure. He insisted it should have been 23. It just proves once again that golf cannot be conquered.

After a lifetime of daily application, the game still has the power to turn and rend the complacent golfer. In realistic terms the game of golf defies

success. Over some forty years, that is to say something like twenty thousand rounds by the world's most accomplished players, the ringer score, or eclectic, for the best eighteen holes at Augusta in the Masters is 38 strokes. Potentially that figure could be reduced by four more shots and doubtless will be in time, as players have the luck to hole out with approach shots. We can say, then, that a score of 34 would represent perfection at Augusta. The course record is 64, which demonstrates that the finest golf by the world's best players is a long, long way from perfect. We are all doomed to failure when we take a golf club in hand. The height of anyone's ambition can only be that his failures be modest. And it is here, surely, that can be found both the source of golf's lunacy and its sanity.

Almost everything in golf is a paradox. The learner discovers through distracted trial and error that in order to make a ball go upward it must be hit downward, and that if the ball is to be hit far it must be struck with a slow swing. At every turn in the game these paradoxes occur. We tell ourselves that golf is a microcosm of life itself, but in truth it is life through the looking glass, life in paradox. And so we come to the comforting thought that the madness which manifests itself in every golfer is really, in our back-to-front world, quite normal. The man who devoted an entire room as a shrine to Arnold Palmer becomes by this interpretation entirely rational, as does the man who has created a large lawn from collected divots torn from golf courses by the clubs of the stars.

By the same token we who shoulder our clubs and seek to master what we know can never be mastered, are perhaps not so irrational as we sometimes fear. For what we are doing is to chase the bitch-goddess Failure. That is golf's ultimate paradox and it could be that we only appear mad from the other side of the looking glass. Maybe we are really the sane ones. And if not, never mind. Golf is fun and that, when you get right down to it, is all that matters.

photo credits

CHAPTER 1
2-3: NS, USGA. 6: NS, Wee Burn; NYPL. 7: Marvin
Newman; JL; Milwaukee Arts Center; U&U; Bill Knight.
10-11: Frederick C. Baldwin. 14-15: *Harper's Weekly.*
16: SS; *Harper's Weekly.* 17: BB. 18-19: NS.
20-21: NYPL (both). 22: Adolph Suehsdorf. 23: Adolph
Suehsdorf; LK; Adolph Suehsdorf. 24: NYPL (all).
26-27: NS; LK. 28-29: Albert Squillace; LK. 30: NS. 31: DR.

CHAPTER 2
38: NYPL. 39: AC (all). 40: AC. 42-43: The Minneapolis
Institute of Arts. 44: "Kolf Player" by H. Brown
from *De Nederlanden.* 46: CP. 46-47: British Museum;
Gloucester Cathedral (both). 49: USGA. 50-51: AC (all).
52. USGA; NYPL. 54-55: AC. 56-57: CP.
59: NYPL. 60-61: BB; BB; CP. 62: CP. 63: NS, USGA.

CHAPTER 3
66-67: Milwaukee Arts Center. 70: USGA. 71: USGA.
72: NYPL. 73: *St. Louis-Globe Democrat.*
74: NYPL. 76-77: CP; BB; BB; BB; SS. 78: JL (both). 79: BB.
80: JL; JL; BB. 81: BB (both). 83: BB; JL. 84-85:
NYPL. 86: NS, USGA. 87: BB. 88: U&U. 89: U&U.
90-91: NYPL; NYPL; JL; JL. 92: CP. 93: JL.

CHAPTER 4
94: UPI. 95: UPI. 97: PP (both). 98: Fitz-Symms.
99: UPI. 100: DR; ABC; ABC. 102-103: ABC.

106-107: British Tourist Authority. 110: LK.
111: Shell Oil Company (both). 113: PP. 114-115: DR.
116: MN. 117: Shell Oil Company. 118: Fitz-Symms (both).
119: Marvin Newman. 120: Shell Oil Company
(both). 121: Australian Consulate General.
122-123: DR (all). 124: Bob Berger.
125: Bob Berger (all). 126-127: Bill Doggrell (both).

CHAPTER 5
130-131: DR. 134: LK. 135: Marvin Newman.
137: NYPL (both). 138: Marvin Newman. 139: LK. 141: UPI.
142: Shell Oil Company (both). 145: ABC; NYPL;
NYPL. 146-147: DR (both).

CHAPTER 6
151-152: NS, USGA. 154: Leo E. McNamara, Walter Hagen
Equipment Co. (both). 155: NS, USGA. 156: U&U.
157: U&U (both). 158-159: U&U; UPI; U&U.
160: U&U. 161: U&U. 162: NYPL. 163: "A Winter Evening"
by W. Dendy Sadler. 164: BB. 165: NYPL (all).
166: U&U; PP. 167: USGA; PP.

CHAPTER 7
170-171: Bill Knight. 175: U&U. 176: U&U. 177: U&U.
178-179: U&U. 180: Associated Press. 181: PP.
182-183: UPI. 184: UPI; ACME. 185: SS. 186: UPI; PP.
188: JB. 189: UPI. 190: JB;
Ken Regan; JB. 191: Bill Knight.

CHAPTER 8
194-195: DR. 199: *Harper's Weekly* (all). 200: UPI. 201: PP.
202: PP. 204-205: Bill Mark. 206-207: Bill Mark (all).
208: UPI. 209: PP. 210-211: Fitz-Symms.
212: DR (all). 214-215: JB (both). 216: PP.
218: Al Satterwhite, Camera 5. 219: UPI.
220: JB. 221: JB. 222-223: JB.

CHAPTER 9
226-227: NS, USGA. 231: NYPL. 233: BB.
234-235: ABC; ABC; ABC; Colgate-Palmolive Co.;
ABC. 236-237: Charles Saxon. 238-239: NS,
USGA. 240: NS, USGA.

index

Caption references in italics

a

Acquasanta (Italy), *110*
Africa, golf in, *112*, 128
Alcan tournament, 90–94
American swing, 178
Anderson, Willie, 203
Apple-Tree Gang, 69, *71*
Archer, George, 178
Armour, Tommy, 169, 197, 243
Arnie's Army, 99–101
Auchterlonie, Lawrence, 203
Augusta National Golf Club, *118,*
  139–140, *141*, 148–149,
  154, 211–213, 243
Australia, golf in, 99, 143–144, 230
Ayrshire, 81
Ayton, David, 196

b

Baffing spoon, 49, 53
Ball(s), 48–49, 50, 64, 65, 129
  featherie, 48, *62*
  gutta-percha, *62*, 64–65
  Haskell, *62,* 65
  variations in size, *240, 242*
Ball, John, 220
Ballybunion, 149
Baltusrol, *60*, 133
Banff, 109
Barnes, Brian, 243
Barnes, Jim, 197
Bemidji (Minn.), *29*
Bendelow, Tom, 75
Berg, Patty, *185*
Betting, 241–242
Big Three, 188
Birkdale, *see* Royal Birkdale
Boros, Julius, 28, 210
Bradshaw, Harry, 198, 200
Brady, Mike, 205
Braid, James, 162, *167*, 169, 197
Brassie, 53

Briggs, Clare, *20*
British Amateur championship, 78
  (1904), 152–153 (1930), *161*
  (1930), *198* (1886), 220, 232 (1904)
British Open championship,
  25 (1926), 65, 82, 87, 128 (1971),
  136 (1968), 144 (1972), *144*
  (1969), 149 (1970), 152 (1930), 153
  (1930), 157, 166, 168, 169, *178*
  (1928), 192 (1971), 200
  (1951, 1953), 196–203 (history),
  197 (1914, 1926), 198 (1934,
  1937, 1947, 1950), 201 (1953), *201*
  (1937, 1965), 203 (1961, 1962),
  209 (1969), 217 (1971), 228 (1965)
Brookline, *88*, 205
Browning, Robert, 37, 69
Bye, 241

c

Caddy(ies), 58, *79*, 167
Campbell, Willie, 203
Capilano (B.C.), 109
Carnoustie, 136, 144, 169, 198, 201
Carter, Ed, 96
Casper, Billy, 174, *188, 206*
Castle Harbour (Bermuda), *110*
Castletroy, *123*
Championships, development of, 64
Charles, Bob, 187–188
Chole, 36–37, *38*, 43
Cleek, 53
Clubs, golf, 44, 49–50, 51–53, 65, *154*
  distance vs. accuracy, 193
  early, 44, 49–50, 53, *152, 154*
  hickory, 172
  illegal, 232, *240*
  limitation of number, 234
  steel, *172*
  women's, 232
  see also clubs by name
Coles, Neil, *96*
Cornelius, Kathy, *234*
Corners (betting), 241

Cotton, Henry, 173, *180*, 198, *201*
Courses, golf, 53, 108, 113-114, 124
  architecture of, 132–149
Crans-sur-Sierre, 109, *110*
Crosby, Bing, 139
Crosse, 37
Curtis Cup, *222*
Cypress Point, 137–139, *196*

d

Daly, Fred, 198
Danecki, Walter, 228
Darben, Althea Gibson, *234*
Demaret, Jimmy, *183*
Desert golf, 108–109
De Vicenzo, Roberto, 187, 217, 236–237
Dey, Joe, 220
Driving ranges (Japan), 121
Dudley, Ed, 198
Dunn, Willie, 203
Dutra, Olin, 210

e

Earnings, 225
Edinburgh Golfers, Honourable
  Society of, 196
El Conquistador (P.R.), 26

f

Faulkner, Max, 200
Feather(ie) ball, 48, *62*
Fife, 81, 121
Foulis, James, 203
France, golf in, 114

g

Gambling, 128, 241–242
Geared, Bob, 229

Geiberger, Al, 219
Glen Cove (L.I.), *82*
Goalby, Bob, 217
Golf
  decree of 1457 forbidding, 36
  earliest depiction, *46*
  evolution of method, 157–161
  origins, 36–65
    in U.S., 68–69, 75–78
  rules of, 13
  see also Clubs, golf
Golf clubs (organizations)
  British compared to U.S., 112–114
  Japanese, 124–128
Golfer's Handbook, The, 228, 230
Grand Slam, 87, 153–154, *159,*
  197, 211
"Great Triumvirate," 162, 164, *167,* 197
Greens, 64, 112, 133, 141–142
Grips, 157
Guldahl, Ralph, 198, 210, 213
Gutta-percha ball, *62,* 64–65

Hagen, Walter, *62,* 65, 101, 172–173, *176,*
  197, 198, 205, 208, 219, 230, 243
Haskell, Coburn, 65
Haskell golf ball(s), *62,* 65
Hassan, King, 128
Hazards, 134–135, 137, 139, *139,* 140,
  142, 144, 147
Heafner, Clayton, 183
Herd, Sandy, 129, 169, 203
Hermitage (Ireland), *147*
Hilton Head (S.C.), *12*
Hines, Jimmy, *183*
Hogan, Ben, 21, 82, *94, 139,* 149, 174,
  178–180, 183, *183,* 184–185,
  190, 191, 200, 201, 213, 219
Holes
  design of, 132–144
  in one, 229
  origins, 44
  number for course, 56–57, 64

Hoylake, 197, 220
Hudson, John, 229
Hutchinson, Horace, 167
Hutchison, Jock, 197

Illegal clubs, 232, *240*
India, golf in, 108
Interlachen, 153
Ireland, golf in, 29, 108, 113, 121,
  123, *147,* 149, 169
Italy, golf in, 114

Jacklin, Tony, *144,* 149, *209*
James I (Scotland), 48
James II (Scotland), 36
January, Don, *205, 206,* 219
Japan, golf in, 28–29, 116–128, *124*
Jeu de mail, 37, 38
Jeu de paume, 37
Jigger, 174
Jones, Bobby, 12, 25, 69, 87, *141,*
  148, 152–154, *157, 159,*
  161, 172, 193, 197, 198, 200,
  213, 220, 236
Jones, Robert Trent, 133

Keeler, O. B., 69
Killarney, 149
Kinsella, Jimmy, 236
Kirkwood, Joe, 173
Kolf, 37, *45*
Kolven, 37, *38, 41, 46,* 68

Lahinch, 149

Lawson, Helen, *176, 178*
Leewood (N.Y.), *29*
Leith, 56, 57
Lema, Tony, 101, *206*
Little, Lawson, 183
Littler, Gene, *206*
Liverpool, *see* Royal Liverpool
Locke, Bobby, *180,* 185–187, 198,
  200, 237
Lockhart, Robert, 68
Long Reef (N.S.W.), *121*
Long spoon, 49
Lowery, Eddie, *88,* 209
Lucan, *123*
Lu Liang-Huan, 128, *217*
Lytham,
  see Royal Lytham and St Anne's

MacDonald, Charles Blair, 75–78,
  157, 232
MacFarlane, Alexander, 69, 75
Mackenzie, Alastair, 148
Maidstone (L.I.), 68
Manero, Tony, 198, 210
Marr, Dave, *206,* 219
Mary, Queen of Scots, 48
Mashie, 53
Masters tournament, *99* (1964), 154, 201
  (1953), *211* (1971), *213*
  (1937, 1942, 1954, 1963), 217
  (1968, 1969), 243
Matched clubs, 156
Match play vs. stroke play,
  57, 217–218
McCormack, Mark, 82–89, *96,* 188
McDermott, Johnny, 203–205
Medinah (Ill.), *117*
Melbourne, *see* Royal Melbourne
Merion, 69, 134, 136, 153
Metz, Dick, *183*
Mid-Ocean (Bermuda), *23*
Milne, A. A., *12*
Money winnings, 225

Montrose, 57
Morocco, golf in, *127, 128*
Morris, ("Old") Tom, *36, 57, 59,* 164,
    166, 196
Morris, ("Young") Tom,
    164, 166, 203
Morro Castle (P.R.), *134*
Mountain golf, 109–112
Muirfield, 144
Musselburgh, 167, 168

n

Nassau (in betting), 241
National Golf Links (L.I.), *134*
Nelson, Byron, 82, 174–178, *183,* 213
Niblick, 53, 173–174
Nichols, Bobby, 219
Nicklaus, Jack, 82–87, *99,* 136–137, 144,
    172, 172, 178, 181, 183,
    188, *190,* 192, 193, 200, *203,*
    213–217, *219*

o

Oakhurst (W.Va.), 69
O'Connor, Christy, 109
Ouimet, Francis, 65, 78–81, *88,*
    164, 205–210

p

Paganica, 37
Palmer, Arnold, 82, 87, *99,* 101, 144–148,
    152, 188–191, *190,* 203, 213, 243
Park, Willie, 168
Pebble Beach, *114, 132, 212*
Perth, 57
Peters, Richard, 232
Picard, Henry, *183,* 198
Piccadilly World Match championship,
    87, *96, 203*
Pine Valley, 144–148

Pirie, Alex, *77*
Player, Gary, 82, *96,* 136–137, 174, *187,*
    188, 191–192, *205, 206,*
    220, 222
Portmarnock, *121,* 149, 200
Portrush, *see* Royal Portrush
Portugal, 114
Pose, Martin, *183*
Press (in betting), 241
Prestwick, 144, 196, 197, 229
Price, Charles, 75
Professional golf
    vs. amateur, 222
    tournament circuit, 222–225
Professional Golfers' Association
    (PGA), 95, 96, 101, 162, 163
Professional Golfers' Association
    (PGA) championship, *188* (1971),
    209 (1962), 217, 219–220
Professionalism, 166–169
    development of, 172–173
Putter(s), 49, 53
Puttie ball, 65
Putting, 64, 184–185, 187
    illegal forms, 232–234

r

Rankin, Judy, *234*
Rawlins, Horace, 203
Rawls, Betsy, 234
Ray, Ted, 81, *88,* 164, *167,* 205–210
Reid, John, 68, 69
Revolta, Johnny, 198
Roberts, Clifford, 154
Robertson, Allan, *59*
Royal Aberdeen, 62
Royal and Ancient Club, *36, 108,*
    114, 203, 232
    see also St. Andrews
Royal Birkdale, 140, 144, 203,
    205, 217, 228
Royal Liverpool, 144, 148
Royal Lytham and St. Anne's, 144,
    144, 197, *209*

Royal Melbourne, 143–144
Royal Portrush, *123, 148,* 149, 200
Rubber-cored balls, 65
Rules of golf, 53, 56
Runyan, Paul, *183*
Ryder Cup, 197, 198, *205, 206*

s

St. Andrews, 36, 41–43, *57, 59, 60,* 64,
    65, *108,* 144, *159,* 166, 167,
    169, 196
    Old Course, 152
St. Andrews Golf Club (N.Y.),
    69, *71*
St. Anne's,
    see Royal Lytham and St. Anne's
Sanders, Doug, 172, 192
Sandwich, 144, *144,* 197, 198, 232
Sarazen, Gene, 148, 173–174, *175, 183,*
    197, 198, 213, 219
Sargent, George, 205
Scared clubs, 154
Seminole (Fla.), *139*
Semmering (Austria), 109–112
Sex in golf, 230
Shinnecock Hills (L.I.), 69,
    74, 117
Shinty, 38, *45*
Shoes, for golf, *81,* 240–241
Shute, Denny, 197, 198
Sifford, Charles, *188*
Simpson, Sir Walter, 13
Smith, Alex, 203, 205
Smith, Garden, 38
Smith, Horton, 183, 198
Smith, Macdonald, 153, 203, 205
Smith, Willie, 203
Smollett, Tobias, 62
Snead, Sam, 174, 180, *183, 190,* 198,
    213, 217, 219, 233
South Carolina Golf Club, 64
Spain, golf in, 114
Spalding club(s), *152*
Spoon(s), 49–50, 53

Spyglass (Calif.), *30*
Steel-shafted clubs, 51
Stranahan, Frank, 198
Stroke play, 56–57, 217–219
  vs. match play, 217–219
Sugarbush (Vt.), *23*
Sunningdale, 144
Superstition, 237–240
Swing technique, 178–183

t

Tait, Freddy, *198*
Taiwan, golf in, 230
Taylor, J. H., 162, *167*, 197
Thomson, Peter, *183*, 187,
  201–203, *201*
Tolley, Cyril, 152, *157*
Tour, professional, 222–225
Tournament(s)
  logistics, 96, 101, *101, 102,* 104, 114
  on television, 105
  watching, 101–104
Tournament Players' Division (PGA),
  219, 224
Travis, Walter, *60,* 65, 78, 232
Trevino, Lee, 128, 144, 172, 178,
  190, 215, 217, 219
Troon, 144, 203
Turnberry, 143

U

Uniforms, wearing of, 240
United States Amateur championship,
  152, 153 (1930), 220, 232
United States Golf Association,
  65, 75, 203, 211, 232
United States Open championship,
  65, 81 (1913), 152, 153 (1930),
  157, *159,* 164, 201 (1953), 203 (1894),
  203–211 (history of), 205 (1910,
  1912, 1913), 208–210
  (1913), 212 (1972)
United States Women's Open
  championship, *234* (1972)

V

Vardon, Harry, 53, 81–82, *88,* 154–164,
  167, 169, 172, 191, 197,
  203, 205–210
Vare, Glenna Collett, *185, 233*
Venturi, Ken, 210

W

Walker Cup, 197
Walton Heath, 144

Walvis Bay (S.-West Africa), *112*
Ward-Thomas, Pat, 129
Water hazards, 134–136
Watrous, Al, 197
Webster, H. T., 25
Wedge(s), 53, 174, *175*
Wee Burn (Conn.), *26, 30*
Westchester Classic, *220, 222*
Westward Ho!, *59,* 144, 162
Wethered, Roger, 152, 153
Williamsburg Inn (Va.), *139*
Wimbledon, 144
Wingfoot (N.Y.), *159*
Women golfers
  compared to men, 231–232
  status of, 230, 232
Wood, Craig, *183,* 213
Wooden balls, 48
World Cup, *219* (1971)

y

Yips, 184–185
Young, Douglas, 36
Yugoslavia, 114

z

Zaharias, Babe D., *185*

E
AT
IES

by William Bayer
Picture research by Marion Geisinger

Editor-in-Chief: Jerry Mason
Editor: Adolph Suehsdorf
Art Director: Albert Squillace
Associate Editor: Moira Duggan
Associate Editor: Barbara Hoffbeck
Art Associate: Mark Liebergall
Art Associate: David Namias
Art Production: Doris Mullane

FOR ELEANOR PERRY

Contents

Introduction **Choosing the Great Movies** 8

1 Westerns 24
Stagecoach   27
The Searchers   32
Red River   35
Shane   38
The Wild Bunch   40

2 Intrigue & Suspense 46
M   48
Rear Window   50
The Third Man   53
Touch of Evil   56
The Big Sleep   60

3 Comedies 64
City Lights   67
The General   70
Duck Soup   73
Dr. Strangelove, or How I Learned
to Stop Worrying and Love the Bomb   76
Tom Jones   81

4 Musicals 84
Top Hat   87
The Wizard of Oz   91
Singin' in the Rain   92
Cabaret   96
A Hard Day's Night   97

5 War 102
La Grande Illusion   104
The Bridge on the River Kwai   108
From Here to Eternity   111
Paths of Glory   114
M*A*S*H   117

6 Adventure 120
Only Angels Have Wings   122
The Seven Samurai   124
The Treasure of the Sierra Madre   129
Casablanca   132
Lawrence of Arabia   137

7 Manners, Morals & Society 142

Rules of the Game   144
Citizen Kane   148
La Dolce Vita   154
Jules and Jim   159
Easy Rider   160

8 Films About Films 164

Sunset Boulevard   167
All About Eve   170
The Bad and the Beautiful   172
Contempt   175
8½   176

9 Cinema of Personal Expression 180

La Strada   183
Viridiana   184
Persona   188
Au Hazard, Balthazar   191
Blow-Up   193

10 Fantasy & Horror 196

Metropolis   198
Psycho   202
The Manchurian Candidate   204
Weekend   206
2001: A Space Odyssey   207

11 The Concerned Cinema 212

The Bicycle Thief   214
The Four Hundred Blows   217
On the Waterfront   219
Hiroshima, Mon Amour   222
Battle of Algiers   223

12 Period Films 226

Les Enfants du Paradis   228
Gone With the Wind   232
Henry V   237
Bonnie and Clyde   243
The Magnificent Ambersons   245

Index 249

RAND

HOTEL

CALUMET
THEATRE TICKET
SERVICE

5

OUGHNUTS

Doughnuts
and Coffee
15¢

1531
TYSON
THEATRE TICKETS

AST
GRETA GARBO·JOAN
GRAN
JOHN AND LIONEL

NEWARK - JERSEY CITY - NEW YORK

STAGE
OR SCREEN
HISTORY!

X OFFICE

THEATRE
AWFORD·WALLACE BEERY
O HOTEL
ARRYMORE - LEWIS STONE
JEAN HERSHOLT

Berney

ADAM
HATS

ADAM
HATS
AMERICAS ONE PRICE HATTER

Choosing the Great Movies

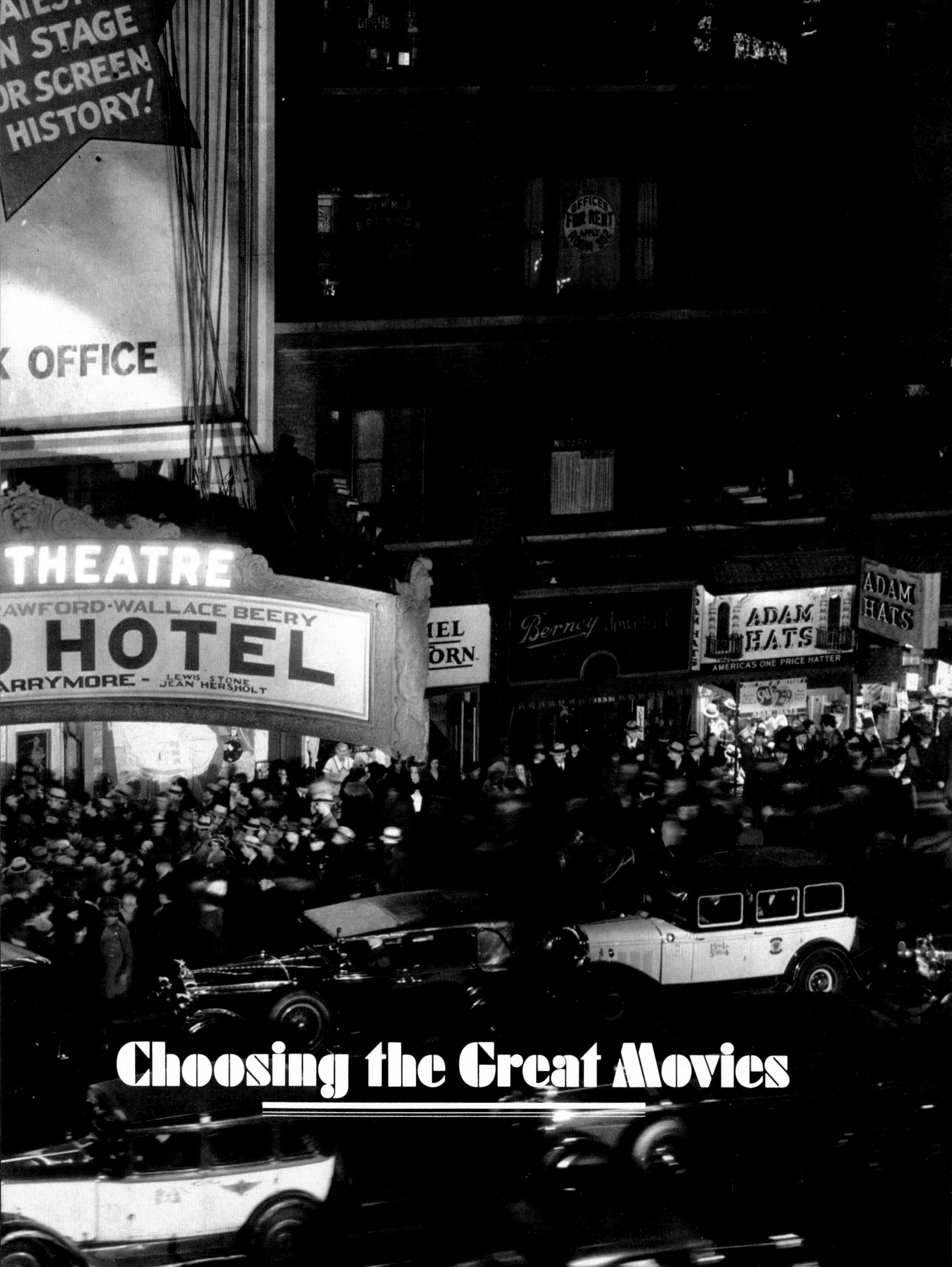

The decision to publish a book on "The Great Movies"
was easy. Picking and choosing the contents was difficult. Pleasantly
difficult — for there is no child of the twentieth
century who is not an instant expert on movies — but difficult.

Once the task was begun, perplexing problems
arose. For instance: What are "The Great Movies"? Are they
the inevitable warhorse classics (INTOLERANCE,
GREED, CITIZEN KANE, THE SEVENTH SEAL), which turn up again
and again in all serious literature on film? Or should they
include the great entertainment films (GONE WITH THE WIND,
THE GRADUATE, THE GODFATHER, even THE SOUND OF MUSIC),
whose popular appeal is undeniable and overwhelming?
Can the collective list of the all-time best films
chosen by the most important international critics, as reported
in the British film magazine, *Sight and Sound,* be
reconciled with the list of all-time box-office champs, as reported
in the American show-business weekly, *Variety?*
Can GONE WITH THE WIND be spoken of in the same breath with
HIROSHIMA, MON AMOUR? There was no simple answer, for
many plebeian movies have had as long a life span, and are
as deeply cherished, as those of the highest artistic accomplishment.

There were other questions. Among the many thousands
of films produced in the seventy-year history of movies,
how many are really "great"? One thousand? Five hundred?
A little research discloses that film history, as
written by experts and critics, focuses on less than two hundred and
fifty titles. Yet even these are far too many to deal
with in a single volume, certainly if anything interesting
or sensible is to be said about them.

Should a film by every important director be included?
What about important screenwriters and stars? How should
the various national schools of cinema be balanced
off, and should equal space be given to each of the seven decades
of the movies' existence? What, when it came to that,
were our premises about film as film? Is the cinema a fine art,
or merely a vulgarian form that has replaced the coliseum
and the circus as the principal source of spectacle in
modern life? Can there be such a thing as a "great masterpiece
of entertainment," or even a "great piece of cinema trash"?

Finding an acceptable set of answers, and establishing
the criteria for them, we decided, should be the

CHARLIE CHAPLIN *in* "THE GOLD RUSH"

Preceding pages: Marquee of long-gone Astor
Theater in New York for premiere of MGM's GRAND HOTEL,
a multistarred big picture in Depression year
of 1932. Based on Vicki Baum's novel, it
was directed by Edmund Goulding and photographed by
William Daniels, Garbo's favorite cameraman.

responsibility of an author committed to movies as a joyful
experience, a matter of cultural importance,
and even as a way of life. We wanted him to be partisan, but not
doctrinaire. We wanted acute observation, fresh insights,
and independent judgment.

Rudolph Valentino

William Bayer has brought all of these qualities
to this book. Although young, he is well versed in the
history of the cinema; he has seen the several thousand
important films, and each of the key two hundred and fifty many times.
He also has an understanding of and sympathy for
the filmmaker's plight, for he has made films himself
and has written a lively and incisive book on the incredible
process by which films are produced today. He is intimately
aware of the clash between money and art in the world of film.

In all, he has chosen sixty movies. They qualify as great,
he says, because "they create a fictional world and give
you access to it. They are films in whose presence
you feel exaltation, whose images you find memorable, whose
elements — whether a scene, a character, a performance,
an idea, a way of looking at the world — move you and stamp
themselves upon your memory. In short, they are pictures
which resolve some segment of experience in some irrevocable way."

Ultimately, Bayer constructed his list in terms
of genres — twelve categories broad enough to accommodate
practically any film ever made, yet specific enough to
permit meaningful comparisons and some judgments on
greatness. Eight of the genres are familiar storytelling forms
which have preoccupied movie makers — and captivated

Garbo and John Barrymore

Garbo as Anna Karenina (1935)

13

Jeanette MacDonald and Nelson Eddy

Betty Grable

Hedy Lamarr

Cary Grant

Bette Davis

Errol Flynn

D. W. Griffith
directing WAY DOWN EAST (1920)

audiences — since THE (less than great) GREAT TRAIN ROBBERY
first showed the way: Westerns, Comedies, War films, Musicals, films of
Intrigue and Suspense, of Fantasy and Horror, Period films, and
films of Adventure. Several — Manners, Morals and Society, Personal
Expression, and the Cinema of Concern — were devised to
organize the unique and intensely personal visions of great directors.
And one — Films about Films — pays tribute to the movie industry's
eternal narcissism and occasional unblinking self-revelation.

The categories make no pretense of precision.
War, or its side effects and aftermath, shows up in four genres
besides War. A number of films in various categories could
be construed as Period pieces. In the end, however, each movie was
assigned its place on the basis of its prevailing
mood and intent. Despite its Civil War setting, THE GENERAL
is innocent fun. The warlike DR. STRANGELOVE, by
taking contemporary militarism to an extreme limit, is really
black comedy. And M*A*S*H, while essentially funny, is
breathtaking by being horribly funny about war.

The principal advantage of the system of genres is that it
permits full and fair consideration of deserving films
that usually are ignored when all-time-anything selections
are being made. Even as the man picking literature
for a desert-island sojourn feels constrained to take Shakespeare
over his favorite junk novel, so movie-list compilers are
likely to dismiss Musicals and Westerns and Adventure films
as inconsequential in their search for the greatest
of the great. Well, maybe SINGIN' IN THE RAIN doesn't rate with
PERSONA, and maybe SHANE isn't KANE. But within the lively,
lovely little world of Musicals, SINGIN' IN THE RAIN is
worthy of some kind of immortality. In the incredibly vast
array of Westerns, SHANE must stand among the top five.
And if PERSONA is to be chosen, it should survive the competition
of the finest, most sensitive films of Personal Expression.

Useful as it was, classification by genre did not solve
all problems. Certain decisions had to be made,
almost arbitrarily, along the way. "Underground films," shorts,
animated films, and documentaries are excluded, without
apology. They are out of the mainstream of movie history.

As for the silents, THE GENERAL, METROPOLIS, and
CITY LIGHTS are in. Nothing else. (THE BIRTH OF A NATION,
probably the greatest single accomplishment in film history,

Al Jolson

Joan Crawford and Neil Hamilton

Margaret Livingston and George O'Brien
in Murnau's SUNRISE (1927)

16

Marlene Dietrich in THE DEVIL IS A WOMAN (1935)

Douglas Fairbanks and Julanne Johnston in THE THIEF OF BAGDAD (1924)

Rouben Mamoulian directs Sylvia Sidney and Gary Cooper in CITY STREETS (1931)

When double features cost 10¢

17

Jean Hersholt, Gibson Gowland, and ZaSu Pitts in GREED (1923)

Barbara Stanwyck

Lana Turner

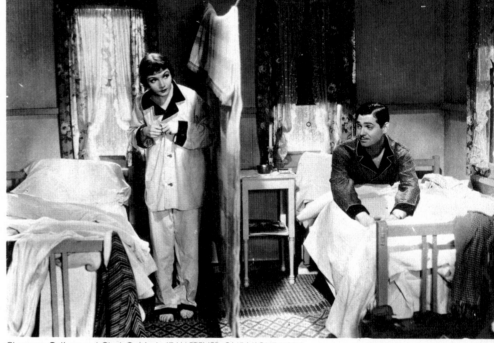
Claudette Colbert and Clark Gable in IT HAPPENED ONE NIGHT (1934)

Spencer Tracy

Jean Harlow

Robert Taylor

Katharine Hepburn

Floodlit opening at Grauman's Chinese

Laurel and Hardy in BRATS (1930)

Filming W. C. Fields in THE OLD-FASHIONED WAY (1934)

Eddie Woods and James Cagney in PUBLIC ENEMY (1931)

Mickey Rooney and Judy Garland

Mae West in I'M NO ANGEL (1933)

is not in only because Bayer felt there was nothing new worth
saying about it.) No disrespect intended. The silents were
the glorious sunlit springtime of the movies. Prodigious
things were done, stars were born, Hollywood make-believe
enchanted the world — not only through the pictures themselves,
but by the splendid magic by which they were made.
Through the stunts, the make-up, the cardboard castles, and the
"special effects," we discovered that the visual possibilities
of movies were limitless, that we not only had a new
form of entertainment, but a whole new way of seeing. Before our
eyes, Doug Fairbanks could ride a flying horse,
Tom Mix could shoot a villain, and John Gilbert could make
love to Vilma Banky. We never got over it.

Still, despite the marvels of the era, the silents —
with rare exceptions, mostly comedies — have become antiques,
valuable but quaint, like a butter churn. Their mechanics
show too easily and their crudities afflict us, particularly those
designed to compensate for the absence of sound.
We bring different expectations into movie theaters today.

Inevitably, much is missing from our book. There is,
for example, no film starring Greta Garbo or, for that matter, Marlene
Dietrich or Joan Crawford. Garbo certainly was greater than
Janet Leigh, who appears in three of Bayer's choices, but PSYCHO,
TOUCH OF EVIL, and THE MANCHURIAN CANDIDATE
are far superior films to ANNA CHRISTIE, CAMILLE, or NINOTCHKA.

The same principle applies to Douglas Fairbanks,
Mae West, W. C. Fields, Lon Chaney, Errol Flynn, and Katharine
Hepburn, all of whom are absent, while Humphrey Bogart,
John Wayne, and William Holden join Miss Leigh with
three selections each. To include the first group would have meant
settling for trivial films, which would be self-defeating
since movies, not stars or directors, are the subject of the book.

And this fact turned out to be another virtue
of the genre system. Strong films survived. Lesser films by famous
names, historic names, critics' pets, and cult favorites

George Raft

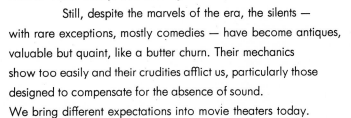

did not. Among directors the casualty rate was high. Jean Cocteau, Satyajit Ray, Joseph Losey, Luchino Visconti, and Max Ophuls — all missing. Also, and regrettably, Sternberg, Cukor, Lubitsch, Rossellini, Vigo, and Bertolucci.

In? Ingmar Bergman, of course; Truffaut, Godard, and Renoir; Bresson and Buñuel, a couple of specialists; and then a rather wide range of Hollywood offspring — Ford, Hawks, Welles, Kubrick, and the inevitable Mr. Alfred Hitchcock. But, as noted, this is not a director's book.

Elizabeth Taylor

Soviet cinema is out. A surprise perhaps, considering the impact Eisenstein and others presumably have had, but Bayer said no. He dismissed THE BATTLESHIP POTEMKIN as a cul-de-sac, EARTH, MOTHER, and STRIKE as overrated, and the spectacles, ALEXANDER NEVSKY, IVAN THE TERRIBLE, and WAR AND PEACE, as appalling.

Marilyn Monroe

In the end, an amazingly eclectic sixty films were selected. Though weighted in favor of the American cinema of the past thirty years, they reflect the developing cinema everywhere. Included are films that no one can ignore (CITIZEN KANE, RULES OF THE GAME, LES ENFANTS DU PARADIS, THE GENERAL, for instance). These are supplemented by popular pictures which some will scorn (THE WILD BUNCH, EASY RIDER, CABARET, M*A*S*H, FROM HERE TO ETERNITY), marginal pictures which many people have forgotten (ONLY ANGELS HAVE WINGS, THE MANCHURIAN CANDIDATE, THE BAD AND THE BEAUTIFUL, THE BIG SLEEP), pictures which now are difficult to see on a full-size screen (THE SEARCHERS, PATHS OF GLORY, TOUCH OF EVIL), and some pictures which few people have seen at all (CONTEMPT; AU HASARD, BALTHAZAR).

Altogether, they represent a coherent vision of the movies, internally logical, extremely solid and energetic in its arguments — and fun to disagree with. As Bayer himself says: "Exactly what these films indicate about my needs for fantasy, how they fulfill my desires for romance, melancholy, music, laughter, diversion, and escape, or why it is my wish to see again and again movies that are inexhaustibly rich and that reflect the most perverse, grotesque, and selfish aspects of man, as well as his warmth and humanity and the glories of comradeship, I cannot begin to explain. That I cannot explain it is, to me, one of the wondrous mysteries of film, a medium of which — even when one tries to write authoritatively — one finds oneself in a state of awe." THE EDITORS

Marlon Brando and Maria Schneider in LAST TANGO IN PARIS (1973)

Sophia Loren PHOTOGRAPH BY DOUGLAS KIRKLAND

Westerns

1

The western, along with the musical and the thriller, is one of the three great escapist genres invented in America. The "spaghetti westerns" of Sergio Leone notwithstanding, Americans can rightly claim that the western belongs to them, that American filmmakers are the only ones capable of exalting the genre to heights of sublimity, and that American audiences are the only ones qualified to judge the greatness of their works. When we hear that Jean-Paul Sartre considers himself a connoisseur of westerns, we must smile slightly at his presumption. We knew more about them when we were sixteen than he can ever hope to comprehend.

More than any other genre, the western is enveloped by rituals and conventions. We are at home in any frontier town. The main street, the cemetery (often called "boot hill"), the saloon, the general store, the stable, the bank, the railway terminal, and the sheriff's office enclosing a jail are all immediately recognizable places. We also know the people who inhabit these towns: the sheriff, the doctor, the prostitute, the telegrapher, the saloon keeper, and the quiet, mysterious stranger who wanders in and may be the fastest gun alive. We recognize the hired killer, the ranching baron, the cardsharp, and the itinerant notion-vender. We know the role of women in this society and we understand the rituals of the posse, the hanging party, the cavalry rescue, the Indian attack (and massacre), the poker game, the cattle roundup, the cattle drive, and the shoot-out on the main street. Whether the story is about law and order, crossing a dangerous territory, an Indian war, ranchers versus homesteaders, cattlemen versus sheepmen, the construction of a railway, the threat of a marauding outlaw band, a stagecoach heist, an Easterner's initiation, a man torn between public duty and private desire, or a hundred other basic situations, we know the parameters and we know what to expect. Because of this knowledge, bred into us since we saw our first movies, we are all connoisseurs of the western, on the lookout for the brilliant variation, the unexpected twist, the expert crossbreeding of themes, the novel vision, the fine points and stylistic ingenuities that will make one western stand out from the herd.

The huge backlog of westerns from which we formulate our expectations and draw our standards is the result of a discovery made quite early by producers that westerns are infinitely marketable, that stories set in the West can be told over and over again without people tiring of the rituals, the characters, and the settings. Thus, there has been an endless stream of works, beginning with THE GREAT TRAIN ROBBERY of 1903, through the pictures starring William S. Hart, Tom Mix, and William Boyd, into the subgenres of the singing westerns of Gene Autry and Roy Rogers (the true horse operas?), the message westerns (THE OX-BOW INCIDENT, 3:10 TO YUMA), the psychological westerns (DUEL IN THE SUN, THE HANGING TREE), the historical westerns (GUNFIGHT AT THE O.K. CORRAL, LITTLE BIG MAN), the comedy westerns (DESTRY RIDES AGAIN, BUTCH CASSIDY AND THE SUNDANCE KID), and the numerous other types represented by such works as RANCHO NOTORIOUS, JOHNNY GUITAR, THE UNFORGIVEN, HIGH NOON, THE SCALPHUNTERS, THE VIRGINIAN, APACHE, WINCHESTER .73, THE COVERED WAGON, THE BIG COUNTRY, THE LEFT-HANDED GUN, and all the stories about the James brothers, Billy the Kid, Wyatt Earp and Doc Holliday, Tombstone, Dodge City, Virginia City, the California Gold Rush, the Alamo, and the other combinations of guns, horses, Indians, cavalry, cattle, frontier towns, and vast and magnificent landscapes which are the threads that bind these many types together into a genre.

Many people have intellectualized the western, studying the mythical and romantic elements that make it so popular. One school of thought maintains that the western provides a moral universe in which violence, supposedly so dear to Americans, can be vicariously experienced without harm. Others believe that the western is an everchanging mirror in which one may read a particular era's perception of itself as reflected in its view of the American past. (The danger of this theory is that it encourages filmmakers to make allegories, almost always self-conscious and deeply flawed.) Still other theorists view it as the terrain of alienation, a peculiarly American syndrome, derived, one is told, from the paradox that the world's greatest democracy was founded on genocide and slaughter, that the settlers who expanded the frontier were disguised imperialists, and that lawmen who lived by the gun were murderers even when they killed on behalf of right. And there is the view that Americans love westerns because of nostalgia for a time when life, which has become so maddeningly complex in urban society, was simple and values were clear. All of these things and many more have been discerned in the western, and though some of them have more merit than others, none of them is relevant to the question of what makes certain westerns great, to such things as filmmaking craft, story, acting, action, the personal vision of a director, his feeling for people and for land, and the dimensions of his spirit which determine his ability to create art.

Because of the richness of the genre it is impossible to pick five great westerns without leaving out works of importance and quality. John Ford is unavoidable (as is John Wayne; he appears in three of the five films dis-

Preceding pages: John Ford's STAGECOACH
(top, l. to r.) — Andy Devine (Buck), George Bancroft
(Wilcox), Donald Meek (Peacock), Claire Trevor
(Dallas); (bottom, l. to r.), — John Carradine (Hatfield),
Chris Martin (Chris), Louise Platt (Lucy),
John Wayne (the Ringo Kid), Thomas Mitchell (Doc).

cussed). Ford not only reinvented the western with STAGECOACH, but he is responsible for THE SEARCHERS, easily the most perfect western ever made. Howard Hawks, master of so many genres, made at least two great westerns, RIO BRAVO and RED RIVER, one of which, at the very least, has to be included. George Stevens made only one western in his career, but SHANE is so exemplary that to leave it out is to ignore the *ne plus ultra* of the mythologizing branch of the genre. And Sam Peckinpah, who, along with Stanley Kubrick, is the most distinguished of the younger American filmmakers, made a western called THE WILD BUNCH which, along with 2001: A SPACE ODYSSEY, may be one of the great films of our time.

But what about Samuel Fuller, Robert Aldrich, Anthony Mann, Henry Hathaway, and Arthur Penn? It is a pity that a picture of each could not be included here. As for the two very popular and defective hits, HIGH NOON and BUTCH CASSIDY AND THE SUNDANCE KID, their exclusion is somewhat less of a pity. But it is with regret that Robert Altman's MCCABE AND MRS. MILLER and Marlon Brando's ONE-EYED JACKS are absent here; though these pictures are, perhaps, outside the western mainstream, there is no doubt that in their unique and sometimes perverse ways they are both masterpieces.

John Ford's Stagecoach 1939

Prior to STAGECOACH, the western was in grievous decline. For a decade it had been a genre unfulfilled. But with STAGECOACH a renaissance occurred. The genre was reinvented, its possibilities as spectacle were reaffirmed, and a new classicism was born. Since 1939, STAGECOACH has been a reference point for anyone who has worked within the genre, as a picture either to be emulated or reacted against, as a treasury of themes and motifs to be worked out in new variations. For John Ford, STAGECOACH was the starting point of that portion of his career most likely to be remembered, and though it may not be true, as some have claimed, that Ford *is* the western, there can be no doubt that his influence upon it has been unprecedented and dominating.

STAGECOACH was the western in which the public first saw Monument Valley, Utah, on film—a place that Ford would revisit again and again, and that became his favorite location for the exterior sequences of his westerns. The rocks and plains of Monument Valley have become a signature on Ford's pictures, immediately identifying a place that plays as meaningful a part in his vision of the West as a certain remote Swedish island plays in the universe of Ingmar Bergman.

STAGECOACH was also the first western to feature John Wayne, the picture that made him a star. Wayne is as deeply merged with the western in the public's consciousness as Humphrey Bogart was with the private-eye film. The amazing thing about Wayne as an actor is the same thing that is so amazing about Bogart: the way he can play a variety of roles maintaining the rough outlines of a single persona, yet transcend those outlines so that each character is individual and unique.

STAGECOACH is so rich it has become a treasury of western characters and motifs. It exemplifies, first of all, a technique especially amenable to the cinema form, the Grand Hotel or Ship of Fools device, whereby characters representing various types are closely confined for a period of time and act out in their relationships with one another the social structure of their era and place. On the stagecoach to Lordsburg, one finds a drunkard doctor, a whiskey drummer, an aristocratic gambler, a woman of quality, a "good" prostitute, a compassionate sheriff, a grizzled driver, a crooked banker, and in the person of the Ringo Kid (Wayne) a good-guy gunslinger.

As for motifs, there is, first, one of Ford's favorite types of scene, a life-ceremony. Sometimes a wedding, sometimes a funeral, in STAGECOACH it is the birth of a child. There are, in addition, cut telegraph lines, an attack by Indians, a chase (with much acrobatics on horses), a cavalry rescue (announced, of course, by a bugle call), a poker game (Luke Plummer holds aces and eights, "the dead man's hand"), a three-against-one gunfight on the streets of a town (the Ringo Kid kills all three Plummer brothers and settles an old score), and a happy ending (the Ringo Kid and the heart-of-gold prostitute, Claire Trevor, ride off to Mexico with Sheriff Wilcox's blessing).

Ford in STAGECOACH thus sets the form for a particular type of folk art, and by his unique ability to use characters both as individual personalities and as social types he singlehandedly gives birth to a mythology that no American can ever escape. The remarkable thing about Ford's westerns, and one sees this process expanded in his later films, is his gift for simultaneously contemplating people as individuals and as representatives of virtues,

Grandeur of Monument Valley,
Utah, became part of the signature
on a John Ford western. Ford
loved this particular piece of
American turf and returned to it
again and again. Another Ford
trademark was appearance of
familiar faces from his ''repertory
company,'' chief among them, John
Wayne's. With his first scene
in STAGECOACH (top), Wayne became
a major star. Above: Cavalry rescue,
pursuing Indians pursuing stage.

29

vices, and other abstract qualities.

For those familiar with STAGECOACH, perhaps the greatest surprise on seeing it again is how small a role the Monument Valley scenes actually play in the whole design. It is a credit to the intensity of these scenes that they expand in one's memory until they seem to dominate the film. Actually, most of STAGECOACH was shot on sound stages with rear-screen process projection, and on sets constructed on a studio back lot. Ford, who in his old age seems to relish the role of the curmudgeon, "Pappy," "the Admiral," or the just plain "guy who made a few westerns," recalls that STAGECOACH cost about $220,000, came in $8,000 under budget, that the chase took two days to shoot, that Wyatt Earp had once personally advised him on how to stage a gunfight, and that the picture was more or less "cut in the camera."

This man, who created STAGECOACH, MY DARLING CLEMENTINE, FORT APACHE, SHE WORE A YELLOW RIBBON, WAGON MASTER, THE HORSE SOLDIERS, THE MAN WHO SHOT LIBERTY VALANCE, and the incomparable THE SEARCHERS, is in no danger of being underrated, thanks to the many who now place him, along with Alfred Hitchcock and Howard Hawks, in a triumvirate of American filmmaker immortals. Two of his most famous pictures, THE IN-FORMER and THE GRAPES OF WRATH, labeled by some as art films, will in time be forgotten, while his westerns will be screened forever.

There is some irony in the fact that though Ford's STAGECOACH rescued the western from decadence in 1939, its remake in 1966 (starring Ann-Margret and Bing Crosby, and directed by Gordon Douglas) evidenced the descent of a new decadence upon the genre. Twentieth Century-Fox, which released the remake, threatened with unparalleled arrogance to prosecute anyone who dared to exhibit Ford's original version. What further proof is needed that the cultural heritage of Americans is in constant jeopardy, that a new breed of barbarians exists willing to ban the showing of a film so great that Orson Welles viewed it (he claims) some forty times while "in training" for CITIZEN KANE?

30

Opposite: Ringo — ''Looks like I got the plague, don't it?'' Dallas — ''No . . . it's not you.'' (Berton Churchill, as pompous banker on run with embezzled funds, is at right.) Pair's mutual isolation leads to romance, culminating in love scene (r.), when they walk past the whorehouses of Lordsburg just before shoot-out with three Plummers. Above & left: John Ford, in black coat and beret, supervising setups on location. Though movie is closely associated with Monument Valley, Ford shot much of STAGECOACH on studio sets.

John Ford's **The Searchers** 1956

It is unfortunate that John Ford's THE SEARCHERS is not widely known, for it surpasses many famous westerns and is among the few pictures in the genre that one can safely label a work of art. Ford would most likely sneer at such a statement, but then it is his very lack of self-conscious artiness, his utter absence of pretension, his singular desire to tell a good story, and his equally fervent wish to avoid delivering a message that ennobles so much of his work and enables him to subliminally transcend the genre. THE SEARCHERS is a picture of such economy of expression and such purity of line that it puts to shame the self-important works of filmmakers who treat the western form as if it were a vessel that anyone who has the nerve to call himself an artist is qualified to fill.

Just as General de Gaulle held "a certain conception of France," so John Ford holds a certain conception of the West. He is not a realist or a buff steeped in the details of western lore, but a fantasist and a stylist who has meditated on the West for a long period of years and has painstakingly, picture by picture, created an imaginary West that is uniquely his own. While other directors sought new locations for westerns, Ford has stayed in Monument Valley, a fact that does not, as some would claim, demonstrate the limits of his imagination, but rather certifies his concern for the refinement of an ideal. One has the feeling that without knowing it, Ford for years was working toward some ultimate western; his continuing reuse of a location and of a company of actors and technicians suggests a quest for a perfect expression. That quest, it seems, was resolved in the film THE SEARCHERS. The pictures that follow, including the fine THE MAN WHO SHOT LIBERTY VALANCE, suggest a cooling off, the beginning of a trek downward from dizzying heights.

There are striking differences between STAGECOACH and THE SEARCHERS, reflecting a change more important than the mere passage of seventeen years. STAGECOACH is a sprawling spectacle; THE SEARCHERS is a confined epic. In STAGECOACH the characters express themselves in speech; in THE SEARCHERS they say more by gestures and glances. STAGECOACH is literary and theatrical; THE SEARCHERS is visual and cinematic. In STAGECOACH the actors come alive while on the screen; in THE SEARCHERS they radiate, from their first appearances, an understanding of who they are that reaches far back into the past. In STAGECOACH the types overshadow the personalities; in THE SEARCHERS the personalities transcend the types. STAGECOACH is a picture

that excites the senses; THE SEARCHERS is a film that moves the heart. And STAGECOACH holds our attention because its story is in constant flux, while THE SEARCHERS entrances us because its story is so single-minded and intense.

For those who know and admire THE SEARCHERS, its opening and ending encourage interminable speculation. A door opens out from the screen while a woman waits in darkness for a solitary man who dismounts his horse and moves slowly from brilliant sunlight toward comforting interior warmth. And when the picture ends that man is again outside, and that same door closes upon him. He is Ethan Edwards, played by John Wayne, the outsider, the wanderer, the quintessential Ford protagonist. He returns to his family from the Civil War, nourishes himself in their domestic warmth, goes on an obsessive five-year rampage of revenge when they are slaughtered and his favorite niece is kidnapped by Comanche Indians, and when he returns, somehow changed and mellowed by the madness of that search, he is still an outsider, still a man alone, shut out from domesticity, destined to wander even more. But that famous door, that opens to beckon him in and then closes at the end to shut him out, is also a door Ford opens for us onto history. It is a means by which he formalizes the distancing that turns the story of THE SEARCHERS into a myth, and the way, too, by which he gives us a glimpse at the enigma of a man's soul.

The five-year search by Ethan Edwards and Martin Pawley (Jeffrey Hunter) for Debbie Edwards (Natalie Wood) is an adventure story encompassing violence, subterfuge, and terror. It is also a story of a strange man, torn between such brutishness that at times he rivals in savagery the very Indians he hates, and such gentleness that at times his "civilization" surpasses that of the family for whom his presence causes such unease. He is admirable for the way he despises money (in contrast to his brother who secretes it), and at the same time he is a man so obsessed with racial hatred that he prefers to kill his own niece rather than allow her to live as a Comanche squaw. He and his brother's wife are unspokenly in love, and this strange, superbly gentle side of his character is revealed in one of the great moments in the western when he embraces Natalie Wood instead of killing her—a moment that Godard has described as so moving that it filled him with love for John Wayne, a man whom he despised politically.

THE SEARCHERS is rich film. Its uses of color, its

John Wayne, badly underestimated as
an actor for many years, gives a towering
performance as Ethan Edwards in Ford's
THE SEARCHERS. Projecting complete conviction
and deep inner torment, he exceeds himself
and becomes a great screen presence.

THE SEARCHERS: Flanking
bands of Comanches (top) close
for the kill — again in
Monument Valley. Above, left:
Wayne grasps Natalie Wood
in culminating scene, when
we and she are certain he will
kill her. Above: In one of
the final frames, Wayne
stands outside the house. In
a moment the door will
shut him out once more.
Left: The funeral sequence,
a favorite motif in
many John Ford pictures.

feeling for the passages of time and the changing of the seasons, the funeral sequence, the recurring use of figures silhouetted against brilliant backgrounds of white and red, its lack of reliance on dialogue, its many moods echoed in landscapes, the supreme eloquence of the gestures of its characters, its strange combination of warmth and hardness, its evocations of terror, and, above all, the sensibility of the unseen man behind it, a man both meditative and wise, are the things that raise it from the level of a fine adventure story into the realm of art.

Howard Hawks' **Red River** 1948

RED RIVER is not a work of art, but it is an extremely good adventure western, justifiably admired despite its controversial ending. A classic series of comparisons have been made between Howard Hawks and John Ford, and though sometimes valuable they often turn out to be less interesting than they seem. For example, there is a theory that while Ford distances his material and places it in an historical perspective, Hawks tends to become directly involved with his and to endow it with a sense of immediacy. As an example of this, one critic contrasts the river crossings in Ford's WAGON MASTER and Hawks' RED RIVER, pointing out that Ford transforms this western ritual into a scene of epic grandeur by shooting it from a distance, while Hawks gets right into it with rapid cutting and close shots, and emphasizes its excitement. This is a valid analysis as far as it goes, but if one recalls the river crossing in Ford's STAGECOACH, quite close in spirit to the one in RED RIVER, one is forced to admit that directors are less consistent than critics might wish.

Hawks and Ford are of the same generation and are both master filmmakers of the American cinema, but while Ford's contribution has been more or less exclusive to the historical film, particularly the western, Hawks has ranged widely over many genres. While Ford has been deeply committed to the western and has treated it as a way of life, Hawks has viewed it as merely one of several modes in which he can work out variations on his long-standing interest in action, adventure, and men in groups. This difference in their commitments shows, for Hawks, good as he is with the western (RED RIVER, RIO BRAVO, THE BIG SKY), has never come close to the intensity of THE SEARCHERS, or ever made anything quite so moving and profound.

Ford's heroes tend to be quiet men. Hawks' tend to be violent. This difference shows in their respective uses of John Wayne. (Ford even made Wayne the hero of a nonwestern, set in Ireland, entitled THE QUIET MAN.) In Ford's westerns Wayne becomes less verbally articulate and more eloquent and more gentle in his strength, while in Hawks' films (Wayne appears in four of them) he plays roles that sometimes border on the unsympathetic, roles in which he is either sloppy or monstrous and nearly always unsubtle.

RED RIVER, the story of a cattle drive up the Chisholm Trail, involves such rituals as the river crossing, the funeral, the cattle stampede, the Indian attack, and that favorite motif of Howard Hawks, the proper role of a leader of men. (See ONLY ANGELS HAVE WINGS.) In RED RIVER we observe the hardening of Tom Dunstan (Wayne) as he carries ruthlessness too far, and we simultaneously observe the personal growth of Matthew Garth (Montgomery Clift), who wrests leadership from Wayne and takes control of the drive. This conflict between Wayne and Clift, father and adopted son, is one of the fascinations of RED RIVER, complicated by the fact that it was Wayne's ruthlessness and implacability years before that led to the death of the woman he had loved and whom Clift symbolizes in his mind. Though we start the film admiring Wayne, we eventually reject him and transfer our sympathy to Montgomery Clift. For this reason, and the fact that their "father-son" struggle is not properly resolved, the ending of RED RIVER is less than satisfactory.

In an interview with Jim Kitses, Borden Chase, who wrote the screenplay and the original story upon which it was based, complains bitterly of Hawks' refusal to use his ending. Wayne was supposed to arrive in Abilene, get badly wounded in a gunfight with John Ireland, proceed to a showdown with Clift, fire half a dozen shots at him, and collapse in a way that makes it clear he is a dying man. He was then to be taken by Clift and Joanne Dru across the Red River, so he could die in his beloved Texas. Hawks, however, did not want Wayne to die, and the result is an artificial ending in which Clift refuses to fire at Wayne, and Joanne Dru intrudes on the showdown, saying something like, "Now, you two boys please stop fighting," which, sheepishly, they do.

RED RIVER, fortunately, is a strong film. The first two hours are so good they cannot be ruined by a bad

Hard, tough, vast in scale, and beautiful in images, RED RIVER is one of the great westerns and among the finest accomplishments of Howard Hawks. Again, John Wayne dominated the screen, but in RED RIVER a major new talent appeared — Montgomery Clift (far right). The love-hate battles of Wayne and Clift, as father and surrogate son, told in the context of a tale of the first cattle drive on the Chisholm Trail, give movie its interesting blend of character conflict and epic sweep. But resolution is badly bungled and the final minutes are disappointing. It took all of Hawks' great feeling for terrain and understanding of men in groups to make RED RIVER work.

final five minutes. However much one may wish to do so, one simply cannot justify Wayne's final actions in this movie in terms of the sort of magical character transformation that occurs in THE SEARCHERS, when he recognizes that he loves Natalie Wood and cannot kill her. His recognition of his love and admiration for Montgomery Clift in RED RIVER is bungled and comes close to being silly.

(In the same interview Borden Chase tells an amusing anecdote about how Wayne, rehearsing the way he will enter Abilene and pass obliviously through the cattle herd, wrecked much of Chase's living-room furniture.)

The aftermath of the stampede is a perfect expression of Hawks' continuing concern with the behavior of men in groups. Bunk Kenneally has caused a stampede by sneaking into the chuckwagon at night and knocking over a pile of pots and pans while in search of sugar. The spooked cattle erupt, and in the ensuing commotion Dan Latimer is overrun and killed. After Wayne has buried Latimer he turns to the business of punishing Kenneally, whom he proposes to tie to a wagon wheel and whip, a perfectly justifiable use of power to Hawks, since in his world a man becomes a pariah and deserves to be pun-

ished when he lets his companions down.

RED RIVER, among other things, was the film that made Montgomery Clift a star. More than five thousand head of cattle (at $10 per day per head) were used in the filming, some of which had their faces painted white. Rainstorms held up shooting and the budget doubled from the original estimate to something close to $3.5 million.

RED RIVER is characterized by Howard Hawks' famous eye-level shooting, and is one of the most beautiful of all black-and-white westerns. Its stupendous shots of the cattle drive, particularly the scene on the morning of the departure from Texas, are spectacular and memorable, and the funeral scene, surprisingly close to similar ceremonial scenes in John Ford films, is embellished by the miraculous effect of a cloud passing the sun and casting a shadow on the background. (This same effect is equally moving in a scene in BONNIE AND CLYDE.) When asked how he achieved it, Hawks admitted that, of course, it was a fortuitous accident. While shooting the funeral he saw the cloud coming, indicated to Wayne that he should hurry up with his speech, and the mountains behind were darkened at just the right moment.

George Stevens' Shane 1953

There can be little doubt that if George Stevens had wanted that cloud-shadow effect in SHANE, he would not have achieved it accidentally but by design, even if that meant setting up the scene and waiting days on end for the proper sun-clouds-mountains conjunction to take place. This is the very thing that annoys some people about SHANE: the aestheticizing, the contrived beauty, the calculated precision, the perfection which, annoying or not, is the picture's major strength.

SHANE is no rough-and-ready western like RED RIVER, nor a meditation on history and character like THE SEARCHERS. It is the most self-conscious attempt ever made to use the western form to create a myth. SHANE is a willed legend, an invented artifact, and as such it represents at one extreme the furthest possibilities of the film as instant mythology—and, at the other, a decadence paralleled in such aspects of contemporary culture as the tattered and patched-up poorboy jacket that costs $600 and is designed by a Parisian couturier. Only a most sophisticated filmmaker could have achieved the studied simplicity of SHANE. Only a man in total control of his medium could have created so perfect a primitive folktale. These things

are mentioned not to put George Stevens down, but, on the contrary, to say that even when one understands exactly what SHANE is, one may still be moved by it, and one most certainly must admire Stevens' mastery of technique.

The dualism between right and wrong in SHANE is central to this technique. Alan Ladd as Shane, the good-guy gunfighter who chooses his cause on principle, is a golden prince, a blond-haired superman in fringed buckskin. His antithesis and enemy, Jack Palance, the bad-guy gunfighter for hire, is dark, dresses in black, and even drinks black coffee from a blackened pot. Ladd radiates spirituality; Palance radiates evil and menace. Ladd is a knight-errant who shoots to kill only when reason fails and after the exhaustion of all other less deadly means of settlement. Palance is a black knight who enjoys killing and has no compunction about shooting an opponent who is clearly unequal to him in fighting skill.

In addition to using dualism, Stevens creates his myth by heightening certain standard western rituals. In SHANE the fistfight, the gun duel, the funeral, and even idealized love are pushed to extremes and then placed in an allegory about the settlement and civilization of the

George Stevens' SHANE is very
much an exercise in
instant myth-making. Every one
of its images is composed
with extreme care:
The deer (below, l.) will raise
its head and frame the
oncoming rider perfectly between
the branches of its antlers.

SHANE is the story of a
duel between good and evil.
Good is represented by
Alan Ladd (l.), the
golden-haired prince in
buckskin. Evil is Jack
Palance, merciless, black-
clad hit-man for the
cattle interests. Above: He
kills Elisha Cook, Jr.

Action sequences of SHANE
are balanced off by the story of
two relationships: unspoken,
desexualized love between Ladd
and Jean Arthur (above, with
Van Heflin as her farmer husband),
and hero-worship of Shane by
Brandon de Wilde. Bottom, right:
Shane says goodbye to Joey
in famous, poignant ending.

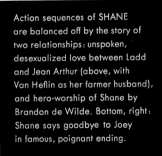

George Stevens' conception of
the West is exemplified in
the funeral sequence (r.) in
which life and death, town
and country, people and the land
all may be grasped in a single
view. Note the austerity
of the town, represented in the
background by a single,
isolated row of frame buildings.

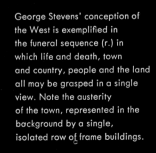

West. The fistfight in SHANE is a Big Fistfight. The gun duel involves some of the fastest gunplay one is likely to see. The funeral in SHANE is much more studied than the funerals in THE SEARCHERS and RED RIVER. The people are grouped more artfully; their buckboards and the covered wagon of the mourning family are positioned with perfection; the reactions of the children and the domestic animals are purified to the point that the dead man's dog actually scratches mournfully at his grave. Cattle graze here and there. The tiny settlement that is the setting of the allegory is lonely on the plain behind, and in the background stands the powerful wall of the Grand Teton mountains of Wyoming, magnificently luminous, captured in perfect light. According to Stevens, this arrangement symbolizes what the West was all about: a continuity between life and death, a positioning of elements, so that all of existence could be grasped at a single glance.

It may be instructive to compare the idealized love between Alan Ladd and Jean Arthur in SHANE with the unspoken love between John Wayne and Dorothy Jordan in THE SEARCHERS. In the latter film, the scene in which Dorothy Jordan caresses John Wayne's army cape and is observed by Ward Bond, who simply notices her gesture and looks away, is typical of the throwaway enrichment of the story. As far as John Ford is concerned, if you pick up on it that's fine, and if you don't then that's all right, too. But in SHANE Stevens makes certain that everything that is unspoken between Ladd and Jean Arthur, every gesture and every glance in every scene, tells us of their impossible and unrealizable love. To make sure we get all the implications, he has the boy, Joey (Brandon de Wilde), make naïve utterances that demonstrate that he senses what has been going on, too. Though one may prefer Ford's subtlety, one must give Stevens credit for having ingeniously inserted a love story into a western—a love story that tantalizes adults and yet does not turn children off the adventure.

The special rhythms of the dialogue of SHANE reinforce all its other myth-making effects. For instance: "Yes, he was fast—he was fast on the draw"; "A man's got to be what he is—you can't break the mold"; and the cadence with which Shane says to Ryker, "I'm a friend of Starrett."

Shane is the ultimate example of that classic character of the western, the melancholic and mysterious stranger who is the fastest gun alive. Take his control, the way he sidesteps a fight until he sees that it is inevitable, and then goes into it without fear. We have seen this kind of man before, the gunfighter with the implied violent past, who will do everything in his power to avoid a showdown and whose avoidance is often misconstrued as cowardice. We want Shane to show Joey how brave and fast he is, and then when Shane does fight, we feel ashamed because we know that the glow of hero-worship in Joey's eyes is there for the wrong reasons, and that Shane knew better than we that once he killed he would be tainted and would have to leave the valley. What is admirable about Shane is not his skill with his gun, but his restraint in using it—something that Joey will understand in time. Joey's famous cry at the end of the picture ("Come back, Shane....") is the cry of all of us for a mythical West that never was, and for a mythical hero so perfect he would not allow himself to be admired by a boy for living by the gun. SHANE is a movie that not only presents its story as a myth, but that evokes nostalgia for itself before it even ends.

Sam Peckinpah's The Wild Bunch 1969

If SHANE makes a myth of the West, THE WILD BUNCH demythologizes it. If SHANE draws sharp moral distinctions that are, literally, black and white, THE WILD BUNCH blurs all moral distinctions, offering us only choices between various modes of immorality. If in SHANE violence is viewed as a necessary evil only to be employed as a last resort, and killing is depicted as swift and clean, in THE WILD BUNCH violence is viewed with exaltation, and killing is prolonged, tormented, and bloody. In short, within the genre of the western, THE WILD BUNCH is the precise opposite of SHANE. Each film may be considered an artifact of a view of the American frontier. SHANE, made during the quietude of 1953, romanticizes and idealizes. THE WILD BUNCH, made fifteen years later in a turbulent time, tells us that the American Dream is dead.

The opening sequence of THE WILD BUNCH stakes out the moral territory. A band of outlaws masquerading as soldiers rides into a town, passing children torturing a scorpion and adults attending a temperance meeting. The band robs a railway office, then finds itself ambushed by a gang of bounty hunters working for the railroad. A ferocious gunfight erupts, many innocent bystanders are killed, and the children afterward wander among the bodies mimicking the dying with glee. We know at once that we are in a terrain that is beyond good or evil, a world of arbitrary violence where the only morality consists of such distinctions as Pike's (William Holden's) pronouncement that "when you side with a man, you stick with him; otherwise you might as well be some kind of animal...."

This moral confusion continues throughout the story as the U. S. Cavalry (the *deus ex machina* in Ford's westerns) is revealed as a mob of bungling fools, the management of the Pacific Railroad (so often the pioneering force in westerns) is depicted as a ruthless enterprise that employs scum as henchmen, children (so often used as symbols of innocence) are shown to be amoral, and the entire myth of the frontier is debunked. If there are any myths left unexploded in the film, they take place on the Mexican side of the border, where the bandits' departure from a village is staged as it might have been in SHANE. (This scene has been criticized as being overly senti-

mental, but that's just the point. The time of the film is 1913, when the American frontier was closing fast. Mexico, on the other hand, was still in a romantic era, the time of Pancho Villa and the Mexican Revolution.)

The credit title for Sam Peckinpah, who directed THE WILD BUNCH, comes on the screen directly after William Holden snarls at his men: "If they move, kill 'em!" This juxtaposition is in keeping with Peckinpah's reputation as a connoisseur of violence. In THE WILD BUNCH he presents the violent scenes passionately, even excessively, and it is his passion and excess that make the picture great. When a man is killed we see blood gush from his body. In THE WILD BUNCH we even see a full frontal view of a man's throat being cut. There are at least two hundred violent deaths in the picture, and Peckinpah often aestheticizes this violence by showing it in slow motion, as Kurosawa did in the early reels of THE SEVEN SAMURAI.

THE WILD BUNCH probably was influenced by the SEVEN SAMURAI, not only stylistically and in terms of its virtuoso sequences of violent action, but also in theme.

41

Robert Ryan (top, c.) and his cutthroat bounty hunters pose for a publicity shot for THE WILD BUNCH. (Strother Martin and L. Q. Jones are top, extreme l. & r.). In Peckinpah's original version, relationship between Ryan and William Holden, the hard-bitten leader of the bunch, was clear, but later studio cuts obscured it.

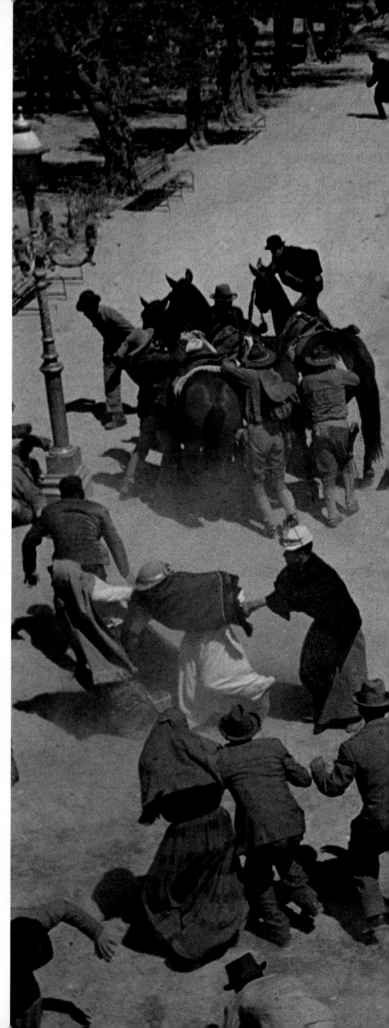

Right: Chaos in the streets, as innocent bystanders get slaughtered in crossfire during attempted robbery of railroad office in opening reels of THE WILD BUNCH. Below: William Holden, flanked by Ernest Borgnine and Warren Oates, leads remnants of the wild bunch against troops of the Mexican despot in an orgy of blood, destruction, and death. Bottom: Scummy bounty hunters crawl over bodies searching for loot at picture's end.

42

The bigger-than-life characters are killed off in both films. If there is a winner at the end of THE WILD BUNCH it is the Mexican peasants who are at last rid of their oppressors, just as the Japanese peasants are said to be the only winners at the end of THE SEVEN SAMURAI.

This "aesthetic of violence," this use of slow motion to prolong dying and turn it into a ballet, has been attributed to a love of violence that Peckinpah is supposed to possess. Actually, it has to do with a legitimate desire to show us what it feels like to kill, sensualizing the killer's pleasure by subjectifying and then prolonging the death of his adversaries. In these terms, the "ballets of death" can be understood as condemnations of violence. Still, one senses an ambiguous attitude in Peckinpah. He, too, seems to be savoring the gyrations of men who have been killed but have not yet bitten the dust.

Another parallel between THE WILD BUNCH and THE SEVEN SAMURAI is in the excellence of the acting. Like Kurosawa, Peckinpah creates his characters in depth, a rare feat in an action movie. Even the smallest parts in

THE WILD BUNCH are superbly played. William Holden has never been better than as the aging outlaw, Pike. The sequence in which he decides to rescue Angel is brilliant. In the hands of most actors and directors, a scene such as this, in which a character is shown making up his mind, is usually embarrassing, especially when actor and director think they can bring it off without dialogue. Holden and Peckinpah have no such difficulty. All the relationships in THE WILD BUNCH are convincing, especially the scenes between Robert Ryan and Albert Dekker, when they argue about the scummy bounty hunters.

The final sequence in the Mexican courtyard is extraordinary. After Holden has shot Mapache, he and his companions stand with drawn guns facing hundreds of surprised Mexicans for several seconds of calm. It is clear that the wild bunch is condemned. They are surrounded, outgunned, as good as dead. They realize it, we realize it. At that point, it is simply a question of how many men they will take with them. The moment passes. Holden shoots Mapache's German advisor between the eyes, and we find ourselves in the greatest scene of bloodshed and slaughter ever filmed, with Peckinpah's excesses carrying us to ever higher plateaus of exaltation (while Lucien Ballard provides brilliant cinematography).

If the story of THE WILD BUNCH is against the classic western, the imagery is in its best tradition. Peckinpah may be the only one of the younger American directors to have the feeling for the grandeur of the West and for the look of men in its landscapes that one finds in the westerns of John Ford. There is a scene in THE WILD BUNCH, when Pike's band holds up and captures an ammunition train, that is staged and shot with the precision and suspense of a great action sequence. There are many directors (e.g., Jules Dassin) who would use such a scene as a culminating sequence. It is as good a heist as one is likely to see on the screen. But Peckinpah does not linger over it. He has many great scenes, such as the long-lens, slow-motion shot of Ryan and the bounty hunters as the bridge explodes, a shot that classicizes a violent moment, prolonging it for eternity. Such is the richness of texture of his film that he can afford to dazzle us for a few moments with the train heist and then move on, more or less throwing a great scene away.

THE WILD BUNCH is a picture that dares to be excessive. Peckinpah courts condemnation and risks disaster by putting so personal and unorthodox a conception upon the screen. Because he is successful, a case can be made that THE WILD BUNCH is not only great within the genre of the western, but may be among the very greatest films of the 1960s.

44

Sam Peckinpah is considered difficult and intransigent when up against ignorant studio personnel and uncooperative crews. Though THE WILD BUNCH was badly mutilated by Warner Brothers, it gained Peckinpah his reputation as connoisseur of violence and reinterpreter of the western.

Credits

The Searchers

U.S.A.; 1956; 119 minutes;
released by Warner Bros.

Directed by	John Ford.
Produced by	Merian C. Cooper.
Screenplay by	Frank S. Nugent, from the novel by Alan LeMay.
Photographed by	Winton C. Hoch.
Art direction by	Frank Hotaling and James Basevi.
Edited by	Jack Murray.
Music by	Max Steiner.
Cast:	John Wayne; Jeffrey Hunter; Vera Miles; Ward Bond; Natalie Wood; John Qualen; Olive Carey; Henry Brandon; Ken Curtis; Harry Carey, Jr.; Dorothy Jordan; Pippa Scott; Antonio Moreno; Pat Wayne; Hank Worden; Lana Wood; Walter Coy; Beulah Archuletta.

Shane

U.S.A.; 1953; 116 minutes;
released by Paramount.

Directed by	George Stevens.
Produced by	George Stevens.
Screenplay by	A. B. Guthrie, Jr., from the novel by Jack Schaefer (additional dialogue by Jack Sher).
Photographed by	Loyal Griggs.
Art direction by	Hal Pereira and Walter Tyler.
Edited by	William Hornbeck and Tom McAdoo.
Music by	Victor Young.
Cast:	Alan Ladd; Jean Arthur; Van Heflin; Brandon de Wilde; Jack Palance; Ben Johnson; Edgar Buchanan; Emile Meyer; Elisha Cook, Jr.; Douglas Spencer; John Dierkes; Ellen Corby; Paul McVey; John Miller; Edith Evanson; Leonard Strong; Ray Spiker.

Stagecoach

U.S.A.; 1939; 105 minutes;
released by United Artists.

Directed by	John Ford.
Produced by	Walter Wanger.
Screenplay by	Dudley Nichols, based on the story ''Stage to Lordsburg'' by Ernest Haycox.
Photographed by	Bert Glennon.
Art direction by	Alexander Toluboff.
Edited by	Dorothy Spencer and Walter Reynolds.
Music by	Richard Hageman, W. Franke Harling, John Leipold, Leo Shuken, Louis Gruenberg (adapted from 17 American folktunes of the early 1880s).
Cast:	John Wayne; Claire Trevor; Thomas Mitchell; Andy Devine; George Bancroft; Donald Meek; Louise Platt; John Carradine; Berton Churchill; Tim Holt; Joseph Rickson.

Red River

U.S.A.; 1948; 125 minutes;
released by United Artists.

Directed by	Howard Hawks.
Produced by	Howard Hawks.
Screenplay by	Borden Chase and Charles Schnee, from the story ''The Blazing Guns on the Chisholm Trail'' by Borden Chase.
Photographed by	Russell Harlan.
Art direction by	John Datu Arensma.
Edited by	Christian Nyby.
Music by	Dimitri Tiomkin.
Cast:	John Wayne; Montgomery Clift; Joanne Dru; Walter Brennan; Coleen Gray; John Ireland; Noah Beery, Jr.; Chief Yowlachie; Harry Carey, Sr.; Harry Carey, Jr.

The Wild Bunch

U.S.A.; 1969; 143 minutes;
released by Warner Bros.

Directed by	Sam Peckinpah.
Produced by	Phil Feldman.
Screenplay by	Walon Green and Sam Peckinpah, based on a story by Walon Green and Roy N. Sickner.
Photographed by	Lucien Ballard.
Art direction by	Edward Carrere.
Edited by	Louis Lombardo.
Music by	Jerry Fielding.
Cast:	William Holden; Ernest Borgnine; Robert Ryan; Edmond O'Brien; Warren Oates; Jaime Sanchez; Ben Johnson; Emilio Fernandez; Strother Martin; L. Q. Jones; Albert Dekker; Bo Hopkins; Bob Taylor.

Intrigue & Suspense

2

Call them films of intrigue and suspense, or crime and punishment, include the subgenres of the gangster flick, the private-eye flick, the spy and espionage story, the *policier* and the thriller—in the end one is talking about the same thing: a certain kind of action picture characterized by certain specific ingredients, criteria, if you will, for greatness within the genre.

1. A great film of intrigue and suspense must be entertaining. Nothing falls so flat as the suspense picture with weak suspense, or the crime-and-punishment film in which the crime is ordinary and the punishment is feeble. Films in this genre must move inexorably, remorselessly. They must take hold of the attention of the audience and not let go. No message is necessary, though it's all right if the director wants to throw one in; the important thing is that he remember always that the raison d'être of his picture is its ability to entertain.

2. A great film of intrigue and suspense must be complex. Nothing simple-minded will do. The more twists and turns the better. Often the story is about a spider web of entrapment, or the double or triple cross. At times it is so complex that the motivations and subplots become impenetrable. It does not matter, because complexity in this genre is an end in itself. The pictures are made for chess players and problem-solvers, who will return a second or third time if necessary in order to unscramble the infernal internal logic of the story.

3. A great film of intrigue and suspense must be strongly visual. Each shot must make a point. Each must be stunning to the eye. Each must move a character or the story forward. Each, above all, must be designed. Intrigue and suspense is a B-picture genre; the object is entertainment, not art. Production budgets are medium or low, and the form is restrictive in that certain conventions must be observed, i.e., police procedures, the chase, the final confrontation, etc. The filmmaker, then, must work under pressure, expressing himself more in visual terms than in terms of message, theme, or meaning. All the great directors who have worked within this genre—Hitchcock, Reed, Lang, Welles, Hawks, Fuller, Siegel, Huston, Walsh—are men whose work has visual distinction. The way in which they stage and shoot what is basically a standard type of event—the way, in short, that they impose themselves on their material—is the way we measure their achievement.

4. A great film of intrigue and suspense takes place in a special sort of urban world. These pictures are often called *films noirs* because they take place in a fictional landscape which might be called the "night city." This is an environment of bars, and back streets, peopled by whores, junkies, psychopaths, henchmen, gunslingers, gamblers, and private eyes. The night city is a world beyond good and evil, estranged from the values of the middle class, a demimonde. The way the night city—the terrain—of a film of intrigue and suspense is depicted is very much to the point in judging its success.

Fritz Lang's M 1932

M is an inevitable choice, a masterpiece in its own right, and in many respects the grandfather of the genre. Unlike other early pictures, it does not seem quaint on account of primitivism. It is as strong and gripping an entertainment as it was the day it opened, and although it is one of the earliest German sound films, it contains some uses of sound which have yet to be surpassed. M is as visually strong a picture as has ever been made, and its depiction of the night city is exceptional.

The screenplay, written by Fritz Lang's wife, Thea von Harbou, was based on the true story of the famous Düsseldorf child-murderer, Kürten. His crimes so upset the underworld that it organized an independent attempt to identify him and track him down. This, basically, is the story. M, the first letter of the word "murderer," is chalked on Hans Beckert's (Peter Lorre's) jacket to iden-

tify him when he is being shadowed by members of the "Beggars Union."

While law-enforcement officials, who are mercilessly satirized, use modern police methods to identify the psychotic Beckert, the underworld employs its own skills and personnel, and succeeds in catching him first. It tries him before a kangaroo court, sentences him to death, and is about to render punishment, despite pleas that "I can't help myself" (shouted, screamed, and whimpered with all the force at Peter Lorre's command), when the police suddenly arrive and take him away to a fair trial.

There is some sort of message here, typical of Lang at the time, probably a result of his thoughts about Nazism, that "the Law" is the only thing that stands between civilization and anarchy. Thus, the battle between the underworld and the police over the destiny of

48

Opening pages: Torment
and claustrophobia in the
final moments of Fritz
Lang's M, as Peter Lorre
pleads for mercy before
underworld tribunal.
Gustaf Gründgens (wearing
derby) plays master criminal
Schränker in this famous
scene set in deserted brewery.
This page: Police aide with
Detective "Fatty" Lohmann (Otto
Wernicke) in sleepless
search for clues; Lorre
finds he is marked as "M";
symbol shot of child victim,
murderer's shadow, and
reward poster. Lang's "night
city" is embellished
with geometric compositions,
draws viewer into an
oppressive world of terror.

49

a murderer, who is himself a split personality, half psychotic, half law-abiding, must be resolved in favor of a merciful court, not the jungle court of the underworld. As in so many films of this genre, the message tends to be simplistic, and comes close to being undercut by the satire. What is important in M is the expression of the story. The visual ideas and formal elements are supreme.

Lang is not a humanist director; he could not be further from Jean Renoir. He is a manipulator, a master puppeteer, and, as a matter of fact, he belongs among the filmmakers who delight in using human beings to make designs. (See METROPOLIS. Busby Berkeley had this obsession, and so did Leni Riefenstahl.) M is full of designs, high shots in which people, along with architectural elements, are used to make geometric patterns. Note the high shot of the children, watching the organ grinder; the shot of Lorre in front of the shop window surrounded by the reflection of geometrically displayed knives, surely a portent of evil; and the configuration of underworld characters in the low-ceilinged basement of the deserted distillery. Lang's choice of certain shop windows that contain a rotating spiral and a sort of jumping-jack puppet echo another of his curious concerns: an obsession with human mechanicalism, automatic and compulsive movements, which is taken in his METROPOLIS to the fringes of madness.

In M the people are puppets, fools, hysterics. The only real exception is Peter Lorre, whose final, heart-rending cries for pity break through Lang's barrier of misanthropy and make the murderer human. No, Lang is not concerned with people, but with designs, traps, visual geometry, and structural irony.

Lang pushes the idea that the underworld and the law are after the same man as far as it will go, cutting back and forth, making ironic comparisons as the lawmen and the outlaws come up with parallel schemes. As the double trap closes tighter around Peter Lorre, the audience is drawn into the frantic hunt, a passionate pursuit carried out by men who swarm like insects. The camera angles become increasingly portentous, suggesting a constant closing-in, and the atmosphere of the night city becomes more and more nightmarish, more and more claustrophobic. An example of the tensions Lang can generate is the famous bouncing-ball sequence. We hear Mrs. Beckmann calling frantically for her lost daughter; then her cries are intercut with shots of Elsie's ball coming to rest and her balloon being caught in telephone wires. The effect is fateful and powerful. We hear the rough nasal whistling of the theme from Grieg's "Peer Gynt" whenever Peter Lorre is hanging around. The effect is ominous and frightening. Such riches, visual and oral, seem less like primitive experiments than contemporary usages. Many of these effects, the use of a child's ball, the use of music, montages of police evidence, and the construction of a trap, turn up in basically the same form, seventeen years later, in Carol Reed's THE THIRD MAN.

Alfred Hitchcock's **Rear Window** 1954

We come now to the man whose name is synonymous with the genre, the towering presence, the supreme champion of intrigue and suspense. We are speaking, of course, of Alfred Hitchcock, who has built a career on films of this sort, and has made nearly fifty of them. If we wished, we could quite easily find five great intrigue-and-suspense films among his works: THE MAN WHO KNEW TOO MUCH (1934 version), THE 39 STEPS, and THE LADY VANISHES from his early English period, and NOTORIOUS, STRANGERS ON A TRAIN, and the very great VERTIGO from his Hollywood years, with SUSPICION, SHADOW OF A DOUBT, SPELLBOUND, and NORTH BY NORTHWEST coming in very strong. Why then choose REAR WINDOW? Simply because it comes very close to being the perfect Hitchcock film, the one that illustrates nearly all his major strengths.

In the first place, Hitchcock is a voyeur, and God knows REAR WINDOW is a film about voyeurism. Hitchcock loves to spy on his characters through windows—this is a recurring motif in his films—and REAR WINDOW comes to grips with the problem once and for all: James Stewart, forced to stay in his apartment because of a broken leg, spies on people through windows in an orgy of voyeurism one hundred and twelve minutes long.

Secondly, REAR WINDOW is an archetypal Hitchcock film for the way it rises to meet a difficult technical challenge. Ninety-nine percent of REAR WINDOW is shot from within James Stewart's apartment, and more than half of the shots simulate his point of view. Hitchcock imposes limitations on himself, as he did in LIFEBOAT, where he used a single location, and in ROPE, where he shot in real continuous time, as though in one unbroken scene. Having boxed himself in, Hitchcock is required to be ingenious,

50

Great master Alfred Hitchcock presides over single
set of REAR WINDOW. James Stewart and Grace Kelly play
the leads in this orgy of voyeurism. Behind them,
on the other side of the "window," are
apertures into the miniature world that reflects
their personal problems in many variations.

to construct a set and people it in such a way that the restriction becomes a strength, that the solution becomes an example of what he likes to call "pure cinema." He has never been more successful in meeting a technical challenge than in REAR WINDOW, which is constantly energized by his imaginative solutions to his problems.

Thirdly, REAR WINDOW represents Hitchcock at his best for the way it works on many levels, yet conceals its own complexity. Many Hitchcock films seem to be light entertainments, but often, particularly in his American period, there is a dark side to them, a psychological probing, an inner exploration that parallels in some way the exterior events. In REAR WINDOW, Stewart is not only restricted to his apartment by his broken leg, but is boxed in, too, by pressure from Grace Kelly, who wants to marry him. Everything he sees out of the rear window of his apartment is related to this problem, though he himself does not seem to realize it. All the people he spies on represent different facets of married life, or the miseries of being single: the older, childless couple who have invested their emotions in a pet dog; the newlywed and ultracarnal lovers; "Miss Lonelyhearts" and her fantasies of entertaining gentlemen callers; and, most important, the couple across the backyard, the bedridden woman and the husband who murders her because he can no longer abide the tyranny of her illness. The murderer and his wife parody Stewart's problem with Grace Kelly on a nightmare scale. While looking out, Stewart is forced to look subconsciously within himself. His backyard view reflects a miniature universe of stories relating to love and marriage, and they relate to his problems, too. The urban backyard setting is the night city terrain of REAR WINDOW, a night city of the soul reflecting the mysterious, unfathomable darkness that lurks inside an ordinary man in an ordinary situation tyrannized by a sick, complaining, difficult wife.

Fourth, REAR WINDOW is visually very strong, reflecting that precise use of designed shots that has made Hitchcock famous. Hitchcock is not a director who arrives on his set and says: "I don't know what to do today. Let's improvise." He knows precisely what he wants to do. His film is completed in his head and in his sketches before he ever steps onto his set. Shooting and editing are for him simply mechanical phases. The creativity has all taken place before.

The first shot of REAR WINDOW is a perfect example of this, and typical of many Hitchcock first shots for the way it visually conveys exposition to the audience. The camera pans from Stewart's face to the cast on his leg to a broken camera on a table to photographs on the wall, including photographs of smashed-up racing cars. We know without a word of dialogue that Stewart has a broken leg, that he is a photographer, that he specializes in action photography, and that he probably broke his leg taking a photo of an auto race.

Hitchcock is a master at using his camera to create suspense. In REAR WINDOW we see Grace Kelly rummaging inside the murderer's apartment, when the murderer appears suddenly in the hall outside his front door. Stewart can see all this from his rear window, and we can see it, too, though neither of the characters under observation is yet aware of the other's presence. Like Stewart in his chair, we are helpless. We cannot warn Grace Kelly. We want to scream out: "Watch out! Escape! Hide!" This is what suspense is all about—not surprise, but helplessness in the face of knowledge that we possess but the characters do not. In this particular scene the suspense is amplified by the fact that we are in the same position as Stewart, restricted inside his apartment. And, of course, this strong suspense is created by purely visual means.

In REAR WINDOW, we find two other Hitchcock specialties: the use of an object as a major clue, and the use of major motion-picture stars. The object is the wedding ring. Grace Kelly says the murderer's wife would not have left town without her wedding ring, so if the ring can be found there is strong reason to believe a murder has been committed. The ring, then, is the giveaway, as was the cut-off finger in THE 39 STEPS, the cigarette lighter in STRANGERS ON A TRAIN, the reversely rotating windmill in FOREIGN CORRESPONDENT, etc., through twenty or thirty pictures. Truffaut points out that the wedding ring in REAR WINDOW has double significance, since Grace Kelly wants to marry Stewart. When she indicates to him that she has found it, the smile on her face constitutes a double victory—another example of complexity and layered meaning in Hitchcock.

As for the use of major film stars, this is something for which Hitchcock is often criticized. He has used Cary Grant, Gregory Peck, James Stewart, Laurence Olivier, Robert Montgomery, Joseph Cotten, Montgomery Clift, Farley Granger, Paul Newman, Anthony Perkins, Grace Kelly, Kim Novak, Doris Day, Janet Leigh, Marlene Dietrich, Ingrid Bergman, Joan Fontaine, and many, many more. The sin here is supposed to be that Hitchcock is dependent on stars because he is weak with actors, a snobbish myth. The fact is that James Stewart in REAR WINDOW, as well as in VERTIGO, ROPE, and THE MAN WHO KNEW TOO MUCH (1955 version), gives the performances of his life, behaving with a naturalness of which more "actorish" actors are not capable. Stewart is the perfect

Hitchcock character, an ordinary-looking, unpretentious man who becomes enmeshed in extraordinary, nightmarish events. An extraordinary thing happening in an everyday situation to an average person is one of the continuing motifs in Hitchcock's films.

Alfred Hitchcock is in fashion now, thanks to his idolization by French critics whose views have been re-imported and have finally made him respectable in his adopted country. For years he was not taken seriously in America. He was the funny little fat man who liked to appear in his own movies, a put-on artist guilty of the worst of all sins, making pictures the public liked, which meant, of course, that his pictures were bad. The incredible thing is that, as late as 1967, Bosley Crowther could write a book entitled *The Great Films* and not discuss a single picture of Alfred Hitchcock in his text.

Carol Reed's The Third Man 1949

THE THIRD MAN is a flawless film of intrigue and suspense, a summit of perfection within the genre. It is one of the most literate thrillers ever made. (The original screenplay was by the great British writer, Graham Greene, who lated adapted his screenplay into a novel.) It is superbly acted by an ensemble working in an understated, effortless style (Joseph Cotten, Orson Welles, Trevor Howard). Its cinematography includes some of the best black-and-white work ever done. (Robert Krasker won the Academy Award against SUNSET BOULEVARD, ALL ABOUT EVE, and THE ASPHALT JUNGLE!) Its score of haunting zither music by Anton Karas is still remembered, instantly familiar to anyone who ever saw the film, and now thoroughly identified with most people's impressions of Vienna. Finally, the producing of Alexander Korda (known for having "saved" the British film industry on account of his "quality" productions) and the direction by Carol Reed are exemplary. Rarely has a motion picture represented the collaboration of so many exceptional talents. THE THIRD MAN may be the greatest film made in Britain since World War II.

The night city terrain of THE THIRD MAN is unique: occupied postwar Vienna, baroque, bombed-out, decadent, patrolled by Jeeps containing representatives of the four occupying powers, an American, an Englishman, a Frenchman, and a Russian. Corrupt, world-weary people hang about its fringes: the overly suave Rumanian, Popescu; the frayed violinist, Baron Kurtz; the atheistic collector of Catholic antiquities, Dr. Winkel; Crabbit, the tired head of the Anglo Cultural Center; and Anna Schmidt, the Czechoslovakian girl friend of Harry Lime, an obscure actress with forged papers. Moving among them are three extraordinary principals, Holly Martins, a typical Greene creation, a hack American writer, a used-up second-rater; Colonel Calloway, a Scotland Yard type, chief of British Military Police; and Harry Lime (Welles),

the corrupt two-bit racketeer, an utterly immoral, totally unreachable villain. These characters wander through rain-slick night streets, in and out of shabby cafés, over the rubble of bombed-out buildings, even into a *terrain vague* dominated by a huge Ferris wheel. The Vienna of THE THIRD MAN is a vast city that seems empty. Its streets are always damp, and water rushes through a system of sweet-smelling sewers underneath. It is a world of slinking cats and biting parrots, of people taking advantage of each other without pity. Its morality is summed up by Orson Welles in lines he wrote for himself. Speaking of his trafficking in stolen and diluted penicillin which has turned children into zombies, Welles excuses himself with the words: "After all, it's not that awful. You know what the fellow said: In Italy for thirty years under the Borgias they had warfare, terror, murder, bloodshed—they produced Michelangelo, Leonardo da Vinci, and the Renaissance. In Switzerland they had brotherly love, five hundred years of democracy and peace, and what did they produce? The cuckoo clock!" Colonel Calloway sums up the sense of entrapment when he speaks to Anna of Harry Lime's chances of escape: "Vienna is a closed city. A rat would have more chance in a closed room without a hole and a pack of terriers loose."

THE THIRD MAN meets the test of complexity. The characters interact, their stories conflict: A man who is supposed to be dead turns up alive, there is a question of whether two men or a "third man" carried off Lime's "body," there are conspiracies, deceits, and double crosses. Martins agrees to be the bait in a trap to catch Harry Lime if Calloway will get the Russians off Anna's back, but when Anna accuses him of being an informer he loses his nerve and decides to leave Vienna. He is only persuaded to be Calloway's "dumb decoy duck" when he is taken to the childrens' ward of a hospital and shown the damage that Lime has done. In the end he kills Lime,

53

Above: Director Carol Reed consults with star Orson Welles on location in the sewers of Vienna during shooting of THE THIRD MAN. Welles' characterization of Harry Lime, corrupt denizen of another atmospheric "night city," is unforgettable. Reed's precise direction, along with a brilliant script, a great score, and fine performances, makes this a nearly perfect film. Reed owes large directorial debts to Lang and Hitchcock, but his own contributions were immense.

his best friend, who in the last moments of his life becomes an almost sympathetic character, wounded, cornered, frightened, trying to crawl out of the sewers, his fingers twitching pathetically in a grille in the center of a moist, wind-blown, empty plaza.

Reed owes debts to Fritz Lang for some of his ideas: the geometrical shots, the montage of evidence, Welles' whistling, etc., but Reed has his own original visual style, particularly his use of a slightly tilted camera to produce so-called "Chinese angles," employed to project danger, foreboding, a twisted universe. He is also capable of providing suspense in the tradition of Hitchcock. One thinks particularly of Martins' mysterious "kidnapping," which turns out to be the result of a misunderstanding. He has been booked by mistake as a speaker to a literary society, and when his incompetence causes the audience to shuffle out, he gets into a verbal duel with Popescu, which only the two of them can understand. As in a Hitchcock film, we in the film audience also understand, but the other characters on the screen do not.

THE THIRD MAN is unique in the genre for its realism. Despite the complexities of plot, the characters are understandable, dimensional, emotionally genuine—a tribute to the fine ensemble playing and special, low-keyed acting style that is the cinematic equivalent of Graham Greene's writing.

Carol Reed was knighted for his excellence as a British filmmaker, and for a body of work that is notable for its good taste. It is this taste, of course, that works so well in THE THIRD MAN, but which has destroyed some of his other films, such as OUR MAN IN HAVANA, which require a certain amount of excess to make them work.

Orson Welles' Touch of Evil 1958

One thing of which Orson Welles cannot be accused is too much good taste. He is flamboyant, excessive, doomed, it seems, to turn a number of films into magnificent failures. He is not known principally for his *policiers*, but his TOUCH OF EVIL must stand beside the very best in the genre. It is unmistakably Wellesian. Its dazzling sound track (a Welles signature since his early days in radio), its long, complicated tracking shots, its low angles, its expressionist lighting, the heightened theatricality of its performances, its dark, brooding photography, its extensive use of the wide-angle lens, its tortuous complexity, and self-contained fictional night-city world, all mark it as the vision of a startling genius of the cinema.

TOUCH OF EVIL may be the greatest B movie ever made. It is the genre film of genre films—in the sense that the French critics refer to the genres of Hollywood B production as places where talented directors work creatively within restrictive modes. On its face, TOUCH OF EVIL is a second-rate *policier,* with some absurd moments that give it the quality of a horror picture. But beneath that veneer it is a brilliant work of a great cinematic mind, exhibiting an encyclopedia of expressionist effects, and containing a tour de force of acting. (What besides tour de force can describe a situation in which the director of a film additionally plays its principal role?)

When Orson Welles is in a film his first appearance is always theatrical. One thinks, particularly, of THE THIRD MAN, when Harry Lime's face is suddenly illumi-nated in a doorway off a wet Viennese street. In TOUCH OF EVIL Welles' first appearance, as the crooked cop Hank Quinlan, is no less startling. A police car pulls up to the scene of a killing and suddenly there is Welles, sitting in the back seat, a huge mound of flesh, bigger than life, a cigar clenched between his teeth, his face unshaven, decadent, flabby, and also vulnerable, revealing that "touch of evil," that suggestion of corruption, that is the key to the fascinating and ambiguous character he plays. From that moment we are caught between admiration of his thousand brilliant directorial effects, and fascination with his characterization of Quinlan, a characterization which constantly energizes the screen.

Stanley Kubrick once said that the first shot of a picture should be the most interesting thing the audience sees after entering the theatre. Certainly, the first shot of TOUCH OF EVIL meets this test. It may be the most dazzling first shot to appear in any film, and Welles complains of having to explain to people how it was done.

In a single, constantly moving crane shot that lasts more than three minutes, we see, first, a close-up of a time bomb being set and a shadowy figure running to a parked car and placing the bomb in its trunk; second, an obviously wealthy businessman and his floozy girl friend appearing from the background, getting into the car, and driving toward the U. S.-Mexican frontier in the fictional border town of Los Robles (by this time the camera has tracked up and back and we have seen several extra-

Orson Welles as Hank Quinlan, the crooked cop, in his TOUCH OF EVIL. Grotesquely fat and bristling with unshaven stubble, swigging soda pop, growling at everyone, planting evidence and improvising the law, Quinlan is the essence of corruption in what is perhaps the greatest ''B'' movie ever made.

ordinary long views of the pseudo-Spanish, colonnaded environment which will contain the story); third, while the car stops at a traffic light the camera swoops back down and we see the Mexican detective, Vargas (Charlton Heston) and his blonde American wife (Janet Leigh) also walking toward the frontier; fourth, the camera tracks them for a while, then picks up again on the car as both Vargas and the car meet at the customs post; fifth, we overhear dialogue between Vargas and the border guard as the car pulls out of frame; sixth, we continue with Vargas and his wife as they walk into the United States until the explosion, which we have been awaiting all this time, overlaps on the sound track.

Unfortunately, Universal-International, which released the film, superimposed main titles over part of this shot, and as a result its fluidity is somewhat diluted. But if we ignore the titles and concentrate on the action we are prepared, by the time the car explodes, to say: "My God, Orson Welles is a genius. He has made the greatest crane shot of all time." In fact, this is precisely what he has done, charging the opening of his picture with unbearable suspense, and setting forth a brilliant visual style that will dominate and at times overwhelm the film. We have spoken of great opening expository shots by Hitchcock; his is the art that conceals itself, while Welles' is the

art that cries out for attention.

Critics have written of TOUCH OF EVIL as if it were of ideological importance, finding great irony in the fact that the duel between the straight, incorruptible Vargas and the tainted, decadent Quinlan only ends when Vargas is forced to used Quinlan's dirty tricks to defeat him. Welles has said that "Hank Quinlan is the incarnation of everything I fight against politically and morally....I firmly believe that in the modern world we have to choose between the morality of the law and the morality of basic justice."

If this is, in fact, the message of TOUCH OF EVIL, it is rather imperfectly expressed in the film. No, TOUCH OF EVIL is not great on account of its ideology, nor does its powerful impact have much to do with its convoluted plot. It is great on account of its succession of brilliantly staged and bizarrely played scenes; its images and its acting and its sound track are that things that make it memorable. Thus, it is a classic B movie. Its greatness lies wholly in how the story is told, and not at all in the message or material.

In addition to its fabulous opening, TOUCH OF EVIL contains other brilliant sequences:

The scene in which Quinlan throttles Grandi with one of Janet Leigh's stockings in a claustrophobic hotel

From TOUCH OF EVIL: Janet Leigh terrorized by motorcycle gang at the Mirador Hotel. Quinlan about to kill Grandi (Akim Tamiroff); he will not use the gun, but one of Janet Leigh's stockings. Right: Charlton Heston (with moustache) as the Mexican detective, Vargas.

room while a neon light flashes outside. Welles moves ponderously and inexorably toward Akim Tamiroff, who scurries about the room; we feel as though an elephant is stalking a mouse.

Two long (four- or five-minute) scenes in single takes in the murder suspect's apartment. Welles manipulates his cast with virtuosity. There is much overlapping dialogue as everyone talks at once, and half a dozen characters are brilliantly delineated.

The appalling terrorization of Janet Leigh at the Mirador Motel by a gang of leather-jacketed teen-agers.

The ambience of the parlor where Marlene Dietrich sits amidst the paraphernalia of her past, and while a pianola tinkles in the background, delivers some marvelous lines: "Darling, you're a mess," she says when she finally recognizes Quinlan beneath his layers of fat. And, when he asks her to tell his fortune: "Your future is all used up."

An extraordinary shot in which the camera dollies back as a group of characters cross a street, tracks them across a hotel lobby, leads them into a cramped elevator, and rides with them up five floors until Vargas, who has left them in the lobby, reappears at the very moment the elevator door reopens.

The final stalking scene in a nightmare world of pumping oil derricks and garbage heaps, with Quinlan's confession echoing off Vargas' receiver.

Perhaps the best thing about TOUCH OF EVIL is the strange, decaying atmosphere of its night city, a fictional space created by Welles out of bizarre locations in Venice, California. It is a weird world of flashing neon, tawdry hotels and night clubs, crumbling arches, peeling walls, twisting alleys, and everywhere, always, heaps of trash.

The history of the film is sad. Welles was hired originally just to play the part of Quinlan, but when the producer discovered that Charlton Heston had agreed to play Vargas only because he'd assumed that Welles would also direct, Welles was quickly signed as director, too. That accidental assignment was destined to change TOUCH OF EVIL from a B movie of average potential into a masterpiece of Gothic expressionism. But the final result confused executives at Universal-International, and when the film opened to poor business, they dumped it.

The box-office failure of TOUCH OF EVIL was harmful to Welles. For years afterward, despite his great critical reputation, no American studio would touch him. "Too eccentric, too grandiose," they'd say, shaking their heads over his "self-defeating genius."

Howard Hawks' **The Big Sleep** 1946

The picture that usually springs to mind when considering that subgenre of intrigue and suspense, the private-eye film, is John Huston's THE MALTESE FALCON, an undeniably taut, tough, first-rate picture about greed and immorality and murder. Once Humphrey Bogart gets going as Sam Spade, emerging as sort of a tough-guy superman, the picture becomes powerfully magnetic. THE MALTESE FALCON (1941) is also the first of the great private-eye films and so is important for the way it stakes out a piece of territory in movie history. If it has faults, they are

that it may take itself a bit too seriously and that it tries to be too logical. There are too many scenes in which characters sit around and explain things so we can follow the complex plot.

Howard Hawks' THE BIG SLEEP, on the other hand, moves so fast and with so little concern for whether or not its complexities are grasped that at times it becomes incomprehensible. For this incredible complexity, and for its speed, its wit, its sophistication, and the fact that for too long it has been ignored, we choose it as a summit in

From THE BIG SLEEP, Humphrey
Bogart about to kiss Lauren Bacall.
After appearing together in
Hawks' TO HAVE AND HAVE NOT
(1944), they became one of Hollywood's
great acting couples. Below: Bogart
as ''shamus'' Philip Marlowe,
is menaced by Louis Heydt's gun,
tied up, and stymied as Elisha
Cook, Jr., inadvertently drinks
poison, thereby adding himself
to a mounting pile of bodies.

the subgenre, without meaning in any way to impugn the excellence of THE MALTESE FALCON. In the end, the question comes down to personal taste: Does one prefer Howard Hawks or the early John Huston, does one prefer a classic private-eye picture or a baroque one, does one prefer Bogart as Hammett's Sam Spade or as Chandler's Philip Marlowe? (The distinction between Dashiell Hammett and Raymond Chandler may not be apparent to the outsider, but to the aficionado of the detective novel it is crucial and basic.)

To speak of complexity in M, REAR WINDOW, THE THIRD MAN, and even TOUCH OF EVIL is to deal on a nursery school level with what is found in THE BIG SLEEP. The plot is so involuted, contains so many twists and turns, with bodies falling so fast, that summary is hopeless and comprehension is dicey. Even William Faulkner, who worked on the script, was confused about the plot. Someone once asked Hawks who had committed one of the murders, and Hawks, who wasn't sure, asked Faulkner. Faulkner wasn't sure either, so he and Hawks called Chandler, who told

them, "The butler did it," to which Hawks is supposed to have replied: "You're crazy; the butler was at the beach house." This anecdote says something very important about THE BIG SLEEP: that though it meets every requirement of the superior thriller, being complex, entertaining, strongly visual, and depicting a demimonde, it is very much a put-on, not to be taken seriously at all.

THE THIRD MAN is a very serious picture. It is, ultimately, about the destruction of children. THE BIG SLEEP is not serious. It has to do with a bunch of whores, pimps, henchmen, killers, blackmailers, gamblers, a debutante who sucks her thumb and gets hopped-up on dope, and a decadent general who holds court in his greenhouse (where Bogart sweats like a pig). It has Mrs. Rutledge (Lauren Bacall), who gets involved with Bogart and with whom he has an incredible conversation, exceedingly daring for the time, in which they discuss sex in terms of horse racing, and it has Bogart as Philip Marlowe, a private eye who can go into a bookstore disguised as a homosexual (hilarious if a little vulgar in these days of Gay Liberation), and then go into a bookshop across the street and have a sexual matinée with a luscious, spectacled, bluestocking nymphomaniac, played by Dorothy Malone. The dialogue is racy, witty, tough, and full of erotic innuendos, so funny that before contemporary college audiences, more than a quarter of a century after its original release, THE BIG SLEEP brings down the house.

To make a critical analysis of THE BIG SLEEP is to take a skillful put-on entertainment too seriously. Suffice to say that it is richly satirical, that Bogart and Bacall together are marvelous, that there is good gunplay, fancy footwork, a Chinese statuette with a camera concealed inside, a pile of bodies, and that Bogart, as the "shamus," is at the top of his form. Perhaps some snatches of dialogue will convey something of the flavor:

Bacall's younger sister to Bogart: "You're a mess, aren't you?" Bogart's reply: "I'm not very tall either. Next time I'll come on stilts, wear a white tie, and carry a tennis racket."

Bogart re some bloodstains on the floor: "Maybe he had meat for dinner; maybe he likes to do his butchering in his parlor."

Bacall to Bogart: "You go too far, Marlowe." Bogart to Bacall: "Those are hard words to throw at a man, especially when he's walking out of your bedroom."

Two private-eye pictures were made in recent years in an attempt to revive the subgenre: Jack Smight's HARPER, starring Paul Newman, and Peter Yates' BULLITT, starring Steve McQueen. Among many other things they teach us that Humphrey Bogart is irreplaceable.

62

Bogart was one of the few actors who didn't look ridiculous holding a gun. For ten years he played minor parts, until in 1941 he appeared as Sam Spade in John Huston's THE MALTESE FALCON. After that he was king of American films noirs, perhaps never so good as in THE BIG SLEEP.

Credits

M
Germany; 1932; 99 minutes;
released in the U.S. by Janus.

Directed by Fritz Lang.
Produced by Nero Film A.G.
Screenplay by Thea von Harbou, after
an article by Egon Jacobson,
in collaboration with Paul Falkenberg,
Adolf Jansen and Karl Vash.
Photographed by Fritz Arno Wagner.
Art direction by Emil Hasler and Karl Vollbrecht.
Edited by Paul Falkenberg.
Music by Edvard Grieg, abstract from ''Peer Gynt.''
Cast: Peter Lorre; Otto Wernicke;
Gustaf Gründgens; Ellen Widmann; Inge Landgut;
Ernst Stahl-Nachbaur; Franz Stein;
Theodor Loos; Fritz Gnass; Fritz Odemar.

Rear Window
U.S.A.; 1954; 112 minutes;
released by Paramount.

Directed by Alfred Hitchcock.
Produced by Alfred Hitchcock.
Screenplay by John Michael Hayes,
from a story by Cornell Woolrich.
Photographed by Robert Burks.
Art direction by Hal Pereira, Joseph McMillan Johnson,
Sam Comer and Ray Mayer.
Edited by George Tomasini.
Music by Franz Waxman.
Cast: James Stewart; Grace Kelly; Wendell Corey;
Thelma Ritter; Raymond Burr; Judith Evelyn;
Ross Bagdasarian; Georgine Darcy; Jesslyn Fax;
Rand Harper; Irene Winston.

The Third Man
Great Britain; 1949; 104 minutes;
released in the U.S. by
Selznick Releasing Organization.

Directed by Carol Reed.
Produced by Alexander Korda.
Screenplay by Graham Greene.
Photographed by Robert Krasker.
Art direction by Vincent Korda.
Edited by Oswald Hafenrichter.
Music by Anton Karas.
Cast: Joseph Cotten; Alida Valli; Orson Welles;
Trevor Howard; Bernard Lee;
Paul Hoerbiger; Annie Rosar; Ernst Deutsch;
Siegfried Breuer; Erich Ponto;
Wilfrid Hyde-White.

Touch of Evil
U.S.A.; 1958; 94 minutes;
released by Universal-International.

Directed by Orson Welles.
Produced by Albert Zugsmith.
Screenplay by Orson Welles, from the novel
''Badge of Evil'' by Walt Masterson.
Photographed by Russell Metty.
Art direction by Alexander Golitzen and Robert Clatworthy.
Edited by Virgil Vogel and Aaron Stell.
Music by Henry Mancini.
Cast: Orson Welles; Charlton Heston;
Janet Leigh; Akim Tamiroff; Joseph Calleia;
Joanna Moore; Ray Collins;
Dennis Weaver; Marlene Dietrich;
Joseph Cotten; Keenan Wynn; Zsa-Zsa Gabor;
Mercedes McCambridge.

The Big Sleep
U.S.A.; 1946; 113 minutes;
released by Warner Bros.

Directed by Howard Hawks.
Produced by Howard Hawks.
Screenplay by William Faulkner, Leigh Brackett and Jules Furthman,
from the novel by Raymond Chandler.
Photographed by Sid Hickox.
Art direction by Carl Weyl.
Edited by Christian Nyby.
Music by Max Steiner.
Cast: Humphrey Bogart; Lauren Bacall;
Martha Vickers; Dorothy Malone; John Ridgeley;
Charles Waldron; Charles Brown;
Regis Toomey; Louis Heydt;
Elisha Cook, Jr.; Bob Steele.

Comedies

3

The genre of comedy is bottom-heavy, which is to say that the "Golden Age of Comedy"—the silent era—has not been surpassed despite the advent of sound, color, and a hundred technical breakthroughs. In almost every other genre it is possible to argue that pictures got better as the art of the cinema developed, and that most old masterpieces look more like artifacts than movies in which a contemporary audience can become involved. But in comedy this is not true. The great silent comedy stars, Charles Chaplin, Buster Keaton, Harold Lloyd, Harry Langdon, and—by extension—Laurel and Hardy (for their style derived from the silents despite their success in the sound era) put Jerry Lewis, Woody Allen, Peter Sellers, and Danny Kaye to shame. One is left with the thesis that the silent screen was particularly amenable to comedy, especially in America; that the tradition of comic mime acting flourished in the early freewheeling days of cinema; and that of all the different types of movies made during the silent period, comedy was perhaps the single one in which silence was an asset. (Chaplin certainly understood this. He continued to make mime comedies long after the advent of sound, and, of course, he was popular enough to get away with it.)

There is something about the sight gag that is universal. Show THE GENERAL to a morose college student today and watch him laugh. Show him IT HAPPENED ONE NIGHT and he'll tell you he can't "relate to it." Of course, he's right. The pictures of Chaplin and Keaton are universal, great, for all time. The situation comedies and screwball comedies of the thirties, forties, and fifties are, no matter how hilarious in their time, now mostly dated.

Mae West and W. C. Fields were very funny people, but their films were not all that great, and their comic attributes are amusing now mostly because of nostalgia. Of the talking comics only the Marx Brothers seem to have staying power. Their total and incorrigible outrageousness is universally accessible. There is something about their irreverent mockery of everything that is not too far from Abbie Hoffman appearing in a Minuteman costume to testify before the House Un-American Activities Committee.

There is a temptation, then, to say that the five

Preceding pages: Buster Keaton as Johnny
Gray on cowcatcher of his beloved locomotive.
THE GENERAL, in which both actor and train starred,
was directed by Keaton and Clyde Bruckman.
Above: Charlie Chaplin meets his opponent at start
of famous boxing sequence in CITY LIGHTS.

greatest screen comedies are THE GOLD RUSH and CITY LIGHTS by Chaplin, THE NAVIGATOR and THE GENERAL by Keaton, and the Marx Brothers' DUCK SOUP. Such a statement treats the last forty years as a comic wasteland, which is, of course, an exaggeration. But if the Frank Capra social comedies, and the Howard Hawks screwball comedies, and the Wilder-Diamond situation comedies, and the British comedies of Guinness and Sellers, the fantasies of Kaye, and the dumbhead movies of Lewis all seem to have lost a lot of their comic savor, and often, if one is not in the precise mood, seem to fall completely flat, there do exist pictures from the last forty years which are funny.

Looking in vain for comic-actor geniuses, one turns to dependable directors. Hitchcock gives us THE TROUBLE WITH HARRY, which may be his worst picture. Welles, Renoir, Fellini, Ford, Buñuel, and Lang, though they may play at times in comic realms, are much too serious. Kubrick, on the other hand, provides an unexpected comic masterpiece—unexpected since he is generally accused of being cold and misanthropic, guilty of what Andrew Sarris calls "strained seriousness." It all adds up, though.

Kubrick's cold formalism finds a voice in the comic mode called "black humor." DOCTOR STRANGELOVE, OR HOW I LEARNED TO STOP WORRYING AND LOVE THE BOMB is the black comedy of cinema. If it does not make us hold our sides, it forces us to smile at the absurdity of the world of men—another way of responding to the vision of Chaplin, Keaton, and the brothers Marx.

There also is Tony Richardson, a director who made his name as the most active filmmaker in the British Neo-Realist Movement, an interesting development in movie history which, unfortunately, produced no masterpieces. Richardson, however, did produce an enormously enjoyable comedy, TOM JONES, a riotous, broad, silly, bawdy costume satire, adapted by John Osborne from the lively eighteenth-century novel of Henry Fielding. It may be hard to argue that TOM JONES is in the same class as DUCK SOUP, or even DR. STRANGELOVE, but it meets the test of a great comedy, which far more subtle and sophisticated works by more proficient directors seem to fail. Years after its release it makes us laugh. And this, indeed, is what comedy is all about.

Charles Chaplin's City Lights 1931

To speak of Chaplin's genius as comic and as filmmaker is to speak of that which everyone knows. The libraries are filled with books that explain him. Every critic has, at one time or another, written a Chaplin appreciation. In 1972, when Chaplin came back to America to receive his Academy Award, and the long overdue apologies of ignorant men who had tried to deprive him of honor, his films began to play again, and crowds flocked to them with pleasure. No comic is as loved as Chaplin. He may be the most famous movie actor in the world; certainly he is in the pantheon of every student of film.

It is almost impossible to locate the Chaplin masterpiece. One must choose from among THE KID, THE GOLD RUSH, THE CIRCUS, CITY LIGHTS, and MODERN TIMES. Which is most vintage? Impossible to say. The problem for the connoisseur of Chaplin is that the most recently seen of these five is always the favorite. The problem is complicated by the fact that the Tramp is always different, sometimes more jaunty and resilient, at other times more depressed, more crushed. And, too, there is the element of social comment. It is always there, but depending on one's taste in Chaplin one will prefer the film that contains the desired quotient. There is something touch-

ingly, naïvely Marxist about MODERN TIMES. THE GOLD RUSH, on the other hand, though on one level concerned with problems of capital, cannot be considered ideological. Ultimately, just how funny does one want Chaplin to be? Purely funny, a comic acrobat, as in the early two-reelers, or with that famous pathos, which gives his characterizations an almost mystical dimension? Charlie the acrobat or Charlie the poet? The Tramp as extrovert or the Tramp who knows himself? Chaplin the fool or Chaplin the breaker of hearts?

The greatness of Chaplin resides in the wealth of possibilities he presents and from which his audience may choose. He did so many things so well, developed and changed so many times, showed so many facets while maintaining such originality, that the richness of his work may be mined by every taste.

Always, lurking behind every great Chaplin film, is Chaplin the director, the filmmaker-genius who understood the actor-genius and depicted him with perfection. With Chaplin we always have the feeling that he is entertaining himself; that he is behind the camera at the same time that he is in front of it, adoring his own antics so honestly that he can photograph himself with utter love.

67

And that love between filmmaker and actor, combined in Chaplin's case within a single man, sends rays out from the screen to pierce the sensibilities of all who watch.

In many ways, CITY LIGHTS is the prototypal Chaplin film, containing most of the important elements of Chaplin's work at or near summits of perfection.

At War with An Object: Chaplin's famous scene along these lines is his extended battle with a Murphy bed, but when he swallows a whistle in CITY LIGHTS the result is the same, and the effect more humorous for being more subtle. He wants to conquer the whistle in his throat, but he cannot. Despite all his ingenuity, its trap is infernal. Variations are played out with perfect timing, hilarity mounts, and then, before there is repetition, Charlie is off to something else. There is a fascinating contradiction in Chaplin's numerous wars against things. While fighting with them, he makes them come alive. In the case of the whistle, he literally breathes life into it. At the same time, the humor derives from the fact that these objects are inanimate, that his wars against them are futile.

Trapped in A Situation: One sees this over and over again in Chaplin, though never so elaborately or comically refined as in the boxing match in CITY LIGHTS. For Charlie the boxing match appears at first to be a marvelous opportunity. He needs money for the blind girl, and there's a fifty-fifty split if he throws the bout. But in the dressing room, as the horror of what *might* happen is revealed, his partner suddenly withdraws and an ominous new combatant appears. The trap springs shut. Charlie is in an impossible dilemma, with no way out. He still needs the money; he must go on; a slaughter

Clockwise from left: Chaplin with blind
flower girl (Virginia Cherrill) in one of their
idealized love scenes. Boxing match is among finest
acrobatic bits in the entire oeuvre of cinema.
Chaplinesque surrealism has street-cleaning Tramp
confronting herculean task posed by elephant.

is imminent. We know the ingenuity of the Tramp. Our wonder at how he will escape this situation fills us with suspense. What happens in the ring is the finest sort of acrobatics, timed perfectly, to the split second. The boxing match in CITY LIGHTS is as good as any stunt sequence in any early Chaplin short. But here, in a film of characters about whom we care, suspended in a story that must have an end, the boxing match is much more than a comic routine. It is a comic sequence wtih dramatic power.

The Girl, Idealized: She is always there, in Chaplin films, and in CITY LIGHTS Virginia Cherrill may be the ultimate example, though there are those who think her spirituality is overdone. Chaplin has a lot of heart, and his films are filled with sentiment, but the idealization of his women can never be considered sentimental, even in CITY LIGHTS where a blind heroine would seem to offer an irresistible opportunity to play for soap opera.

Social Comment: There is plenty of it in CITY LIGHTS: the millionaire, generous when drunk, hard-nosed when sober; his butler, who is a snob; the pomposity of the officials and patrons at the unveiling of the statue; the night-club sequence, which is brilliant social satire. Comparing the social comment in CITY LIGHTS and MODERN TIMES, one can say that in CITY LIGHTS the satire is less bitter and therefore more poignant.

Surrealism: Certainly a trademark of the Chaplin film is the controlled surreality of the world in which the action takes place. Chaplin's sets are always stylized, but not so much as to look artificial. In CITY LIGHTS he has created a city that is no city in particular, but which is every city in general, a city that is oppressive and also believable, a perfect place of torment for the Tramp.

Top: Scenes of social satire between
Tramp and the Millionaire (Harry Myers),
who is friendly when drunk (l.) and
hostile when sober (r.). Genteel drink is ruined for
Tramp by hiccups and chirruping whistle
stuck in throat. Right: Prototypical Tramp.

Pathos: There is no better example of the famous pathos of Chaplin than in the final minutes of CITY LIGHTS. The comedy, the slapstick, is somehow transscended. Suddenly one is in the realm of poetry. The expressions on Chaplin's face and on the face of the girl say so much on so many levels that they defy analysis. In fact, to try to analyze them is to risk the destruction of the poetry. Is this a sudden realization in which the Tramp grasps his own unworthiness? Has his gift of sight to the blind girl, for whom he has suffered and gone to prison, produced a gaze upon himself whose pity makes him wither? And are his teeth, bared through his grin, the remnants of a defense that has just been breached? Surely, there is here some moment of truth, some confrontation between a Tramp who is lovable and a Tramp who is pathetic. But to unravel it all is to know things which must forever be wrapped in mystery: Who is the Tramp? What are his origins? Why, above all, is he a tramp? For all the mystery, one thing in these final frames becomes clear to every Chaplin fan. The Tramp is much more than a lovable fool—much, much more.

What of Chaplin as filmmaker? In his autobiography, he writes that he spent more than a year shooting CITY LIGHTS because he had worked himself "into a neu- rotic state of wanting perfection." The Tramp's discovery that the flower girl is blind, a scene that lasts seventy seconds, took five days to shoot. The movies of Chaplin, which look so simple, are among the most carefully crafted of films. Mack Sennett had accidentally discovered —accidentally, because he really had no aesthetic—that the best way to shoot a comic sequence was to set up a camera, turn it on, and shoot the scene performed in front of it in long, single takes. Chaplin took this idea, totally opposed to the concept of montage, and carried it out with artistry. His shots are always perfectly framed. When he chooses an angle it is not merely to cover his antics, but to frame his scenes for eternity, to place a music-hall proscenium around them in the most perfect way he can devise.

The reason, perhaps, that people speak of Chaplin as a genius is that they cannot understand where he learned such things, how he was able to transform himself from a clown into an artist. Genius is the only word there is for talent that comes from sources deep within the self that can neither be traced nor understood. Chaplin's fall into the self-pity of LIMELIGHT, and the flatness of MONSIEUR VERDOUX, would not be noticeable in a man who had not reached dizzying heights in earlier years.

Buster Keaton's The General 1926

Chaplin and Buster Keaton ruled the Golden Age of Comedy, while Harold Lloyd, Harry Langdon, and Laurel and Hardy worked within the territory they staked out. Chaplin and Keaton often have been compared, and the belief exists that they represent antipodes of expression. No one has stated their differences quite so eloquently as the film critic, Andrew Sarris, who wrote:

"The difference between Keaton and Chaplin is the difference between poise and poetry, between the aristocrat and the tramp, between adaptability and dislocation, between the function of things and the meaning of things, between eccentricity and mysticism, between man as machine and man as angel, between the girl as a convention and the girl as an ideal, between life as farce and life as fantasy."

James Agee came close to putting the essence of Buster Keaton's comic character into words when he wrote: "In a way his pictures are like a transcendent juggling act in which it seems that the whole universe is in exquisite flying motion, and the one point of repose is the juggler's effortless, uninterested face."

This repose, this sense of self-containment, this indifference to the madness of the world, this aloofness while pursuing some private goal, combined with the beauty of his face and his famous dead-pan look, endows his pictures with a unique quality perhaps nowhere better illustrated than in his masterpiece, THE GENERAL.

The first thing one notices about this film is its sense of cinema. While Chaplin's conceptions are often theatrical, Keaton seems to have had an instinctive grasp of the potential of the screen. Throughout THE GENERAL, in which Keaton plays a railroad engineer in Civil War times, there is a manipulation of trains running back and forth, while violent, comic, and extraordinary actions take place upon them, that gives the picture an enormous sense of movement. We see Keaton, poised against backgrounds that are constantly in motion, engaging in feats of acrobatics and in startling and ingenious comic stunts. Simultaneously, he is enmeshed in a dramatic story of strong suspense and epic grandeur. THE GENERAL, among

70

Buster Keaton performing with locomotive and cannon in a series of his famous battles with machines. At times they defy him, at other times they overwhelm him, and then there are sublime moments when he and they are in perfect harmony.

other things, is a comedy, an historical reconstruction, a chase movie, a war movie, and a film that exhibits the major theme of Buster Keaton's work: Man versus The Machine—a struggle between himself and a locomotive which resolves, at times, into a delicious harmonization.

The story is based on an actual incident of the Civil War, the so-called Anderson Raid, a daring exploit by a Northern spy who captured a Confederate train and tried to ride it back to Union lines, wreaking havoc along the way. Keaton was fascinated by the story and wanted to shoot it as authentically as possible, even going so far as to explore the possibility of shooting on the original Alabama-Tennessee railway line, where it had taken place. In the end, he shot in the lumber country of Oregon on a narrow-gauge track with Civil War-type wood-burning engines. (One of these started a forest fire which Keaton's extras, four thousand members of the Oregon National Guard, put out under his direction.) One of the extraordinary things about THE GENERAL is its sense of historical authenticity. It has the look, particularly in the Northern railway yard scene and in the great ambush scene, of photographs by Mathew Brady.

Throughout the film we are fascinated by the constant back-and-forth movement of the trains and the comic scenes played out upon them. After a series of increasingly ingenious pranks (including a phenomenal sequence in which Keaton barely avoids having his head blown off by a cannon) there suddenly appear alongside Keaton's train whole armies, literally thousands of men, a retreating Confederate force and a pursuing Union regiment, in one of the epic throwaway scenes in movie history. Keaton ignores this extravaganza with total composure and thus confirms Agee's description of his essence.

We are moved by Keaton and the films he designed, co-directed, and always edited himself, because of something ineffably human and poised in his being that tells us about ourselves and our weaknesses with good humor and infinite grace. There is a remarkable scene in THE GENERAL—a film filled with remarkable scenes and playful inventiveness—that illustrates this especially well. Keaton is furiously stoking his locomotive to escape two pursuing Union trains, and is desperate on account of his dwindling supply of wood fuel. He turns to find his girl, Annabelle Lee, nonchalantly sweeping wood chips out of the locomotive cabin and rejecting pieces of wood that do not please her eye. Keaton looks at her, mimics her gestures, grasps her by her neck, makes as if he is going to throttle her, and then embraces her with a loving kiss. No one can fail to be moved by so gracefully executed a sequence of gestures, illustrating that special combination of fury and love which men sometimes feel toward the women they adore.

Buster Keaton had the misfortune to fall from public favor. Billy Wilder dug him up as a "waxwork" for SUNSET BOULEVARD and Chaplin used him as an extra in LIMELIGHT. In the early days of television he was trotted out for variety shows, and nostalgia buffs were pleased to recognize his ruined face. In the last few years his genius has been recognized by many young critics, who have resurrected him to the pantheon. In a poll conducted by *Sight and Sound* magazine in 1972, THE GENERAL was voted the eighth greatest film of all time.

The Marx Brothers' **Duck Soup** 1933

Like Chaplin and Keaton, the Marx Brothers came out of a background of poverty and a childhood on the vaudeville circuit, which may or may not say something about the origins necessary to become a great comedian. But while Chaplin and Keaton rose high above their vaudeville music-hall backgrounds, recasting themselves as great mime artists, the Marx Brothers, if anything, reduced vaudeville slapstick to its most debased level. In other words, they reveled in their vulgarity. Rather than try to rise above it and elevate themselves to artistry, they took lowbrowism and shamelessly pushed it to extremes.

They were neither poised nor poetic, not sublime or mystical, not skilled acrobats or breakers of hearts, or deeply tragic beneath their comic masks. They were cheap, sophomoric, scatological, reckless, excessive, lunatic, and asinine, all to such extremes that they turned everything impossibly bad into something extremely good. By being so thoroughly second-rate, without embarrassment or remorse, they made art out of the tawdry. And, of course, as much as they are loved by the hardhats, their greatest admirers are the intellectuals, whose best-kept secret is the acknowledgement that trash like DUCK SOUP is superior to phony art like DEATH IN VENICE because, when all is said and done, the Marx Brothers give pleasure by blasting at pretension, while Visconti is insufferable when he is sucking up to Art.

73

Keaton in cab; during rescue of his girl,
Annabelle Lee (Marian Mack); and receiving
hero's reward while taking salute. In final sight gag,
the General starts to move, and couple — still
seated on side rod and still in clinch — rise and
fall, rhythmically and unheedingly.

Top: "If you think this country's bad off now, just wait 'til I get through with it," sings Groucho in opening reel of DUCK SOUP. Right: Four Marx Brothers (Zeppo at left) play at war. Far right: Groucho calls his troops collect. Below: Chico and Harpo ruin Louis Calhern (Ambassador Trentino). Comic genius of Marxes lies in special brand of contrived chaos and arrant lowbrowism.

The problem with the intellectuals' adoration of the Marx Brothers is that they feel they must justify their response by analysis and elevation—like the distinguished professor of English who enjoyed the music of the Beatles, and used methods of literary criticism to discuss them. By applying the self-conscious standards of official, certified art to material that is opposed to art, self-consciousness, and official standards, his analysis makes the Beatles sound unbearably pretentious. The situation is analogous to attempts to make sense out of the Marx Brothers, to explain their appeal in anything but the most obvious terms. The Marx Brothers give pleasure because, in addition to every other adjective heretofore applied to them, *they are outrageous.*

As for DUCK SOUP, it is undoubtedly the brothers' funniest film. This is not so much on account of its surrealism, well noted by intellectuals, or of the historical analysis which views it as striking a blow against fascism and war, but for the purity of its anarchy and absurdity, more valid than the self-conscious handling of these themes by Ionesco and Beckett.

Groucho plays Rufus T. Firefly, newly elected President of Fredonia, a self-contained universe of insanity. In other pictures Groucho played Captain Jeffrey T. Spaulding, Professor Quincey Adams Wagstaff, Otis B. Driftwood, Dr. Hugo Z. Hackenbush, J. Cheever Loophole, S. Quentin Quale, Wolf J. Flywheel, Ronald Kornblow, and Sam Grunion. Margaret Dumont, who in DUCK SOUP plays the wealthy Mrs. Teasdale, in other Marx Brothers' pictures played Mrs. Rittenhouse, Mrs. Potter, Mrs. Claypool, Mrs. Emily Upjohn, Mrs. Dukesbury, and Martha Phelps. The juxtapositions of these names explain all one needs to know about the famous Groucho-Dumont relationship. Their exchanges are legendary, sequences of put-downs and deflations seemingly without end. In DUCK SOUP, Firefly and Teasdale speak:

GROUCHO: What about your husband?
DUMONT: He's dead.
GROUCHO: He's just using that as an excuse.
DUMONT: I was with him to the end.
GROUCHO: No wonder he passed away.
DUMONT: I held him in my arms and kissed him.
GROUCHO: So—it was murder?

DUCK SOUP is filled with such delicious garbage, so stuffed with it, in fact, that the viewer barely has time to catch his breath. A random sampling should give a notion of the texture of the picture, and perhaps will convince the reader who has not seen it to rush out next time it comes around and laugh his head off.

The antics of Harpo and Chico: They are double

agents in DUCK SOUP, spies of Ambassador Trentino of Sylvania, and cronies of President Firefly, as well. In their great scene with Trentino, Chico freaks him out with a spiderweb of verbal non sequiturs, while Harpo takes over the physical side, cutting off his tie, his coattails, and when asked to produce Firefly's "record," pulls out a phonograph record, throws it at the ceiling, fires at it with a pistol, and reduces it to crumbs. Harpo also uses a welder's torch as a cigar lighter, glues a newspaper to Trentino's derriere, and indulges in so many other acts of controlled violence that when the two depart Trentino's office they leave behind a man who has been wrecked.

In another scene, outside Firefly's presidential palace, which has nothing to do with anything in the picture but is more in the nature of an entr'acte skit in a vaudeville show, Harpo plays out his smiling hostility with a lemonade vender acted by slow-burning Edgar Kennedy. Again the physical and psychological destruction is total.

In a long sequence of interlocking slapstick scenes in Mrs. Teasdale's mansion, the three brothers have an opportunity to play together. One piece of mischief tops another until the three meet in what has become one of their two most famous scenes: the mirror sequence. (The other one is the jammed-stateroom sequence in A NIGHT AT THE OPERA.) In the mirror sequence, Groucho has just escaped from being locked in the bathroom, an inevitable consequence of the brothers' scatological tendencies. Chico and Harpo have taken turns impersonating him with the bewildered Mrs. Teasdale, and when Groucho confronts Harpo, dressed as himself, Harpo must evade detection by pretending to be Groucho's mirror-image. This routine is an old vaudeville stunt, done many times before and since DUCK SOUP, but for some reason, in this particular context, it is hilarious beyond belief, culminating when the two do a half circle and thus pierce through the "mirror," and breaking apart when Chico arrives, also dressed as Groucho. Suddenly there are three Grouchos staring at one another on the screen.

This kind of nonsense reaches depths of excess when Fredonia and Sylvania go to war. Harpo does a parody of a Paul Revere ride to awaken the threatened citizenry, Groucho sends orders to his troops "collect," and Chico deserts Trentino's headquarters after the following exchange:

TRENTINO: "There's a machine-gun nest on Hill 22. I want it cleaned out."
CHICO: "Good, I'll tell the janitor."

To put a film critic's problem vis-à-vis the Marx Brothers into perspective, consider the following possibility: Forced to attend a double feature consisting of Bergman's HOUR OF THE WOLF and the Marx Brothers' A NIGHT AT THE OPERA, and being deeply moved in the first instance by the anguish suffered by the creative mind, and in the second by a sore stomach caused by excessive belly-laughing, the critic can only reconcile his schizo-phrenia by concluding that the cinema is both a fine art and a debased, vulgarian entertainment form. No amount of pantheon-erecting, or theory, or inventing of *politiques* will ever explain this anomaly away. If there is anything beside pure pleasure to be derived from the films of the Marx Brothers, it is this essential lesson.

Stanley Kubrick's **Dr. Strangelove,** or How I Learned to Stop Worrying and Love the Bomb 1963

In the late 1950s, we were confronted with books by technocrats instructing us to "think about the unthinkable."

In DR. STRANGELOVE, Stanley Kubrick does not ask us to "think about the unthinkable." He asks that we laugh about it. America's military and political leaders, hot-lines and fail-safe points, Strategic Air Command (whose motto, incredibly, is "Peace Is Our Profession"), computer technology, obsessions with Communist plots, former Nazi scientists, and the entire military-industrial complex are used by Kubrick as objects for merciless mockery. These things are funny all right, but we don't laugh too long. At the end of DR. STRANGELOVE, as we watch a lyrical sequence of mushroom clouds and listen to Vera Lynn sing "We'll Meet Again," we chuckle a little and then hold our guts.

DR. STRANGELOVE, then, employs the comic values of the 1960s. It mocks the most serious things, turns a death rattle into gales of laughter, makes us titter and then makes us bleed. It is what some intellectuals would have us find in DUCK SOUP, a surrealist comedy, an outrageous tract against war, power, and pretension. But the difference between these pictures could not be more consequential. Rather than being anarchic, open-ended and absurd, DR. STRANGELOVE is put together like a fine watch, charged with suspense, and, despite the claims of the U. S. Air Force, believable. In addition, because it was created intellectually, as opposed to being improvised from a series of slapstick sketches, it is, unlike DUCK SOUP, subject to analysis.

The action takes place at three locations: Burpelson Air Base, ruled by its insane commander, General Jack D. Ripper, a man obsessed with the idea that fluoridation is a plot hatched by Communists to taint the purity of "our precious bodily fluids"; the War Room at the Pentagon where President Merkin J. Muffley and Chairman of the Joint Chiefs, General "Buck" Turgidson, enact a duel of ideologies in exchanges that employ the equally fatuous language of Cold War liberals and conservatives; and the cockpit of a B-52 bomber, commanded by Major T. J. "King" Kong, flying toward military targets in the Soviet Union. These three locations, which are physically realistic, become the stages for outrageous if internally logical events.

The suspense of the picture is dependent upon the way Kubrick (and his editor, Anthony Harvey) cut back and forth between the locations. We become involved in a race against time: Will Group Captain Mandrake obtain the recall code from General Ripper? Will the President reach Major Kong in time? Will the B-52 be recalled, or will it drop the bomb and set off the "doomsday device"? Whenever a scene at Burpelson or the War Room comes to an end, Kubrick cuts to the B-52, flying ever closer to its target over snowy Arctic terrain. Computers click, the pace quickens, the cuts are faster, and suspense plays against comedy until, despite our better judgment, we find ourselves at the edge of our seat. The comic thrust of DR. STRANGELOVE is not open-ended. It fights against a clock.

Into this tight drama about the destiny of man, Kubrick installs a half-dozen fine comic performances. Peter Sellers, the most famous comic actor of the day, plays three parts. As Group Captain Lionel Mandrake he is the epitome of the British officer, calm in the face of disaster, a satirical composite of all the Group Captains we've seen in an endless succession of movies about the Battle of Britain. As President Muffley he is the platitudinous liberal ("Gentlemen, you can't fight in here; this is the War Room!"), and when he gets on the hot-line with the Soviet Premier he talks like a resident in pediatrics trying to reason with a sick child. As Dr. Strangelove, he is a crippled ex-Nazi whose black-gloved wooden arm constantly threatens to give President Muffley a Nazi salute, and even tries to strangle Strangelove himself. When the "doomsday device" is triggered, Strangelove's withered legs are miraculously cured. "Mein Führer," he says to Muffley, "I can walk!"—surely one of the great

George C. Scott as General "Buck" Turgidson and Peter Sellers as President Merkin J. Muffley in DR. STRANGELOVE, OR HOW I LEARNED TO STOP WORRYING AND LOVE THE BOMB. Although Sellers was the famous comedian and played three parts, Scott gave the comic performance of the year.

Director Kubrick worked with a brilliant cast (l. to r.): Peter Sellers as Dr. Strangelove ("Mein Führer, I can walk!"); Scott as General Turgidson ("You got to watch them Ruskies"); Sterling Hayden as General Jack D. Ripper ("We must protect our precious bodily fluids. . . ."); Sellers as Group Captain Mandrake; Keenan Wynn as Colonel "Bat" Guano ("If you want to know what I think, I think you're some kind of deviated prevert"). Below: The War Room. (Muffley: "You can't fight in here. This is the War Room!") Opposite: Slim Pickens as Major Kong in cockpit of unrecallable B-52 bomber which will set off "doomsday device."

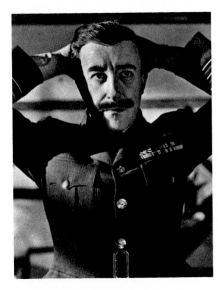

moments in screen comedy.

As General "Buck" Turgidson, George C. Scott—not known up to that time as a comedian—gives the comic performance of the decade, screwing up his face, broadly satirizing the emotions of cunning and rowdiness, at times assuming ape-like stances, often ending his speeches with his gestures frozen.

Turgidson, however, is the lightweight "heavy" of the film. General Ripper (played by Sterling Hayden) is the brooding maniac. Hayden is very good, and would be even funnier if it weren't for the fact that shortly before the release of the film a U. S. Army general was retired from active duty for spouting similar paranoic sentiments. Keenan Wynn, as Colonel "Bat" Guano, gives a marvelous performance as the man who won't shoot the lock off a Coke machine to retrieve a dime to make a phone call that might save the human race, and Slim Pickens, as Major "King" Kong stunningly satirizes a plane commander, particularly in his pep talk to his crew.

The film is rich in sexual humor, making a constant equation between sexuality and war. Under the opening titles we see one jet plane refueling another in an aerial ballet devised to resemble copulation. General Turgidson is reluctant to go to the War Room, despite the possibility of nuclear war, because he wants to conclude a sex session with his secretary. "Bat" Guano speaks obsessively of "deviated preverts." General Ripper tells Mandrake that he first suspected the fluoridation plot when he found himself impotent during sexual intercourse. Major "King" Kong rides the phallic-shaped bomb orgasmically whooping his Stetson. And Dr. Strangelove's plan to save a sampling of the human race by installing high military and political leaders at the bottom of mine shafts with attractive women at a ratio of one to ten puts gleams of sexual avarice into the eyes of everyone.

Kubrick has said that he started out with the intention of making a serious film about the problems of accidental nuclear war, but that the longer he allowed his imagination to dwell on this theme the more apparent it became that "the only way to tell the story was as a black comedy, or, better, a nightmare comedy, where the things that make you laugh are really the heart of the paradoxical postures that make a nuclear war possible."

His film is not only daring in its subject matter, but is stylistically ingenious, too. The scenes inside the B-52, for example, are staged as they might have occurred, with source lighting and an overpowering sense of realism. The attack against Burpelson Air Base is shot in a *cinéma-vérité* style with hand-held cameras, mostly operated by Stanley Kubrick himself. The effect is like a newsreel, perhaps the first staged battle scene to look totally convincing.

This stylistic realism heightens the impact of DR. STRANGELOVE, making us laugh and think at the same time. Like the picture's suspense, it works against the comedy, making us choke on our laughter, and leaving a bitter taste—the inevitable effect of "black humor."

Stanley Kubrick with machine gun and camera. He himself shot much of the attack on Burpelson Air Force Base (r.) with hand-held camera in *cinéma-vérité* style. Although wildly comic, DR. STRANGELOVE is a disciplined film, brilliantly edited to heighten suspense.

Tony Richardson's **Tom Jones** 1963

TOM JONES appeared the same year as DR. STRANGELOVE. Both pictures survive as great comic entertainments, and yet are totally different in terms of comic thrust. STRANGELOVE is intellectual; TOM JONES is silly. STRANGELOVE is futuristic; TOM JONES is historical. STRANGELOVE is controlled; TOM JONES is wild. The sexual humor of STRANGELOVE is witty; the sexual humor of TOM JONES is bawdy. STRANGELOVE is cold; TOM JONES is warm. The differences between them are the differences between irony and slapstick, the drawing room and the burlesque hall, the cool grin and the belly laugh, a comedy that matters and a comedy of manners. At one point, Kubrick decided to end his final war-room sequence with a custard-pie fight. He actually shot the scene and then dropped it from his final version because he realized it was out of place. In TOM JONES a custard-pie fight would have been consistent with the style, whether relevant or not.

TOM JONES was a popular success and as a result has been attacked by highbrow critics. The principal fault they find is that the picture is academic. Though appearing to be a helter-skelter comedy, it is academically contrived. The charge of academicism is valid, but irrelevant to the picture's success as a comedy. Certainly, TOM JONES self-consciously employs the full gamut of New Wave devices: speeded-up action, frozen frames, superimposed titles, an ironic narrator, spiral wipes, iris dissolves, etc. (which were not, of course, invented by New Wave directors, but were resuscitated by them from the Mack Sennett comedies). And, of course, these devices are not employed with abandon, but with the calculation of filmmakers trying hard to produce an entertainment.

Perhaps the most academic thing about the picture is the warm, rich, precise cinematography of Walter Lassally, which, combined with very careful costuming and a certain amount of Neo-Realist historicism, gives the picture its famous "Hogarthian" look.

But it seems a little silly to find fault with TOM JONES because it does not look shabby, or because it lacks the spontaneity of silent two-reelers, or to question, for example, the use of a helicopter shot in the stag-hunt sequence because such a shot does not simulate an eighteenth-century point of view. Whatever faults the picture may have, it is redeemed by the fact that it makes no attempt to take itself seriously, or even to remain very faithful to Henry Fielding. TOM JONES is a film that mocks itself, its own devices, its own origins. It even allows its characters to turn to the lens and address the audience, thus breaking down the barrier between audience and screen, and disrupting suspension of disbelief.

The most marvelous of these to-the-camera moments occurs when Mrs. Waters receives the news (which turns out later to be false) that the Tom Jones with whom she has made delightful love is really her son. She shrugs at us as if to say: "Oedipus, schmoedipus!"

There are great sequences in TOM JONES (the nocturnal machinations at Upton Inn, the stag hunt at Squire Western's estate, etc.), but the dining sequence between Tom and Mrs. Waters is the high point of the film, and must be counted among the all-time great comic scenes in movie history. Their devouring of food is so erotic that the scene outclasses, on a purely sexual level, any of the frank, nude lovemaking scenes which began to appear on the screen in the 1970s. Lobsters, chickens, oysters, and fruits are sucked, gobbled, licked, and bitten with riotous obscenity.

In TOM JONES, Tony Richardson has no cast of comic geniuses like Chaplin, Keaton, or Groucho Marx, or even Peter Sellers and George C. Scott. His actors— Albert Finney, Hugh Griffith, Susannah York, and Edith Evans—are all fine straight performers, but are not breathtakingly poised (like Keaton) or hopelessly sloppy (like Groucho). The pleasure of TOM JONES does not derive from watching the people so much as from becoming entranced by the absurd and complex situations and the parodies of eighteenth-century manners. By cutting the picture fast, and employing every trick he knows, Richardson keeps TOM JONES going at a feverish pitch, much like a juggler performing an absurdly complicated balancing act. If his social satire has sometimes too bitter a taste (as in the bloody spur-bitten flanks of the horses in the stag hunt, or the poor farmer incredulously holding up his trampled goose), Richardson manages to subdue his social conscience long enough to produce an extraordinarily entertaining comedy, funny enough to blot out thoughts of its trivial flaws.

It is interesting that Richardson manages to do this, because his best-known pictures—LOOK BACK IN ANGER, A TASTE OF HONEY, THE LONELINESS OF THE LONG-DISTANCE RUNNER—all were made in the Angry Young Man mood that cries out its commitment and importance. Richardson may be one of those filmmakers who are corrupted by Art. When he tries to make statements he fails to be moving; when he merely tries to entertain he can make people laugh.

Albert Finney as Tom Jones in Tony Richardson's period comedy. Below: Tom and Mrs. Waters (Joyce Redman) in hilarious eating sequence in which they swallow oysters, bite meat, suck at lobster, and gobble fruit in a magnificent parody of the sexual delights to come.

Credits

City Lights
U.S.A.; 1931; 87 minutes;
originally released by United Artists.

Directed by	Charles Chaplin.
Produced by	Charles Chaplin.
Written by	Charles Chaplin.
Photographed by	Rollie Totheroh, Gordon Pollack, and Mark Marklatt.
Art direction by	Charles D. Hall.
Music by	Charles Chaplin.
Cast:	Charles Chaplin; Virginia Cherrill; Florence Lee; Harry Myers; Allan Garcia; Hank Mann; Albert Austin; Henry Bergman; John Rand; Jean Harlow.

The General
U.S.A.; 1926; 80 minutes;
originally released by United Artists.

Directed by	Buster Keaton and Clyde Bruckman.
Produced by	Joseph M. Schenck.
Screenplay by	Al Boasberg and Charles Smith.
Photographed by	J. Devereux Jennings and Bert Haines.
Cast:	Buster Keaton; Marion Mack; Glen Cavender; Jim Farley; Frederick Vroom; Charles Smith; Frank Barnes; Joe Keaton; Mike Denlin; Tom Nawm.

Duck Soup
U.S.A.; 1933; 70 minutes;
released by Paramount.

Directed by	Leo McCarey.
Screenplay by	Bert Kalmar and Harry Ruby, with additional dialogue by Arthur Sheekman and Nat Perrin.
Photographed by	Henry Sharp.
Art direction by	Hans Dreier and Wilard Ihnen.
Edited by	LeRoy Stone.
Music and Lyrics by	Bert Kalmar and Harry Ruby.
Cast:	Groucho Marx; Harpo Marx; Chico Marx; Zeppo Marx; Margaret Dumont; Louis Calhern; Raquel Torres; Edgar Kennedy; Edmund Breese; Leonid Kinsky.

Dr. Strangelove, or How I Learned To Stop Worrying and Love the Bomb
Great Britain; 1963; 94 minutes;
released by Columbia Pictures.

Directed by	Stanley Kubrick.
Produced by	Stanley Kubrick.
Screenplay by	Stanley Kubrick, Terry Southern, and Peter George, from the novel ''Red Alert'' by Peter George.
Photographed by	Gilbert Taylor.
Art direction by	Ken Adam.
Edited by	Anthony Harvey.
Music by	Laurie Johnson.
Cast:	Peter Sellers; George C. Scott; Sterling Hayden; Keenan Wynn; Slim Pickens; Peter Bull; Tracy Reed; James Earl Jones.

Tom Jones
Great Britain; 1963; 125 minutes;
released by United Artists.

Directed by	Tony Richardson.
Produced by	Tony Richardson.
Screenplay by	John Osborne, based on the novel by Henry Fielding.
Photographed by	Walter Lassally.
Art direction by	Ralph Brinton.
Edited by	Antony Gibbs.
Music by	John Addison.
Cast:	Albert Finney; Hugh Griffith; Susannah York; Edith Evans; Joyce Redman; Joan Greenwood; David Tomlinson; Jack MacGowran; Diane Cilento; Wilfrid Lawson; Peter Bull; David Warner; Julian Glover; Rosalind Knight; Lynn Redgrave; George Devine; George A. Cooper.

Musicals

4

People seem either to adore musicals or to detest them, and logic will not sway their opinions on this not-too-crucial issue. People either go to the movies to be entertained and to escape reality, or else they go to be engaged by themes and to be moved by art. To the first group (a vast majority), musicals are the raison d'être of the cinema, and to the second they are evidence of its debasement. Of course, both groups are wrong.

It is important to give musicals their due and to honor them in proportion to their worth. Some bridge the gap by claiming that Europeans are best at making art films, and that Americans are preeminent in escapist genres. Hollywood was a dream factory, their argument goes, and its greatest products were escapist fantasies: thrillers, westerns, musicals.

Though this position is much too doctrinaire, and has a patronizing air about it, one must risk the wrath of the musical cultists and say that it comes fairly close to the truth. Musicals are the most escapist of genres, and Americans seem to be most excellent at making them. This may be accounted for by the size of the country and its traditions, the quality and diversity of American song-writing and of its singing and dancing entertainers, plus the reservoir of material and people provided by the musical stage. And though the Hollywood studio system had many defects, most of them deriving from the fact that movie-making was considered above all else a business, no one can deny Hollywood's technical expertise, the craftsmanship and inventiveness of its artisans, and the respective sizes of its budgets and sound stages. Combine American talents, American expertise, American budgets, and a desire to manufacture an escapist product, and you come up with a peculiarly American genre, perhaps not an art form, but an entertainment form that must be admired. It generated, perhaps more by accident than design, a certain number of delightful works a cultist would call "masterpieces," but which a civilized person must recognize as belonging with such charming and minor things as Fabergé Easter eggs. At their very best, this is what musicals are. At their worst (and there are plenty of examples), they can be impossibly vulgar, akin to such awful things as plastic suction-cupped Madonnas, or as totally lifeless as lead balloons.

It has been pointed out that the first sound film, THE JAZZ SINGER, was, essentially, a musical. Also that Busby Berkeley was the first original talent to grace the genre with a fantastic vision, his elaborate and grandiose choreographies. From that time to the present, the history of the musical has been a history of famous names, stars, composers, and even some directors: Fred Astaire and Ginger Rogers, Jeanette MacDonald and Nelson Eddy, Shirley Temple, Judy Garland, Barbra Streisand, Julie Andrews, Doris Day, Cyd Charisse, Mickey Rooney, Bing Crosby, Frank Sinatra, Gene Kelly, Cole Porter, Harold Arlen, Irving Berlin, Richard Rodgers, Jerome Kern, George Gershwin, Ernst Lubitsch, Rouben Mamoulian, Vincente Minnelli, Stanley Donen, George Cukor, and many more. These people are the American musical, as are certain art directors, costume and set designers, choreographers, cameramen, and sound technicians. All of this says something important about musicals. As much as one may try, it is difficult to prove that great musicals can be attributed to great filmmakers, or that musicals are even a filmmaker's medium. Sometimes it is the star (a Fred Astaire, a Judy Garland) that makes a musical work. Other times it is the composer (a Jerome Kern, a Cole Porter), or a producer (an Arthur Freed), or a director (a Vincente Minnelli). But the number of superior film-

Preceding pages & above: Fred Astaire and
Ginger Rogers in TOP HAT. In their marvelous duets, the
most magical dancing ever seen on the screen, they enacted
the conflicts between men and women, romance and sex.

makers who have failed with good musical material (Carol Reed with OLIVER!, Joshua Logan with CAMELOT, William Wyler with FUNNY GIRL, George Cukor with MY FAIR LADY, etc.) suggests that a musical is a precarious balance of many ingredients, and that filmmaking ability is not always the most important.

What, then, are the qualities that make a great musical, keeping in mind, of course, that the best of musicals are minor works? It is easier to say what these qualities are not. It is not necessary, for example, as some have said, that a great musical be an organic whole with the songs growing naturally out of the story (the Astaire-Rogers musicals do not meet this test and they are great; Fred Zinnemann's OKLAHOMA does and it is not). A great musical doesn't have to be an original work as opposed to a Broadway adaptation (originals like THE WIZARD OF OZ and SINGIN' IN THE RAIN are great, but so are adaptations like CABARET and ON THE TOWN; the original AN AMERICAN IN PARIS is about as pretentious as a musical can be, and

the adaptation of WEST SIDE STORY is a feeble reminder of its glory upon the stage). A great musical need not emphasize dancing at the expense of singing, or, for that matter, the other way around. (Is Streisand less marvelous than Ginger Rogers? Is Fred Astaire better than the Beatles?) These are the kinds of assertions that devotees use to justify their favorites.

No, the criteria for a great musical are among the most elusive of things, for though it is obvious that a musical must work, that its diverse elements must come together in some way, this "way" remains mysterious and seems to depend upon something called "chemistry," which is a word used to describe a phenomenon that people recognize but can't rationally explain. Still and all, a great musical gives pleasure because of its lightness and artistry and the ebullience of its fantasy, because, like the Fabergé egg, or a trompe l'oeil ceiling, it is "right." And that, admittedly, is as dubious and subjective a standard as one can employ.

Astaire and Rogers in **Top Hat** 1935

There can be no better example of pictures being "right," of things "working," and of "chemistry" in musicals than the films of Fred Astaire and Ginger Rogers. Their partnership is legendary, and the ten films they made together are remembered not for their stories (which were mostly inane), nor for the brilliance of their filmmaking (they were workmanlike, but not extraordinary), nor even for their music (some of which was extremely fine as popular music goes), but for the way Fred Astaire and Ginger

Rogers moved together. He was sophisticated, elegant, graceful, and supple. She was fresh, charming, speedy, and engagingly maddening. Together they were sublime.

She made him vulnerable and he gave her class; she made him sexy and he made her look like a lady—these are the usual explanations for their famous chemistry. Like Spencer Tracy and Katharine Hepburn, Humphrey Bogart and Lauren Bacall, Fred Astaire and Ginger Rogers together combusted into something greater than

the sum of their separate selves, and that is saying something, since Rogers alone could be magnificent and Astaire was and is the greatest dancing star in motion pictures. However, it is interesting that unlike Tracy-Hepburn and Bogart-Bacall, Astaire-Rogers had little use for each other off the screen, which may say something about the special nature of musicals: that at their best they are worlds of fantasy where things can happen that are impossible in real life. Astaire and Rogers were impossible—impossibly well-matched, impossibly enchanting, an exemplary pair that could only exist in the dream-world of luminescent screens in darkened halls.

They came together by accident as second leads in FLYING DOWN TO RIO in 1933, and they stole the show from Gene Raymond and Dolores del Rio with their "Carioca," the first of a series of spectacular and innovative dances they premiered usually at the end of their pictures. ("The Continental" in THE GAY DIVORCEE, 1934; "The Piccolino" in TOP HAT, 1935; the wild "Yam" in CAREFREE, 1938; etc.) For five years they flourished until in the last number of CAREFREE, "I Used to Be Color-Blind," they kissed for the first time. The dance and the kiss were shot in slow motion, a tantalizing reply to the demands of their fans that the time had come for Fred to kiss Ginger. After CAREFREE, THE STORY OF VERNON AND IRENE CASTLE in 1939 was something of a letdown, and a decade later, when they played in THE BARKLEYS OF BROADWAY, their duets were but a pale reprise of magic that was lost and could not be recaptured.

The kiss in CAREFREE was, quite possibly, the logical end to their collaboration. When Astaire and Rogers danced together they achieved a delicate tension between reality and abandonment, infatuation and realization. Astaire was always in pursuit of Rogers and she always pretended she wasn't interested. In their duets things usually proceeded to the point where it seemed as though

Astaire could sweep her away, that after dealing with her many rebuffs he could carry her to the point of capitulation. And then, on the verge of oneness, there would occur one of their famous pauses, and Rogers would charmingly pull back. It is in these heightened moments of pause, when fantasy (his) and earthiness (hers) lie in the balance, that one may observe the essence of their chemistry. By his seductiveness and her feigned indifference and haughty withdrawals they enact wooing patterns, dance out the basic duel between men and women, and symbolize the conflict between romance and sex. Watching them swirl together, one feels them approaching a oneness of deep intensity. It is clear that they belong together, that they perfectly fit. But the source of their power to enchant is the tension between them, and once it was released in the kiss at the end of CAREFREE that power was gone. It had to happen. Their magic was too delicate a thing to last forever. It is remarkable that it lasted through eight films and five years.

To select the best of these films is a difficult task. One searches for the picture with the greatest number of great duets. TOP HAT is a likely choice, for here, as in FOLLOW THE FLEET and CAREFREE, one finds an additional empathy between Astaire and Irving Berlin to reinforce that of Astaire and Rogers. One also finds Astaire's trademark solo, his famous "Top Hat" number, that sums up better than anything else he ever did the elegance and élan of his screen character.

Astaire and Rogers were genuine stars, so it was appropriate that their films were viewed by producers as "star vehicles." It didn't much matter what the story was, as long as it provided opportunities for the pair to dance. The story of TOP HAT is as forgettable and irrelevant as the story of any Astaire-Rogers film: A dancer falls for a haughty model and chases her up and down Europe, tap-dancing most of the way. The journeyman direction of Mark Sandrich (who directed five of their ten pictures) is appropriate for this sort of material. No mastermind, no Busby Berkeley, he does not manipulate people like pawns. No heavyweight director, no Vincente Minnelli, he does not impose a fantasy concept or try to impart a strong directorial style. Rather, Sandrich does the only logical thing that a director can do with Astaire-Rogers—he lets them dance.

TOP HAT may be the best of the Astaire-Rogers films, because in addition to the songs of Irving Berlin and the excellence of the dances, it is the simplest and most pure. And it was made early enough in the collaboration that Astaire's and Roger's elation at the miracle of their chemistry shines through and adds to its prevailing charm.

"Isn't It A Lovely Day" number in London
bandbox (above) and ebullient "Top Hat" solo (opposite)
were among picture's many delights.
"Chemistry" between Astaire and Rogers has never
been surpassed by another screen couple. Any
of six films could be judged their best.

The Wizard of Oz 1939

Nineteen thirty-nine was a key year in the history of motion pictures. In France, Jean Renoir was depicting the social confusion of Europe in his biting and satirical RULES OF THE GAME. At Columbia Studios, Howard Hawks was staking out the themes and motifs of the adventure film with ONLY ANGELS HAVE WINGS. In Monument Valley, John Ford was reinventing the western with STAGECOACH. And at MGM, Victor Fleming was directing a sheerly pleasureful bit of fluff called THE WIZARD OF OZ. One can only speculate on whether there is significance in any of this, and particularly in the fact that while Europe was threatened by war and the depression was not yet over in America, Hollywood was turning out escapist fantasies.

THE WIZARD OF OZ was the first of a series of musicals produced for MGM by Arthur Freed which would give that studio dominance in the genre for many years. Freed, who encouraged and gave free rein to such people as Vincente Minnelli, Gene Kelly, and Stanley Donen, and who produced such remarkably fine musicals as CABIN IN THE SKY, MEET ME IN ST. LOUIS, ON THE TOWN, SINGIN' IN THE RAIN, IT'S ALWAYS FAIR WEATHER, and a good thirty more of varying quality but consistent commerciality, harbored a definite conception of what a musical should be.

It should be an organic whole, an entertainment in which story, songs, and dances are integrated and unified by a strong dramatic line. Songs, according to Freed's concept, must flow out of the dramatic material and advance the story, rather than serve merely as intermezzos between action that stops when music begins and resumes when music is finished. An obvious corollary to his theory was that a song, no matter how tuneful or pleasure-giving, that did not advance the story should be scrapped, which is precisely what happened to "The Jitterbug" in THE WIZARD OF OZ, and which almost happened to the picture's most famous song "Over the Rainbow." In addition, Freed believed that the transition from dialogue to music should be as smooth as possible, triggered usually by the emotion of a character whose enlarged exuberance would make a burst into song natural and inevitable. Freed's influence lay not so much in the novelty of his ideas, but in the fact that he formulated them into a definite concept, and then applied that concept to all the musicals under his jurisdiction. The result of his success was a clamp upon the musical so binding that new approaches have emerged only in recent years.

THE WIZARD OF OZ was the first musical calculatedly fashioned according to this formula, and therefore it is important for historical reasons. But it is also special on several additional counts. It has a magnificent score: songs by Harold Arlen and lyrics by E. Y. Harburg. Arlen's elaborate and sophisticated music combusts "chemically" with the teasing *joie de vivre* of Harburg's rhymes, and the result is one of the few scores that appeals equally to children and adults. Also, the very idea of making a musical out of L. Frank Baum's classic was brilliantly inspired, akin to Disney's use of "Snow White" for his first feature-length cartoon. Baum's book contains the very fantasy elements that the musical film is best equipped to deliver: special architecture, magical effects, and the distortion of normal space-time. Finally, and especially notable about THE WIZARD OF OZ, is the performance of Judy Garland.

Garland: Her place in the history of the American musical is as important as that of Fred Astaire. THE WIZARD OF OZ, by no means her greatest work, is representative of the first phase of her remarkable career. She almost didn't get the part. Originally it was to go to Shirley Temple, who was to be borrowed from Twentieth Century-Fox in exchange for Jean Harlow and Clark Gable. When Harlow died the deal fell through, and MGM decided to risk everything on Garland. She was sixteen years old at the time, but was able to look eleven or twelve and to exude a wholesome, innocent, bouncy freshness that was charming because she achieved it without being cute. As Dorothy she was perfect, and one squirms now at the thought of Shirley Temple in the role. Garland's performance in THE WIZARD OF OZ endeared her to the public. People watched with fascination as her adolescent wholesomeness gave way to the all-heart sincerity and emotional directness of her performance in MEET ME IN ST. LOUIS in 1944, and then mutated again until, by the time of A STAR IS BORN in 1954, she had become urgent, electric, quivering, self-destructive, and altogether stunning for the way she made these qualities work for her in what may be the greatest piece of dramatic acting in the history of the musical genre. Garland was unique in movies. No other singer, with the possible exception of Edith Piaf, has ever matched her musical passion.

THE WIZARD OF OZ begins in black and white in a bitterly real America of stern faces and endless plains.

From left, Ray Bolger (Scarecrow), Jack Haley (Tin Woodman), Frank Morgan (The Wizard), Judy Garland (Dorothy), and Bert Lahr (Cowardly Lion) posed for studio publicity shot before a giant copy of L. Frank Baum's THE WIZARD OF OZ. Bit player Margaret Hamilton won enduring fame as Wicked Witch.

Dorothy, the innocent dreamer, is swirled from this place to a Technicolor dreamland "somewhere over the rainbow." Here she eludes peril, overcomes enemies, and finds loving friends. And when she returns her innocence is intact. THE WIZARD OF OZ is one of those films, like Disney's SNOW WHITE and Douglas Fairbanks' ROBIN HOOD, on which people are brought up and which they never forget. Children and parents who go to see THE WIZARD OF OZ year after year never seem to tire of it. How to account for this timeless appeal? There is no way except to repeat that like all great escapist fantasies it is, somehow, "right."

Kelly and Donen's **Singin' in the Rain** 1952

SINGIN' IN THE RAIN is considered by those who are connoisseurs of the genre to be the summit of the Hollywood musical. Perhaps they are right, for SINGIN' IN THE RAIN is light, frothy, unpretentious, and funny, contains good songs, good dances, good performances, and is unified by an inspired idea.

It was produced for MGM by the ubiquitous Arthur Freed and meets his conception of the film musical more completely than any of his other calculated efforts. Freed also wrote the lyrics to the songs, and they are fine, especially the title number "Singin' In the Rain," which Stanley Kubrick reprised with such fascinating perversity in A CLOCKWORK ORANGE. But the magic and strength of SINGIN' IN THE RAIN lie in its story, written by Betty Comden and Adolph Green, whose chemistry was also responsible for ON THE TOWN, IT'S ALWAYS FAIR WEATHER,

and BELLS ARE RINGING. SINGIN' IN THE RAIN is a satire on show business and Hollywood, an exposé of the ruthless ambition of idolized stars, and it is built around the comic possibilities implicit in the problems faced by actors and studios making the transition from silent films to talkies in the late 1920s. This situation, in which an industry that deals in fantasy and illusion must adapt itself to a new technology, was actually tragic for several film stars who, because of lack of diction and disparity between image and voice, were undone by the demands of the talking film. Whoever decided to use it as the unifying theme of a musical comedy (Freed, Comden and Green, or whoever) must receive credit for enormous inspiration. Hollywood is often at its best when feeding upon itself.

SINGIN' IN THE RAIN is the tale of a sex goddess, played by one of the great impersonators of the "dumb

92

Sequences of Dorothy's Kansas home are in black and white, Oz is in color. Movie has timeless quality of a fairy tale, a magnificent score by Harold Arlen and E. Y. Harburg, and a lovable performance by Judy Garland. Clara Blandick was Auntie Em, Charley Grapewin was Uncle Henry.

blonde," Jean Hagen, who cannot sing, cannot talk, cannot enunciate a single word without creating mounting hysteria in an audience. The Hollywood where she and her co-star, Gene Kelly, work, is depicted as a lovably phony place. Hagen, of course, is thoroughly despicable, and is in love with Kelly who cannot stand her and is himself in love with the lovely, modest, and talented Debbie Reynolds. Kelly is unscrupulous and superficial, though there are plenty of indications that he knows he is involved in a put-on business. Anyway, Hagen achieves stardom on Debbie Reynolds' voice, dubbed in for her execrable singing, grows vicious and arrogant, and is mercilessly debunked by the machinations of Kelly and Donald O'Connor. Debbie, in the end, is reconciled with Gene, who, it turns out, is not such a bad guy after all.

SINGIN' IN THE RAIN is rich in references to the old days of Hollywood, and the satire on moguls, stars, and show business is sharp and sometimes devastating. It is also rich in musical film styles. Each of its three great production numbers is presented differently, and their juxtaposition gives the picture its notable qualities of variety and lightness. "Singin' In the Rain" is a simple and emotionally direct Garlandesque solo by Gene Kelly. "You Were Meant for Me," in which Kelly and Reynolds sing and dance their love duet on an empty sound stage is more in the Astaire-Rogers tradition. And the big production number, "Broadway Ballet," is a surrealistic Busby Berkeley-type extravaganza filled with magic, un-

expected transitions, a huge cast, and spectacular uses of light, color, costumes, and sets, plus marvelous balletic dancing by Kelly and Cyd Charisse. In addition, there is Donald O'Connor's acrobatic and amusing "Make 'Em Laugh," and a couple of other numbers which enrich the mixture, heighten the ebullience, and make the picture an anthology of musical styles and techniques.

The Comden-Green collaboration is reinforced in SINGIN' IN THE RAIN by the chemistry between Gene Kelly and Stanley Donen, who co-directed the film. Kelly as a performer is nearly as important in the history of the musical as Astaire-Rogers and Judy Garland, although he never achieved their popularity. People liked Kelly for his brashness and his very American brand of charm, his extraordinarily virile footwork, and their feeling that he was on the verge of winking at them from the screen. But for some reason he was difficult to love. Perhaps his famous grin seemed painted on. But if he was important as a performer, he became legendary as a choreographer and director. With Stanley Donen, in addition to SINGIN' IN THE RAIN, he made ON THE TOWN and IT'S ALWAYS FAIR WEATHER, all of which were produced by Arthur Freed and based on screenplays by Comden and Green. Taken together, they constitute an *oeuvre* of such lightness and dazzle that they must be considered the ultimate works of a certain kind of film, the apotheosis of the organic, unified, smooth-flowing musical developed and nurtured at MGM.

93

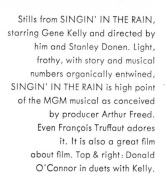

Stills from SINGIN' IN THE RAIN, starring Gene Kelly and directed by him and Stanley Donen. Light, frothy, with story and musical numbers organically entwined, SINGIN' IN THE RAIN is high point of the MGM musical as conceived by producer Arthur Freed. Even François Truffaut adores it. It is also a great film about film. Top & right: Donald O'Connor in duets with Kelly.

Cabaret 1972

The musicals of the 1960s were characterized by bigness, expensiveness, and the degeneration of an outmoded principle. Some made fortunes, like Robert Wise's THE SOUND OF MUSIC, perhaps the most perfectly contrived piece of sticky, sentimental, tear-jerking kitsch ever manufactured by Hollywood. Others, like WEST SIDE STORY and MY FAIR LADY, typified Hollywood's knack for ruining great properties, in the first instance when an expressionist fantasy was staged in the streets of New York instead of on a sound stage (an example of the tyranny of the notion that a film will be good if it is made on location), and in the second by such rigid direction and lifeless staging that one can only think of it as an embalming. Still others, like STAR, SWEET CHARITY, and DR. DOOLITTLE, have so little to recommend them that they are significant only as casebook studies of failed "chemistry." No matter how elaborate the production numbers, how engaging the stars, how successful the Broadway productions (when they were adaptations), or how talented the choreographers imported from New York, something in the musicals of the 1960s was lacking and that something was life force.

Arthur Freed's conception of the integrated musical, by then imitated by producers at all the studios, was worn out. The time had arrived for a new formulation, and when it finally came it turned out to be in fact two separate concepts, sufficiently interesting to cause one to quit shaking one's head over the demise of the genre.

The first new approach came from the recognition that there were great filmic possibilities in the new music called rock. The second, and the one that concerns us here, involved a rejection of the Arthur Freed principle. Taking off from the premise that there is nothing wrong with an unintegrated musical, a musical in which songs and dances are separated from story, the thinking went that since the natural transition from dialogue to music had become a cliché, why not simply abandon it and start again from scratch? The breakthrough musical of this type was CABARET, and though it is still too early to know whether or not it is a freak, its quality and success may establish it in movie history as a pivotal work.

CABARET, in the first place, is tough, stinging, satirical, and acid. None of the sweetness of Rodgers and Hammerstein here; none of the wholesome goodness of THE SOUND OF MUSIC in which life is depicted with utter falsity as one big happy songfest. CABARET owes more to the Weill-Brecht spirit of THE THREEPENNY OPERA, an un-compromising, hard-nosed look at life consistent with the coming of age of America in the 1960s. CABARET is the first musical to exploit the notion, now generally recognized by the public and for too long ignored by the industry, that life is fascinating because it is ambiguous, and that the intensity of a character's experiences is more interesting than an imposed wholesome personality. This is not to say that CABARET is some kind of thinking man's musical, and that because it confronts the facts that (a) people use one another, (b) homosexuality exists, (c) Nazism had its seductions, (d) decadence can be fun, etc., it is any less escapist than THE WIZARD OF OZ. On the contrary, CABARET is an escapist fantasy of a new kind. If the wholesome fantasy of THE WIZARD OF OZ is the sort that audiences needed when the reference points of American culture were midwestern and small town, CABARET is the sort they need and crave now that urban and political turmoil are the hallmarks of the age.

CABARET uses music in an exciting new way. Characters do not burst into song to express their emotions. Rather, a sleazy night club called the Kit Kat becomes a place where satirical comment on the lives and problems of these characters is made in striking, entertaining, and often savage dances and songs. Unlike a street in Spanish Harlem or a meadow in the Austrian Alps, the Kit Kat Klub is a logical place for music, and yet the entwining of the music performed in the cabaret and the story of Sally Bowles and her friends is as unnatural as the drama-music mix in any musical. The difference is that the fantasy in CABARET is not disguised by the pseudo-naturalism of the integrated musical. It is clearly artificial and no attempt is made to have it any other way.

Moreover, like all great musicals, CABARET is "right." Liza Minnelli (daughter of Judy Garland and Vincente Minnelli) is the catalyst. She enlivens the story by her gifts for dramatic acting, and becomes bigger than life when belting out songs on the Kit Kat Klub stage. She is the force that unifies the sly, cruel satire of Joel Grey (the cabaret's emcee and the personification of a decadence beyond good and evil), the superbly stylized art direction inspired by German expressionist painting, the handsome and intricate camerawork, and the choreography and dramatic direction of Bob Fosse. CABARET is not unforgettable, it is not profound, it is not great art, but it is great entertainment, a daring piece of diverting escapism that hopefully will revitalize a tired form.

Richard Lester's **A Hard Day's Night** 1964

And then there came rock....

For many years the split in pop music was between the tawdry trash beloved by teen-agers and the kind of classy pop known as "show music" (the songs of Porter, Berlin, Rodgers, etc.). But in the 1960s a reversal took place. Rock-'n-roll flourished with a brilliance that even exceeded the flourishing of the cinema in the same decade. People like Bob Dylan, the Beatles, The Rolling Stones, The Who, The Grateful Dead, Crosby, Stills, Nash and Young, and countless other artists and groups took over rock, refined it, and raised it from its more or less barbaric origins to the level of an art form.

Though many rock music cultists sincerely believe that this process sapped the greatest strength of rock—its primitive power—and that sophistication in this sort of music is more of a curse than a triumph, to the unbiased ear it is clear that the new rock music has transcended itself and has become the new "class" pop, and that conventional "show music" has gone into decline.

The cinema has not yet come firmly to grips with rock. Its potential as a new base for filmed musicals has been recognized, but the final form of these musicals has yet to be devised. Documentaries like WOODSTOCK, MONTEREY POP, DON'T LOOK BACK, and the very great GIMME SHELTER are, in a sense, a new kind of musical film, though not of the sort we are discussing here. Rock has been used, too, to embellish and heighten certain dramatic films. One thinks of the important contribution of Simon and Garfunkel to THE GRADUATE and the "score" of EASY RIDER made from preexisting rock songs written and recorded by a variety of vocalists and groups. One film, Richard Lester's A HARD DAY'S NIGHT, starring the Beatles, stakes out new ground. It synthesizes the new music with the new cinema in an exciting way, suggests a new format, and is, moreover, a great musical film.

Some would deny to A HARD DAY'S NIGHT the right to be called a musical. It was not made in Hollywood, after all, and contains no dream sequences, no dancing, no fantasy, and was not even shot in color. In fact, A HARD DAY'S NIGHT is a truer musical than the embalmings that have been passed off as musicals in recent years.

Like any Astaire-Rogers film, A HARD DAY'S NIGHT was contrived as a star vehicle. It was commissioned in frantic haste by United Artists as an exploitation film about the Beatles. Executives of UA were convinced that the group's popularity would crest in 1964 and were most anxious that the film be completed before the bubble burst. (How badly they misunderstood the temper of the times. There is no question that the Beatles' place in musical history is more secure than that, for example, of Julie Andrews, but then film-industry executives, whose business presumably is fantasy fulfillment, rarely have shown much understanding of what the public craves.)

A HARD DAY'S NIGHT, like any great musical, is totally informed by music. It is a musical about music, a pseudodocumentary about an immensely popular rock band whose members' lives center around music and who attempt both to escape from and build rapport with their many thousands of screaming fans. There are plenty of songs, some played voice-over, some rendered live from the concert stage; the final seventeen minutes, which were shot in a single day with six movie cameras and three TV cameras, is as much of a fantastic extravaganza as anything ever cooked up by Busby Berkeley.

Fantasy? The whole film is a fantasy, an entertaining vision of how the Beatles live and the absurd claustrophobic world they inhabit.

Comedy? The Beatles are natural-born comedians of the Mack Sennett school, and Lester has used many revitalized Mack Sennett devices to reinforce and heighten their comedic personalities.

Lightness? Exuberance? Froth? Escape? A HARD DAY'S NIGHT has all of these, and is surrealistic and satiric as well. The rising shot of the Beatles as they cavort around a field in a kind of mad ballet is a perfect example of lightness of touch in musical filmmaking. Their final concert is the picture's great escapist production number. Their relationships with each other, the "clean old man," their managers, and their public are enriched by put-down dialogue delivered with ingenuous charm. Only the most obtuse viewer believes that A HARD DAY'S NIGHT is a documentary. It is clearly contrived and a good deal of the froth and fun of the film lies in the way it calls attention to its many contrivances, and, in fact, flaunts them.

Magic? Chemistry? If seeing is believing, then the evidence is on the screen, both of the chemistry among the Beatles (which the bitterness of their breakup further confirms) and between them and their fans. A HARD DAY'S NIGHT is a filmmaker's film, a bold, inventive work by Richard Lester, whose flashy, jumpy style combusts with the exuberance of his stars into an explosion of joy at being young and alive.

From Kit Kat Klub sequences
of CABARET. Liza Minnelli (l.)
as Sally Bowles; Joel
Grey is the bawdy emcee.
CABARET represents a departure
from ''integrated musical''
of Arthur Freed. Singing and
dramatic elements are
separated, and wholesomeness
(as in THE SOUND OF MUSIC)
is finally abandoned
in favor of adult themes.

Scenes from A HARD DAY'S NIGHT, with Director
Richard Lester (bald) posing with the Beatles
during shooting (bottom l.). With decline
of show music, it was inevitable that the filmed
musical would turn to rock 'n roll. Lester's
"documentary" approach was another breakthrough.

Credits

Top Hat
U.S.A.; 1935; 105 minutes;
released by RKO.

Directed by Mark Sandrich.
Produced by Pandro S. Berman.
Screenplay by Dwight Taylor and Allan Scott.
Photographed by David Abel and Vernon Walker.
Art direction by Van Nest Polglase.
Choreography by Hermes Pan and Fred Astaire.
Songs by Irving Berlin.
Cast: Fred Astaire; Ginger Rogers;
Helen Broderick; Edward Everett Horton;
Eric Blore; Erik Rhodes.

The Wizard of Oz
U.S.A.; 1939; 101 minutes;
released by MGM.

Directed by Victor Fleming.
Produced by Mervyn Le Roy and Arthur Freed.
Screenplay by Florence Ryerson, Noel Langley and
Edgar Alan Woolf, from Frank L. Baum's story.
Photographed by Harold Rosson.
Art direction by Cedric Gibbons and William Horning.
Choreography by Bobby Connolly.
Songs by Harold Arlen and E. Y. Harburg.
Cast: Judy Garland; Ray Bolger; Jack Haley;
Bert Lahr; Billie Burke; The Singer Midgets;
Frank Morgan; Margaret Hamilton.

Singin' in the Rain
U.S.A.; 1952; 103 minutes;
released by MGM.

Directed by Stanley Donen and Gene Kelly.
Produced by Arthur Freed.
Screenplay by Betty Comden and Adolph Green.
Photographed by Harold Rosson.
Art direction by Cedric Gibbons and Randall Duell.
Choreography by Stanley Donen and Gene Kelly.
Songs by Nacio Herb Brown and Arthur Freed.
Cast: Gene Kelly; Debbie Reynolds;
Donald O'Connor; Cyd Charisse; Jean Hagen;
Millard Mitchell; Douglas Fowley; Rita Moreno.

Cabaret
U.S.A.; 1972; 122 minutes;
released by Allied Artists.

Directed by Bob Fosse.
Produced by Cy Feuer.
Screenplay by Jay Allen, based on the musical
drama ''Cabaret!'' written by
Joe Masteroff
and based on the play ''I Am A Camera'' by
John Van Druten and stories by
Christopher Isherwood.
Photographed by Geoffrey Unsworth.
Art direction by Rolf Zehetbauer.
Choreography by Bob Fosse.
Songs by John Kander and Fred Ebb.
Cast: Liza Minnelli; Joel Grey;
Michael York; Helmut Griem;
Marisa Berenson; Fritz Wepper.

A Hard Day's Night
Great Britain; 1964; 87 minutes;
released by United Artists.

Directed by Richard Lester.
Produced by Walter Shenson.
Screenplay by Alan Owen.
Photographed by Gilbert Taylor.
Songs by The Beatles.
Cast: John Lennon; Paul McCartney;
George Harrison; Ringo Starr; Wilfrid Branbell;
Norman Rossington; Victor Spinetti; John Junkin;
Anna Quayle; Kenneth Haigh; Richard Vernon;
Eddie Malin.

War

5

More movies have been made about war than about any other subject. War stories are so amenable to the cinema that in other chapters of this book there are at least fifteen pictures from which one could draw several perfectly acceptable lists of great examples of the genre: DR. STRANGELOVE, THE SEVEN SAMURAI, HIROSHIMA, MON AMOUR, THE GENERAL, and THE WILD BUNCH, or DUCK SOUP, GONE WITH THE WIND, LAWRENCE OF ARABIA, THE BATTLE OF ALGIERS, and HENRY V, etc.

There are so many good war films that it is difficult to make a valid selection. One may choose from such Second World War action classics as Howard Hawks' AIR FORCE, John Ford's THEY WERE EXPENDABLE, and William Wellman's STORY OF G. I. JOE, Sergei Eisenstein's great war pageant ALEXANDER NEVSKY, such antiwar warhorses as John Huston's THE RED BADGE OF COURAGE, Lewis Milestone's ALL QUIET ON THE WESTERN FRONT, and Bernard Wicki's THE BRIDGE, plus many films about people caught up in the drama of war: Edward Dmytryk's THE YOUNG LIONS, Vittorio De Sica's TWO WOMEN, Roberto Rossellini's GENERAL DELLA ROVERE, William Wyler's THE BEST YEARS OF OUR LIVES, Don Siegel's HELL IS FOR HEROES, and so on.

War is a subject that invites every sort of portrayal by every sort of filmmaker, usually with the common goal of condemning its pain, uselessness, and waste. The history of the war film is mostly a history of well-meaning attempts to save the world. Henry King shows us that he comprehends the anguish of war but can also justify its cost in TWELVE O'CLOCK HIGH. Mike Nichols is fascinating and pretentious in his black-comic CATCH-22. Carl Foreman's ironies are simple-minded but strong in THE

VICTORS. Stanley Kramer's moralizing is graceless but convincing in ON THE BEACH. Darryl Zanuck and Co. are exploitive in THE LONGEST DAY, but many of its scenes are forceful. Even the Sanders brothers deserve some credit for their self-righteous short film, A TIME OUT OF WAR.

The purpose of these critical remarks is not to condemn these pictures (flawed, but still better than ninety-five percent of the genre), but to debunk the widely held belief that a great war film must, by its very nature, be antiwar. In fact, this is probably true, but not in the sense that most filmmakers think—namely, that if their war movies are antiwar they are half-way to greatness already. Since it is so easy these days to be antiwar, one is inclined to admire the now unfashionable, prowar propaganda films of Hawks, Ford, and Wellman, and to be suspicious of the exploitation of antiwar sentiment by filmmakers who justify depiction of the most violent and revolting details of combat on the grounds that since their message is noble their vulgarity can be excused.

It is not enough that a war film be antiwar, or that it be measured solely on the basis of the skill of its scenes of combat, its verisimilitude or its politics. (The five pictures discussed here contain, all together, fewer minutes of actual combat than a single reel of THE DIRTY DOZEN.) To be great, a war film must view the madness that is war in the context of characters in conflict; then it must probe that madness, take its measure, and render it convincingly on the screen. The five selected films do these things well, and each, too, is the work of a unique sensibility that has come to grips with the endemic phenomenon of war in an original way.

Jean Renoir's **La Grande Illusion** 1937

The question surrounding the legendary LA GRANDE ILLUSION is what, precisely, is the "great illusion" of its title? Is it the belief, widely held after 1918, that the First World War was the war that would end all wars? Is it the idea that war is a noble enterprise? Is it the myth that nation-states are the things that separate men, when, in fact, it is social differentiation? Or is it the "illusion" that these disparities of class can be overcome? The beauty of this title is that it is open to so many lines of interpretation, and thus reflects the richness and complexity of a film that probes the nature of war in the compassionate and profound style so characteristic of Jean Renoir.

But since 1936, when LA GRANDE ILLUSION was con-

ceived and shot, a new interpretation of the title has emerged, an interpretation which the makers of the film did not anticipate. This is the possibility that Jean Renoir and his co-writer Charles Spaak suffered from a "great illusion" in thinking that they could change the world by making a work of art which would also be one of the strongest and most luminous pleas ever made for peace and brotherhood between men. Jean Renoir put it most poignantly when he made a written reply to a question posed by Robert Hughes, who was assembling a book about films having to do with war and peace, and who asked, in effect, whether such films ever really altered the public consciousness. Renoir wrote: "In 1936 I made a

Preceding pages: Alec Guinness staggers from sweatbox
in THE BRIDGE ON THE RIVER KWAI. Opposite: Stills
from LA GRANDE ILLUSION. Bottom: Erich von Stroheim as
von Rauffenstein and Pierre Fresnay (also at top,
hand in pocket) as de Boeldieu. Portraits, from top:
Jean Gabin, Marcel Dalio, Director Jean Renoir.

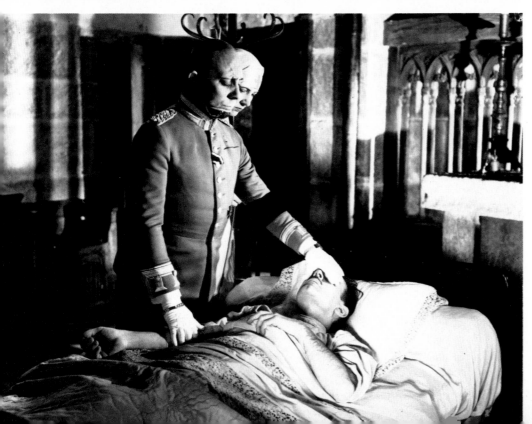

picture named LA GRANDE ILLUSION in which I tried to express all my deep feelings for the cause of peace. Three years later the war broke out. That is the only answer I can find to your very interesting enquiry." Could, then, in this ironic and retrospective way, the film itself have been a "great illusion"?

LA GRANDE ILLUSION is of that subgenre of war films which does not deal with combat or the horrors of war, but with the effects of war upon men removed from the fighting fronts, in this case men who are prisoners.

Though the settings of LA GRANDE ILLUSION are German prisoner-of-war camps in World War I, and the plot contains many of the motifs of prison-camp films, the real story of this picture is not escape, brutality, etc., but the interlocking and ambiguous relationships of four men, and the way these relationships illuminate the nature of human conflict. The men are the German aristocrat, von Rauffenstein (Erich von Stroheim), the French aristocrat, de Boeldieu (Pierre Fresnay), the former French mechanic and now officer, Maréchal (Jean Gabin), and the rich Jewish French officer, Rosenthal (Marcel Dalio). Their relationships are complex on account of social differences (important, but overcome), and differences in nationality (meaningless, but not overcome). In this sense LA GRANDE ILLUSION is about the stupidities of war rather than its horrors. In Jean Renoir's own words, it is "a sort of reconstructed documentary, a documentary on the condition of society at a given moment."

Jean Renoir, goes the cliché, is humanistic. But the cliché is true. The story, acting, and theme of LA GRANDE ILLUSION are permeated by compassion, warmth, and humanity, as is the very particular, steady, unblinking gaze of Jean Renoir's camera upon the faces of his actors while they perform with a genuineness of emotions and a generosity of spirit that is so luminous it nearly blinds us to their faults. The scene between Rosenthal and Maréchal in the snow is one of the perfect examples of this. Their split-up after their escape, Maréchal's anti-Semitic outburst and then the two men's reconciliation are a deeply moving dramatization of Renoir's belief that the nobility

of a man is best demonstrated in moments when his most human failings are exposed.

Renoir is concerned with what he calls "the interior truth which is the one vital thing." In effect, he says, "it has to do with knowing what someone is really like, what stuff he has in him. Then, once one has got at him, one has to make the audience see it too...." This is the principle upon which all great Jean Renoir films have been built, and when brought to bear in LA GRANDE ILLUSION upon the subject of men in war, it results in something that is unique, tranquil, and altogether extraordinary.

The key to finding the interior truth of a character was, for Jean Renoir, resolved by the way he dealt with his actors. When Renoir cast Jean Gabin, he was the biggest star in France. Pierre Fresnay was extremely popular, and Erich von Stroheim was to Renoir something like a god. Stroheim and Renoir did not meet until after Stroheim accepted the role of Rauffenstein. They got along beautifully, Stroheim freely making suggestions, Renoir agreeing to build up his part. (The idea that Rauffenstein should wear an iron corset and a chin brace was Stroheim's.) Stroheim has written of Renoir's patience with his actors, the delicacy of his manners, his fervor, and his patience, too, in the face of enormous production difficulties. Every actor who has worked with Renoir has commented upon these qualities, and the intense and warm gaze with which he inspired their confidence and which is paralleled in his shooting style.

LA GRANDE ILLUSION was released in 1937, at a time when war in Europe seemed inevitable. It was applauded by the public as a plea for peace, and was later banned by Goebbels. All existing prints were confiscated during the German occupation. Of course, the Nazis hated this film. Its message that national boundaries are meaningless was taken as a direct attack upon the expansionist policies of the Third Reich. Renoir refers to the Nazis as men "who almost succeeded in making people forget that Germans are also human beings." His use of the word "almost" is characteristic. Despite the fact that his life's work was nearly destroyed by them, and they ridiculed his fondest dream of human brotherhood, his conviction that war and conflict are but the ignoble acts of an otherwise noble creature, remained unshaken.

In the early 1950s, Renoir bought back the rights to LA GRANDE ILLUSION, which was being shown in various mutilated versions. He discovered an untouched print in Munich, and from that reconstructed the picture in time for the 1958 Brussels World's Fair, at which it was judged one of the dozen greatest movies ever made.

Alec Guinness leads his ragged troops into Japanese prison camp in BRIDGE. Bridge blows up in dramatic finale (l.) which camp physician calls ''madness, madness . . .'' William Holden (above) is American commando killed along with Guinness in bloody Japanese counterattack. Opposite: Gabin and Dalio in LA GRANDE ILLUSION.

David Lean's The Bridge on the River Kwai 1957

Like LA GRANDE ILLUSION, THE BRIDGE ON THE RIVER KWAI is an antiwar war film set in a prisoner-of-war camp milieu. But there the similarities cease. THE BRIDGE ON THE RIVER KWAI is an action movie in which the nature of war is explored in a contrived story executed by a director who is more concerned with spinning a climactic yarn than in making a social statement in an open-ended form. And if in LA GRANDE ILLUSION the characters are depicted by a great artist who cherishes their common humanity, in THE BRIDGE ON THE RIVER KWAI they are pushed to fulfill their destinies by a superb craftsman who values above all else suspension of disbelief.

The Japanese prison camp located near the Kwai River in Burma is an enclosed universe in which many familiar prison-camp motifs are played out. Escape is impossible but there is the inevitable talk of an escape committee; the prisoners are organized by their native commanders and are abused by brutal guards; the camp commandant is a psychopathic sadist; conditions are terrible—disease, poor food, a bad climate; morale fluctuates; the prisoners put on a musical in which they dress up as women; there are no significant female characters.

Into this essentially familiar situation comes Colonel Nicholson, a brave and admirable British officer, deeply concerned for the welfare of his men. Nicholson wants to prove to the Japanese that the British soldier is superior; he is convinced that if he can prove this his men will achieve a victory in their defeat. After an initial and fairly conventional struggle between Nicholson and the Japanese commandant over an obscure point of honor, the major situation of the story is introduced. Nicholson agrees to help the Japanese construct a bridge, and in his passion to find victory in defeat, loses sight of the fact that this bridge, which he insists must be a "proper bridge," will be used to further the war aims of the Japanese against other British troops.

In addition to the usual contending forces of a prison-camp picture, captors versus captives, and an interesting moral dilemma posed by the issue of the bridge, a third element is introduced: a commando force, led by a British major and an American escapee from the camp, whose mission is to blow up the bridge.

The film works to a climax. A Japanese train and the commando force converge on the bridge being completed by the British captives. The film cuts back and forth between the camp and the commandos, and the motives of Nicholson, the Japanese commandant, and the British major are fully explored. Each character has a perfectly valid reason for what he is doing, and each develops a relationship to the bridge that increases to proportions that are slowly and subtly revealed to be insane. Eventually, the suspense is relieved by a sensational climax in which the bridge is blown up, the Japanese train hurtles into a canyon, two of the commandos are killed, the commandant who was planning to commit hara-kiri is killed, and Colonel Nicholson dies, too, but not before he falls upon the plunger that sets off the explosives that destroy the bridge he has tried to save. In the words of a British medical officer who observes this finale from a hilltop, it is "madness, madness...."

Thus, THE BRIDGE ON THE RIVER KWAI deals with war in the form of a single incident in which well-developed and rational characters march reasonably and logically into an orgy of self-destruction. This, the film tells us, is what war is all about.

There are certain standard complaints leveled against THE BRIDGE ON THE RIVER KWAI, all of which seem to revolve around questions concerning the ending. Does Colonel Nicholson fall upon the exploder mechanism by accident or design? If by accident, is not the story ruined by a coincidence that is too farfetched, and if on purpose, is not his character inconsistent and absurd? If David Lean were really so precise a craftsman, his critics say, he would not have bungled an ending that must be clear in order to justify his film.

Let those who question the craft of David Lean's choreography look at the picture again. Many things happen very quickly at the end of THE BRIDGE ON THE RIVER KWAI, but a close inspection makes it clear that Nicholson finally realizes the insanity of what he has done, and is groping, in panic and shock, toward the plunger when he is shot. Perhaps it is a coincidence that he happens to fall upon it, but films of this kind are built around coincidences, possible in fictional terrains where internal logic creates a suspension of disbelief. The only valid question about a scene like this is not whether it is realistic, but whether it works as entertainment. Since the climax of THE BRIDGE ON THE RIVER KWAI is one of the most gripping finales in cinema, one must say that it works extremely well.

Frank Sinatra's singing career was in shambles when he entreated Harry Cohn of Columbia Pictures to cast him as Maggio in FROM HERE TO ETERNITY, then set for Eli Wallach. Wallach withdrew, Sinatra got part, won an Oscar, and made a phenomenal comeback.

Fred Zinnemann's **From Here to Eternity** 1953

Unfortunately, FROM HERE TO ETERNITY is principally remembered for its role in the now legendary career of Frank Sinatra. "FROM HERE TO ETERNITY?" people say. "Oh, yes, wasn't that Sinatra's comeback film?" And recently the whole story has been sensationalized and distorted in THE GODFATHER. The real significance of FROM HERE TO ETERNITY is that it was one of the best pictures produced in America in the 1950s, a superb entertainment that has in common with THE BRIDGE ON THE RIVER KWAI a well-wrought war story about people with whom audiences can become intensely involved.

It may seem odd to refer to FROM HERE TO ETERNITY as a war film, since so much of it deals with the peacetime army. But war is very important to this film. The December 7 attack on Pearl Harbor is its end point, the culmination of a merciless attack on the military mind.

FROM HERE TO ETERNITY views war as the monstrous cloud that hangs over its characters' lives. Throughout the film one feels a terrifying sense of déjà vu. One knows that the Japanese attack on Pearl Harbor will be the climax of the story, but since the characters do not know this and cannot anticipate the momentous event that will so deeply affect their destinies, one's inclination is to shout a warning to them.

When the attack comes it is brilliantly staged, one of the superb action sequences in war films. The Japanese planes are first only heard. Then there are explosions. Confused men rise from Sunday breakfast; the planes dive and strafe the quadrangle of the barracks while men run back and forth. When a noncom refuses to issue arms the men break down the door, take machine guns to the roof and blaze away. When they finally shoot down a plane they are exhilarated by their first taste of combat.

With this one powerful scene all the interlocking relationships which have been the substance of the story (between the bugler, Prewitt, who lives by his own very special code of honor—Montgomery Clift; Prewitt's buddy, the tough little guy, Maggio—Frank Sinatra; the sadistic Sergeant of the Guard at the stockade—Ernest Borgnine; Sergeant Warden, the man who cannot imagine himself as an officer—Burt Lancaster; Warden's lover, the estranged wife of his company commander—Deborah Kerr; her husband, a Captain whose principal concern is winning a divisional boxing tournament; and Donna Reed, Prewitt's girl friend, a paid companion at the New Congress Club) are permanently altered. A huge event diminishes these characters' sufferings and passions. World War II is a force that changes everything. Clift, Sinatra, and Borgnine die, the company commander resigns from the Army, Donna Reed and Deborah Kerr return to the mainland without their lovers, and Burt Lancaster has ahead of him an heroic career. War, in this picture, is bigger than people, and its sinister nature is explored by way of the relationships of the characters in the remote, confined, peacetime world of Schofield Barracks.

James Jones' novel, which sold millions of copies, was considered so offensive by the military that it took considerable pressure before the Department of Defense agreed to help with the filming of the attack. Daniel Taradash, who wrote the screenplay, has written that Harry Cohn of Columbia Pictures felt (undoubtedly by that infamous sense of instinct ridiculed by Herman Mankiewicz in his marvelous quip: "Imagine—the whole world wired to Harry Cohn's ass!") that Prewitt should blow his bugle before the sequence when he plays taps for Maggio. This led to one of the picture's more interesting scenes, when Montgomery Clift, perhaps the most brooding and introspective of American movie stars, plays a flamboyant and mournful blues in an enlisted man's club to express his rage at the way his beloved army is mistreating him. Other fine scenes include the great romantic-erotic encounter between Lancaster and Kerr at twilight on a beach (perhaps the most remembered sequence in the film, and quite daring in its day); Maggio's various encounters with Borgnine; and many short scenes of army life, in the barracks, on the drill field, and at the enlisted man's haven, the New Congress Club.

Fred Zinnemann's film closely follows James Jones' novel in style and technique. The omniscient and realistic direction of FROM HERE TO ETERNITY is Zinnemann's trademark. At the peak of his form (not apparent in HIGH NOON), he is capable of merging naturalistic acting and theatrical staging with a discipline that controls the first and prevents the second from looking phony. FROM HERE TO ETERNITY, his best picture, is one of those rare films in which the characters seem to have lives beyond the confines of the scenes in which they appear. The intersection of the attack on Pearl Harbor and the lives of Prewitt, Maggio, Warden, and the two women is a moving and eloquent statement of how war (a disinterested force) collides with the destinies of people and hurls them into a maelstrom.

111

Montgomery Clift as the bugler-boxer Prewitt in FROM HERE TO ETERNITY. Fred Zinnemann refused to direct the picture unless Clift played the lead, in which Cohn wanted to cast Aldo Ray. Cohn conceded, and Clift gave an extraordinary performance, perhaps the best of his career.

Burt Lancaster (l.) as
Sergeant Warden, Deborah
Kerr (above) as Karen
Holmes. FROM HERE TO ETERNITY
was one of greatest hits
of the 1950s. Costing little
more than $2 million, it
earned a fortune and
won eight Academy awards.

Stanley Kubrick's **Paths of Glory** 1957

In PATHS OF GLORY war is viewed in terms of power. This urgent, pulsating film about an episode in World War I combines Jean Renoir's idea that class differences are more important than national differences with the cannon-fodder theory of war, the theory that soldiers are merely pawns in the hands of generals who play at war as if it were a game of chess.

PATHS OF GLORY is a great film despite certain serious defects. The dialogue has an overwritten, literary quality that is not enhanced by the flat American accents of actors who sometimes seem out of place in French uniforms and kepis. Because of the strong ideological content of the story, many of the characters seem to represent ideas rather than personalities. One does not find here the kind of naturalistic acting that leads to audience identification as, for example, in FROM HERE TO ETERNITY. But perhaps the major failing of this film is that its story—basically about three men ceremoniously court-martialed and executed to justify the incompetence of their corrupt commanders—is a thoroughly stacked deck. A picture about the consequences of military tyranny, power plays by generals, corruption in high places, blind obedience, men using one another ruthlessly for professional advancement, and class struggle between officers and men (officers dance while poor men wait to die, etc.), it often has the stink of a heavy-handed antiwar message picture. And its ending, when Colonel Dax (Kirk Douglas) watches while a German girl (Susanne Christian, later to become Kubrick's wife) is forced to sing for drunken French troops, and then stirs recognition in them of her and their shared humanity—a scene that is either moving or sentimental depending upon one's taste—is a forced and too-symmetrical windup to an already overly symmetrical structure.

Despite these faults, which all are arguable, PATHS OF GLORY is redeemed by the brilliant filmmaking of Stanley Kubrick. Even if one objects to the ideological formality of PATHS OF GLORY—the fact that the generals are too inhumane and corrupt, the enlisted troops too innocent and used, Colonel Dax, the man in the middle, too torn on account of his peculiar blend of obedience and moral outrage, and a forced, pseudohumanistic ending—one can still admire the formality of its execution. Imagine, for an instant, the result if Stanley Kramer had made this film; consider how bland, soft and dull such a version would be. In the hands, however, of another Stanley the visual excitement of PATHS OF GLORY is so great that it overwhelms the viewer and covers up the defects of the material. PATHS OF GLORY is a director's film. One feels in every scene that one is in a director's hands. The

From PATHS OF GLORY: General Mireau (George Macready) inspects trenches (l.). Kirk Douglas as Colonel Dax (above). Opposite: Futile attack on "the anthill"; General Broulard (Adolphe Menjou) arrives at château; the trial sequence.

115

power of the picture lies in what the French call the *mise en scène*, the way it is all put together.

This power is the result of the way Kubrick uses his camera to express visually the content of his scenes. No one who has seen PATHS OF GLORY will ever forget the long travelling shots through the trenches, first when General Mireau inspects the troops, and then when Colonel Dax walks the trenches before the attack on the Ant Hill. While these wide-angle moving shots convey the claustrophobia of the trenches and the oppressed conditions of the soldiers, the elegant compositions inside the huge rooms of the chateau convey the coldness of the commanders and also their luxurious condition. The Ant Hill attack is a marvel of realistic filmmaking; one feels the confusion and desperation of an impossible assault. And the execution sequence, in which the camera moves relentlessly closer and closer to the stakes through lines of formally arranged troops, is one of the most suspenseful, geometric formulations in cinema. Alexander Walker has pointed out that the various shots of the Ant Hill assault made through binoculars express the way the commanders view the battle as a spectator sport. Similarly, the black-and-white squares of the château floors and the hierarchic arrangements of people in the court-martial scene express the way this occasion is a power play, a game of chess in which enlisted men are pawns

being sacrificed to further the advancement of more powerful pieces.

This amazing film, which Winston Churchill is said to have admired for the verisimilitude of its combat sequence, cost a mere $900,000, of which more than one-third went to Kirk Douglas. It was shot in Germany, with German policemen cast as extras. Six cameras were used to shoot the attack on the Ant Hill; there were five "dying zones" and each extra had a slip of paper which told him in which one he should "die." For a while after it opened, PATHS OF GLORY was banned on American military bases, and it is still banned in France, where the military establishment considers it a vicious slander against its honor.

In Kubrick's career, PATHS OF GLORY is a formative work that shows traces of the influence of Max Ophuls, so famous for his endless dolly shots, and also of the Soviet cinema, with its formal framings, rhythmic cutting, and dialectically balanced stories. It led to Kubrick being hired by Kirk Douglas to direct SPARTACUS, which in turn led to his being taken seriously as a director, presumably on the theory that a man who directs a $10 million picture has got to be serious. The result has been the emergence of one of the great talents in contemporary cinema, the master who created 2001: A SPACE ODYSSEY, and whose greatest work is yet to come.

116

Priest comforts ''cowards'' before rifle squad
receives order to fire. Entire execution
sequence is elaborately choreographed
and cut for maximum ''build.'' Kubrick staged scene
in formal geometric compositions in keeping
with hierarchical themes of film.

Robert Altman's M*A*S*H 1970

When Stanley Kubrick dealt with war again, in DR. STRANGELOVE, OR HOW I LEARNED TO STOP WORRYING AND LOVE THE BOMB, he pushed the absurdity he had described with such seriousness in PATHS OF GLORY into the realm of black comedy. M*A*S*H has also been described as a black comedy about war, but is actually part of the "service comedy" tradition, of which NO TIME FOR SERGEANTS and MISTER ROBERTS are probably the most famous examples. The "service comedy," a cross between the war film and the comedy, usually emphasizes the amusing aspects of being thrust into unfamiliar military situations, while minimizing the sinister realities of combat. But M*A*S*H is different. It combines broad, farcical routines with a significant and unblinking look at the nature of war, and is thus a film unto itself, perhaps the first picture in a new sub-subgenre that one might label the "blood comedy" on account of the large amount of scarlet fluid that dominates this movie's "look."

The Mobile Army Surgical Hospital, where most of the action in M*A*S*H takes place, is three miles from the front of the Korean War. Although we never see actual combat, we do see, over and over again until we are nauseated, the bloody results of fighting. War, in M*A*S*H, is a slaughterhouse, a huge, vicious machine that literally chews men up into so much bloody meat. It is against this situation, so gruesome and so horrendous, that the comedy is played. To stay sane the surgeons and nurses must indulge themselves with raucous and elaborately erotic games.

M*A*S*H is a very special film for reasons that elude those who shrug it off as trash. It is the first important film of Robert Altman, a highly original talent who develops here techniques he will use again in his superb western, MCCABE AND MRS. MILLER. These techniques, which result in a unique texture, may constitute one of the few original approaches to filmmaking in the last decade. The special look of M*A*S*H is the result not only of the lavish use of blood, but of its huge set constructed on mud flats at the Twentieth Century-Fox ranch in Malibu, California. The confused, asymmetrical arrangements of tents, supply dumps, field surgeries, and motor pool, crisscrossed by telephone wires, heaped with junk, and dominated by a public-address system that becomes, in effect, a major character, has the authentic feel of a mobile army surgical hospital, just as the town in MCCABE AND MRS. MILLER, in the very process of being built during the filming, conveys the sensual texture of the frontier. These sets do not look like sets. They are real spaces in which people live and work. And Altman, in both pictures, uses them this way. His casts actually inhabit these constructed environments, build up relationships with one another in them, improvise scenes and conversations, and literally live out their roles.

The extras in M*A*S*H were drawn from ensemble companies in San Francisco. Their realistic playing works in counterpoint to the foreground slapstick. In both of Altman's films one hears inconclusive pieces of conversation (often mumbled or cross-faded), and one glimpses relationships often left unresolved. Characters are revealed in bits and pieces rather than in conventional "character scenes." One has the sensation of exploring a particular world in a manner that is akin to one's experience in real life. In M*A*S*H one wanders through an environment, grasping its structure and meaning through the senses.

M*A*S*H was a big commercial hit. Despite the fact that it required more work from audiences than a more conventional film, it earned back its cost many times over. Like PATHS OF GLORY, it was considered an affront to the U. S. Army and was initially banned on American military bases. There is no solemnity in M*A*S*H, none of the heavy-handed pretentiousness that one finds in the brooding black comedy, CATCH-22, released in the same year. M*A*S*H has the vitality, the exaltation of life, that is typical of the American cinema at its best, and though its "Last Supper" sequence, derived from Leonardo da Vinci's famous painting, is not used with the same power as in Luis Buñuel's VIRIDIANA, it has in common with that great iconoclastic work the intention of mocking religion. M*A*S*H may have been the first commercial American film to do this openly. Religion—in the form of the "Last Supper," an incompetent surgeon who ludicrously prays, and a sanctimonious chaplain who wanders about giving spiritual comfort to men and women hourly confronted by blood and gore —is ridiculed without mercy. Religion, says Altman and his screenwriter, Ring Lardner, Jr., is of no comfort in the face of the insane carnage that is war. The only comforts, according to them, are the belly laugh, the sexual leer, and the marijuana cigarette.

From M*A*S*H: Elliott Gould and Donald Sutherland interrupt golf practice (l.) to examine X-rays. Bottom left: ''Last Supper'' sequence (compare with Buñuel's in VIRIDIANA, page 185). Bottom center: Director Robert Altman (with beard). M*A*S*H is notable for its ensemble playing, constructed environment, and bizarre blend of free-flowing blood and slapstick comedy.

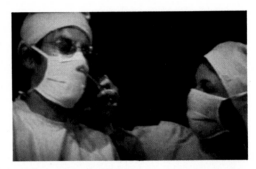

Credits

La Grande Illusion
(The Great Illusion)
France; 1937; 117 minutes;
originally released in the U.S. by
World Films.

Directed by Jean Renoir.
Produced by Frank Rollmer and Albert Pinkovitch.
Photographed by Charles Matras and Claude Renoir.
Screenplay by Charles Spaak and Jean Renoir.
Edited by Marguerite Renoir (Marguerite Marthe-Huguet).
Art direction by Eugène Lourié.
Music by Joseph Kosma.
Cast: Jean Gabin; Pierre Fresnay; Erich von Stroheim; Marcel Dalio; Julien Carette; Gaston Modot; Jean Dasté; Georges Péclet; Jacques Becker; Sylvain Itkine; Dita Parlo; W. Florian.

The Bridge on the River Kwai
U.S.A.; 1957; 161 minutes;
released by Columbia.

Directed by David Lean.
Produced by Sam Spiegel.
Screenplay by Carl Foreman and Michael Wilson, based on the novel by Pierre Boulle.
Photographed by Jack Hildyard.
Edited by Peter Taylor.
Art direction by Donald Ashton.
Music by Malcolm Arnold.
Cast: Alec Guinness; William Holden; Jack Hawkins; Sessue Hayakawa; James Donald; Geoffrey Horne; Andre Movell; Peter Williams; John Boxer; Percy Herbert.

From Here to Eternity
U.S.A.; 1953; 115 minutes;
released by Columbia.

Directed by Fred Zinnemann.
Produced by Buddy Adler.
Screenplay by Daniel Taradash, from the novel by James Jones.
Photographed by Burnett Guffey.
Edited by William Lyon.
Art direction by Cary Odell.
Music by Morris Stoloff.
Cast: Montgomery Clift; Frank Sinatra; Burt Lancaster; Deborah Kerr; Ernest Borgnine; Donna Reed; Philip Ober; Mickey Shaughnessy; Harry Bellaver.

Paths of Glory
U.S.A.; 1957; 86 minutes;
released by United Artists.

Directed by Stanley Kubrick.
Produced by James B. Harris.
Screenplay by Stanley Kubrick, Calder Willingham, and Jim Thompson, based on the novel by Humphrey Cobb.
Photographed by George Krause.
Art direction by Ludwig Reiber.
Edited by Eva Kroll.
Music by Gerald Fried.
Cast: Kirk Douglas; Ralph Meeker; Adolphe Menjou; George Macready; Wayne Morris; Richard Anderson; Joseph Turkel; Timothy Carey; Peter Capell; Susanne Christian.

M*A*S*H
U.S.A.; 1969; 116 minutes;
released by 20th Century-Fox.

Directed by Robert Altman.
Produced by Ingo Preminger.
Screenplay by Ring Lardner, Jr., from the novel by Richard Hooker.
Photographed by Harold E. Stine.
Art direction by Jack Martin Smith.
Edited by Danford Greene.
Music by Johnny Mandel.
Cast: Donald Sutherland; Elliott Gould; Tom Skerritt; Sally Kellerman; Robert Duvall; Jo Ann Pflug; Rene Auberjonois; Roger Bowen.

Adventure

6

The adventure film, like the western and the suspense picture, is a degraded genre, a genre of B pictures. Its purpose is to entertain an audience and make money, not to illuminate human experience and be honored as art. But like the western and the suspense picture, the adventure film can be a work of art. A great director, working within the conventions of the genre, can rise to heights of expressiveness.

The adventure film stands for everything that is anathema to Women's Liberation, a closed male world whose values the women's movement finds false and ugly. The pictures are always about men, alone or in groups, engaged in difficult action enterprises that reveal the male attributes of the characters. The enterprises are such things as the accomplishment of a difficult or impossible mission (a heist, a rescue, a search for treasure, a military campaign, or an act of revenge), involving encounters with harsh terrains (jungles, mountains, deserts), extremes of danger (natives, bandits, wild beasts, terrifying storms), and various forms of human baseness (killing, torture, betrayal, war). The revealed attributes are such things as bravery, ruthlessness, physical superiority, the assertion of power, and other aspects of machismo currently in disrepute.

If the story is about a solitary adventurer, it will concern his attempt to meet his own standards of honor. If it is about a group, it will concern camaraderie, the need for each man to measure up to the group code. The men of adventure films are hard, tough, determined, and physically skilled. The women, if they exist at all, are usually minor characters, sex objects, sometimes degraded, other times impossibly romanticized, or outsiders who must prove themselves before they can be admitted to the male world. A final convention is a subterranean stream of male love—love of man for man, expressed in an acceptable way, never tinged with effeminacy—which some observers cannot resist labeling latent homosexuality.

It is possible that the adventure story derives from some archetypal myth residing in the collective unconscious of man. From the time of Homer, stories of male exploits have been enormously popular. From the earliest days of the human race, men have sat around fires listening to other men tell stories of adventure. Someone once said that the cinema is the most perfect means ever devised to tell a story. Adventure films have been one of the economic pillars of the industry. Perhaps because they fulfill some need for vicarious experience they rarely fail to find an audience.

Ask someone to name his favorite films, and chances are he will give you a list of works which have been officially certified as art. Narrow the question and ask him to name the films he has most enjoyed, and chances are he will name one or more of the following five pictures, all of which are masterpieces of entertainment.

Howard Hawks' Only Angels Have Wings 1939

ONLY ANGELS HAVE WINGS is, perhaps, the basic adventure film of the American cinema, demonstrating all but one of the conventions of the genre in full development. The convention that is not fulfilled is the convention of great action sequences. In terms of production values, ONLY ANGELS HAVE WINGS is a modest film in which the subject is the meaning and consequences of adventure, rather than the adventures themselves.

It is a film with a very special mood. Most of the action takes place at the Dutchman's saloon, but this one-set arena is surrounded by a dark world of dangerous mountains, treacherous storms, and sudden, lonely death. The characters, civil aviators working for a small mail-run outfit in the port town of Barranca, presumably near the high Andes region of Peru, form an enclosed, all-male world in which the performance of work—getting the mail through and thus measuring up to standards set by the group—is the substance of life. In this world a man's self-respect determines the poise of his behavior. Here personal honor is a function of his professionalism and the esteem of his peers.

In this isolated masculine world a cast of adventurers is assembled: Cary Grant, the stoical commander of the unit who must conceal his deep feeling for his men lest he lose the poise necessary to inspire their respect; Grant's best friend, a character called Kid (Thomas Mitchell), older than Grant and subordinate to him, a man who will not admit that his vision is failing because flying and the camaraderie of the group are his life; another flier named Bat McPherson (Richard Barthelmess), who must prove to himself his right to be part of this elite because of a shameful incident in his past; and the pilots, Joe, Les, Tex, Sparks, and others.

Bat's wife (Rita Hayworth) knows the subordinate

122

Preceding pages: Tim Holt, Humphrey Bogart, and Walter Huston in John Huston's THE TREASURE OF THE SIERRA MADRE. Opposite: Cary Grant and Jean Arthur in Howard Hawks' archetypal adventure melodrama ONLY ANGELS HAVE WINGS. At rear: Victor Kilian, Thomas Mitchell, Allyn Joslyn.

role that a woman must play in this sort of world. Jean Arthur, who becomes involved with the young flier, Joe (and later with Grant), does not understand and threatens its cohesion. When Joe dies because he takes an unacceptable risk in order to get back in time to meet her for a dinner date, Jean Arthur's outburst disrupts the cool, hard way the pilots know they must respond to the death of one of their own. In a world where death lingers everywhere, where the threat of death hangs over every one of them at every moment he is in the air, an outward callousness toward disaster is the only way to cope. At first Jean Arthur is appalled by this. When she comes to understand it, when she is initiated into the special world of Barranca, she becomes one of the guys.

The male attribute of not showing pain, of not weeping over the death of a friend, of maintaining the unspoken code that says that the way Joe died proved he

wasn't "good enough," didn't have the character to give proper precedence to the job and the people who were counting on him to fulfill it—this code, finally, becomes her own, and when she understands it, we do, too.

ONLY ANGELS HAVE WINGS exemplifies the masculine ethos which is at the core of all great adventure films. This ethos is delineated by scenes which have become part of the vocabulary of films of this sort: camaraderie exhibited in the group sing; the initiation of a woman into a male world; the stoical hero who finally breaks down because even he, and therefore no one, can really take such pressure; the scenes which show why the job is more important than the individual; the austere life style of the adventurer who leaves no possessions behind, nothing except the status of his honor at the time he falls; and, finally, the scenes where a single man tests himself against danger, tempts death, and then defies it.

There are people who find ONLY ANGELS HAVE WINGS a corny film, filled with clichés, stock characters, and embarrassing moments whose excess makes them cringe. In a sense they are right. The film has blemishes, amplified perhaps by the fact that its ethos has become unfashionable. But its flaws are not important enough to obscure its brilliance as a film of conflicting relationships, played out in a strange and special world, in which the nature of adventure and the consequences of being an adventurer are laid bare.

If there is a literary equivalent of ONLY ANGELS HAVE WINGS it is in the works of Antoine de Saint-Exupéry, particularly *Night Flight,* in which the same philosophy of life is spelled out. It is also the philosophy of Howard Hawks, himself a physical adventurer, hunting companion of Hemingway, single-seat aviator, racing-car driver, and supreme technician of cinema, who made so many fine films over a period of many years, always denying that he was trying to do anything except tell a good story. In his career he created the parameters of the adventure film, not only with ONLY ANGELS HAVE WINGS, but with his two great westerns, RIO BRAVO and RED RIVER (which see), his Hemingway adaptation, TO HAVE AND TO HAVE NOT, his action war film, AIR FORCE, and many others. Hawks' pictures place him in the elite of Hollywood directors. Like the heroes of his adventure films he is a professional among professionals, the highest compliment that can be paid in the Hawksian universe.

Akira Kurosawa's **The Seven Samurai** 1954

A totally different kind of adventure film is Akira Kurosawa's THE SEVEN SAMURAI. It is a classic action movie following the exploits of a group of men accomplishing an impossible mission at great expense—i.e., the death of most of the adventurers. We have seen this story many times, in Peckinpah's THE WILD BUNCH, Brooks' THE PROFESSIONALS, Aldrich's THE DIRTY DOZEN, etc., but never in the history of the cinema have we seen it told so well, with such intensity and passion.

ONLY ANGELS HAVE WINGS is a confined entertainment. THE SEVEN SAMURAI is a vast work of art. While Hawks is concerned with the psychology of adventurers, Kurosawa is concerned with their physical exploits. Both pictures deal with camaraderie and the code of men under stress, but while Hawks demonstrates the meaning of the code, Kurosawa shows it in full practice, played out, literally, on the battlefield. Intelligence, bravery, physical superiority, self-sacrifice—the "male" values are all here, imbedded in a great outdoor action picture. THE SEVEN SAMURAI is about the vanity of human endeavor: how the brave and the mighty, who dare risk all to perform exemplary deeds and who fling themselves into life without caution, must always lose in the end, before the timeless circles of existence as played out by lesser men.

It is ironic that this best-loved of all Japanese films has rarely been seen at its original three-hour, twenty-minute length, and doubly ironic that the worst of three butchered versions was distributed in the United States under the title, THE MAGNIFICENT SEVEN, only to be withdrawn in 1960, when John Sturges made a picture with the same title, transposing Kurosawa's story to the American West. (The only resemblance between Takashi Shimura and Yul Brynner is that they both have shaven heads.) Such are the vicissitudes of filmmaking. For a long time the original of THE SEVEN SAMURAI was thought to have been lost, but now that it has finally been uncovered, we can only marvel at the fact that it stands up for every one of its two hundred minutes, a feat most rare in the history of the very long film, and certainly not true of the most famous of "lost" originals, the full-length GREED.

Kurosawa has said of THE SEVEN SAMURAI: "I wanted to make a film which would be entertaining enough to eat." After a year of difficult shooting ("we didn't have enough horses;...it rained all the time"), clashes of temperament, threats by Toho Studios to close down the production, and the expenditure of over half a million dollars (which, till then, was the greatest sum ever spent on a Japanese movie), Kurosawa had in his hands an extraordinary vision, which he proceeded to edit himself.

Kurosawa had created what amounted to a film repertory company. His actors and technicians had worked with him over and over again, and the essence of this sort of collaboration (unique in the world, with the exception of Bergman's group in Sweden) was that he was able to put his vision onto film as close as possible to the way he harbored it in his mind.

With this sort of atmosphere, and the addition of many innovative techniques (a consistent and audacious use of the long lens to telescope action, give the impression that men moving toward the camera are running in place, and thus bring action into the viewer's lap; constantly tracking and panning his camera; and a surprising use of slow motion in the early reels during moments of great stress), Kurosawa was able to create a universe, people it with characters from his imagination, set them against one another in a story of conflict, and stage all action so that his film forecloses any extraneous thoughts that might cross a viewer's mind. With THE SEVEN SAMURAI he literally possesses us, grabs hold of our attention, and does not let it go until the last frame has faded from the screen. As Pauline Kael has written: "Kurosawa achieves...the excitement of the senses."

One of the impressive things about this picture is that we always know precisely what is going on, even in the last rapid and chaotic moments of combat, when much of the action is obscured by a driving rainstorm, the cutting is swift, and the camera is constantly in motion. This is partly the result of Kurosawa's skill as an action director, his use of multiple cameras for each scene, and also his use of a clever map of the village and its defenses. The device enables Shimura to explain his tactics simply and to record the progress of the fight by brushing out a symbol each time an enemy bandit is killed.

(If anyone should question the importance of this point, he need only look at Richardson's THE CHARGE OF THE LIGHT BRIGADE, in which the culminating battle scenes are so badly staged that it is impossible to know what is happening, and, for that matter, who is fighting whom.)

Among the superlative moments of action in this film: the duel when we first see Kyuzo, the master swordsman; the awe of the villagers when they go to town and see the samurai marching back and forth on the streets, swords over their shoulders; Toshiro Mifune's antics when he goes out to steal a rifle from the bandits (his sloppy and comic adventure is beautifully contrasted with Kyuzo's austere approach to the same mission); and, of course, always the battles—great swirling contests of charging horses, rushing enemies, thrusting spears, fired arrows, and slashing swords, including an incredible final sequence in wind and rain.

Woven into all this action are subtle intimations of character. We know and understand each of the seven samurai, and are particularly fascinated by Mifune, the half-comic, half-serious madman whom we finally come to understand the best. His finest character scene is so moving that it bears description in detail.

Mifune has discovered that the villagers have

125

Six of THE SEVEN SAMURAI in Akira Kurosawa's remarkable film. Takashi Shimura is at left. Toshiro Mifune, whose performance is one of the greatest in Japanese film history, is second from right. Bottom: Bandits attack the village defenses.

Furious action and fantastic battle
sequences form the backbone of
THE SEVEN SAMURAI. But the film is rich,
too, in characterization and in
philosophical dialogue on the doomed role
of the superior samurai and the
survival of the downtrodden farmers.
Below: Shino and Katsushiro in love scene.
Opposite: At burial of Heihachi,
Mifune plunges sword into grave mound.
Above & right: Typical scenes. Kurosawa
revels in the use of telephoto shots
of men running toward his camera;
illusion of running in place may suggest
his attitude toward violence and war.

secreted away many samurai weapons and suits of armor. He brings these things to the other six, who are instantly appalled, since they know that these objects were stripped off dead samurai, whom the villagers, their employers, may even have killed. Mifune answers them in a stunning speech, most of it addressed to the lens of the camera, so that we feel he is speaking to us, too.

"Well, what do you think farmers are? Saints? They are the most cunning and untrustworthy animals on earth. If you ask them for rice, they'll say they have none. But they have! They have everything! Look in the rafters. Dig in the ground. You'll find rice, salt, beans, sake. Look in the mountains—there are farms hidden everywhere. And yet they pretend to be oppressed. They are full of lies. When they smell a battle they make bamboo spears and then they hunt. They hunt down the wounded and defeated. Farmers are miserly, craven, mean, stupid, murderous. You make me laugh so hard I'm crying. But then who made animals out of them? You!

You samurai! All of you damned samurai! And each time you fight you burn villages and destroy fields, steal food, rape women, enslave men. You kill them when they resist —you damned samurai!"

Mifune has delivered this speech while shouting, crying, laughing, full of hate and spite and irony and compassion. It is a fantastic scene, because after it we know that he is a farmer's son who, sickened by the craven cowardice of farmers, and wishing to be proud and noble, has proclaimed himself a samurai warrior. Yet at the same time he hates being a samurai, because he knows that the cowardice of farmers is caused by them. Thus his character is boxed. All his snorting bravado, his enormous rage, huge stamina, and boundless humor come out of the pressure of this paradox. Here, in the midst of a film of action and high adventure, we find a revelation of character as profound as any in any film made anywhere. This is Kurosawa's art: a rare combination of fully developed characters participating in violent action.

John Huston's The Treasure of the Sierra Madre 1948

THE SEVEN SAMURAI deals with the impossible mission. Another great theme is the search for treasure. Here, again, a group of men face an ordeal where courage, stamina, and sacrifice must carry them through. THE TREASURE OF THE SIERRA MADRE is a story about a search for treasure, but the adventurers do not measure up to their ordeal. THE TREASURE OF THE SIERRA MADRE is a picture about the breakdown of the adventurer's code. Under pressure the principal character becomes cowardly and selfish, the adventure fails, the treasure is lost, the camaraderie dissolves. As an action film THE TREASURE OF THE SIERRA MADRE works extremely well; it holds the audience by providing vicarious exhilaration. But there is more to it than that. Besides being an action picture it is a psychological thriller with a moral bias, always human and never allegorical.

Indisputably, the success of the picture is due to the talents of its writer/director, John Huston, and its star, Humphrey Bogart, who collaborated on no less than six films over a period of fifteen years. Bogart's performance in THE TREASURE OF THE SIERRA MADRE is unique in his career. In the course of two hours we see him change from a likable and fair-minded guy on the bum, into a nervous paranoic, and finally into a madman capable of killing his best friend in cold blood. And the cause of his de-

terioration is gold, the cursed metal whose quest is the plot and whose ability to corrupt is the story of the film.

In an early scene, Bogart is sitting in a flophouse in Tampico, Mexico, with his friend Curt, listening as a wiry old prospector named Howard (Walter Huston, the director's father) says that once a man has had a taste of gold, he is never satisfied until he has more. "No," says Bogart, "that wouldn't happen to me—not to Fred C. Dobbs." Thus the theme of the movie is laid bare. Despite fair warning of what is to come, Dobbs is corrupted and then devoured by greed. His gold destroys him, and at the end, insane with fear and thirst, he is cornered and slaughtered by ruthless bandits, and his treasure is scattered to the winds.

The production of TREASURE was an adventure in itself. Huston had wanted to make the film for years, and chose it as his first production after returning from World War II, where he had honed his craft making documentaries for the Army. He wrote a screenplay based on the novel by the elusive author B. Traven. Huston mailed his screenplay to Traven, and when he received back a long letter, he asked to meet with the author to further discuss the filming of his book. He was instructed to appear at the Hotel Reforma in Mexico City for an interview. Huston waited there several days, but Traven

Hand-to-hand combat in a driving rainstorm: Spears are thrust, arrows fired, horses slip, and swords slash in the phenomenal climactic battle as samurai lead embattled peasants to victory over the bandits — perhaps the greatest action sequence ever filmed.

Bottom, far right: John Huston, director of THE TREASURE
OF THE SIERRA MADRE, sits between Humphrey Bogart and father
Walter Huston. Both Hustons won Academy awards, John
for screenplay and direction, Walter as best supporting actor.
Above (on burro): Alfonso Bedoya scored in small, juicy
role of Gold Hat, the sinister Mexican bandit.

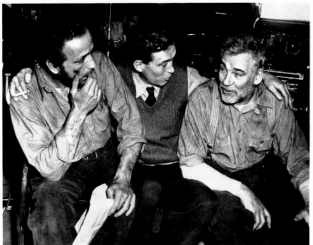

didn't show up. As he was about to return to Hollywood a man handed him a card which read "H. Croves, translator, Acapulco," and a note from Traven saying, "This man knows my work better than I do." Huston hired "Croves" as a technical advisor on the film, but throughout the production "Croves" refused to be photographed. When the filming was over Huston somehow got hold of a rare photograph of Traven and showed it to Bogart. "That's Croves," said Bogart, but the "mysterious" author had disappeared and Huston never saw him again.

The film was one of the first major postwar Hollywood productions to be shot entirely on location, for which Huston had to have the special permission of Jack L. Warner, president of Warner Bros. The shooting was difficult and the conditions primitive. While Huston was casting extras his Mexican production manager told him that the men would normally receive ten pesos a day, but if Huston was willing to pay them fifty, he could shoot them in an arm or a leg. He was warned, however, that they were not to be killed!

There were many battles with the studio as costs mounted to nearly $3 million and Jack Warner insisted that the Bogart character not die. (Huston's early films always seemed to climax in difficult and bitter fights with his backers. Then, for a long period, he seemed to lose his will to fight and became involved in mediocre projects.)

B. Traven's novel rambles along through a thicket of Marxism, while Huston's film is a direct and hard-hitting attack on the accumulation of wealth, without once mentioning the word "capital." This may constitute its superiority over Erich von Stroheim's GREED. Stroheim hits his audience over the head with a long, ambitious attempt to make a Great Statement. Huston conceals his statement in a comparatively modest and austere story of believable characters, whose obsession grips the audience and becomes their own. In THE TREASURE OF THE SIERRA

MADRE we seldom feel that we are watching a "message film." The picture is pure entertainment, and its ironic ending, in which the gold dug out with such difficulty blows back into the hills where it was mined, is barely tarnished by the final echoing laughter of Walter Huston on the sound track. This laughter may represent less the irony of John Huston than the triumph of a wise old man whose predictions have come true.

The film is striking for its purity of technique—its clean cuts and avoidance of tricky angles and attention-calling shots. Its sense of movement is as great a credit to Huston the screenwriter as it is to Huston the director. His construction is economical, spare, always correct. We feel that each shot and each scene is exactly as it should be.

Many of the moments in THE TREASURE OF THE SIERRA MADRE have become classic: the glint in Bogart's eyes as Walter Huston weighs out the gold; the night the three adventurers decide that each man will take care of his own "goods"; Walter Huston's trusting look back when he is taken off by peaceful Indians; the shadow of the desperado, Gold Hat, when he appears behind Bogart at the water hole; the way the bandits seem to pick over Bogart, even before they kill him.

There is one sequence that is rarely mentioned, and that seems to sum up the artistry of this film especially well. This occurs when Gold Hat and the remnants of his band go into town to sell Bogart's burros. Someone spots a brand on one of the burros, a boy runs to the police, people in the marketplace stall the thieves, surround them, and then turn them over to the Federales for immediate execution. The scenes goes on for nearly a reel, the entire dialogue is in Spanish, not one word of English is spoken, and yet every moment is comprehensible, and we are never really aware that we are listening to a foreign language. In a scene like this, Huston is telling his story visually, at the highest level of film art.

Michael Curtiz' **Casablanca** 1943

The Casablanca of CASABLANCA is a unique piece of fictional turf. The picture opens on maps while a narrator explains that Casablanca is the second-last resting place on the long, tortuous refugee route from war-torn Europe. (The last resting place is Lisbon; the mecca is New York.) As one character puts it: "The scum of Europe has gravitated to Casablanca." Another says: "Human beings... they're Casablanca's leading commodity." "In Casa-

blanca," says the Nazi Major Strasser, summing it all up, "human life is cheap." It is a place, in short, where anything is possible and everything is negotiable, a place of drama, adventure, and intrigue, a place where a man may be shot on the street in front of a portrait of Marshal Pétain, or where an attractive young lady may secure an exit visa by spending the night with the Préfet de Police.

The center of the action in this world is Rick's

133

Humphrey Bogart in his quintessential
adventurer's role, posing before Rick's Café Américain
in a publicity still for CASABLANCA. Rick's
café is an arena of incredible adventures, harboring
arrogant Nazis, Free French, black marketeers,
idealists, murderers, refugees, and S. Z. Sakall.

As Time Goes By: Bogart presides over his domain
while Dooley Wilson plays piano. Center: Bogart with Paul Henreid,
Ingrid Bergman, and Claude Rains. Bottom: Bogart about
to kill Major Strasser (Conrad Veidt). Opposite: Bogart
and Bergman in one of their "with-the-whole-world-crumbling-
we-pick-this-time-to-fall-in-love" moods.

Café Américain, conveniently located across the street from the airport, which is where most of the people in Casablanca want to go. Rick's café is an incredible place, owned and operated by Humphrey Bogart, a combination bar, night club, and gambling casino, where the pastry chef formerly was the leading banker of Amsterdam, and where the rooms seethe with conspiracies, black-market activities, and plots and counterplots of all sorts. A member of the Free French underground circulates with a ring that conceals a Cross of Lorraine; a marvelous black singer-pianist named Sam plays nostalgic tunes; and the roulette wheel is fixed to stop at number 22 on command.

CASABLANCA is one of the few adventure films where the adventures take place indoors. There are no fights, no outdoor adventures here. There are, instead, adventures of verbal jousting, of dialogue and innuendo, and they are dominated, in fact ruled, by a supreme adventurer, Rick.

Rick is the quintessential Bogart character, who has absolutely nothing in common with the psychopathic Fred C. Dobbs of THE TREASURE OF THE SIERRA MADRE. He is more urbane than Sam Spade in THE MALTESE FALCON or Philip Marlowe in THE BIG SLEEP. The Bogart of CASABLANCA is the Bogart who has been posthumously idealized by the young, resurrected by them from a temporary oblivion.

In the 1940s, audiences who attended Bogart films thought of him as a good actor who appeared in interesting movies. Since the mid-1950s, however, when informally arranged Bogart festivals were booked into college movie theatres, he has been rediscovered and his cult born. Youngsters had never seen his like before. They adored him, the way he smoked and talked out of the corner of his mouth and held a gun as if he knew how it worked and meant to use it. Girls found him sexy and young men wished to emulate him. He was idolized for his toughness, his vulnerability, and his implicit freedom. He had the aura of a man who did what he liked doing; he didn't work for wages and he was nobody's patsy. Of all the Bogart characters (and most of them were facets of the same man), none stirred these young audiences so much as the Bogart of CASABLANCA. Who is this Rick/Bogart? What is his magic? What is the secret of his appeal? Portions of dialogue from CASABLANCA give hints. When added together they make something of a portrait of a supreme adventurer.

His Irony:

Asked to explain why he came to Casablanca, Rick says: "I came to Casablanca for the waters."

"What waters? We're in the desert."

"I was misinformed," he says.

His Politics:

We learn that in 1935 he ran guns to Ethiopia, and in 1936 fought on the Loyalist side in Spain. "I was well paid on both occasions," he says, but the Préfet de Police points out that "the winning side would have paid you twice as much." Rick, we come to understand, is on the Nazi blacklist—their "role of honor."

His Erudition:

Rick is a man who can tell by the sound that a piece of distant artillery is "the new German 77." Listening a little more closely he can estimate its distance from Paris at thirty-five miles "and moving closer every minute."

His Sex Life in Casablanca:

A brief exchange with a girl explains a lot:

"Where were you last night?" she asks.

"That's so long ago I don't remember."

"Will I see you tonight?" she insists.

"I never make plans so far in advance."

His Cynicism:

Twice he says: "I stick out my neck for nobody." When asked who he thinks will win the war, he replies: "I haven't the slightest idea.... The problems of the world are not my department—I'm a saloon keeper," he says. And on another occasion, when pressed for a commitment, he replies: "Your business is politics—mine is running a saloon."

His Fastidiousness:

He never drinks with his customers.

His Sentimentality:

To Ingrid Bergman in Paris: "With the whole world crumbling we pick this time to fall in love...."

To Bergman and her husband at the Casablanca airport: "The problems of three little people don't amount to a hill of beans in this crazy world."

His Pain:

The look on his face when he throws away Ingrid Bergman's letter as his train pulls out of Paris. (The rain has washed away the ink of her hurtful words.)

The look on his face when Ingrid Bergman appears in his café. "Of all the gin joints in all the towns in all the world," he says, "she walks into mine."

His Bitterness:

When he accuses Ingrid Bergman of having had other lovers: "Were there others in between? Or aren't you the kind that tells?"

His Urbanity:

"What is your nationality?" asks Major Strasser.

"I'm a drunkard," says Rick.

His Mystique:

Claude Rains explains it to Ingrid Bergman: "Rick is the kind of man that if I were a woman I would be in love with Rick."

Bogart dominates CASABLANCA, but there are other characters too, fascinating ones, revealed at breathtaking speed in the first few reels, delineated clearly by snatches of their own dialogue, by comments others make about them, or by their own peculiar and very striking presences:

Claude Rains, the police prefect, infinitely charming, infinitely corrupt: "I blow with the wind; the prevailing wind blows from Vichy."

Conrad Veidt, the Nazi major who has come to Casablanca to impose the influence of the Gestapo: "You speak of the Third Reich as if you expect there to be a fourth."

Paul Henreid, the goody-goody character, underground resistance leader, Bergman's husband, stiff and pompous. As Claude Rains says of him: "He succeeded in impressing half the world; it's my job to see that he doesn't impress the other half." At the same time that Henreid refuses to tell the names of the underground leaders in the capitals of Europe, he assures Veidt that if the men are caught "from every corner of Europe hundreds, thousands will rise up to take their places."

Sidney Greenstreet, owner of the Blue Parrot and chief of the black market: "As the leader of all illegal activities in Casablanca, I am an influential and respected man."

Peter Lorre, a psychotic, two-bit black marketeer and murderer: "You despise me," he says to Rick. "I trust you because you despise me."

A girl who has apparently slept with every man in the story: "In her own way she may constitute an extra second front."

A refugee couple: "We hear very little and we understand even less."

Ingrid Bergman, Bogart's lover: She is simply there—beautiful, soft, remote, warm, mysterious, the impossible object of an impossible romance, the dream lover of every man.

Of course, the interaction of these adventurers results in some moments of pure corn: the Paris flashbacks; the Marseillaise versus the Horst Wessel Song sequence; the "Here's looking at you, kid," toasts; the "Play it, Sam" pleas of Ingrid Bergman; the discarded bottle of Vichy water at the end; the line of Paul Henreid: "Welcome back to the fight. This time I know our side will win"; and the lyrics of "As Time Goes By." But all this corn is delivered with enormous style, and is satisfying in an uncanny way. It is conventional now to admire CASABLANCA for its camp qualities. "It's so good it's bad," is what a lot of people like to say. Actually, CASABLANCA is good on its own merits. It is extremely well written and very well directed by Michael Curtiz. The two long sequences at Rick's Café, in which a dozen characters and nine or ten subplots are developed with wit and clarity, are unbeatable examples of shorthand storytelling. Obviously, it is not a work of art, but just as obviously it is a masterpiece of entertainment.

CASABLANCA was big when it opened thirty years ago, a week before the wartime Casablanca Conference, and it has been big ever since, particularly on campuses. In fact, it is possible that CASABLANCA has ruined the summer vacations of many college students who have gone to the city expecting to find the glamor and excitement of the movie, and have found instead a huge, impersonal metropolis, the Chicago of Morocco.

David Lean's Lawrence of Arabia 1962

I consider myself an entertainer....
I like a good strong story. I like a beginning,
a middle, and an end....I like to be
excited when I go to the movies.
                    —David Lean, in an interview on
                         the CBC, March, 1965.

No amount of critical analysis will sum up the aesthetic of David Lean better than that quotation. Lean does not merely pay lip service to well-constructed, exciting stories. He makes them. His greatest achievement, in a career that has included the poignant romance, BRIEF ENCOUNTER (1946), the splendid period film, GREAT EXPECTATIONS (1947), and the great war picture, THE BRIDGE ON THE RIVER KWAI (1957), is undoubtedly LAWRENCE OF ARABIA, the adventure film of adventure films, one of the best-constructed and most exciting adventure stories ever to fill a screen.

LAWRENCE OF ARABIA has in common with THE SEVEN SAMURAI a rare combination of deep character penetration and enormous epic sweep. It is a masterpiece of

137

Opposite: Peter
O'Toole as T. E.
Lawrence crossing
the ''sun's anvil.''
This page: Lawrence
leads charge; ''El
Awrens''' guerrillas
attack dynamited
train; Anthony
Quinn as desert chief
Auda Abu Tayi; Alec
Guinness as King
Feisal. All the
actors in LAWRENCE OF
ARABIA are superb,
but so is supporting
cast — the sun
and the desert.

139

intimate moment and spectacular largesse. But while THE SEVEN SAMURAI is about a group of men, LAWRENCE OF ARABIA is the story of a solitary adventurer who lived, was romanticized, and has lately been debunked. Throughout the picture one has a sense of a man discovering his own unique dimensions. Lawrence always knew he was different, but in Arabia he discovered that his proportions were heroic. Perhaps this is the secret of LAWRENCE OF ARABIA—that at the bottom of all the violent action is a protagonist about whom one cares, an intriguing, enigmatic personality whom one glimpses but never fully understands.

All the conventional elements of the genre are at peaks of excellence here: a difficult terrain (the desert—when Lawrence leads men across the sun's anvil we pant with thirst); danger (it is everywhere, for LAWRENCE OF ARABIA is a film about guerrilla warfare); prowess (Lawrence crosses Sinai on foot!); torture (Lawrence in the hands of the Turkish bey); an impossible mission (to take Aqaba from behind); a rescue (Lawrence returns to the sun's anvil to pick up a man who has fallen from his camel); ruthlessness (Lawrence must kill the man he saved to give justice to his Arab allies; he shouts "take no prisoners" when his men decimate a Turkish column); austerity (Lawrence is an adventurer uninterested in possessions; for him glory is enough and he even renounces that when he returns to England and seeks anonymity); the subordinate role of women (there are none in the film, unless one counts the nurse who appears at the end and speaks one line). Every component is here, everything one needs for a great adventure film, and in addition there is a fascinating pivotal character whose mystery is grasped though never solved.

The usual complaint against David Lean is what some critics call his "impersonal style." What they really are objecting to is his superlative technique, craftsmanship that never calls attention to itself, but always serves the telling of his stories. LAWRENCE OF ARABIA represents an enormous achievement, a film, like THE SEVEN SAMURAI, that literally excites the senses.

There are many spectacular sequences in LAWRENCE OF ARABIA, each of them flawless: Lawrence's trek to rescue the fallen man (Lean cuts to the sun again and again, turning it into a character); the scene in Feisal's tent when Lawrence first talks with the King (as the characters pace and move into different pools of light the camera tracks back and forth with at least a dozen changes of focus, but the conversation flows with an effortless grace that obscures the technical accomplishment); Lawrence striding on top of a captured train,

parading before rows of cheering Arabs; Lawrence in his encounters with Allenby and Bentley (to Allenby he confesses discovering a perverse pleasure in killing; when Bentley asks him what attracts him personally to the desert, he looks the man up and down and says, "It's clean"); the scene when Ali Ibn el Kharish (Omar Sharif) appears on his camel, an excruciatingly long take in which an ominous figure is first resolved out of waves of heat and then, as he draws closer, becomes a deadly threat to Lawrence's escort; the great slaughter scene when Lawrence discovers himself caked with blood and becomes horrified at the barbarism lurking beneath his civilized veneer; and the scene between Lawrence and Jose Ferrer illuminating Lawrence's strange perversity, a mixture of masochism and repressed homosexuality. (Some critics have complained that this scene is a copout because Lean doesn't show what happened. It is difficult to know what they want to see, why a literal act of sodomy is necessary when Lawrence's look and gestures, before and after, make absolutely clear what took place.)

There is not much more one can say about LAWRENCE OF ARABIA other than that it meets every test of the great adventure film and passes it with honors. The photography by Freddy Young, the script by Robert Bolt, and the acting by Peter O'Toole, Alec Guinness, Anthony Quinn, Jack Hawkins, Jose Ferrer, Anthony Quayle, Claude Rains, Arthur Kennedy, and Omar Sharif are so superb that LAWRENCE becomes one of the very rare breed, the superexpensive picture that is also good, the lavish spectacle that is deep, the big film that didn't get away from the director whose control one can feel in every frame.

140

Director David Lean (in white hat) on location
in Jordan during filming of LAWRENCE. Raid on Aqaba
and blasting of railroad were shot in Spain,
slaughter of Turks in Morocco. Scenes of Cairo,
Damascus, and Jerusalem, which had become too modern
for period of film, were recreated in Seville.

Credits

Only Angels Have Wings
U.S.A.; 1939; 121 minutes;
released by Columbia.

___

Directed by Howard Hawks.
Produced by Howard Hawks.
Screenplay by Jules Furthman,
from a story by Howard Hawks.
Photographed by Elmer Dyer and Joseph Walker.
Art direction by Lionel Banks.
Edited by Viola Lawrence.
Music by Dimitri Tiomkin and Morris W. Stoloff.
Cast: Cary Grant; Jean Arthur;
Richard Barthelmess; Rita Hayworth;
Thomas Mitchell; Sig Rumann; Victor Kilian;
John Carrol; Allyn Joslyn; Donald Barry;
Noah Beery, Jr.

The Seven Samurai (Shichinin No Samurai)
Japan; 1954; 200 minutes;
released by Toho.

___

Directed by Akira Kurosawa.
Produced by Shojiro Motoki.
Screenplay by Shinobu Hashimoto,
Hideo Oguni, and Akira Kurosawa.
Photographed by Asakazu Nakai.
Art direction by So Matsuyama.
Edited by Akira Kurosawa.
Music by Fumio Hayasaka.
Cast: Toshiro Mifune; Takashi Shimura;
Yoshio Inaba; Seiji Miyaguchi; Minoru Chiaki;
Daisuke Kato; Ko Kimura; Kunmnori Kodo;
Kamatari Fujiwara; Yoshio Tsuchiya;
Keiko Tsushima; Yukiko Shimazaki.

The Treasure of the Sierra Madre
U.S.A.; 1948; 126 minutes;
released by Warner Bros.

___

Directed by John Huston.
Produced by Henry Blanke.
Screenplay by John Huston,
from a novel by B. Traven.
Photographed by Ted McCord.
Art direction by John Hughes.
Edited by Owen Marks.
Music by Max Steiner.
Cast: Humphrey Bogart; Walter Huston;
Tim Holt; Bruce Bennett;
Alfonso Bedoya; Barton MacLane.

Casablanca
U.S.A.; 1943; 102 minutes;
released by Warner Bros.

___

Directed by Michael Curtiz.
Produced by Hal B. Wallis.
Screenplay by Julius J. and Philip G. Epstein
and Howard Koch.
Photographed by Arthur Edeson.
Art direction by Carl Jules Weyl.
Edited by Don Siegel and James Leicester.
Music by Max Steiner.
Cast: Humphrey Bogart; Ingrid Bergman;
Claude Rains; Paul Henreid; Conrad Veidt;
Sidney Greenstreet; Peter Lorre;
Marcel Dalio; Helmut Dantine; Dooley Wilson;
S. Z. Sakall; Joy Page; Leonid Kinsky;
Madelaine LeBeau; John Qualen.

Lawrence of Arabia
Great Britain; 1962; 221 minutes;
released by Columbia.

___

Directed by David Lean.
Produced by Sam Spiegel.
Screenplay by Robert Bolt.
Photographed by F. A. Young.
Art direction by John Box.
Edited by Anne Coates.
Music by Maurice Jarre.
Cast: Peter O'Toole; Alec Guinness;
Anthony Quinn; Jack Hawkins; Jose Ferrer;
Anthony Quayle; Claude Rains;
Arthur Kennedy; Donald Wolfit; Omar Sharif.

Manners, Morals & Society
7

anners, Morals and Society" is not, of course, a classic motion-picture genre. It is a phrase that serves as a catchall, a means of linking pictures whose makers enjoyed a common desire to describe a social milieu. These are not the "message films" that take positions on specific issues or speak for those who have no voice. They are dealt with later on, in a chapter on "The Cinema of Concern." Here the focus is on movies which express filmmakers' visions of society, in widely varying styles and at different levels of artistic achievement.

This matter of artistry may present a problem. It is a fair question to ask why a sublime work like RULES OF THE GAME should be linked in any way with so crude a work as EASY RIDER. The question begs an answer. Otherwise, it might seem as though some fragile link between fine and popular art is being forged in order that the author might secure himself a base in each of the two great opposing critical camps, the camp of the highbrows,

oriented toward the art cinema of Europe, and the camp of the slobs, who exult in the pop cinema of Hollywood.

Let that charge now be firmly met. The fact that the vision of Jean Renoir is refined and complex, and the vision of Dennis Hopper is crude and simplistic, has no bearing when it comes to judging the emotional strength of their respective works. It is the contention here that these distinctions are not relevant to "greatness." Who would now say that a "great" painting by Raphael is either better or worse than a "great" primitive sculpture by an unknown African Bushman? However wide the gulf between RULES OF THE GAME and EASY RIDER in matters of quality, style, and commercial success, they share an intensity that is rarely found in film.

Intensity—that, ultimately, was the basis for choosing the pictures in this chapter. Each of them is an enormously powerful vision of society, a picture which once seen cannot be shaken from the mind.

Jean Renoir's **Rules of the Game** 1939

RULES OF THE GAME is a social comedy in the tradition of certain classics of the French theatre, the comedies of manners of Beaumarchais and Marivaux. An opening title protests that "This entertainment...does not aspire to be a study of morals"—a protestation one must rapidly dispute. Morals, or rather the absence of them, is what the picture is all about.

Renoir has spoken of his mood at the time he conceived the film: "It was between Munich and the beginning of the Second World War, and I was deeply disturbed by the state of mind of French society and the world in general." Clearly, he is referring to the well-known aimlessness and social corruption of that period, the macabre dance of a society headed for cataclysm. (His use of Saint-Saëns' "Danse Macabre" during the fête sequence is a stroke of genius.)

Rather than express his distress directly in the form of a serious protest film, Renoir decided to use the more subtle form of the comedy of manners. A large number of characters, representing many types, are confined in the Château la Colinière. In this miniature universe they become a ship of fools, and play out the manners and morals of society at large in a diverting, farcical, and tragic-grotesque style. In RULES OF THE GAME, Renoir does not allow us to identify too closely with any single individual. Rather, he paints on a broad canvas which we

observe from an amused distance. And, as in French plays of this sort, when we laugh at the posturings of the characters we are really laughing at ourselves.

Like LA GRANDE ILLUSION, RULES OF THE GAME is an enigmatic title, a device of which Renoir, in the thirties, was especially fond. Just as the first question about LA GRANDE ILLUSION is what, exactly, is the "great illusion," so the first problem of RULES OF THE GAME is to identify the "game" and to understand what is meant by the word "rules."

The game is life. Life becomes a game in a society when human behavior has no meaning beyond pleasure and diversion. The rules are the manners and morals, the social code, by which such a society expects its members to live. In the world of La Colinière these rules are closely allied with the metaphor of poaching. There is no morality, everyone cheats, everyone trespasses, everyone lies. Politeness is more important than sincerity. Being amusing is more important than being honorable. Discretion and charm are highly valued, commitment and honesty are in disrepute. The Marquis de la Chesnaye rescues the rabbit-poacher Marceau from the clutches of his gamekeeper Schumacher, and hires him to serve inside the house where he poaches on Schumacher's wife. The aviator, Jurieu, who has himself been poaching on la Chesnaye's wife, Christine, no longer can abide a hypocritical

144

Preceding pages: Peter Fonda as Wyatt and Dennis Hopper as Billy discover America on choppers in Hopper's EASY RIDER. Despite dubious values, such as dope-selling heroes, film was an enormous hit, created the myth of "youth-oriented films." Opposite: Actor-director Jean Renoir in RULES OF THE GAME.

relationship; he wants to marry Christine after settling the matter honorably with la Chesnaye. The great irony of the film is that the two characters, Schumacher and Jurieu, who live by the rules of an earlier time, when personal honor was paramount and poaching in all its forms was a crime, become the protagonists in the final tragedy. Schumacher shoots Jurieu after a series of absurd misunderstandings. When Jurieu is killed, la Chesnaye informs the other guests that there has been a "deplorable accident"—a startling euphemism for a grotesque tragedy that is the logical ending to a preposterous tale. The game is finished because two of the players, Schumacher and Jurieu, played by different rules.

RULES OF THE GAME is an admirably complex picture in which a number of characters are closely observed and an exceedingly large number of subplots are intricately entwined. The parallel lines of the story, scenes between nobles and scenes between servants, games played at the top of society and at the bottom, are reconciled at the end when the social boundaries merge and Schumacher kills Jurieu. It is not just the upper class that is on display in RULES OF THE GAME. It is the entire world whose blurred stratification was mourned by Boeldieu and Rauffenstein in LA GRANDE ILLUSION.

Much has been written about Jean Renoir's improvisatory methods, carried further in RULES OF THE GAME than in any of his other films. He and his writers share credit for the script with the members of the cast. Evidently, much of the dialogue and many of the characterizations were worked out during shooting. The spirit of collaboration, inspired by Renoir, may account for the picture's extraordinarily fine ensemble playing.

Special mention must be made of Marcel Dalio's performance as the Marquis de la Chesnaye. He is the central character, master of the château, arbiter of the world of La Colinière. Strange, at times absurd, almost desperately polite, he loves and collects automatons, and yet is able to make tenuous contact with human beings. Because his lies are softened by the style with which he lives them, he ultimately becomes a sympathetic character, perhaps the most rounded in the story.

In an interview with Dalio and Renoir made by French television in 1961 at locations where the picture was shot, actor and director reminisce and then agree that in the brief instant when la Chesnaye stands before his huge mechanical organ, his entire character is revealed, a "mixture of humility and pride, of success and doubt." Renoir goes as far as to say that those few seconds amount to "the best shot I've done in my life." This tells us much about Jean Renoir. To him the human being is the essen-

tial element in a film; the quality of an actor's performance is always more important than some use of the camera that will dazzle the audience, call attention to the director, and distract from the revelation of character.

The hunting scene and the fête are the two remarkable sequences in the film. At the hunt we are again confronted with a game played by certain rules. While servants beat the forest trees with sticks, driving birds and rabbits from their nests and holes, the nobles wait at their stations with ready guns. Renoir dwells upon the death throes of these little animals, the way their bodies crumple and twitch, until he evokes enormous anguish and pain. To those involved in this hunt, an extraordinary combination of pictorial beauty and merciless slaughter, the massacre is another game.

The fête is a grand farce, or rather a combination of so many farces that when le Chesnaye tells his major-domo to "Get this comedy stopped!", the confused Corneille must ask his master, "Which one, Monsieur le Marquis?" While Schumacher chases Marceau through the chateau and fires his revolver, the guests think it is just another of the amusing little skits that have been organized for their pleasure. At the fête, La Colinière becomes a merry-go-round: happenings, relationships, misunderstandings, and fights flare up and explode at breathtaking speed.

One marvels at the intensity of Renoir's vision, and his ability to filter his dismay through irony and present it in a classical theatrical form. Only a Frenchman could have made RULES OF THE GAME, and only Frenchmen could hate it. When the picture opened in Paris in 1939 it was poorly received. Audiences booed and hissed, and a perplexed Renoir, watching from the projection booth, could not still the furor no matter how many cuts and changes he made. Something about his vision cut too deep. During the Occupation the film was confiscated and banned, and in 1942 the original negative was destroyed when the GM film laboratories were hit by Allied bombs. After the war the picture could only be seen in mutilated prints until two Frenchmen, Jean Gaborit and Jacques Durand, reassembled it in 1958 from bits and pieces into its original form. The world owes these gentlemen an extraordinary debt.

Aristocrats and servants play various "games"
by various "rules" in Jean Renoir's brilliant film about
manners, morals, and society. Renoir acted role of
the pompous failure Octave (this page, top). Film was
booed at its premiere, was only recognized as
a masterpiece when reconstituted twenty years later.

Orson Welles' Citizen Kane 1941

It has been said many times, but let it be said again: Orson Welles' CITIZEN KANE is the greatest film ever made.

Let it also be said that CITIZEN KANE is not perfect. RULES OF THE GAME comes closer to perfection; the minor gem, THE THIRD MAN, is perfection itself. CITIZEN KANE is a work of great excess. It is an extravaganza, and like all extravaganzas it is riddled with imperfections. But it is interesting that when one uncovers and lists its flaws one's admiration remains undiminished. Who really cares that some of the characters recount incidents they could not possibly have observed? What difference does it make to a person sophisticated in film technique that many of the special effects, particularly the miniatures, are technically weak? Who is much bothered by the occasional patches of hokey dialogue, and the few overdrawn characterizations? Give Welles a B for precision, but give him A's for force, bravado, originality, effort, richness of texture, ability to entertain, power to compel, intensity of vision and personal expression. CITIZEN KANE is the greatest film ever made, and that is a fact there is no way around.

CITIZEN KANE is probably the most discussed film of all time. Books have been written about it, and those who are interested in balanced critiques and labored analyses should turn to them. Since almost everything there is to say about CITIZEN KANE has already been said, it seems appropriate to note down some random thoughts.

What is CITIZEN KANE about? It is about William Randolph Hearst, not literally, of course, but in the form of a fictionalized fantasy produced with the intention of exploiting public interest in a controversial man, and becoming, like Welles' "The War of the Worlds," a *succès de scandale*. One of the most delightful things about CITIZEN KANE is the way it uses Hearst against himself. CITIZEN KANE exploits him the way his papers exploited everyone else. CITIZEN KANE is yellow journalism. It sacrifices the truth about Hearst for the sensational aspects of his story.

CITIZEN KANE is also about money and power, aging and time, love and marriage, business and politics, and the futility of human aspirations.

CITIZEN KANE is a mystery story, a search, a quest. One of its themes is that the more one finds out about someone, the less one understands his character.

CITIZEN KANE is a mighty exposition of American society and a devastating critique of the American Dream.

CITIZEN KANE is a version of Faust, the story of a man who gains the world and loses his soul.

CITIZEN KANE is a circus. Many acts take place at once. One is diverted. One is amused. There is a leitmotif of comedy, and an exhilarating razzle-dazzle style. Welles is like a huckster pitching a fantastic notion. We know he is overselling but we are charmed by his spiel.

Orson Welles has said that CITIZEN KANE is "a portrait of a public man's private life," and that may be the best summary of all.

The jigsaw puzzle is the great metaphor of the story. The picture is about a journalist named Thompson trying to work out the puzzle of Charles Foster Kane. He collects various pieces from various persons, but at the end he cannot fit them together. With an actual puzzle in his hand he says: "I guess Rosebud is just a piece in a jigsaw puzzle—a missing piece." Crates of the things that Kane has accumulated in his life lie about like disconnected pieces. The puzzle of Kane, like the giant puzzles that Susan Alexander could never finish, cannot be solved. CITIZEN KANE does not pretend to explain the character of Charles Foster Kane. It offers glimpses but leaves the center murky. Just as it begins with the camera penetrating mists, then passing through the barriers around the mysterious world of Xanadu, so it ends with the camera withdrawing until mists cover the lens. Like the photographer in BLOW-UP, the closer we look the less we see.

Rosebud: It is too glib to call it parlor Freudianism. Rosebud is a powerful idea. The irony of Rosebud, of course, is that it doesn't make any difference that Thompson never finds out what it means. He finds out more on the route of his quest than Rosebud could ever tell him. But having set up Rosebud as the object of a search, Welles cannot leave us dangling. He explains Rosebud in a way that makes it clear that it is not the key piece, but at best a minor fragment of the puzzle. Yet the shot when the camera moves over the crates and toward the furnace where flames lick at the lettering on the sled is one of the most powerful in all of cinema. Those crates are the ruins of a life and say better than any words how greatly Charles Foster Kane had failed.

Some things that CITIZEN KANE is not: It is not the first film to use deep focus; it is not the first to use overlapping dialogue; it did not cost millions of dollars; it was not poorly received by critics when it opened.

148

Orson Welles, aged twenty-five, made the most impressive debut in cinema history as producer, director, star, and co-author of CITIZEN KANE. Opposite: Kane speaks at rally as candidate for governor before scandal wrecks his political career. This is perhaps the most famous movie still of all time.

Opposite: Welles at head, Everett Sloane (Bernstein) and Joseph Cotten (Leland) at foot of table. Note depth of field created by cameraman Gregg Toland. This page: Kane becomes newspaper publisher; scene from montage of Kane's failing marriage; Kane's wife (Ruth Warrick) confronts his mistress (Dorothy Comingore); Boss Jim Geddys (Ray Collins) in background.

Some facts about CITIZEN KANE:

Louis B. Mayer offered to reimburse RKO for the cost of the picture, if RKO would destroy its negative and all existing prints. The difference between him and General Hans Speidel is that the general didn't want to go down in history as the man who blew up Paris, but Mayer would have been content to be remembered as the man who destroyed CITIZEN KANE.

The production cost of CITIZEN KANE was either $686,033 or $842,000, depending upon one's source.

The apparently continuous shot when the camera passes through a neon sign, then penetrates a skylight and descends into the "El Rancho" cabaret, was achieved by a combination of miniatures and a life-size set, joined by an invisible cut camouflaged by a flash of lightning and a lap dissolve matched to the misting of the skylight by rain. Of all the virtuoso effects in the film this shot is the most phenomenal. One is tempted to stand up in the theatre and shout to everyone: "My God, Welles' camera has just passed through glass!"

All rumors to the contrary, Orson Welles, not Herman J. Mankiewicz, was responsible for CITIZEN KANE. Film is a collaborative art and many artists contributed to CITIZEN KANE. Without the brilliant camera work of Gregg Toland, the superb music of Bernard Herrmann, the astute editing of Robert Wise and Mark Robson, and the superior performances of the Mercury Theatre Company, CITIZEN KANE would not be the same film. The same thing applies to the work of the sound men and scenic artists at RKO, and the very important contribution of Herman Mankiewicz' screenplay. But CITIZEN KANE is Welles' film. He produced it, he directed it, he stars in it, and he worked on the script. Attempts to prove otherwise are as futile as attempts to prove that Shakespeare did not write Shakespeare's plays. CITIZEN KANE and Orson Welles are inseparable. As annoying as it is that Welles was only twenty-five years old at the time, and as annoying as it is that we cannot all be prodigies and create works of genius, facts are facts and credit must be given where it is due.

CITIZEN KANE is an encyclopedia of the cinema. Its flashbacks, its montages, its deep focus, its sound track, its sets, its structure, its camera moves, its cuts make it a treasury of superb examples of almost everything one can do in a film. One can look at CITIZEN KANE a dozen times and still not mine its riches. One can look at it fifty times —as many people have—and still enjoy its story. Familiarity does not make it tiresome. CITIZEN KANE remains unpredictable at each separate viewing. It is impossible to think of another film that gives so much pleasure so many times.

CITIZEN KANE is not a difficult picture; it is accessible to nearly everyone. Let those who think that a great picture must contain exotic symbols, be produced in a foreign language, and deal with abstract themes, think again. Let those who think that CITIZEN KANE is shallow name a picture that has a scene more profound than that in which Welles smashes up Susan's room.

152

Top, left: Another example of great depth of
field in CITIZEN KANE. Top, right: Camera set up in pit
for low-angle shot; KANE is notable for its
visible ceilings. Opposite: At Xanadu, Susan Alexander
(Dorothy Comingore) works huge jigsaw puzzle
which is central metaphor of the film.

One of the great charms of CITIZEN KANE is its flamboyance. Its excesses, its bravado, its look-Ma-no-hands effects are forgivable and actually warm the heart because Welles delivers them with a wink. CITIZEN KANE is not as subtle as LA GRANDE ILLUSION, or as difficult as PERSONA, or as self-effacing as THE SEARCHERS. It proclaims its genius from every frame with the stylishness of a brilliant show-off magician whom we admire for taking enormous risks.

The newsreel sequence: Charles Higham reports that the aging of the early shots was achieved by rubbing the negative with sand. The newsreel, an amusing satire on "The March Of Time," is a brilliant device for the way it provides the structure of Kane's life in linear terms, making the nonlinear puzzle quality of the main body of the film scrutable.

A speculation: CITIZEN KANE is the watershed work of the cinema, approximately halfway between Griffith and now.

A question: Try to think of a personage in contemporary life who would be a suitable model for an updated Kane? Howard Hughes? The late Joseph Kennedy? Lyndon Johnson? Or don't they make them like Hearst anymore?

Another question: If you were the head of a Hollywood studio—not a patron of the arts, but a man concerned with profit and loss—would you give Welles the kind of total freedom he had at RKO, and which he claims he needs to make another masterpiece?

Some thoughts upon watching Orson Welles on a television talk-show: The great filmmaker has become the great pontificator. The twenty-five-year-old could play the old man, but the old man cannot play the twenty-five-year-old. The charm is still there, but something is missing—perhaps recklessness. If Welles made CITIZEN KANE today it might be ponderous.

A thought upon visiting San Simeon: It was more insane than Xanadu.

The first films of most great filmmakers are usually faltering and talented. One looks at them to discover the themes and motifs that are worked out with greatness in later pictures. Welles' first film is different. It is the monument of his career. CITIZEN KANE is an ultimate first film for the way it shouts out to the world that a new presence is at large in the cinema, that a giant has arrived and that the dwarfs had better scatter. Unfortunately, this announcement was not heeded, and the giant suffered when the dwarfs ganged up. Welles, of course, made other masterpieces: THE MAGNIFICENT AMBERSONS, LADY FROM SHANGHAI, TOUCH OF EVIL, CHIMES AT MIDNIGHT. But his career faltered after CITIZEN KANE until he became a symbol of the artist ruined by philistines.

There is a quotient of Charles Foster Kane in Orson Welles; there are rages and there are ruins left behind, grandiose schemes and a fall from glorious heights. One does not want to stress this point and say that CITIZEN KANE prophesied Welles' own life, but the parallels that exist are poignant.

Federico Fellini's La Dolce Vita 1959

Looking at LA DOLCE VITA today, more than ten years after its original release, it is possible to find it quaint. Recalling the lines outside the theatres where it played, recalling the conversation piece it became, recalling its power as an exposé of the decline and decadence of European intellectual and aristocratic circles, recalling what a heavy indictment it then seemed of the boredom, uselessness, and self-hatred of people at the top, one is tempted to ask what all the hoopla was about. LA DOLCE VITA today seems positively tame. It is amazing how fast the world has changed, how what seemed so daring and depraved in 1959 appears now to be almost innocent and restrained. But who in 1959 would have predicted that by 1969 sexual intercourse could be legally shown upon the commercial screen?

Remember the scandal of LA DOLCE VITA? How it was attacked by the Vatican as an outrageous sacrilege, and championed by the Left as a profound exposure of ruling-class decadence? Remember the articles which described how the film was convulsing Europe, how anticipation built as the American opening neared, and the backlash when the highbrow critics discovered it was going to be a popular success? Remember the adjectives that were flung about: journalistic, superficial, hallucinatory, disturbing, putrid, Ziegfeldian, cinematic, breathtaking? While the educated bourgeoisie feverishly studied the dialogue in the Steiner sequence which, it was rumored, revealed important clues to the picture's meaning, intellectuals scoffed that the Steiner character was absurd, because none of them had ever been to a gathering where "intellectuals" spoke that way. Fellini was either a philosopher or a fraud, an artist or a huckster, and LA DOLCE VITA was either the greatest film ever made or a hulk of laborious trash.

Fellini, himself, must have been amused. In one stroke he had created a scandal and at the same time become the most famous and talked-about director in the world. And all of this for merely, as he put it himself, taking "the temperature of an ailing society, a society that has every appearance of running a fever."

Like Jean Renoir in RULES OF THE GAME, Fellini took on the task of describing the manners and morals of a society in a certain time and place. But unlike Renoir he was successful in making a picture of enormous influence. What LA DOLCE VITA may have lacked in aesthetic power, it more than made up for in popular accessibility. Despite its apparent tameness a decade after the fact, LA DOLCE VITA should not be underestimated. As a film of social comment it is extremely important, an opening wedge, the first in a phalanx of pictures that dissected the milieu of the rich and the successful, and helped to smash public confidence in the social order. It is possible to argue that the disorientation that characterized the social tensions of the 1960s, and the subsequent rejection by a good many people of what it is now fashionable to call "the establishment," may be attributed to the influence of certain films of which LA DOLCE VITA was the first.

Federico Fellini, like most filmmakers who have created popular hits, was ahead of his audience with LA DOLCE VITA—not so far ahead that they were left behind, but just enough ahead that he could carry them along as he showed them things which they had always suspected, but had not yet come around to articulating for themselves. Fellini in LA DOLCE VITA says that the "sweet life" that can be purchased with money and fame is dreary and ugly, that people who are beautiful and successful are

154

Pack of *paparazzi* signifies falseness
and emptiness of life in modern Rome in Federico
Fellini's influential LA DOLCE VITA. Photographers
callously crowd around characters in moments of
stress, invading privacy and turning life
into an outrageous gossip column.

boring and neurotic, that sin is rampant in society, that sophistication is a curse and innocence a treasure, and that vulgarity and greed—symbolized by the refuse of the media, the *paparazzi* of Rome with their pitiless flashbulbs and cameras—have tainted everything and ruined even the most intimate moments of human feeling. So negative a message was enormously gratifying to people who wanted to discover that the people they envied were worse off than themselves, and who could enjoy the delicious taste of a gossip column at the same time. As a piece of fantasy fulfillment LA DOLCE VITA was more than satisfactory. It confirmed the secret desire of the filmgoing public for a put-down spectacle about a world they could never know.

LA DOLCE VITA is filled with what one calls Felliniisms: empty piazzas at midnight, satiric anticlericalism, scenes set near the sea, clarity in the light of dawn after long night voyages of the soul, a young girl symbolizing innocence, elaborate scenes involving unexpected actions by groups of people, and the inevitable Fellini signature, the constant use of the "interesting" face.

It contains sequences which, though beautifully staged, are sometimes a little too self-conscious and overburdened with meaning: the opening, for example, in which one helicopter carries a huge statue of Christ over Rome, while Marcello in a second helicopter cannot communicate with the sunbathers on the apartment roof. The lack-of-communication motif recurs throughout the film. Marcello cannot hear the words of the innocent girl who calls to him at the end. Marcello ends up confessing his love from the echo-chamber at the aristocrats' villa to an uninterested woman kissing another man, etc. But this fashionable strain of alienation should not distract from the social satire, brilliantly displayed in such amazing and memorable sequences as the one in which Anita Ekberg runs up the staircase of St. Peter's in a dress that is a modified version of priestly attire, or the anguish implicit in the sequence when Steiner's wife learns of her husband's and childrens' deaths in front of a pack of camera-clicking *paparazzi*.

The false miracle is one of the supreme sequences in all the films of Fellini. The exploitation by television and the press of two little children who claim to have seen the Madonna, the milking of a neurotic aberration for publicity and profit, may say more about the manners, morals, and society that Fellini was depicting than any of the famous orgies, or the sequence where Anouk Aimée insists upon making love in a whore's bed.

Fellini based many of the incidents in LA DOLCE VITA on incidents he read about in newspapers. He said in an interview: "I just thought of it as a vast fresco...and then gradually characters and incidents merged to fill it in...." This may account for the film's fragmentary quality, a series of blackout sketches bound together by the recurrent figure of Marcello Mastroianni, the journalist mired in the "sweet life," who wanders through the inferno of modern Rome. But there is also in LA DOLCE VITA a strong personal dimension, a renunciation by Fellini of the world in which he became involved by virtue of being a well-known film director in an ultra-film-conscious town.

LA DOLCE VITA is a big film filled with bravura, but it is dwarfed by CITIZEN KANE. It is an omniscient view of a collapsing social milieu, but not so fine a one as RULES OF THE GAME. What it does have in common with these pictures is a swirling intensity, a life force. Despite the way time has blunted the impact of its "scandal," LA DOLCE VITA is still alive.

Scenes from LA DOLCE VITA
(top to bottom): False
"miracle"; striptease and
orgy; Marcello Mastroianni
(r.) as journalist Marcello
Rubini; encounter with
sea monster. Opposite: Anita
Ekberg as Sylvia. LA
DOLCE VITA was a scandal
when it opened in
1959, principally because
of its sexual candor
and open anticlericalism,
but it looks tame today.

François Truffaut's **Jules and Jim** 1961

"My films are gambles," says Truffaut. "For me shooting a film is like laying a bet. People took a strong dislike to the script for JULES AND JIM. Distributors said: 'The woman is a tart; the husband will be grotesque, etc.' The gamble for me was to make the woman moving (without being melodramatic) and not a tart, and to prevent her husband from seeming ridiculous."

Truffaut gambled and won, for JULES AND JIM is one of the best of all postwar French films, a miracle of storytelling, acting, filmmaking, and audience involvement.

JULES AND JIM is, admittedly, a period film. It recreates the spirit and moods of the times before and after World War I with a remarkable economy of means. The past is recaptured not so much by costumes and sets but by newsreel segments, an ironic, omniscient narrator, brilliant performances, and a calculated, ebullient, and mannered style of filmmaking. Within the first few minutes we feel the Paris of pre-1914. Throughout the picture, silent-film devices (iris dissolves, masking off of portions of the frame, etc.) and a restless, probing camera (including the use of swish-pans with a wide-screen process—a hitherto "forbidden" technique on account of its tendency to induce nausea) become in Truffaut's hands a bag of cinematic tricks by which he conveys a period flavor.

But to think of JULES AND JIM primarily as a period film may be to miss its real point. On one level, of course, it is a romance. Two close friends meet a *femme fatale*, and an impossible triangular relationship begins as an idyll and ends in tragedy. But on a deeper level it is a film about three social outlaws and the price they must pay for living free of social restraint and by improvised and mostly self-serving standards. As far as manners and morals are concerned, Jules, Jim, and Catherine invent their own and suffer the consequences.

They are bohemians. They live spontaneously in permanent isolation from the social mainstream. It is interesting that we see neither of the men perform a particle of "useful" work, nor do we ever observe Catherine make a single compromise toward the standards of society at large. Even when Jules and Jim must fight (on separate sides) in the war, they maintain a distance from the grit of the trenches, and an alienation from the issues (if, indeed, there were any) over which the war was fought. To the degree that JULES AND JIM is a film about society, it is about a tiny privileged sector, the bohemian subculture that flaunted the manners and morals of the bourgeoisie.

Jules, Jim, and Catherine play life as if it were a game. Even in a movie theatre, watching footage of the Nazis burning books, they are more interested by the amusing coincidence of being in the same place at the same time than in the political reality descending upon their world. By the end it is clear that they have played too long. The fake world of joy and tenderness, freedom and spontaneity, which they have created is impossible to maintain. The rules they have improvised do not serve, jealousy and neurosis intervene, their dream existence decays and the cost is frightful: sorrow and isolation for Jules, death for Catherine and Jim.

But despite the fact that their *ménage à trois* becomes grotesque, Catherine's charming dominance turns perverse, Jules' passivity descends into self-pity, and Jim's *joie de vivre* crumbles into anarchy, they are sympathetic characters. They live with such passion that it is impossible not to be fond of them. Their attempt to create their own life style is brave, and they must be admired for

159

Opposite: Jim (Henri Serre) and Catherine (Jeanne Moreau) in François Truffaut's JULES AND JIM. Jim, Catherine, and Jules (Oskar Werner) appear at separate bedroom windows suggesting their *ménage à trois*.
Above: Three principals with Truffaut.

having made it. Though in manuscript form they may have seemed repulsive to distributors, in Truffaut's hands they come alive and exude a warmth that makes their tragedy chilling. At one time or another everyone has wanted to live in total freedom; these three who tried and failed evoke nostalgia for our long-lost dreams.

JULES AND JIM begins as an ode to bohemianism and gradually turns dark. We are charmed when the two friends, whose relationship is so tender and sincere, rush off to Greece just to see the smile on a statue. When they meet up with Catherine, whom they instantly adore for having the same smile, we are enchanted by their romps, their outings on bicycles and to the beach, their runs across bridges and meadows. They are living at the highest of degrees, and despite the fact that the world is crumbling around them, their attempt to turn life into a "fiesta," to use Hemingway's word, is irresistible.

Of course, their idyll cannot go on forever. Social isolation leads to madness. Destructive traits within the human psyche cannot be willed away. When Catherine drives herself and Jim off the end of a broken bridge, following through on the self-destructive urge hinted at in earlier and jollier scenes, she smiles the enigmatic smile of the Greek statue, which is revealed to have been a smile of selfish triumph. All the innocence turns out to have been a fantasy. JULES AND JIM is like a seductive dream that suddenly turns into a nightmare and jars the sleeper awake.

There are brilliant and memorable scenes in this picture: the one (said to be improvised) when Jim tells of the soldier who fell in love with a girl he had known for half an hour on a train; Thérèse listing her lovers for Jim when he meets up with her again in a café; Jeanne Moreau listing all the great wines of France in response to Jim's delight in German beer; Catherine jumping into the Seine; the burial sequence in which black comedy reinforces the shock of the finale; and the amazing scene when Catherine's dress catches fire from the flames of her burning love letters, and she remarks to Jim that she carries around a bottle of vitriol for "lying eyes."

Dennis Hopper's Easy Rider 1969

A not-so-imaginary conversation:

"You're not serious about EASY RIDER being a great film?"

"I'm absolutely serious."

"But it's nothing but a chain of poorly executed sequences patched together with shots of a couple of guys riding motorcycles. When a director needs that many musical transitions you know he's in trouble."

"It doesn't matter what a director needs, or even if his work is uneven. The only important thing in a film of this kind is the final result. EASY RIDER is a powerful experience. If Dennis Hopper has only one-tenth the film craftsmanship of François Truffaut that does not in itself disqualify him from making a great film. Besides, the lunchroom sequence, the George Hanson scenes, and the finale are not 'poorly executed.'"

"What do you mean when you say 'a film of this kind'? Are you sure you're not creating special standards to make your case?"

"Not at all. By 'a film of this kind' I mean a film of such consequence that imperfections (which might be crucial in a picture that was self-consciously 'finely wrought') become trivial in relation to impact."

"Aren't you confusing the phenomenon of EASY RIDER with its stature?"

"No. The phenomenon of EASY RIDER is well known: The picture cost a few hundred thousand dollars and earned many millions; it destroyed the idea once held sacred in Hollywood that a few isolated executives could determine the fantasies the public was willing to buy; it caused innumerable firings of personnel who, in the light of the success of EASY RIDER, were rightfully considered useless; it inspired a series of imitations, pictures calculatingly manufactured for the 'youth audience,' which failed and are now rightfully referred to as 'youth culture rip-off pictures.' These things are facts, the side effects or the 'phenomenon' of the film. But today, several years after its release, when the phenomenal aspect has cooled down and the political and social environment is considerably different, EASY RIDER is still powerful and still unnerving. This is what I mean by 'impact' and this certainly has to do with the film's stature."

"But the premise is faulty. This idea that if you're free in America you're going to get killed, that if you have long hair some redneck will shoot you down—it's paranoic. And the idea that two cocaine dealers can be heroic is immoral and absurd."

"We can argue endlessly about the morality of

motion pictures. People hate Peckinpah's THE WILD BUNCH because they say it's immoral, too violent, etc. What would they have him do? Make a picture like MARY POPPINS? Would Dennis Hopper be any more moral if he had made DR. DOOLITTLE? The whole point of being a filmmaker is to express oneself, and God knows, EASY RIDER expresses the convictions and vision of Hopper and Peter Fonda. Call the premise paranoic, but in the context of various assassinations and violent urban outbreaks it seems pretty realistic to me. Anyway, it's pointless to argue about the premise of a film. Some people can't stand the worlds of Hitchcock or Fritz Lang, but very few people deny the richness of these worlds or the power with which they are expressed. Give Hopper credit for having articulated a world that had never before been articulated on film. His is the first and only authentic picture about the youth culture. His perceptions—that America is violent, that the spirit of the counterculture descends from the spirit of the pioneers, that the one thing that enrages people trapped by their lives is the flaunted freedom of outsiders—may seem clichés now, but before EASY RIDER they had not been expressed on the screen."

"Aren't they expressed better by all that pop music he uses, than by anything he did himself?"

"He chose the music. What's the difference between using someone else's music and basing a picture on someone else's novel? The job of a filmmaker is to mold the work of collaborators toward a specific personal goal. This Hopper does admirably well. All those pop tunes certainly enrich the vision, and as a matter of fact one could say that Hopper's use of music is almost classic in the sense that the music becomes a chorus that comments on the action and defines its meaning."

"Aren't you confusing a film of fantasy fulfillment with a work of art when you put EASY RIDER in the same chapter as RULES OF THE GAME and CITIZEN KANE?"

"What is a movie? Some miles of celluloid and some chemicals arranged so that light projected through them will render images and sound. Film is fantasy, and a successful film is a form of fantasy fulfillment. As for CITIZEN KANE and RULES OF THE GAME, they too are based on arguable interpretations of society.

"To say that a picture is great is not the same thing as to say that it is a great work of art. It can be a great work of entertainment, a great articulation of an idea, a great example of a new technique, or a great work of personal expression. Let's simply think of the word 'great' as a superlative to be applied to pictures that distinguish themselves in an important way. EASY RIDER is one of the most distinguished pictures of fantasy fulfillment of the 1960s, for it certified an apprehension about America that was harbored in a vague form in many people's minds, and when they saw it rendered so intensely in this particular story they instantly recognized that it was true."

"You keep using words like 'powerful' and 'intense.' Do you think these are really the most important qualities in films?"

"In films that are interpretations of society—yes. A delicate and sensible EASY RIDER, or a thinking man's EASY RIDER would not be very interesting. By its very nature EASY RIDER must be polemical; the only way it can enforce its vision is to describe it on the most emotional and visceral level. To create two protagonists, a gentle 'Captain America' and a discontented 'Billy' (who, by the way, are not meant to be 'heroic'), to mount them on two incredible, gleaming motorcycles, to send them down the roads of America, first past some of the most spectacularly beautiful scenery in the world, and later down roads that border ecological and neon wastelands, to arrange for them to intersect with various social alternatives en route, and then, after several adventures, to have them gunned down gratuitously, is to engage in highly imaginative mythmaking on a powerful emotional level. It only seems easy and obvious after the fact. I think the thing that really bothers people about EASY RIDER is that it was cooked up by a couple of long-haired acid-trippers, instead of by a self-appointed artist like Losey or Visconti. And that lines like, 'We blew it,' and the recurring use of the word 'man' don't go down with people who think civilized movies must contain elegantly written dialogue. I'll tell you one thing, though. The image of the motorcycle exploding into flames contains as many cultural cross references as Renoir's use of French theatrical farce in RULES OF THE GAME: self-immolations and napalmings in Vietnam, for example, and the American Dream going up in smoke. Besides, it is an unforgettable image, as strong in its own primitive way as the final sled-burning in CITIZEN KANE. EASY RIDER is a primitive work, but then 'primitive' has perhaps ceased to be a pejorative word."

"If I read you correctly, you are saying that it is the primitive power of EASY RIDER that makes it great."

"You are reading me correctly. You can rip EASY RIDER apart for poor technique and dubious morality, but you cannot fault the intensity of its vision, even if you think it is sophomoric. It is authentic, a film that is true to itself. The people who made it were sincerely concerned about what they were saying, and the emotion they put into it rushes out each time it is projected. As Penelope Gilliatt put it (and no one can accuse her of lacking 'civilized values'): 'EASY RIDER is the real thing.'"

Dennis Hopper (top), whose
articulation of alienation was
bought by youth audience.
Although not a great director,
he affected national
consciousness deeply. Above:
Jack Nicholson's engaging
acceptance of offbeat heroes
gave picture a boost.
Right: Hopper freaks out at
New Mexico commune.

Credits

Rules of the Game (La Règle du Jeu)
France; 1939; 113 minutes;
released in the U.S. by Janus.

Directed by	Jean Renoir.
Produced by	Jean Renoir.
Screenplay by	Jean Renoir, Karl Koch, Camille François and the cast, derived from "les Caprices de Marianne" by Alfred de Musset.
Photographed by	Jean Bachelet.
Art direction by	Eugène Lorié.
Edited by	Marguerite Houlet-Renoir.
Music by	Monsigny, Chopin, Saint-Saëns, Rosi, Salabert, and J. Strauss, arranged by Roger Désormières.
Cast:	Marcel Dalio; Nora Grégor; Roland Toutain; Jean Renoir; Mila Parély; Paulette Dubost; Gaston Modot; Julien Carette.

Citizen Kane
U.S.A.; 1941; 119 minutes;
released by RKO.

Directed by	Orson Welles.
Produced by	Orson Welles.
Screenplay by	Herman J. Mankiewicz and Orson Welles.
Photographed by	Gregg Toland.
Art direction by	Van Nest Polglase and Perry Ferguson.
Edited by	Robert Wise and Mark Robson.
Music by	Bernard Herrmann.
Cast:	Orson Welles; Joseph Cotten; Dorothy Comingore; Agnes Moorehead; Ruth Warrick; Ray Collins; Erskine Sanford; Everett Sloane; William Alland; Paul Stewart; George Coulouris; Fortunio Bonanova; Gus Schilling; Philip Van Zandt; Georgia Backus; Harry Shannon; Sonny Bupp; Buddy Swan; Richard Baer; Joan Blair.

La Dolce Vita (The Sweet Life)
Italy; 1960; 175 minutes;
released in the U.S. by Astor.

Directed by	Federico Fellini.
Produced by	Giuseppe Amato and Angelo Rizzoli.
Screenplay by	Federico Fellini, Tullio Pinelli, Ennio Flaiano and Brunello Rondi.
Photographed by	Otello Martelli.
Art direction by	Piero Gherardi.
Edited by	Leo Cattozzo.
Music by	Nino Rota.
Cast:	Marcello Mastroianni; Walter Santesso; Anouk Aimée; Anita Ekberg; Yvonne Furneaux; Lex Barker; Alan Dijon; Alain Cluny; Valeria Ciangottini; Renée Lonarini; Annibale Ninchi; Polidor; Magali Noël; Giulio Questi; Nadia Gray.

Jules and Jim (Jules et Jim)
France; 1961; 105 minutes;
released in the U.S. by Janus.

Directed by	François Truffaut.
Produced by	Les Films du Carrosse/SEDIF.
Screenplay by	François Truffaut and Jean Gruault, based on the novel by Henri-Pierre Roché.
Photographed by	Raoul Coutard.
Edited by	Claudine Bouche.
Music by	Georges Delerue.
Cast:	Jeanne Moreau; Oskar Werner; Henri Serre; Marie Dubois; Vanna Urbino; Sabine Haudepin; Boris Bassiak; Jean-Louis Richard; Michel Varesano; Pierre Fabre; Danielle Bassiak.

Easy Rider
U.S.A.; 1969; 94 minutes;
released by Columbia.

Directed by	Dennis Hopper.
Produced by	Peter Fonda.
Screenplay by	Peter Fonda, Dennis Hopper and Terry Southern.
Photographed by	Laszlo Kovacs.
Art direction by	Jerry Kay.
Edited by	Donn Cambern.
Music by	Numerous pop artists.
Cast:	Peter Fonda; Dennis Hopper; Jack Nicholson; Luana Anders; Luke Askew; Toni Basil; Karen Black; Warren Finnerty; Sabrina Scharf; Robert Walker.

Films About Films

8

11454-103

Just as novelists have written novels about novelists, and playwrights have written backstage plays, so filmmakers have made films about films. These are partly the products of their desires to clarify their lives and their relationship with their industry, to express their rage at the system in which they work, to savor the sweetness of vengeance against prototypal enemies, and to make personal statements, to describe the world they know best, and to create self-portraits on celluloid. The motion-picture business is notorious for being cruel, and these films about films are often visions of that cruelty, reflecting with varying degrees of intensity the filmmaker's dilemma.

What, exactly, is that dilemma? One finds it described often by filmmakers interviewed in freewheeling and bitter moods. It is first the constant struggle for financing, and then the struggles with philistine studio chiefs, stupid and overbearing producers, difficult and temperamental stars, and the corrupt and vicious practices of a corrupt and vicious industry. Throughout the short history of the cinema, the filmmaker has been confronted with the problems of having his work altered, reshot or re-edited without his consent, being cheated out of a fair share of the money earned from his successes, and, when his films have failed with the public, being ignored and driven to exhaustion and collapse. The horror stories are endless and when filmmakers get together tales of double crosses, abuses of power, and various mutilations are exchanged.

Why has Elia Kazan turned to writing novels? Why do so many people speak of Orson Welles' career as "tragic"? Why was Francis Ford Coppola fired five times during the shooting of THE GODFATHER? Why was Fred Zinnemann's MAN'S FATE cancelled? What has happened to the announced projects of Richard Lester? What about the struggles of Sam Peckinpah? Why was Dennis Hopper's second film "dumped"? Why was George Cukor fired from GONE WITH THE WIND? Why did John Huston resign from A FAREWELL TO ARMS? What happened to Erich von Stroheim and David Wark Griffith? What about blacklisted screenwriters, actors who commit suicide, multimillion-dollar litigations, works massacred for television? Why so many feuds, embargoes, scandals? Why have so many fine talents been degraded? What is the process that so softens filmmakers of promise that corruption actually seems to ooze out of works made only a few years after their promising early efforts? One could go on forever with the questions, and, of course, in each case there is a specific answer. But the general answer to all of them may reside in the peculiarities of the movie industry, engaged in the manufacture of products that have no saleable value beyond their ability to entertain, and thus dependent for survival on the unpredictable force of public taste. Unlike the steel or coal or automobile industries, the movie industry is, by its very nature, subject to economic extremes, and these extremes create vicissitudes and pressures that tear at people, turn them into monsters, and sometimes destroy them.

The movie business is corrupt, capricious, and ruthless because, among other things, all the problems inherent in any sort of show business (and movies are just an extension of the carnival and circus businesses) are combined with the problems inherent in big-money speculation. When big money is at stake artists always suffer. The demands of box office success and artistic self-fulfillment are nearly impossible to reconcile. One could examine the relative positions of filmmakers in the American cinema solely in terms of the ways each has tried to reconcile his artistic aspirations with the demands of his backers that his pictures make money. In short, American filmmakers have always been stretched on a rack, pulled from one side by money and from the other by art.

From time to time, when the opportunity arises, filmmakers have made films about the filmmaking process and depicted their dilemma. Such films are widely scattered through the years, but they have themes in common, and when examined together and treated as a genre one may discern in them a streak of cynicism, and, particularly in American films about films, a large quotient of self-hatred. Hollywood loves to lacerate itself, and the proof of that much-repeated axiom is to be found in the Hollywood films about the Hollywood filmmaking milieu. A sociologist from another galaxy would deduce from an examination of these films about films that Hollywood is one of the most terrible places on earth, not, like the American West, a territory for contending forces of good and evil, but a place where viciousness and cruelty are to be found at exalted heights.

A few words about the pictures chosen for this chapter. The word "great" has been expanded in this book to embrace pictures ranging from "great works of art" to "great masterpieces of entertainment," "great personal visions," and even impaired works which have "great emotional intensity" or which are "great" by reason of some technical or stylistic innovation, or on account of their prophetic power. When it comes to choosing films about films this word "great" must be stretched even more. THE BAD AND THE BEAUTIFUL, for example, discussed here with several other films of which it is an outstanding example, can only be construed as great if one accepts the

166

proposition that there can be such a thing as a "great piece of trash." THE BAD AND THE BEAUTIFUL is a film that revels in and insists upon its trashiness, and therein lies its fascination.

As for Godard's CONTEMPT, not many people have seen it, but of those who have many despise it greatly.

CONTEMPT is one of the few films that actually encourages its audiences to walk out. Aside from the fact that it has something important to say and says it interestingly, CONTEMPT is a nadir of entertainment, and for this reason, and because it is one of the most alienated and alienating films ever made, one can choose to call it great, too.

Billy Wilder's **Sunset Boulevard** 1950

Of all the films about films, none exhibits so much self-hatred and cynicism as Billy Wilder's SUNSET BOULEVARD:

1. This story about an aging silent-movie queen, her former director/husband-now-butler, and their grotesque existence, is told against a background of the then (1950) alive, youthful Hollywood. Yet this background ambience, used as a contrast to the grotesqueries in the mansion on Sunset, is a disgusting, vile world of arrogant producers (Sheldrake cannot remember his story editor's name), ruthless agents (Morino never returns William Holden's calls; when cornered on the golf course he refuses to loan him $300, and threatens him with a softly muttered, "Maybe you'd better get yourself another agent"), and a hierarchy of fools (when Norma Desmond arrives at Paramount to visit Cecil B. De Mille, word is phoned from the gatehouse, through a series of lackey assistants, until it finally reaches the "great" De Mille, who takes a condescending interest). Not only are the characters vile, but the dialogue of the picture is filled with put-downs and self-disgust. Holden refers to one character as a "yes-man at Metro," to his agent as "the big faker," cringes before the producer Sheldrake, and says of the best script he ever wrote: "It was a beautiful script about Okies in the dust bowl. When it reached the screen it took place on a torpedo boat."

2. When casting the freaks for his "old Hollywood," Wilder comes up with the following cynical ideas: Gloria Swanson, biggest of the real silent-movie stars, will play Norma Desmond, biggest of the fictional silent-movie stars, who wants to make her comeback. In fact, Swanson's appearance in SUNSET BOULEVARD did represent a comeback, but unlike Norma Desmond's it was not a fiasco. It was brilliant. This grotesque, Norma Desmond, is to be served by a butler who is to be her former husband and director, Max von Meyerling. Who does Wilder cast? Erich von Stroheim, the most famous of the early directors broken by the Hollywood system. At one point Stroheim says: "In the early days there were three direc-

tors of great promise: D. W. Griffith, C. B. De Mille, and Max von Meyerling." True, perhaps, if one thinks of Meyerling as Stroheim, who is here forced, in effect, to play out his own degradation. And whom does Wilder dig up for his "waxworks," the has-beens with whom Norma Desmond plays bridge? H. B. Warner, Anna Q. Nilsson, and Buster Keaton! (Keaton gets applause in the theatres now when SUNSET BOULEVARD is re-run. In 1950, however, he was in such decline that his appearance as a "waxwork" was something of a sick joke.)

3. Against this weird typecasting of the "old Hollywood" Wilder creates a character with whom he, presumably, identifies. This is the hack writer Joe Gillis (William Holden), a man with a certain small amount of integrity and a huge amount of self-disgust. Though Gillis speaks wistfully of returning to his profession of newsman in Dayton, Ohio, he is too far gone, too deep into the Hollywood money trap, performing hack work, but too lethargic to give up the rat race. This may well have been the collective dilemma of Billy Wilder, Charles Brackett, and D. M. Marshman, Jr., the writers of SUNSET BOULEVARD. Although they were highly successful, big-time screenwriters, there is in their creation of Gillis the idea that movie writing is a phony profession and that "real" writing takes place in newsrooms in Dayton.

4. Are the rats in the empty pool at Norma Desmond's estate any more a proof of decadence than the frantic phoning of the younger characters from booths in Schwab's Drugstore? Are Hedda Hopper and Cecil B. De Mille any better, because they are involved in the phony-real world of Hollywood, than Norma Desmond and Max von Meyerling, living in painful seclusion in the mansion on Sunset? Is the Gloria Swanson film, QUEEN KELLY, actually directed by Stroheim, which Norma projects in her house and which makes William Holden squirm, really any worse than the exploitive "spectacular" that De Mille is making at Paramount? The answer to all these questions is an ambivalent no. SUNSET BOULEVARD is like two

mirrors facing each other, reflecting images of "good" and "bad," the neurosis of recluses and the neurosis of the rat race, back and forth until all values are blurred and the reflection is infinite.

5. Indeed, what could be more cynical than to write a story for a film that will be told as a flashback by a character who is already dead? The suspension of disbelief required is incredible, yet the picture is so involving that we forgive the intentional fallacy of having William Holden, whom we first see as a corpse floating in a swimming pool after being shot by Norma Desmond, narrate the story. Presumably we should be grateful that Wilder didn't use a sequence he actually shot. The film was to open with the camera tracking down a row of corpses stretched out on slabs in the morgue. When it reached Holden's body he was to sit up suddenly and address the audience!

These notes on the cynicism of SUNSET BOULEVARD are by no means meant as an attack on the picture. Like all great films about films it deals with the insanity of the picture business, the difficulty of doing good work in the face of madness, and the cruel cynicism of its scenes and dialogue helps clarify this theme. We will always remember certain scenes from SUNSET BOULEVARD:

Gloria Swanson's marvelous imitation of Chaplin, interrupted by a call from Paramount. "Paramount!"

she snarls at Stroheim. "Let 'em wait! *I've* waited long enough!"

When Holden recognizes her for the first time and mentions that she used to be "big," she replies, "I *am* big. It's the pictures that got small!"

When she stands up in the cone of light thrown by the projector in her living room, places her hands on her face, and says, "They don't make faces like that anymore!" Or when she visits De Mille at the studio and an old-time grip turns a brute arc on her, making her cringe before its blinding glare, we are moved and disgusted, filled with pity and terror.

The monkey burial by candlelight is one of the more grotesque scenes ever filmed, and it provided Wilder with the opportunity to make one of his most famous *bons mots.* An assistant approached him and asked him how he planned to stage the scene. Wilder is alleged to have shrugged and answered: "You know—the usual monkey-funeral sequence."

The last scene of SUNSET BOULEVARD is unforgettable. As Gloria Swanson comes down the stairs to face the newsreel cameras, she is urged on by Stroheim, whom in her madness she mistakes for De Mille. The final close-up of her face, and her fingers twisted like fangs, is as cruel a comment as has ever been made on what the movie business is all about.

From SUNSET BOULEVARD: Swanson (opposite) to
William Holden: ''They don't make faces like that anymore!''
Erich von Stroheim (I.) plays out his degradation as Norma
Desmond's butler. Swanson and Cecil B. De Mille.
The monkey funeral. Swanson and captive
Holden dance in mouldering mansion on Sunset.

Joseph L. Mankiewicz's **All About Eve** 1950

ALL ABOUT EVE was released in the same year as SUNSET BOULEVARD. Although strictly speaking not a film about films, since it deals with the world of the Broadway stage, and is therefore not really fair game for exhaustive analysis or even inclusion in this chapter, ALL ABOUT EVE nevertheless is worth at least cursory examination, for it is a magnificently entertaining work that says more about the mythical ruthlessness and temperament of performers, and says it better than movies set in Hollywood that deal with these same themes.

Like SUNSET BOULEVARD, ALL ABOUT EVE is structured as a flashback. It is even better written than SUNSET BOULEVARD, employing biting and witty dialogue. The story, told almost exclusively in set-piece interiors, shows how Anne Baxter's sneaky Eve uses Bette Davis' bigger-than-life Margo Channing to achieve stardom. It ends on a flamboyant image of narcissism that rivals the flamboyant ending of SUNSET BOULEVARD. A new "Eve," who

has slipped into Anne Baxter's suite, postures before the star's full-length dressing mirrors with Baxter's "Sarah Siddons" award in her hands. She falls into a dynamic reverie in which she dreams of great fame and savors the sweetness of imaginary applause. What we know (and she does not, as she admires her endlessly reflected self) is that her destiny is monstrous, that she will be just another in a long line of stars to whom fame has brought loneliness and for whom old age brings the kind of grotesquerie-on-a-staircase that ends the life of Gloria Swanson's Norma Desmond.

Between them, Mankiewicz and Wilder spent the year 1950 carving up the theatrical worlds of the East and West coasts, each creating a legend about the unscrupulous female star who will do anything to advance her career and whose talent is great enough to justify her temperament. SUNSET BOULEVARD tells us that old forgotten stars are bundles of megalomaniacal nerves; ALL

ABOUT EVE tells us how they get that way.

Bette Davis as Margo Channing may even surpass Gloria Swanson as Norma Desmond; George Sanders plays his trademark role as the cad; Marilyn Monroe stands out in a small part as the dumb blonde at a party— a role she spent her life trying to overcome; and Thelma Ritter epitomizes the personal maid-confidante. Though ALL ABOUT EVE has about as much relation to the actual ways of the New York theatre as ON THE WATERFRONT has to what really happens on the New York waterfront, it is nevertheless a lively fiction, true unto itself, reveling in its artificiality and gloating over the unscrupulousness of the world it so magnificently depicts.

Four years after he completed ALL ABOUT EVE, Mankiewicz offered up his film about films, THE BAREFOOT CONTESSA. The two pictures together constitute his best work. THE BAREFOOT CONTESSA expands upon the myth of the female star, in this case Ava Gardner, who ascends to stardom from the gutter, presumably the place from which all stars, including Anne Baxter's Eve, come. It includes many of the stock characters of the genre, the ruthless buys-and-sells-human-beings producer, the boot-

licking and permanently sweating press agent, and the once-great-but-now-discarded director, mournfully played by Humphrey Bogart.

What is interesting about THE BAREFOOT CONTESSA is that it is a funny prophecy-in-reverse of the Grace Kelly movie-star-to-princess story. Gardner's Cinderella story turns black. Lustily waiting in bed on her wedding night, she is approached by her as yet untasted continental husband-count, Rossano Brazzi. "There's something I haven't told you," he says and hands her a medical report that documents his impotence. Just as a star uses people, people use a star.

The wages of stardom, as depicted in SUNSET BOULEVARD, ALL ABOUT EVE, and THE BAREFOOT CONTESSA, are loneliness and sexual frustration. The difference between Anne Baxter and Ava Gardner, however, is that Baxter really wants to be a star and is willing to pay the cost and sit around lonely night after night puffing moodily on cigarettes. Gardner, on the other hand, is willing to give it all up, to satisfy her cravings by sleeping with the servants and, ultimately, to pay for her corruption with her life.

171

From ALL ABOUT EVE: Gary Merrill (l.) comforts Bette Davis, who plays the star Margo Channing; Anne Baxter as Eve (r.) accepts her "Sarah Siddons Award." Little does she know that another "Eve" is lurking in her apartment, ready to do to her what she did to Margo Channing.

Vincente Minnelli's **The Bad and the Beautiful** 1952 and Other Things.

THE BAREFOOT CONTESSA is one of a series of films about Hollywood which are perhaps best described in order of trashiness. Of these, Preston Sturges' SULLIVAN'S TRAVELS (1942) is probably the least. The story of a director who runs away from the phony world of Hollywood in order to find "real" material for a "real" movie about "real" people, it is a mildly amusing film combining gentle satire and serious social comment. Its net effect, however, is to tickle Hollywood with a feather. Better (i.e., trashier) pictures of this school lash at Hollywood with a whip.

There is Paul Mazursky's ALEX IN WONDERLAND (1970), a film that failed pitifully at the box office. ALEX IN WONDERLAND is so pretentious that one cannot rightfully call it trash. Sort of a poor man's 8½, it is part homage to Fellini (who appears as himself and in his embarrassment seems to put the whole thing down), part film of social comment (it contains extended fantasies on the three Great Social Issues of the age: ecology, race relations, and the Vietnam war. The last is by far the best: The war is staged on Hollywood Boulevard), and partly it is the story of a successful director going through a personal crisis. This portrait of the artist on celluloid is rather tiresome, but it contains an interesting twist that makes it an important film in the subgenre. Mazursky casts himself as one of the new breed of producers whose hipness is merely a façade covering that monstrousness so essential in a producer character in a Hollywood film about films.

William Wellman's A STAR IS BORN (1937) may have been the first and most famous picture in the subgenre. The story of a marriage between stars, which fails when the career of one ascends and the career of the other declines, was evidently considered strong stuff in its day, though in retrospect it looks more like the sort of fantasy about Hollywood harbored in the hearts of the readers of 1930s fan magazines. (When remade into a musical in 1954, George Cukor's filmmaking and Judy Garland's performance transcended the material, and the story seemed altogether extraordinary.)

One truly enters the universe of trash with John Cromwell's THE GODDESS (1958). Cromwell's gift for working with actresses shows in Kim Stanley's remarkable performance as the neurotic and unhappy sex goddess, Rita Shawn, incapable of giving or receiving love. Stanley is married to Lloyd Bridges, a prizefighter and television addict, and the whole thing looks a lot like Marilyn Monroe and Joe DiMaggio though, naturally, everyone concerned denies it. THE GODDESS is clearly another attempt to portray those miseries of stardom suffered by the heroines of SUNSET BOULEVARD, ALL ABOUT EVE, and THE BAREFOOT CONTESSA.

THE OSCAR (1966) is probably Hollywood's most horrible exercise in self-laceration, for in this film the town's most precious icon, which cannot be depicted on the screen without the permission of the Academy of Motion Picture Arts and Sciences, is made the butt of an enormous joke. An Oscar, says THE OSCAR, can be "arranged." Horror of horrors! One wonders how the producers got away with it, how they got Burt Lancaster, Richard Burton, Frank Sinatra, Hedda Hopper, and even the costume designer, Edith Head (who has won just about as many Oscars as anyone else), to play themselves in this delicious monstrosity. THE OSCAR is notable for its heightened use of cliché Hollywood types, as well as for two immortal lines: "The Oscar is a symbol and we don't like it tarnished," and "When you sleep with pigs you come up stinking of garbage."

There are many other devastating films about films: Stuart Heisler's THE STAR (1953), starring Bette Davis; Gordon Douglas' HARLOW (1965), starring Carroll Baker; Robert Mulligan's INSIDE DAISY CLOVER (1966), starring Natalie Wood; Edward Dmytryk's THE CARPETBAGGERS (1964), from the same company that brought us HARLOW and THE OSCAR, etc. But the biggest and the best are the two pairs of masterpieces by Robert Aldrich and Vincente Minnelli, which do for Hollywood in trash what SUNSET BOULEVARD did for Hollywood in quality.

Robert Aldrich is primarily known as the master of *film noir*, and his first film about film, THE BIG KNIFE (1955), is very much in that style. THE BIG KNIFE was knocked off by Aldrich in a mere sixteen days of shooting. The result is an austere, tough, cruel, electric, and highly theatrical charcoal-sketch of Clifford Odets' play. This is the film that enraged Harry Cohn and brought tears to the eyes of Louis B. Mayer, each of whom thought he was the model for the odious movie mogul so brilliantly played by Rod Steiger.

In 1968, Aldrich made THE LEGEND OF LYLAH CLARE, a lavish, florid, self-indulgent, and magnificently trashy film about film that represents a departure from the tough

style of his earlier work and is in keeping with the decadence of his THE DIRTY DOZEN. In THE LEGEND OF LYLAH CLARE, one finds such familiar types as the has-been director (Peter Finch), the starlet who is discovered and turned into a star (Kim Novak), the two-bit agent (Milton Selzer), the brutal producer (this time played by Ernest Borgnine), and all sorts of lesbians and gossip columnists, and Sidney Skolsky playing himself. In the tradition of Ava Gardner in THE BAREFOOT CONTESSA, Kim Novak sleeps with the gardener. The most interesting thing about this picture is the aspect that reflects its total trashiness. It is a film about film in which a character is making a film about film.

To Vincente Minnelli, however, must go the crown. His infamous pair of films about films, THE BAD AND THE BEAUTIFUL (1952) and TWO WEEKS IN ANOTHER TOWN (1962), are unmatched in the entire history of the sub-genre, as well as in the history of the cinema of trash.

Minnelli, of course, is best known for his musicals, which include the very fine MEET ME IN ST. LOUIS and the much-admired but incredibly pretentious AN AMERICAN IN PARIS. But his later films—stylish, melodramatic, decadent, and lavish—are of equal interest, and THE BAD AND THE BEAUTIFUL and TWO WEEKS IN ANOTHER TOWN are of this type.

THE BAD AND THE BEAUTIFUL trashes CITIZEN KANE. There are flashbacks as characters narrate different versions of the same series of events. (It is interesting that Minnelli's producer was John Houseman, who had

worked on the script of CITIZEN KANE until he and Welles had a falling out.) Kirk Douglas plays the monster-producer Jonathan Shields, who, among other fiendish things, double-crosses directors, dumps a big alcoholic star (Lana Turner—"tossed on the ash heap by this town"), and entices a Pulitzer Prize-winning novelist (Dick Powell) to Hollywood, where his wife is lured into an affair with an actor, so Powell will be able to give his full attention to screen writing.

Jonathan Shields, it seems, was the son of a movie tycoon who died poor and despised, and by this his ruthless character is psychologically explained. Of course, some people think that Charles Foster Kane's character is explained by the fact that as a child he was separated from his beloved sled, but the difference here is that Minnelli offers his explanation as a camp effect which his audiences accept as a convention, while Welles uses Rosebud as an ironic reminder that human character is impenetrable and mysterious.

THE BAD AND THE BEAUTIFUL is filled with magnificent characters and set-pieces. Two-bit agents, directors, stars, and moguls abound—and there is an institutional Hollywood cocktail party, a quintessential Hollywood funeral, lots of movie lingo, and scenes set in famous places on Hollywood Boulevard and in Beverly Hills.

Ten years later Minnelli, Kirk Douglas, John Houseman, and the screenwriter Charles Schnee got together and cooked up another film about film based on Irwin Shaw's novel, TWO WEEKS IN ANOTHER TOWN. In this

Kirk Douglas and Lana Turner in Vincente Minnelli's trash masterpiece film about film, THE BAD AND THE BEAUTIFUL. Minnelli later used bits of this film to embellish TWO WEEKS IN ANOTHER TOWN, thus piling trash upon trash to create an infinite resonance.

Clockwise, from top left: Kirk Douglas exhibits producer's ire in THE BAD. Gaynor-March A STAR IS BORN (1937). Robinson-Douglas in TWO WEEKS. Kim Stanley, THE GODDESS. Finch-Novak in LYLAH CLAIRE. ALEX IN WONDERLAND. Mason-Garland A STAR IS BORN (1954). Opposite: Jack Palance embraces Brigitte Bardot in CONTEMPT.

picture Douglas plays a once-big star recovering from a nervous breakdown. (In a bureau drawer in his hotel room he keeps an Oscar which he brings out from time to time and regards strangely.) Douglas has come to Rome to play a bit part in a movie being directed by his old "friend" the paranoic Maurice Kruger (Edward G. Robinson). Kruger has a heart attack, Douglas replaces him as director, and when he shows he has talent, Kruger turns against him and accuses him of trying to "steal my film." (Kruger, according to the dialogue, is famous for his inimitable "Kruger sound." Could this be another dig at Orson Welles?)

Just as THE BAD AND THE BEAUTIFUL trashed CITIZEN KANE, so TWO WEEKS IN ANOTHER TOWN trashes the European cinema, putting down with great satiric effect both LA DOLCE VITA and LAST YEAR AT MARIENBAD.

Among its more amusing scenes is one in which Douglas, replacing Kruger on the set, turns to his cameraman and says something like: "I'm stumped. Can you think of a good angle?" The cameraman replies: "Well, how about putting the camera over here?" As if this is the way that directors work and movies are really made.

But by far the most incredible thing about TWO WEEKS IN ANOTHER TOWN, and the utter proof, if any is needed, that it is a trash masterpiece, is Minnelli's use of footage from THE BAD AND THE BEAUTIFUL. Even Billy Wilder at his most cynical seems positively innocent compared to Minnelli, who has the outrageous nerve to use clips from his first trash masterpiece film about film as examples of exemplary filmmaking in his second trash masterpiece film about film. That the has-been characters in TWO WEEKS IN ANOTHER TOWN view pieces of THE BAD AND THE BEAUTIFUL, and then speak of them nostalgically as examples of their greatness in the days when they were all winning Oscars, is some sort of summit.

Together THE BAD AND THE BEAUTIFUL and TWO WEEKS IN ANOTHER TOWN make an extremely entertaining double feature. Their pleasures are the pleasures of wallowing in decadence and trash, pleasures that the moviegoer should never underestimate.

Jean-Luc Godard's **Contempt** 1963

Just as 1950 was a golden year in the American cinema for films about films, 1963 was that sort of year in Europe. Two extraordinary pictures were released: Godard's CONTEMPT and Fellini's 8½.

When it was announced that Jean-Luc Godard, favorite director of the New York Film Festival, was going to direct a million-dollar, wide-screen spectacular for Carlo Ponti and Joseph E. Levine, starring Brigitte Bardot and Jack Palance, and based on a novel by Alberto Moravia, the underground held its collective breath. Had the revolutionary genius of the cinema finally sold out? Had the philistines finally captured the soul of the most startling and independent hope of the New Wave?

Well, they needn't have feared. The picture that Godard delivered to his producers had the production values of the lowest of low-budget features. ("My God," they must have exclaimed in the posh screening rooms of Rome and New York. "There's a scene here, more than half an hour long, that takes place in one apartment! We send Godard to Capri and he comes back with half an hour in a deserted house! Where are the crowds? Where are the extras? Where's our million bucks?")

Not only did CONTEMPT look cheap, it was a total rip-off of the men who had financed it. Godard had made

a film in which the most vulgar traits of his producers were unmistakably satirized, and in which the crux of the filmmaker's dilemma (should he sell out to the slobs?) was laid bare once and for all in merciless and austere vignettes. In short, Godard had used the million dollars of his unsuspecting backers to tell the story of his relationship with them, and he had done so with the help of the most famous sex kitten of the time, within the confines of a story they had approved, and in a way best contrived to make the whole thing fail at the box office, and make

175

their million forever irretrievable. The result: Of all the films about films, CONTEMPT may be the most piercing, most alienating, most alienated, and least entertaining.

Paul Javal is a writer who wants to write for the stage, but his beautiful ex-typist wife, Camille (Brigitte Bardot), wants a middle-class style of life. Paul has used his savings to buy her an apartment and is now financially enslaved. The American film producer and tycoon, Jeremy Prokosch (Jack Palance), has offered him a job as screenwriter of THE ODYSSEY, to be directed by the great German filmmaker Fritz Lang (played by Fritz Lang!).

Paul sells out, signs the contract with Prokosch, and earns the eternal contempt of his wife, who drifts into a liaison with Prokosch (it is not clear whether they actually have an affair), and who is killed when Prokosch smashes his sports car against an enormous truck.

Prokosch is The Great Vulgarian Producer. He wants Lang to direct THE ODYSSEY because "A German, Schliemann, discovered Troy." Prokosch buys and sells mens' souls, shows his contempt for Lang by knocking film cans out of his assistant's hands, and even heaves one can across the screening room in the manner of a discobolus. He rushes around the film studio in a flashy red sports car, and reads asinine and pretentious maxims from a red book he carries in his breast pocket. When someone mentions the world "culture," Prokosch says, "Whenever I hear that word I know it's time to pay somebody," and brings out his checkbook.

The story of the dissolution of the Javals' marriage and Camille's contempt for Paul is entwined with the legend of Ulysses (in ways that are sometimes obscure), and also with a sort of documentary look at what it's like to make a movie: the compromises, the idiocy, the bore-dom, and the fatigue. There are references to film and filmmaking throughout the picture: posters on walls for Howard Hawks' HATARI and Hitchcock's PSYCHO, glances at the inside of a movie studio, and the goings-on in a screening room. But perhaps the most interesting and mystical element in this film are its first and final shots.

The film opens with a profile view of a movie camera tracking a girl. We see a sound man holding a microphone, and the tracks for the camera lead toward us to the foreground plane. The camera and the girl slowly move closer until the camera fills the screen. Then it slowly turns and tilts until the lens is staring directly at us in the audience.

The precise meaning of this shot is not clear until the end of the picture. Javal, who just learned of the deaths of Prokosch and Camille, goes to the roof of the villa in Capri to say goodbye to Fritz Lang. Lang is directing a short scene from THE ODYSSEY production, and Jean-Luc Godard himself is acting the role of Lang's assistant director. We watch as Lang sets up the shot, and Godard relays his instructions to the crew—homage to Lang, perhaps, but there is a strange duality here, since we know that Godard really is directing both shots. Lang's camera slides out of frame, Paul goes to the edge of the roof, and the camera that is telling us the story of CONTEMPT (as opposed to Lang's camera that is telling the story of Ulysses) settles upon a vision of the sea, infinite, tranquil, mysterious. We are no longer looking at any of the characters of the story, but at a symbol of the oneness of the universe. On Godard's instructions we are forced to turn inward, to think, to contemplate. Godard seems to be telling us that the story of CONTEMPT is really a story about us all.

Federico Fellini's 8½ 1963

Our profession . . . is one of 'lives that have been bought.' There are no bad movies that were not made because of some fault of the producer or through intellectual affectation, or good films that were not made despite the producer. . . . The cinema (commercially speaking, and only from that point of view) is like a well-organized heroin racket (when you think of the money some people make out of it) but one that has unjustly been made legal.
      —*Federico Fellini in "L'Express," 1957*

So, relatively early in his career, did Federico Fellini characterize his chosen profession. For Fellini, too, the producer has been the villain, and so have the financiers.

In 1963, with the world at his feet after the enormous success of LA DOLCE VITA, he faced the challenge of topping a spectacular hit. Setting out to make a sequel to LA DOLCE VITA which would explore the world of the innocent girl who called to Marcello at the end of that film, Fellini found himself creatively blocked, and while his producer, his staff, his collaborators, the press, and ten thousand other people wanting statements, favors, audiences, roles, and portions of his time pressured him

176

Marcello Mastroianni as Guido in Federico Fellini's great autobiographical film about film, 8½. As Fellini's alter ego, Guido suffers the miseries of being a famous filmmaker, passes through a convergence of crises and emerges, miraculously, intact.

to the point of a breakdown, he decided to make a film about film that would be, in his own words, "more than a confession—my testament."

8½ is the greatest of all films about films, and it is also the first great filmed self-portrait. It is as rich, complex, endlessly analyzable, and endlessly seeable as CITIZEN KANE, with which it must stand as one of the summit works in cinema, a picture that expands the possibilities of the form.

8½, like CITIZEN KANE, is one of those few films that makes people want to become filmmakers. And also, like Welles' masterpiece, it deals with a huge number of subjects in a comprehensive way, entwining them with the story of a single dominating character. 8½ is not merely a film about film. It is about power, art, corruption, manners, morals, money, love, marriage, friendship, failed ambitions, disillusionment, religion, childhood, and how a man should live. But unlike many self-portraits by artists in various media it is totally without self-pity, and in this way, too, it is unlike the films about films that have poured out of Hollywood. 8½ has the charm, exuberance, and life force that one has come to expect in a Fellini film, and that one so rarely finds in this age of existential melancholy, self-disgust, and creative ennui.

In a way, all of Fellini's pictures have been about entertainers: carnival performers, journalists, prostitutes, etc. When Fellini decided to make a picture about the subject he knew the best, filmmaking, the motif of the performer could at last be resolved in the form of a filmmaker-protagonist who could only be himself.

8½ is, first of all, a film about the making of 8½. By telling the story of its own production (not the shooting, but the psychic process by which the film was conceived), 8½ becomes a film about itself. It is a measure of the complexity of this work and the skill of its inventor that this idea, already complicated, is allowed to resonate with a self-portrait on celluloid in which scenes of reality, fantasy, and memory are mixed, and the resulting mosaic used to illuminate the character of a filmmaker pondering his next picture (in fact, this picture) while immersed in a personal and professional crisis. Fellini has often been compared to a conjurer, and has himself said that he would like nothing better than to be a magician (though at times, surely, he has given the impression that he would prefer to be a clown). With 8½ he realizes this ambition. In it he conjures up memories of great

warmth, such as the La Seraghina sequence, in which Guido observes the fat whore dancing on the beach, and the wine-making in the farmhouse sequence which, in many ways, is the ultimate Fellini scene. He creates fantasies of delicious intensity, such as the orgy scene, the interview with the cardinal in the subterranean baths, the hanging of his despicable screenwriter collaborator, etc. And he constructs an imaginary world, building, for example, a useless and incredibly expensive space-platform tower which, in effect, he then uses as a throwaway prop, an example of his alter ego's directorial wastefulness. Like Welles in CITIZEN KANE, Fellini provides us with an enormously entertaining circus in which numerous acts take place in numerous rings, with the end result that our heads spin even as we are being moved.

Within the circus that is 8½, the world of filmmaking is depicted in all its cruelty, made even more unbearable than it actually is by Fellini-Guido's goodnatured acceptance. When Guido's producer appears with his entourage in the lobby of the hotel, Guido runs to him, salaaming—an ironic expression of his awe in the presence of an omnipotent force. His relationships with his collaborators are full of strain. He must endure the chatter of the intellectual writer who anticipates almost

every criticism that one can make of 8½, and the tired whines and annoying reproaches of his production manager Conocchia. People thrust scripts into his face, laugh at him as they pronounce the collapse of his career, demand explanations of his latest film, accuse him of this, threaten to break him on account of that, behaving with either exaggerated sycophancy or unbearable hostility, pushing him until he is about to crack. Never has the world of a famous film director been so truthfully presented. In no other film about film has the chaos and almost psychotic anarchy that surrounds motion-picture work been so accurately described. In this sense 8½ is a study of the problems of making a film like 8½, and, for that matter, the problems of making any film at all. If one were to sum up 8½ as a film about film (and, of course, it is much more than that), one would have to say that it depicts the insanity of its own enterprise, yet justifies that insanity on the ground that out of it can come a masterpiece. 8½ is the sort of picture that gives filmmakers hope. Even as it describes all the horrors they must endure, which they speak of so often and describe in their films about films, it demonstrates the potentials of the medium on such an inspiring level that it justifies their endurance and proves that their profession is worthwhile.

Credits

Sunset Boulevard
U.S.A.; 1950; 111 minutes;
released by Paramount.

Directed by Billy Wilder.
Produced by Charles Brackett.
Screenplay by Charles Brackett, Billy Wilder
and D. M. Marshman, Jr.
Photographed by John F. Seitz.
Art direction by Hans Dreier and John Meehan.
Edited by Arthur Schmidt.
Music by Franz Waxman.
Cast: William Holden; Gloria Swanson;
Erich von Stroheim; Nancy Olson; Fred Clark;
Lloyd Gough; Jack Webb;
Franklyn Barnum; Larry Blake; Charles Dayton;
Cecil B. De Mille; Hedda Hopper;
Buster Keaton; Anna Q. Nilsson; H. B. Warner;
Ray Evans.

The Bad and the Beautiful
U.S.A.; 1952; 118 minutes;
released by MGM.

Directed by Vincente Minnelli.
Produced by John Houseman.
Screenplay by Charles Schnee,
based on the story by George Bradshaw.
Photographed by Robert Surtees.
Art direction by Al Ybarra.
Edited by Tony Martinelli.
Music by David Raksin.
Cast: Kirk Douglas; Lana Turner;
Walter Pidgeon; Dick Powell; Barry Sullivan;
Gloria Grahame; Gilbert Roland;
Leo G. Carroll; Vanessa Brown; Paul Stewart;
Sammy White; Elaine Stewart.

All About Eve
U.S.A.; 1950; 138 minutes;
released by 20th Century-Fox.

Directed by Joseph L. Mankiewicz.
Produced by Darryl S. Zanuck.
Screenplay by Joseph L. Mankiewicz,
adapted from the story and radio play,
''The Wisdom of Eve,'' by Mary Orr.
Photographed by Milton Krasner.
Art direction by Lyle Wheeler and George Davis.
Edited by Barbara McLean.
Music by Alfred Newman.
Cast: Bette Davis; Anne Baxter;
George Sanders; Celeste Holm; Gary Merrill;
Hugh Marlowe; Thelma Ritter;
Marilyn Monroe; Gregory Ratoff; Barbara Bates;
Walter Hampden.

Contempt (Le Mépris)
French-Italian Co-production; 1963;
100 minutes.
Released in the U.S. by Embassy Pictures.

Directed by Jean-Luc Godard.
Produced by Georges de Beauregard, Carlo Ponti,
and Joseph E. Levine.
Screenplay by Jean-Luc Godard, from the novel,
''Il Disprezzo,'' by Alberto Moravia.
Photographed by Raoul Coutard.
Edited by Agnès Guillemot and Lila Lakshmanan.
Music by Georges Delerue.
Cast: Brigitte Bardot; Michel Piccoli;
Jack Palance; Fritz Lang; Giorgia Moll;
Jean-Luc Godard; Linda Veras.

8½ (Otto e Mezzo)
Italy; 1963; 138 minutes;
released in the U.S. by Embassy Pictures.

Directed by Federico Fellini.
Produced by Angelo Rizzoli.
Screenplay by Federico Fellini, Ennio Flaiano,
Tullio Pinelli and Brunello Rondi
from a story by
Federico Fellini and Ennio Flaiano.
Photographed by Gianni Di Venanzo.
Art direction by Piero Gherardi.
Edited by Leo Cattozzo.
Music by Nino Rota.
Cast: Marcello Mastroianni; Anouk Aimée;
Sandra Milo; Claudia Cardinale; Rossella Falk;
Barbara Steele; Guido Alberti;
Madeleine Lebeau; Jean Rougeul; Caterina Boratto;
Annibale Nichi; Giuditta Risson.

Frolicking schoolboys enjoy La Seraghina's
lascivious dance in 8½. The fat, bittersweet
whore is a recurring character in
Fellini films, coloring the
sexual attitudes of his protagonists who never
forget their initiations at her hands.

Cinema of Personal Expression

9

A great film, by definition, expresses the world view of its maker and is an artistic expression of his personality. Sometimes, however, it is difficult to locate this directorial personality, to isolate it from the restrictive conventions of motion-picture genres. For example, when a man makes a western he usually deals with the terrain of the American West, the period and costumes of the 1880s and 1890s, and such conventions as the showdown gunfight, the ambience of the saloon, the role of the sheriff in the frontier town, etc. If he is to express himself, his personal vision must be squeezed through these conventions.

In the cinema of personal expression there are no such problems. The personal vision of the filmmaker is the raison d'être of his film. He does not have to impose himself upon his material. His vision, his personality, are his picture's subjects.

The trouble with personal films—films that are conscious expressions of a filmmaker's self—is that they constitute a luxury few people can afford. Attempts to make the screen serve art often lead to bankruptcy. Such pictures are called "art-house films" or "chamber films,"

which is another way of saying that their appeal is to a relatively small segment of the audience. Because film production is very expensive a mass audience is usually necessary in order to recoup an investment and turn a profit. The personal film is only possible in countries where production costs are relatively low, or where there exists some form of government subsidy.

It would have been inconceivable for a John Ford or a Howard Hawks or an Alfred Hitchcock to go to the head of a Hollywood studio and demand production funds because, "I want to make a picture that will express me as an artist." These men have obtained financing by saying, "I want to make a western [or an adventure film, or a thriller]. Here's the story. We can star so-and-so, bring it in for a million seven and project profits at four million eight." The head of the studio could then make a business decision without any meaningless talk about art and self-expression. Yet Ford and Hawks and Hitchcock, being artists, put so much of themselves into their pictures that their personal signatures are always evident, even if they have to be deciphered from what Peter Wollen, in *Signs and Meaning in the Cinema*, calls the

182

Preceding pages: Giulietta Masina as
Gelsomina in Federico Fellini's great filmic poem,
LA STRADA. Above: With Anthony Quinn as the
strong man Zampano, performing their
circus act for villagers. Masina's performance has
been compared to best of Keaton and Chaplin.

"noise" of the star, the studio, the story, or the genre.

In the cinema of personal expression there is no "noise." The filmmaker is up front and on the line. His picture is presented for what it is: a work of art expressing his vision of the world.

Much has been written in recent years about the emergence of the personal film. Actually, the personal film has been a part of cinema since the beginning. What could be more personal, for example, than the early works of Fritz Lang, Carl Dreyer, F. W. Murnau, Griffith's INTOLERANCE, Jean Vigo's ZÉRO DE CONDUITE, and every thing made by Charles Chaplin? No, the personal film is not new. What is new is a self-conscious approach to it, possible only because in recent years the economies of the film industry have been favorable in a few places.

The five pictures discussed here all were made by European directors. They were all, in addition, austerely produced. (Only one, BLOW-UP, is in color.) Bergman, Buñuel, and Bresson are inconceivable in Hollywood. The pictures they make are incompatible with the financial realities of the American film industry. Fellini, though probably the most famous living director, has difficulty obtaining financing because, although some of his pictures have become hits, he is not dependably commercial. Antonioni's flirtation with Hollywood resulted in ZABRISKIE POINT, a financial and artistic failure. The point is that although these five men are among the dozen most interesting directors around, their collective fame is less than one hundredth of John Wayne's, and their bankability is resultingly limited.

Do not look, then, in their work for spectacle, lavishness, an exciting story, or escapist entertainment. Be prepared for seriousness, self-revelation, and even obscurity. The artists of the American cinema necessarily had to produce popular works in order to survive. In Europe it has been possible for artists to use the screen without giving their highest consideration to popular taste. Nothing is more useless than to set up hierarchies in which a man like Robert Bresson is placed above or below John Ford; or Luis Buñuel, at his most alienated and eccentric, is said to be greater than or inferior to Alfred Hitchcock. The wonder of the cinema is that it is flexible enough to embrace all who can use it well, including the man who uses it directly to express his inner self.

Federico Fellini's **La Strada** 1956

The career of Federico Fellini is one of the most remarkable in the history of the cinema. He is and has for some years been the most famous filmmaker in the world, with movie audiences in Europe and America at his feet. In this way he bears a resemblance to Pablo Picasso, the most famous painter in the world, and in another and very important way, too: both men have recreated themselves many times. Each has had a tendency to adopt a style, carry it to heights of accomplishment, and then abandon it for something new. In fifteen years Fellini has made at least five great films (three of them discussed in this book), a personal accomplishment that no other filmmaker can claim. I VITELLONI is a surpassing autobiographical film; LA STRADA is a lyrical film, a great personal poem; LA DOLCE VITA is an influential film of social comment; 8½ is probably the greatest self-portrait of an artist on celluloid; and SATYRICON is an extraordinary film of fantasy, an incredible fictional vision. Fellini is now in his early fifties, at the height of his powers. We can only wonder what he will do next, what new territory he will explore and dominate.

LA STRADA won the Academy Award for Best Foreign Film in 1956, and has collected a good fifty more prizes besides. It is the favorite movie of many people, including filmmakers as diverse as Sam Peckinpah (whose "tough" outlook is about as far as one can get from Fellini) and the documentarian Albert Maysles (who doesn't like fiction films much at all).

LA STRADA is a film with an uncanny power to move people to tears. It is simple and modestly produced, and it haunts members of the toughest audiences. It is a poem about marginal people living on the fringes of society. It takes place, literally, "on the road," in deserted lots, on beaches between highways and the sea. Its message—that everyone needs someone; that loneliness and solitude are unbearable—is almost simple-minded, yet it is exquisitely expressed. LA STRADA is episodic, unpredictable, spontaneous. It is filled with seemingly gratuitous scenes linked together in the most casual way, yet they add up to a rich and powerful vision of life, an offering from a filmmaker to a public that adores his every crumb.

One has the feeling about the Fellini of LA STRADA (and of the other pictures of the same early period, IL BIDONE and NIGHTS OF CABIRIA) that his films are bear hugs, that he is grasping his public to him in a powerful and warm embrace, rubbing his rough whiskers against the smooth cheeks of his audiences as if to say: "I give you a world from my heart; may it move you and may you taste in it the rough-warm flavor of life."

The story of LA STRADA is so simple that one feels certain that in screenplay form it would have been rejected by every studio in the United States, just as it nearly was by Carlo Ponti and Dino de Laurentiis. They agreed to produce it only when Fellini told them he would employ the American actor, Anthony Quinn.

A strange, half-mad girl is "bought" from her mother by a second-rate carnival strongman, and the two go on the road. Zampano (Anthony Quinn) brutalizes Gelsomina (played by Fellini's wife, Giulietta Masina, in a weird pantomimist style that has been compared to the styles of Keaton, Chaplin, and Marcel Marceau). When they join a provincial circus, Gelsomina meets the tightrope walker, Matto the Fool (Richard Basehart). Zampano hates Matto, who taunts him mercilessly, and when, after provocation, he pulls a knife, he is arrested and sent to jail for the night. Gelsomina wants to leave Zampano, but Matto convinces her to stay with him. With a pebble in his hand he tells her: "All in this world serves some purpose…even this little stone." So Gelsomina stays with Zampano. Later, when they meet up again with Matto on the highway, Zampano beats him up and accidentally kills him. Gelsomina goes mad and Zampano abandons her on a roadside. Years after, Zam-

pano hears a girl hum the tune that Gelsomina used to sing. He discovers that Gelsomina has died, he goes out on a drunk, and that night he falls to his knees on a beach and weeps over the loss of her warmth and the misery of his own solitude.

This little story is enriched by a series of extraordinary episodes having to do with the experiences of Gelsomina as she discovers and marvels at the world:

When Zampano abandons her in front of a trattoria and goes off to sleep with a whore, she spends the night weeping. In the morning she is amazed when a riderless horse strolls by her down the street.

At a country wedding, where she and Zampano have done their act, she is taken by some children to an attic room to see a deformed child named Oswaldo, who peers strangely at her from his bed.

When Gelsomina runs away from Zampano and is sitting by a roadside wondering what to do, three musicians surrealistically appear in a single file and lead her to a village where she sees a religious procession. She watches it with awe, and later that night sees the aerial ballet of Matto the Fool for the first time.

With such apparently gratuitous scenes Fellini suffuses us with his rough warmth. In a context of clowns, carnivals and circuses—a continuing motif in his movies, derived, we are told, from his own adolescent experiences as a member of a carnival troupe—he sings us an exquisite poem about an innocent girl, a brutal man, and an artist-fool. It is a poem that haunts.

Luis Buñuel's **Viridiana** 1961

Nothing could be further from the warm humanism of Federico Fellini than the ironic misanthropy of Luis Buñuel. The differences between them are compounded by the fact that the world of Fellini is accessible to everyone (even children), while the world of Buñuel is the delight of a small, devoted cult which must constantly defend him against self-appointed guardians of the public morality. For Luis Buñuel has been accused of almost every sin, every sort of political extremism, every variety of sexual perversion. He has been accused of being the Marquis de Sade of cinema, even of being a man who dines upon live ants. His films, filled with paranoia, anticlericalism, foot-fetishism, and cruelty, are presented with the rage and passion of a man who seems set upon the alienation of the public. Call him bizarre, violent, scan-

dalous, outrageous, he remains one of the tremendous personal voices of the cinema, a hurricane that howls from the normally vacuous screen, a man who clearly does not give a damn for anyone, who is thoroughly committed to nothing but the violent expression of his tormented self. Buñuel with a camera is an iconoclast with a blowtorch.

He has been making scandals since 1928, when he collaborated with Salvador Dali on UN CHIEN ANDALOU, and shocked the public with a shot of a razor blade slicing through a woman's eyeball. In 1930, he established himself as the master of the surrealist cinema with L'AGE D'OR, a picture that so enraged audiences that they tore its first-run theatre apart. There followed various odd jobs: producer of antifascist films in Spain, resident docu-

184

mentarian at the Museum of Modern Art in New York, dubbing director in Hollywood, and then a long period as a filmmaker in Mexico, where he created more than fifteen works, some brilliant, some mediocre, all stamped with the brand of his unique sensibility.

Since UN CHIEN ANDALOU and L'AGE D'OR, the highpoints of his career have been the socially committed LOS OLVIDADOS (1950); a paranoic fantasy on jealousy, EL (1952); a satanic farce, THE LIFE OF CRIME OF ARCHIBALD DE LA CRUZ (1955); and the cryptoreligious masterpiece, NAZARIN (1958). In 1961 Buñuel created his greatest film, the masterpiece in which every sin and outrage of which he had been accused was exhibited in its fullest development. VIRIDIANA, like other Buñuel films, was an enormous scandal. He had returned to Spain for the first time in twenty-five years in order to make it, and had worked under the supervision of Spanish censors. When it won the grand prize at the Cannes Film Festival, the Spanish government was forced to ban and disown it. Somehow, by some route of deviousness too complex to trace, Buñuel had sneaked by his censors a picture that was an abomination to the Fascists he despised and whose regime his work officially represented.

It is impossible to describe the visual texture of this film and its extraordinary force. VIRIDIANA is a picture that must be seen. Certainly the orgy of the beggars (destruction, copulation, and sacrilege) is a stunning sequence, shattering, violent, as perverse as anything that has ever been rendered on the screen. (It makes brilliant contrast with the now-standard "decadent party" sequence, inevitable in films about alienation, and usually so boring.) It climaxes when the beggars form a tableau, in imitation of Leonardo's painting of the Last Supper. Christ is played by an evil blind man, a scratched recording of Handel's "Messiah" plays on an antique Victrola, and the moment is "photographed" by a demented whore,

who snaps it with her "box camera"—revealed when she abruptly lifts her skirts.

VIRIDIANA is an indictment of charity, mercy, all Christian virtues, and all the paraphernalia of the Catholic church. (Viridiana travels with certain personal props: a cross, a hammer and nails, and a crown of thorns, which she burns when she renounces Catholicism for sensualism.) It is filled with seemingly gratuitous shots of feet, insects, cruelty, and other Buñuelian obsessions, including a particular emphasis on the maid's daughter's jump rope, an instrument used alternately for play, strangulation, and bondage. The decaying estate and the perverse happenings on it are probably symbolic of Buñuel's vision of the condition of his native Spain. And the whole picture is shot through with Buñuel's cruel irony, perhaps no place better illustrated than in the famous sequence of the dog and the cart.

Jorge takes pity on a wretched dog tied to the undercarriage of a peasant cart, which he rescues by buying from its owner. As he walks away, Buñuel shows us another dog, even more wretched, trotting tiredly along under another cart coming down the road from the other direction. This scene illuminates the ethos of Buñuel's universe: the innate cruelty of the world, and the stupidity and hypocrisy of performing good deeds. It is a devastating indictment of liberalism, with revolutionary implications: The world cannot be changed by a fine gesture. If it can be changed at all, which is doubtful, it will be by a total destruction of every existing system. Buñuel's message, if one can call it that, seems to be that since everything is awful, and nothing anyone does can make any difference, an amusing solution is to laugh at life's cruelties. This is an extremely unpopular notion, calculated to alienate almost everyone. But Buñuel's hatred is immense, and in VIRIDIANA, at the age of sixty-one, it is as stone-hard and knife-sharp as in any of his outrages.

Ultimate in anticlericalism, as dwarfs, whores, and half-wits re-enact the Last Supper in an orgy of destruction, copulation, and sacrilege at climax of Luis Buñuel's VIRIDIANA. Even after forty-five years of filmmaking, Buñuel's hatred of the church has not softened.

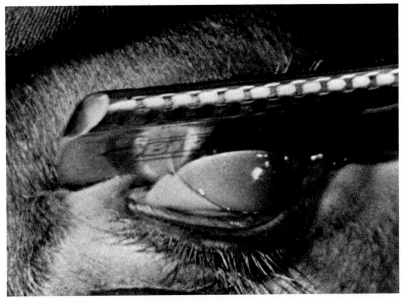

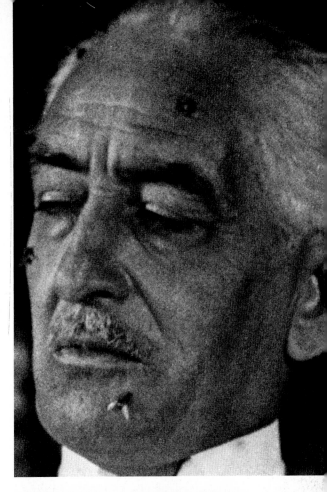

Opposite: Fernando Rey makes love to Silvia
Pinal (Viridiana) and performs an obligatory act
of foot fetishism. This page: Sadism, as a
razor blade slices through a woman's
eyeball in UN CHIEN ANDALOU, made in 1928 by
Buñuel and Salvador Dali. Insects,
another recurring obsession, are endured by a
character in L'AGE D'OR (1930). More
foot fetishism, with Jeanne Moreau. Portrait
of Buñuel, the "devil" of the cinema.

187

Ingmar Bergman's **Persona** 1966

If Buñuel is the Spanish Director—the only one of international repute, and typically Spanish on account of his fascination with the grotesque, reminiscent, in ways, of the vision of Goya—Ingmar Bergman is the Swedish Director, and, for that matter, the most famous living Swede. Though Buñuel is sometimes slipshod in his work, Bergman is fastidious, a perfectionist with a supreme command of the film medium. And while Buñuel bran-

dishes a blowtorch and throws acid on the conventions of society, Bergman explores the dark recesses of his psyche, and there fabricates fantasies that illuminate his personal anguish.

The Bergman freaks, or Bergmaniacs, as they are sometimes called, believe their man to be the greatest filmmaker of all time. If ever a Nobel Prize is given for cinema they will holler if it is not given to him. Bergman

Left: Bibi Andersson (foreground)
and Liv Ullmann in scene
from Ingmar Bergman's PERSONA.
Note resemblance to each
other. Below, Andersson as nurse,
Ullmann as mute stage
actress. Scene from a dream
sequence. Bottom, right: Bergman
conferring with his
actresses (Ullmann facing).

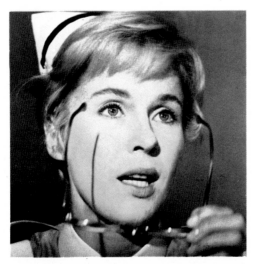

has his detractors, too, people who are bored by his obscurity, and irritated by his heavy symbolism and his austere, icy, Scandinavian melancholy. Both admirers and detractors have their points. Bergman is one of the very few filmmakers who has consistently treated the cinema as a fine art, and has expanded its possibilities as a medium of personal expression. On the other hand, he is just as certainly uncompromising when it comes to providing entertainment. Bergman may be an artist, but he is not a showman; the audience at a Bergman film is forced to work very hard without much certainty that its hard work will provide much penetration into the fog.

Unlike Fellini, Bergman does not give up much warmth to the public. His is a pure blue flame. He makes his films, they get better and better, and his personal odyssey, his search for meaning in life, is there for anyone who wants to observe it, but in the end Bergman doesn't much care what people think. Each of his pictures is a part of a long dialogue with himself.

PERSONA may be his masterpiece, though there are people who are devoted to SMILES OF A SUMMER NIGHT, THE SEVENTH SEAL, WILD STRAWBERRIES, THROUGH A GLASS DARKLY, WINTER LIGHT, THE SILENCE, and THE PASSION OF ANNA. His pictures can be arranged into trilogies, and his development traced and measured in phases. In his later work the intrusion of himself—interrupting action while actors speak about their parts, allowing equipment to be seen along the fringes of the frame, leaving in clap-sticks, using deliberately shoddy and transparent special effects, and repeating takes so as to suspend progression of action—suggests an interest in establishing the artificial "made" quality of his films, in stating very clearly that he is not presenting reality in a manner that requires suspension of disbelief, but is rendering experience in the form of art. The fact that PERSONA opens with shots of the lighting up of an arc lamp in a projector and of film leader being fed onto sprockets, and closes with the film running out and the arc lamp dying, suggests a deliberate attempt to say: This is a film, an artifact, a thing I made and dreamt, not a document of reality I observed. In addition, this opening and closing may represent a definitive statement by Bergman that he is not providing escapist entertainment.

In PERSONA, a stage actress, played by Liv Ullmann, is being treated for catatonia. During a performance of "Electra" she suddenly stopped acting, the next day she fell silent, and she hasn't spoken since. Her doctor sends her to a house by the seashore in a remote area of northern Sweden, accompanied by a nurse-companion (Bibi Andersson). The faces of the two women are strikingly similar, and as the film progresses their clothes, their gestures, even their expressions begin to merge. The actress, the artist, is totally silent; her behavior could be conventionally described as mentally diseased. The nurse is talkative, unmiserable, effusive, an equally conventional projection of a normal young woman. In the house by the sea the relationship between them develops in a strange and fascinating way. As the nurse babbles and reveals herself, and the actress listens, there comes a point where the normality of the nurse becomes questionable and the silence of the actress explicable. It is as if the actress is infecting the nurse, and some process of reversal is taking place; as if the talkative nurse is becoming hysterical, and the silent actress is becoming eloquent.

The turning point comes when the actress gives the nurse an unsealed letter to mail. The nurse reads it and discovers that the actress has been toying with her. Hostility erupts. The nurse leaves a shard of glass on the terrace of the house and is pleased when the actress cuts herself on it. There are fights between them, unexpected outbreaks of physical violence, intimate caresses, even a bloodsucking episode suggesting lesbianism and also a complete merging of identities. At last, after a terrifying nightmare in which the nurse dreams of making love to the actress' husband while the actress stands by like a voyeuse, the two women part, the actress still silent, still uncured, the nurse apparently returning to the normal world.

What does it mean? Impossible to say. Bergman gives very little in PERSONA, not enough to clarify its many obscure points. However, it seems clear that this story, realized so perfectly, rendered with enormous skill and acted and photographed with astonishing brilliance, constitutes some sort of speculation about the role of the artist and the meaning of art. The symbiotic relationship between artist and audience, the way life and art feed upon one another, fight, merge, exchange and separate, the madness that is at the core of art—these seem to be the abstract themes symbolized by the relationship between the actress and the nurse, whose faces Bergman actually combines, at one point, in a strange, surreal superimposition. In another sense, one could say that PERSONA is a justification for the personal film. If the artist does not discharge his agony in the constructive form of art, his silence will destructively infect the public. Art, then, thrives upon disease, and Bergman's films are the product of his neurosis.

It is not his obscurity that is so frightening about Bergman. It is his intensity. There is such tension in PERSONA that it comes at times to be an almost unbearable experience. One senses a man revealing his anguish at the furthest extremes of cold fire, compelling attention by the blazing sting of total chill. In PERSONA the faces of Liv Ullmann and Bibi Andersson are incandescent with this intensity. Their interchange is so intimate that at times we want to avert our eyes.

The mystery surrounding Bergman is whether he himself knows what his pictures are about. In PERSONA one has the feeling that something very personal is being revealed, wrenched out of himself and placed with great creative agony upon celluloid. Bergman seems to be hovering very close to some momentous revelation, or to some irreversible fall into an abyss of obscurity and unresolved symbolism. His future work will reveal whether he can fully communicate his anguish, or whether his attempts to communicate it are burning him out.

Whether one likes him or not, Bergman cannot be dismissed. His craftsmanship is impeccable, his skills with actors and camera enormous. In his films he offers himself up as few men ever have. In each succeeding work there is a sense of a man straining against the limits of his abilities and the limits of his art, using the screen as a diary, not of his exterior life, but of the life of his tormented soul.

Robert Bresson's **Au Hasard, Balthazar** 1966

Robert Bresson has been called the Ingmar Bergman of France, a description that is much too facile and that prevents real understanding of a unique directorial personality. Both filmmakers are intensely austere, Bresson perhaps even more so than Bergman. His pictures are severe in the manner of a Jansenist Catholic, redeemed from utter coldness by an innate Gallic warmth. But while Bergman's films are saturated with symbolism, Bresson's films are more realistic, and while the struggles of Bergman's characters mirror struggles within Bergman's own soul, the struggles of Bresson's characters are the struggles of real people whose humanity is never denied. Bergman exhibits great inner anguish; Bresson, in his films, exudes a composure, a self-containment that suggests a man at peace with himself.

Robert Bresson is a master of total control in the cinema. His every shot is precise and his spare images are indelible. Every move, every gesture, every utterance of his players (usually nonprofessional actors) is dictated with precision. Bresson is a puppeteer and his players are marionettes. It is said that he gives precise line-readings and enforces his will by making innumerable takes, wearing down anyone who contradicts him until all resistance is dissolved. The famous downward glances of his people, their avoidance of eye contact, and the famous Bres-

son monotone in which all the characters speak in more or less the same rigid, styleless way, are evidences of the very special sensibility he imposes.

Like Bergman, Bresson is utterly uncompromising when it comes to matters of public taste. He decidedly does not produce works of escapist entertainment, nor cater in any way to current fashions. But unlike Bergman he is not well known—a national monument, even a national treasure in France, perhaps, but virtually unrecognized in the rest of the world. AU HASARD, BALTHAZAR, his greatest film, has received only the most cursory distribution in the United States. Bresson, who has made no more than ten films in forty years, is perhaps the most obscure great filmmaker around, content to be the darling of film festivals and the object of a small, devoted cult, totally uninterested in personal fame or mass adulation.

It is not easy to gain access to the world of Bresson. His films require an audience to work. He leaves many things unsaid, removing everything from his stories that is not essential. His characters are usually revealed only in moments that illuminate their natures. These people are often vile, sometimes evil, always sinful, yet they are depicted with compassion, for they are human and are therefore blessed with grace. In this sense Bresson is very much a Catholic filmmaker, a man interested in truth-

191

Balthazar the donkey dies amid a flock of sheep at end of Robert Bresson's AU HASARD, BALTHAZAR. Among other enormous accomplishments of this film is the fact that it is nearly impossible not to feel moved; after all that happens this death seems a final outrage.

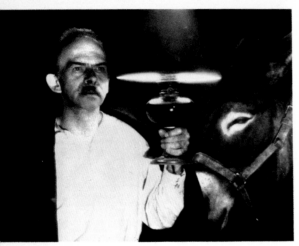

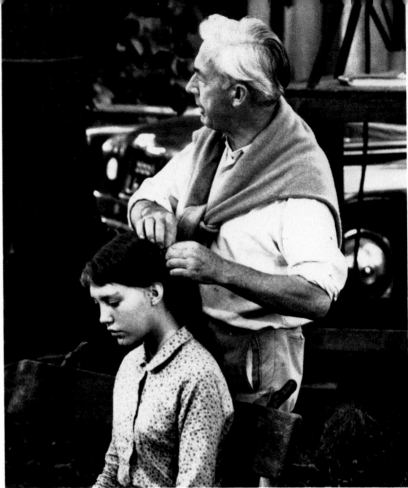

fully illuminating the predicament of people of whose eventual salvation he has little doubt. A Bresson film is spare and episodic, characterized by short, intense scenes linked together by dissolves. The narrative voice is staccato, and the special quality of the performances, from which every attempt at "acting" has been removed, endows his characters with an aura of spirituality that the makers of Biblical epics never seem to obtain.

AU HASARD, BALTHAZAR is set in rural France, a brooding frontier region, where human life is mostly taken up by toil. A donkey, Balthazar, is the central character. His life intersects with the lives of humans who either own him or use him at various times. The lives of these human characters also intersect, and thus through the device of the donkey a complicated story of human entanglements and struggles is told. The principal characters are Marie, a sullen girl who first adopts and names Balthazar (she is torn between spirituality and sensuality, sensuality wins out, and at the end she is gang-raped and dies); Gérard, a young sadist, leader of a motorcycle gang, a sinister youth who is the first seducer of Marie, and who torments Balthazar by setting fire to his tail; and Arnold, a half-witted drunken tramp, who owns Balthazar for a while, is alternately cruel to and solicitous of him, and who also dies in the course of the film.

When Balthazar is young he is loved and caressed by children. Later, turned into a beast of burden, he is tormented by men. In his middle age he becomes a stunt donkey in a circus and is applauded for his brilliance. And in his old age he is regarded by his final owner as a saint. Gérard is ultimately responsible for his death. He steals Balthazar, uses him on a smuggling expedition, and then deserts him when he is shot by a border guard.

It is difficult to convey the intensity of this film and its ability to evoke emotion. When Balthazar dies in a high meadow, amidst a flock of sheep, slowly sinking to the ground, the depth of one's feelings for him is remarkable. There have been many pictures about animals, and most of them have been sentimental. AU HASARD, BALTHAZAR is not one of these. It is a hard, tough picture about suffering and cruelty, human vice and human struggle. The fact that one can come out of a theatre unashamedly moved by the death of a donkey suggests some special power in Robert Bresson. He brings off an almost impossible feat, a picture in which the agony of the human race is convincingly illustrated by the life story of an animal which, by its end, becomes the bearer of the enormous weight of all unexpiated human guilt.

AU HASARD, BALTHAZAR, as Jean-Luc Godard has said, "is really the world in an hour and a half."

192

From AU HASARD, BALTHAZAR: Downward glance of
Anne Wiazemsky (Marie) is typical of
Bresson's style. Pierre Klossowski as the corn merchant,
with Balthazar. Right: Robert Bresson
tends Marie's hair. His relationship with his actors
is that of puppeteer to his marionettes.

Michelangelo Antonioni's **Blow-Up** 1966

The warm embrace of Federico Fellini is opposed by the cool elusiveness of his fellow countryman, Michelangelo Antonioni. Antonioni is not misanthropic like Buñuel, or heavily symbolic like Bergman, or severe like Robert Bresson. His universe is fashionably existential, peopled by characters embroiled in crises of despair. The Antonioni hero is a man or a woman who has acquired all the possessions that society regards as the accouterments of success, but whose inner life is empty, whose spirit is voided, and whose ability to alter his predicament is curtailed by ennui. The world of Antonioni is the world of T. S. Eliot's "The Wasteland": Love is illusory and the meaning of life is elusive. Modern urban society is a wasted landscape through which he wanders, unsatisfied by money, sex, relationships, a strange place where all conversations are elliptical, contact with other humans is strained, matters arise that are never resolved, and life is bounded by boredom and meaninglessness.

For many years Antonioni was obscure. He filmed his existential tales, mastering motion-picture technique and evolving a personal style, and the public yawned. Eventually, in 1960, his L'AVVENTURA became a *succès de scandale* when it was booed and hissed at the Cannes Film Festival. An excruciatingly slow but perfectly told story of modern despair, it enraged audiences by neglecting to explain the disappearance of a girl on a deserted island. A backlash against those who had booed swiftly developed. "But of course he doesn't explain it! That's just the point! That's how life is! Nothing can be explained!" Those who had hissed were relegated to the category of philistines. Suddenly the public was ready for a filmmaker who raised questions and then refused to answer them. LA NOTTE in 1961 and ECLIPSE a year later completed Antonioni's trilogy about alienation, and established one of the contemporary cinema's most characteristic and easily satirized motifs: the long, meditative walk through an urban wasteland, interrupted by unlinked and random events that evoke futility and despair. By the time of the release of Antonioni's first color film, RED DESERT, in 1964, he had established himself as the master of alienation—perhaps not so financially rewarding a position as Hitchcock's master of suspense, but infinitely more chic.

With BLOW-UP (1966), Antonioni created a genuine hit. The sort of picture that would normally have been seen only on the art-house circuit a few years before,

it was widely played, even in small towns, and became a compulsory conversation piece in its year of release. The public was finally ready for Antonioni; his particular brand of avant-gardism had finally become fashionable. Perhaps it was the picture's milieu—"swinging" London, youth pop culture, a few then-daring scenes of erotic sex—but Antonioni had at last surmounted the barrier that had always lain in the personal filmmaker's path: He became a commercial success.

BLOW-UP concerns a successful mod photographer in London whose world is bounded by fashion, pop music, marijuana, and easy sex. His inner life is as bored and despairing as that of any classic Antonioni hero, but in the course of a single day he stumbles upon an event that challenges his ennui, evokes for a few moments the possibility that he may overcome it, but leaves him in the end much as he was before.

While snapping photographs in a park he accidentally captures on film the commission of a murder. The fact that he has photographed a murder does not occur to him until he studies and then blows up his negatives, uncovering details, blowing up smaller and smaller elements, and finally putting the puzzle together in a masterful sequence which in visual strength and suspense would be a credit to Alfred Hitchcock. Whether out of moral weakness, or something in modern life beyond his control, the photographer cannot follow through on his discovery. In the end his photographs are stolen, all evidence of the crime disappears, and he himself begins to question the truth of what he thinks he has seen.

Antonioni's telling of this story is perfection. He is said to have screened every print of BLOW-UP before release to assure himself that the quality of the color met the standards he brought to the production. Many of the scenes, including the simplest, were shot over and over again. The backgrounds—left by many filmmakers to chance or to uncaring assistants—are meticulously controlled. (Note the turbaned Hindu and the foursome of Nigerians who appear in two of the street scenes.) Background buildings were painted in hues that Antonioni believed would evoke specific emotional responses. The behavior of the actors is characteristically Antonioniesque: They move languorously, deliver their dialogue in carefully arranged tableaux of alienation, faces averted, stances opposed, lines left incomplete. Their faces are often suddenly distracted by unexplained noises or random events outside, and they play their sex scenes with chilly intensity. The sound track, too, is a marvel of perfection. Antonioni listened to hundreds of recordings of wind blowing through trees before settling on the mixture that produces the special texture of the scenes set in the park.

The meaning of BLOW-UP has been widely debated, and an entire book of speculations about it has been assembled. Though most critics are convinced that a real murder was committed, there are some who believe the murder was only an illusion of the photographer. Interpretations have been suggested ranging from the thesis that the more one looks at something the less one knows about it (the very process of blowing-up a photograph renders it increasingly abstract); that life is an illusion while art is substantial; that the interaction between life and art is ambiguous and ungraspable; to the idea that it is impossible to know the difference between what is true and what is false in the contemporary world.

Whatever the precise meaning of BLOW-UP, its effect upon audiences was intense. For the first time an extremely personal and difficult film was bought as entertainment. One wonders, however, how long Antonioni will remain in vogue. It is possible that for a brief time his personal obsessions coincided with public taste, but that the public, forever in pursuit of the novel, has moved on to new areas—extreme violence, perhaps, or the "wholesome" escapism of "family" pictures.

Antonioni may be left, like Bergman, Bresson, and Buñuel, with a small, devoted audience. This is the dilemma of the personal filmmaker. While he may spend a lifetime working out his personal themes, refining them, working toward an ultimate film that fully expresses them, the public is constantly on the lookout for new forms of escapism, and the personal fantasies of a single man are not of popular interest for very long. This is the main reason that the personal film is a great luxury, almost unknown in America except, perhaps, immediately after a director has made an enormous commercial hit. Film is just too expensive to be a fine art. The personal film is one of the side shows of cinema. The mainstream lies elsewhere, in the popular genres.

194

From BLOW-UP: Intimacy without passion as
David Hemmings (Thomas) photographs high-fashion model
Verushka in balletic sequence of opening reel.
With Vanessa Redgrave. Michelangelo Antonioni at
work. Opposite: Seemingly split Thomas
contemplates studio setting for photograph.

Credits

La Strada (The Road)
Italy; 1956; 108 minutes;
originally released in the U.S. by
Trans-Lux.

————

Directed by	Federico Fellini.
Produced by	Dino de Laurentiis and Carlo Ponti.
Screenplay by	Federico Fellini,
	Tullio Pinelli, and Ennio Flaiano.
Photographed by	Otello Martelli.
Edited by	Leo Cattozzo and Lina Caterini.
Music by	Nino Rota.
Cast:	Anthony Quinn; Giulietta Masina;
	Richard Basehart; Aldo Silvani; Marcella Rovere;
	Livia Venturini.

Persona
Sweden; 1966; 81 minutes;
released in the U.S. by
Lopert Pictures Corp.

————

Directed by	Ingmar Bergman.
Produced by	Ingmar Bergman.
Screenplay by	Ingmar Bergman.
Photographed by	Sven Nykvist.
Art direction by	Bibi Lindström.
Edited by	Ulla Ryghe.
Music by	Lars Johan Werle.
Cast:	Bibi Andersson; Liv Ullmann;
	Gunnar Björnstrand; Margaretha Krook.

Viridiana
Spain; 1961; 91 minutes;
originally released in the U.S. by
Kingsley International.

————

Directed by	Luis Buñuel.
Produced by	Gustavo Alatriste.
Screenplay by	Luis Buñuel and Julio Alejandro.
Photographed by	José Aguayo.
Art direction by	Francisco Canet.
Edited by	Pedro del Rey.
Music:	Handel's "Messiah."
Cast:	Silvia Pinal; Francisco Rabal;
	Fernando Rey; Margarita Lozano; Victoria Zinny;
	Teresa Rabal; José Calvo; Joaquín Roa.

Au Hasard, Balthazar
(Look out, Balthazar)
France; 1966; 95 minutes;
released in the U.S. by
New Line Cinema.

————

Directed by	Robert Bresson.
Produced by	Mag Bodard.
Screenplay by	Robert Bresson.
Photographed by	Ghislain Cloquet.
Art direction by	Pierre Charbonnier.
Edited by	Raymond Lamy.
Music by	Franz Schubert Piano Sonata No. 20.
Cast:	Anne Wiazemsky; François Lafarge;
	Philippe Asselin; Nathalie Joyaut; Walter Green;
	J.-C. Guilbert; François Sullerot;
	M. C. Frémont; Pierre Klossowski; Jean Remignard;
	Jacques Sorbets; Tord Paag; Sven Frostenson;
	Roger Fjellstrom.

Blow-Up
Great Britain; 1966;
111 minutes; released by MGM.

————

Directed by	Michelangelo Antonioni.
Produced by	Carlo Ponti.
Screenplay by	Michelangelo Antonioni and Tonino Guerra;
	English dialogue in collaboration with
	Edward Bond; inspired by a short story by
	Julio Cortázar.
Photographed by	Carlo di Palma.
Art direction by	Assheton Gorton.
Edited by	Frank Clarke.
Music by	Herbert Hancock.
Cast:	David Hemmings; Vanessa Redgrave;
	Sarah Miles; John Castle; Peter Bowles;
	Jane Birkin; Gillian Hills; Harry Hutchinson;
	Verushka.

Fantasy & Horror

10

Because the photographic process makes it possible to simulate reality, realism has been the mainstream of the cinema. But fantasy has been a subterranean stream since the earliest days of the medium, since the late nineteenth century, when Georges Méliès made L'EVENTAIL MAGIQUE. Méliès was a magician, and his interest in cinematography was in its potential to create magic through special effects. This magical aspect of filmmaking has been basic to the cinema of fantasy down to our own time and the greatest masterpiece of the genre, Stanley Kubrick's 2001: A SPACE ODYSSEY.

The great horror film overlaps the great film of fantasy. Neither, in this discussion, concerns mad scientists (except, of course, for the inescapable Rotwang), Frankenstein monsters, and evil beings with fangs dripping blood, staples of the enormous category of exploitation films that frighten children, amuse adults, and quickly desert the memory. The best horror pictures, the ones made by master filmmakers, extrapolate from the horror that coexists with normality in everyday life, and fantasize worlds which inspire terror because they are so plausible. The macabre characterizations of Lon Chaney are an interesting phenomenon, but Godard's vision in WEEKEND is ten times more terrifying than THE HUNCHBACK OF NOTRE DAME or THE PHANTOM OF THE OPERA. It is a fantasy that cannot be disregarded because it could come true.

In this same sense, 2001: A SPACE ODYSSEY is a horror film. The magic of its technology and its matter-of-fact tone are infinitely more terrifying than all the devices of menace in ROSEMARY'S BABY. 2001 is truly frightening because an amoral universe is more plausible than a cabal of witches, and an unseen manipulative intelligence is scarier than a flesh-and-blood demonic doctor.

Hitchcock's PSYCHO is the cinema's greatest horror-murder film, though it includes only two murders and most pictures of the genre usually deal with many more. It doesn't take decapitations and gore, a leering paranoid with a reverberating chuckle, or Vincent Price in a wax museum, to make people scream. All it takes is a sympathetic character in an ordinary situation, suddenly confronted by the violence that resides just beneath the surface of everyday life. In a Transylvanian castle, committed by a wolf man or an anthropomorphic vampire, a knife murder would be merely hokum. In the shower cubicle of a shabby motel it is a stroke of genius.

Great horror is not to be seen on the Japanese monster-insect-King Kong-Dracula circuit, but in the subtler films that have a basis in real life. The cheapie horror pictures of the quick-kill commercial cinema wear the tawdry trappings of the carnival freak show. The great horror films, the fantasies of great filmmakers, are gripping and powerful because even their components of magic are personal and visionary.

Fantasy is a realm which fascinates every filmmaker, even those who are not true fantasists at heart. Fellini's SATYRICON, Welles' THE TRIAL, Bergman's THE MAGICIAN, and Charles Laughton's NIGHT OF THE HUNTER are just a few of many phantasmagoric creations which are not included here. Works have been included which are peaks of achievement in various subcategories of the genre: METROPOLIS, a futuristic fantasy produced on an epic scale; PSYCHO, the absolute summit of screen terror, perhaps the most manipulative film ever made; THE MANCHURIAN CANDIDATE, a prophetic work of political science-fiction; WEEKEND, a vision of horror so personal that it may constitute the first nervous breakdown ever recorded on celluloid; and 2001: A SPACE ODYSSEY, a great magic show, a frightening horror story, and a distinguished work of motion-picture art.

Fritz Lang's **Metropolis** 1926

METROPOLIS has been called absurd, a work of insanity, and, by H. G. Wells, "quite the silliest film I have seen." It is all of these things, and also a strikingly visual, monumental production, and an important landmark in the history of motion pictures.

Charges of absurdity are usually leveled against the story of METROPOLIS—its tyrant master, its mad scientist Rotwang, Freder, Maria, revolution and floods and a final reconciliation between capital and labor, with love in the end conquering all. Not a very promising story, perhaps, but this tale of a mechanical world in which men are enslaved by machines, becomes the excuse for Fritz Lang to build enormous sets, employ all sorts of screen magic, and visualize an incredible future with all the technical and financial resources of the German cinema at his command.

Lang is said to have received the inspiration for METROPOLIS when he first came to New York in 1924 and

198

Preceding pages: One of the vast, mechanistic sets used in METROPOLIS (1926). Robot-like class of worker-slaves tends the underground machines that supply energy to the city of Metropolis. Opposite: Director Fritz Lang (r.) and cameraman Karl Freund carried by assistants in gag shot on flood set.

beheld the Manhattan skyline from the deck of his ship. His wife, Thea von Harbou, wrote *Metropolis* as a novel, and then developed it into a screenplay. Lang turned the paper story into a vast celluloid monument of personal excess.

Everything about METROPOLIS is big. It even rivals Griffith's INTOLERANCE in volume of spectacle. The picture cost more than $1.5 million, an enormous sum in 1926. Nearly two million feet of film were exposed; twenty-five thousand men (eleven thousand with shaven heads), eleven thousand women, seven hundred and fifty children and twenty-five Chinese played the extras; the shooting time was three hundred and ten days and sixty nights. During the course of the production rumors were widespread: Lang was doing something monstrous, the UFA Company (Germany's largest motion-picture firm) was going bankrupt, the wild director had even discovered a way to achieve epic grandeur by some sort of magical process that combined miniature sets with real actors. (This was a reference to Lang's use of the Shuftan Process, a special-effects technique invented by the same Eugene Shuftan who, years later, won the Academy Award for Cinematography for THE HUSTLER.)

Lang was the director originally assigned to the now legendary film, THE CABINET OF DR. CALIGARI, ultimately directed by Robert Wiene. CALIGARI, so famous and so fundamental to the whole German Expressionist Movement, is something of a disappointment today because, though its motifs are rather interesting, it contains very little that could not have been done on a theatrical stage. METROPOLIS, on the other hand, is a cinematic miracle,

reflecting Lang's special ability to create an atmosphere by visual means, and to propel a story by using a moving camera and by staging scenes in strong geometric patterns. Among its more brilliant and purely visual sequences is the scene in which Maria struggles against Rotwang's power, an unrelenting beam of light in which she is imprisoned and which forces her to make a long, terrifying run through a dark labyrinth of catacombs beneath the city.

The production excesses of METROPOLIS were matched by its excessive length: seventeen reels in the original version. Many of these reels are taken up by long, tormenting shots of workers arranged in architectural tableaux, or marching in ornamental unison, like dancers in a Busby Berkeley musical.

As a fantasy METROPOLIS has been called prophetic. The choreography of its geometrically arranged people is to be seen in Leni Riefenstahl's Nazi documentary, TRIUMPH OF THE WILL. It is as if Lang prophesied the manipulative, mechanistic world of National Socialism. (It is also interesting that Goebbels told Lang that he and Hitler had seen METROPOLIS years before they came to power, in a small provincial theatre. Hitler had turned to Goebbels and said: "Lang is the man to make our films" —which Lang, of course, refused to do when Goebbels offered him the job in the course of the same conversation.) The prophetic power of METROPOLIS may not yet have been spent. There are those who believe human society is headed toward an ultimate split between masses of toiling have-nots and an elite of decadent pleasure-seekers. Lang's "absurd" vision may yet prove valid.

METROPOLIS employs many of the themes which Lang worked out later in his suspense-thriller M. There is his characteristic mood of oppression, his favorite device of contending forces and an enclosing trap, individuals struggling with omnipotent mobs, and a prosaic ending to a bizarre situation, which is usually a disappointment to contemporary audiences.

METROPOLIS, quite unlike THE CABINET OF DR. CALIGARI, is not a cul-de-sac. It began a tradition of great personal screen fantasies displaying the excesses of directors making incredible demands upon studios, usually because these directors had recently achieved commercial success and the studios involved were afraid to say no. 2001: A SPACE ODYSSEY is very much a part of this tradition. Like METROPOLIS, it is a highly personal, utterly fantastic futuristic vision, produced on a gigantic scale, in which machines rule humans, implacable forces contend, robotism is a leit-motif, and the location in time is almost the same. (METROPOLIS is set in the year 2000.)

Fantasy and horror expressed
on a vast scale are the
essence of METROPOLIS. Above:
Freder (Gustav Frölich) grapples
with evil inventor Rotwang
(Rudolf Klein-Rogge), while Maria
(Brigitte Helm) hangs
precariously from cathedral roof.
Right: Shooting the flood
sequence. Though Lang worked
with miniature models and
employed trick photography, much
of METROPOLIS was shot on
huge sets. Opposite: Wedge of
workers at cathedral doors
in final reconciliation scene.
Rotwang with rig for transferring
Maria's form and substance
to robot. Freder's agony at
inhuman conditions of workers.
False Maria burns at stake.

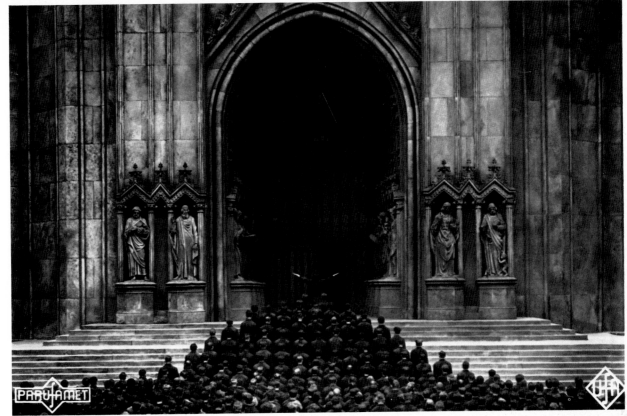
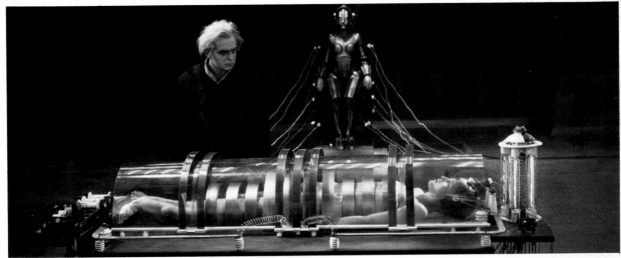

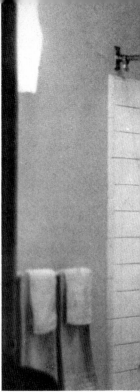

Alfred Hitchcock's **Psycho** 1960

PSYCHO is the most astounding, audacious, and successful horror film ever made. There are films which contain more killings, more bloodshed, and more frightening and ludicrous characters, but no film has ever gripped an audience and induced it to scream with quite the same force as this most expertly crafted masterpiece of murder and psychosis.

Hitchcock is very clear about his motives. "It was rather exciting to use the camera to deceive the audience," he says to Truffaut, in the latter's famous study of his favorite American director. "The game with the audience was fascinating. I was directing the viewers. You might say I was playing them, like an organ." And later: "I didn't start off to make an important movie. I thought I could have fun with this subject and this situation. . . . PSYCHO cost us no more than $800,000 to make. It has grossed some $15 million."

"My main satisfaction," he says, "is that the film had an effect on the audiences; . . . [it] made the audience scream. I feel it's tremendously satisfying for us to be able to use the cinematic art to achieve something of a mass emotion. And with PSYCHO we most definitely achieved this. It wasn't a message that stirred the audiences, nor was it a great performance or their enjoyment of the novel. They were aroused by pure film. That's why I take pride in the fact that PSYCHO, more than any of my other pictures, is a film that belongs to filmmakers."

And then Hitchcock turns to Truffaut, a young man famous for his films of high culture, though of perhaps limited appeal, and says: "That's what I'd like you to do—a picture that would gross millions of dollars throughout the world. It's an area of filmmaking in which it's more important for you to be pleased with the technique than with the content . . . it won't necessarily get you the best notices, but you have to design your film just as Shakespeare did his plays—for an audience."

Ah, ha! At last the secret is out. Alfred Hitchcock, who for years has denied that he is an artist, who has claimed over and over again that he considers himself merely an entertainer, who confesses to having taken enormous pleasure in manipulating an audience and milking it for millions of dollars, now speaks of his most manipulative and successful picture as a "filmmaker's film," and equates himself by inference with the greatest artist of all time. Well, he may be right, on every count.

Never in the history of the cinema has a filmmaker so audaciously played his viewers "like an organ." For the first forty-five minutes of PSYCHO, Hitchcock carefully, meticulously builds up sympathy and audience identification with Janet Leigh. She is young, attractive, in love, and has problems that money can solve. She cannot resist when tempted by the possibility of stealing $40,000 from a disgusting and dishonest old man. Will she get away with it? Will she be caught? Or will she come to

202

Left to right: Tony Perkins brooding beside
house in PSYCHO. Notice his posture, indicative
of his unique mincing walk. Perkins
terrorized by bloody sight on bathroom floor.
One of the images from the shower-murder
sequence that took seven days to shoot.

her senses, return the money, and salvage her life? We cringe as she blunders. We pity her for her naïveté when she draws herself to the attention of the police. When she stops at the Bates Motel and has the sort of intimate conversation with Anthony Perkins that is only possible with a sympathetic stranger, we are relieved that she sees the error of her ways and decides to return the money, making up for what she's spent out of her own meager savings. She has redeemed herself, and when she returns to her room and takes a shower, we feel as though the dirt of her crime is being washed away.

And then, after caring for her and identifying with her for three quarters of an hour, we watch with amazement as she is brutally slain, knifed to death in the shower by a maniacal woman who slashes at her again and again. Her blood mixes with the water and swirls down the drain, and when that shot is matched to a spiraling pullback from an extreme closeup of one of her dead eyes, her world, so carefully and lavishly built for us, is gone. The center has dropped away. Every convention of storytelling has been defied. Our heroine is dead and the film is only half done. We are horrified by her death, and even more horrified by the breakdown of narrative. We know we are in a nightmare world where anything is possible. What Hitchcock has done has been outrageous. Now he has us completely in his hands. (Hitchcock experimented with killing off a heroine in VERTIGO, where we see Kim Novak killed twice! But because our main identification is with Jimmy Stewart, the effect is not so strong as in PSYCHO, where our total attention is on Janet Leigh.)

With Janet Leigh gone, we must transfer our loyalties to Anthony Perkins, the pleasant, modest, charming young man, who gains our sympathy, Truffaut insists, by the way he cleans up the bathroom and protects his mother. Yes, incredible as it may seem, when Perkins mops up the shower stall we begin to root for him.

This is another Hitchcock trick, of course, because we have no reason to suspect that Perkins' mother does not exist. We are certain we have seen her murder Arbogast, the detective, and Hitchcock confesses with delight that the high-angle shot he uses for her mad, knife-brandishing rush from her bedroom, and the similar shot when Perkins carries her to the cellar, are ingeniously designed so that we will never ask ourselves why we have not been allowed to see her face. It never occurs to us that she is a mummy, preserved by her friendly young taxidermist son, the matricidal maniac. And when he is revealed as the killer, our world is shattered again. It's all tricks, yes, and manipulation, yes, and yes, indeed, Hitchcock does play us "like an organ."

PSYCHO is one of the most strangely constructed films ever made. It goes against every expectation of the audience, and thus reduces it to a trembling, fearful, screaming mass. It is a demagogic work by a master craftsman of the film medium, who knows precisely what he is doing and why he is doing it. To gross $15 million, to have "fun" with the camera (he spent seven days shooting from seventy camera set-ups to make the shower-murder montage), to demonstrate the power of the screen, and, like Shakespeare, to please an audience—these are the things that Hitchcock is all about.

203

John Frankenheimer's The Manchurian Candidate 1962

THE MANCHURIAN CANDIDATE is a political fantasy, a warped extension of conditions inherent in the American political scene. Its horror resides in its relation to events that have occurred since its release: a series of political assassinations, the Vietnam War, the emergence of extreme violence in everyday life, an expansion of political extremism, and the interchangeability of the far Right and the far Left. Its much-criticized perversity—that Joe McCarthy could have been a Communist agent; that a Presidential candidate could be assassinated; that a captured soldier could be brainwashed and turned into a walking time bomb—unfortunately no longer seems so farfetched. When John Kennedy was assassinated many people believed that Lee Harvey Oswald was some sort of "Manchurian candidate." His sojourn in the USSR suggested that perhaps, in his case, life was imitating art.

The fantasy is the creation of the novelist Richard Condon. It is his vision, one of a series of fascinating speculations he has made in novels with the common themes that anything is possible, that peoples' motives are usually the opposite of what one might suppose, and that social facts can be the basis of outrageous possibilities. But the visualization of THE MANCHURIAN CANDIDATE must be credited to John Frankenheimer, who brought to it superb élan, created many dazzling sequences, and piled his own embellishments upon the excesses of Condon, and the screen-writer George Axelrod.

Frankenheimer has contributed brilliant touches to this fiendish and paranoid story of the brainwashed Raymond Shaw, used by his mother as a tool to gain control of the United States. When Shaw kills Senator Jordan he uses a silenced pistol. The bullet enters Jordan through a carton of milk he happens to be carrying. The milk that runs out is a grotesque and satirical symbol of the proverbial milquetoast liberal.

Another fine sequence is the press conference held by the Secretary of the Army, who has been accused by the demagogic Senator Iselin of harboring Communists in his department. The scene is covered partly through the monitoring screens of television cameras, a device that not only supplies verisimilitude—being similar to scenes set in Senate hearing rooms that one sees on evening news shows—but also brings the faces of the protagonists into striking juxtapositions.

The Madison Square Garden sequence is brilliant, filled with political hoopla, mass hysteria, and the terror of assassination. (When Iselin is shot, one cannot help but be reminded of portions of the Zapruder film of the Kennedy assassination in Dallas.) The political drama combined with the subjective vision of the assassin through the cross hairs of his telescopic sight is worthy of Hitchcock and makes for a tense dramatic finale.

But by far Frankenheimer's best sequence is the brainwashing. Here he dollies his camera around and around as the scene shifts back and forth between the brainwashing as it actually took place, and the woman's garden-club milieu in which the brainwashees believe themselves to be.

It is interesting that Frankenheimer has not surpassed THE MANCHURIAN CANDIDATE, which came fairly early in his career. He seems to have given up a pyrotechnical approach and attempts at dazzling sequences in favor of a solemn and sometimes heavy-handed narrative style which is certainly more pure, but just as certainly more tiresome. The sort of material that seems to attract him now is less commercial and more arty than THE MANCHURIAN CANDIDATE, less dazzling and more profound in an academic sense. Since he evidently was close to Robert Kennedy, who spent the last day of his life at Frankenheimer's house in Malibu, it is possible that his recent austerity represents a reaction against the razzle-dazzle associated with that particular tragedy. Then again such a speculation may be unfair to a man who continues to make worthy films within a difficult commercial system, and from whom the credit for THE MANCHURIAN CANDIDATE, a great work of political fiction, cannot be taken away.

204

John Frankenheimer (above) at work.
Opposite: Sergeant Raymond Shaw (Laurence Harvey) kills a comrade during brainwashing sequence of THE MANCHURIAN CANDIDATE, while Major Bennett Marco (Frank Sinatra) sits in a daze. Both victim and chair are knocked across the room.

Jean-Luc Godard's **Weekend** 1967

Like the other films of horror being considered here, Jean-Luc Godard's WEEKEND is a fantasy extrapolated from the real world. It reflects a personal view of existence, a view of the roles of art and politics in life, and, in addition, a special, deeply felt, highly personal hatred of the bourgeoisie. WEEKEND is passionate, chaotic, a marred work of genius by a man who made more innovations and affected the cinema more deeply in the eight years prior to this work than any other filmmaker of his time. With WEEKEND we have the impression that Godard may have burned himself out, so incandescent, so passionate, so intense is the vision and so hellish is the horror.

WEEKEND begins with a long, casual description of a sex orgy that is so disorienting and so obscene that one is tempted to leave the theatre. It observes the adventures of a young couple evidently out to murder the wife's

rich mother for an inheritance, and proceeds through a long series of satirical sequences in which life is seen in terms of a weekend, a hell of rape, murder, traffic jams, automobile accidents, blood, and carnage. It then offers a mystical sequence in which a pile of smashed-up cars is transformed into a herd of sheep, a pastoral interlude in which we watch a man playing a Mozart sonata in a farmyard, on-camera interviews with a Negro and an Algerian who drive a garbage truck filled with the refuse of western civilization, and ultimately it plunges into a milieu of hippie-guerrillas who kill and literally eat the flesh of the bourgeoisie. There are appalling scenes along the way: a pig having its throat cut, a goose being decapitated, a fish being inserted into the vagina of the anti-heroine, and at the end a scene in which she eats pieces of her husband's chopped-up body. WEEKEND is excessive. Among other things it is a vision of life as horror, a premonition of the youth revolution, a dissertation concerning the contending views of Mao Tse-tung and Lyndon Johnson, a stylized reference to the Vietnam War, a social satire, a poem of hatred, and the ultimate in audience alienation.

What is one to make of all this bloodshed, butchery, carnage, this satire on the aspirations of the middle class (when the antihero and antiheroine are asked to make three wishes, they respond: "A better car, naturally blond hair, a weekend with James Bond!"), this finale of anarchy and cannibalism? There is only one thing to make of it: A filmmaker has carried his obsessions so far, and expressed his rage with such intensity, that filmmaking for him may afterward be impossible. Although Godard has made other films since WEEKEND, they have mostly been political diatribes, agitprop pictures in the service of what he calls "the Revolution." The real clue to the personal meaning of WEEKEND may be the title on its final frame. "End of Film" the caption reads, and then, "End of Cinema." For Jean-Luc Godard, most influential filmmaker of the 1960s, most innovative groundbreaker of the French New Wave, WEEKEND is perhaps "the end of cinema." His view of existence is so horrible that cinema—film in the service of art—may no longer be possible for him. With WEEKEND Godard destroys everything he hates in a bloody massacre, and very possibly he also destroys himself. WEEKEND is a brilliant psychopathic work, a horror story containing strong evidences of a filmmaker's self-destruction.

Above: Butchery in the woods and carnage on the highway — scenes from Godard's WEEKEND. Opposite: The "Starchild" of Stanley Kubrick's 2001: A SPACE ODYSSEY. Inscrutable to some, deeply meaningful to many, the Starchild is one of the memorable screen images of the 1960s.

Stanley Kubrick's **2001: A Space Odyssey** 1968

2001: A SPACE ODYSSEY was the most controversial and misunderstood film of the 1960s. When it opened it "disappointed" many reviewers who found it slow and tedious, and who felt that its resolution was phony-profound. Actually, the real deception concerning 2001 was not the result of Kubrick's lightweight metaphysics, but the critical establishment's inability to deal with a new kind of picture in a new kind of way. The backlash against this initial hostility was quick to come: first, when the "youth audience" discovered that 2001 was a great "trip," and then when younger critics used it as an excuse to flog the "liberal-arts mentalities" of their older rivals. As a result, an enormous amount of nonsense has been written about 2001 on both sides of the generation gap.

By now the controversy has passed and 2001 has been more or less accepted as one of the very few great films of our time. As a science-fiction fantasy it remains unexcelled. No other picture in the genre even comes close. As a horror story, too, it is a towering achievement, not on the same scream-inducing level as Hitchcock's PSYCHO, but in a subtler and far more haunting way. There are many elements of horror in 2001, but perhaps the most overwhelming one is the picture's vision of man, a creature that mutates from the spontaneous, frightened, wretched, clumsy, murderous apes of the "Dawn of Man" section into the controlled, unemotional, sterile, competent, dehumanized technologists of the moon visit and the Jupiter mission. Somewhere in between, civilization came and went. In Kubrick's fantasy the Golden Age of man was a negligible instant between an ape's exaltation at discovering the first weapon, and a satellite carrying a nuclear weapon floating in a graceful orbit around the earth. A future containing an astral Howard Johnson's is so horrible that it is enough to make one long for the dissolution and cannibalism of Godard's WEEKEND.

Almost everyone who has seen 2001 has been struck by the fact that the HAL 9000 computer is the most "human" character in the movie, that its preference to commit murder rather than admit an error is less sinister and more "human" than the unfeeling logic of HAL's astronaut-caretakers. When Keir Dullea lobotomizes HAL by unscrewing his higher mental functions, one feels considerably more sympathy for the victim than when HAL discontinues the life functions of the hibernating astronauts.

As a spectacle 2001 is a marvel. There are no great crowd scenes, no massed armies, but millions of dollars' worth of glittering machinery that works. From story to completion the picture took five years to make. The special effects alone occupied a year and a half. The great device

that made possible the unusual shots in the spaceship, particularly the phenomenal one of Gary Lockwood jogging and shadow-boxing through 360 degrees, was a $750,000 centrifuge ten feet wide and thirty-eight feet high. Throughout 2001, one is faced with computers and control panels covered with read-out display screens; all of them are active with authentic material, the result of intricate rear-screen projections of numerous specially made animated films. The landing at the Clavius Base on the moon, in which the Aries craft enters an airlock and passes tiers in which tiny human figures can be seen at work, was achieved by a most painstaking and elaborate use of matte processes.

Kubrick was assisted by a huge staff of designers and scientific advisers, and induced hundreds of corporations, government agencies, and research institutions to help work out the technology of the year 2001. All the devices one sees are supported by the finest and most thorough scientific research. The result is that in 2001—as opposed to other science-fiction films—one is surrounded by a totally believable futuristic environment. Its technical perfection gives substance to Kubrick's speculations. The mysterious dimension of the story is backstopped by a sensual dimension in which one can actually feel the texture of the future.

2001: A SPACE ODYSSEY is not a linear film. It is more like a sensory experience which one either rejects or accepts, depending on one's instincts. Kubrick has called it a "mythological documentary." Though its many details are logical, its grand design is not. It is very much a speculation about time, intelligence, and human destiny, and its open ending, into which Kubrick urges viewers to read whatever they like, is but one example of a new film language deliberately opposed to the tight construction of the conventional three-act story. Of course, 2001 is not the first nonlinear film, but the fact that everything is not neatly tied up at its end annoys many people. They demand clarity where there can only be mystery; they insist upon an answer where there can only be a question.

Arthur C. Clarke, who wrote the original story and collaborated on the screenplay, has pointed out that if a fifteenth-century man were transported to our time, he would think of our airplanes and television as feats of magic, because he would not understand the logic of the technology we have devised. By the same token, Clarke points out that an encounter between a man of 2001 and a vastly more advanced technology would result in the same sensation of magic. On this basis alone one can justify the mysterious ending of 2001. When Keir Dullea

encounters a slab—similar to the one which inspired the apes to use weapons, and another which was set up as some sort of sentinel on the moon—everything that happens to him must be magical. For those who can accept this premise, the ending of 2001 is deeply moving. Some have even called it a religious experience. For those who resist it, for whom mysticism is unacceptable, the final powerful and haunting "star-child" image is a source of endless infuriation.

2001 is a film filled with riches—brilliant sequences and extraordinary moments: the stunning first half-hour in which the story of the apes is told visually, without a single line of dialogue (the apes were played by dancers and mime-artists, and two live baby chimpanzees); the restrained satire of the scenes aboard Orion, the space station, and Aries (the zero-gravity toilet, the smiling stewardess); a stewardess on Aries turning upside-down (actually she is on a treadmill, it is the spaceship set and camera that turn); the banality of all human exchanges (the chitchat with the Russians, Gary Lockwood's canned birthday greeting from his family, Dr. Floyd's conversa-

tion with his daughter on the picturephone); the terribly frightening moment when we realize that HAL is reading the astronauts' lips; the tension leading to the moment when Dullea must pass through total vacuum, and the actual image of him being sucked toward us (achieved by having him fall upon the camera, his fall broken by wire restraints); HAL singing "Daisy, Daisy" in his death throes; the magical alignments of sun, moon, and earth, and of Jupiter and its moons, that occur whenever the slab appears.

One must view 2001 ultimately as a personal triumph for Stanley Kubrick, who devoted himself to it for five years. At a time of grave economic trouble within the picture industry, when the grandiose projects of equally famous directors were being canceled right and left, and when MGM, the film's sponsor, was passing through near-bankruptcy and debilitating proxy fights, Kubrick held on. Think of him, spending $10.5 million, and sending back tens of thousands of feet of frolicking apes to executives who could not hope to understand how such scenes could be transformed back into money.

209

Glittering hardware that doesn't look like cardboard is one of the attractions of 2001. Production values of the picture were exemplary. Kubrick induced corporations and scientists to help him create an environment with the texture of the future.

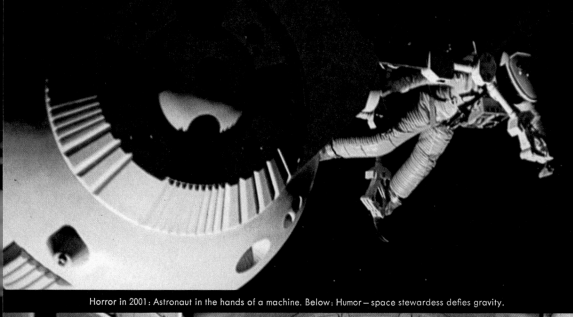

Horror in 2001: Astronaut in the hands of a machine. Below: Humor—space stewardess defies gravity.

Bowman (Keir Dullea) enters "time slot."

Space station orbits moon in Kubrick's cosmic ballet.

Credits

Metropolis
Germany; 1926; 94 minutes
(U.S. version); released by UFA.

Directed by	Fritz Lang.
Produced by	Erich Pommer.
Screenplay by	Thea von Harbou from her novel.
Photographed by	Karl Freund and Gunther Rittau.
Art direction by	Otto Hunte, Erich Kettelhut
	and Karl Vollbrecht.
Cast:	Alfred Abel; Gustav Frölich;
	Brigitte Helm; Rudolf Klein-Rogge; Fritz Rasp;
	Theodor Loos; Erwin Biswanger;
	Heinrich George; Olaf Storm;
	Hans Leo Reich; Heinrich Gotho.

Psycho
U.S.A.; 1960; 109 minutes;
released by Paramount.

Directed by	Alfred Hitchcock.
Produced by	Alfred Hitchcock.
Screenplay by	Joseph Stefano, from the novel
	by Robert Bloch.
Photographed by	John L. Russell.
Art direction by	Joseph Hurley,
	Robert Claworthy, and George Milo.
Edited by	George Tomasini.
Music by	Bernard Herrmann.
Cast:	Anthony Perkins; Janet Leigh;
	Vera Miles; John Gavin; Martin Balsam;
	John McIntire; Simon Oakland;
	Frank Albertson; Patricia Hitchcock;
	Vaughn Taylor.

The Manchurian Candidate
U.S.A.; 1962; 126 minutes;
released by United Artists.

Directed by	John Frankenheimer.
Produced by	George Axelrod and John Frankenheimer.
Screenplay by	George Axelrod,
	based on the novel by Richard Condon.
Photographed by	Lionel Lindon.
Art direction by	Richard Sylbert.
Edited by	Ferris Webster.
Music by	David Amram.
Cast:	Frank Sinatra; Laurence Harvey;
	Janet Leigh; Angela Lansbury; Henry Silva;
	James Gregory; Leslie Parrish;
	John McGiver; Madame Spivy.

Weekend (Le Weekend)
France; 1967; 105 minutes;
released in the U.S. by Grove Press.

Directed by	Jean-Luc Godard.
Screenplay by	Jean-Luc Godard.
Photographed by	Raoul Coutard.
Edited by	Agnès Guillemot.
Music by	Antoine Duhamel.
Cast:	Mireille Darc; Jean Yanne;
	Jean-Pierre Kalfon; Valerie Lagrange; Paul Gegauff;
	Virginie Vignon; Jean Eustache;
	Ernest Menzer; Jean-Pierre Léaud.

2001: A Space Odyssey
Great Britain; 1968;
141 minutes; released by MGM.

Directed by	Stanley Kubrick.
Produced by	Stanley Kubrick.
Screenplay by	Stanley Kubrick and Arthur C. Clarke,
	based on Clarke's story ''The Sentinel.''
Photographed by	Geoffrey Unsworth.
Art direction by	Tony Masters,
	Harry Lang, and Ernie Archer.
Edited by	Ray Lovejoy.
Music by	Richard Strauss, Johann Strauss,
	Aram Khatchaturian
	and György Ligeti.
Cast:	Keir Dullea; Gary Lockwood;
	William Sylvester; Daniel Richter;
	Douglas Rain (voice of HAL 9000);
	Leonard Rossiter; Margaret Tyzack; Robert Beatty;
	Sean Sullivan; Frank Miller.

The Concerned Cinema

11

The concerned cinema is the cinema of social commitment, the cinema that confronts an issue or a problem, the cinema that speaks for those without a voice.

Its pitfalls are many: political bias; making a statement at the expense of emotional involvement; cardboard characters enunciating ideologies; the notion that good and honorable intentions and a sincere desire to straighten out the world are an excuse for bad art. Among the worst mistakes that a filmmaker can make is to think that because his point of view is just, his nobility of heart will move an audience, or that because an issue is important its form is not. Subject matter will not redeem a bad film. Sincerity of purpose is not sufficient.

The great film of concern is not propagandistic, is not made in the service of a state-owned cinema, or a political party. It does not manipulate the truth in order to convince its audience of the correctness of a political line, nor does it impose an ideology to which its characters and scenes must conform. If it has a bias, it is not intellectual; it is the bias of the filmmaker's soul. If it is concerned, the concern is not applied a priori; it derives from the material, the story, and the characters of the film.

The concerned film serves art, not politics. It produces emotion on account of its story, not its issue. Its antagonists are not depicted as bad merely because they happen to be on the "wrong" side. The great film of concern is, above all else, compassionate. It reveals its characters in their many-sided complexity, not merely as automatons reflecting points of view. In this sense great films of this genre are humanitarian. Their concern is with people. And if they are critical of the social order, their criticism is implicit and not imposed.

Everyone who is sane is against war, poverty, crime, fascism, slavery, lynching, anti-Semitism, and the oppression of minority groups. It's not very difficult to be right about the basic issues of society. What is difficult is to reflect one's rectitude or one's rage in terms that can move an audience. Nothing is more tiresome than the film which tells us what we already know in terms we have seen a hundred times. Originality of expression is very important in this kind of film. The how is more important than the what, the depth of concern is more important than its existence.

Many people are afraid of the cinema because it seems such a powerful medium. Lenin recognized this and spoke of it several times. Hitler turned to Leni Riefenstahl after he had seen and been impressed by THE BATTLESHIP POTEMKIN, because he wanted a filmmaker who would serve him the way he thought that Eisenstein had served the USSR. Because the cinema seems so powerful, there are people who fear the men who have mastered its art. Surely the worst stain on the history of Hollywood is the blacklisting and purges of the 1950s.

It would be vulgar to demean the suffering of people who were deprived of their right to work on political grounds, and that is not the intention here. But aside from the issue of whether such people were guilty or innocent of the biases of which they were accused, the truth is that their power to alter political and social consciousness was vastly overrated. Many men have made films of social concern, but very few have made films that were great. It takes enormous excellence to make a truly moving film, a film that captures a dilemma, crystalizes it in human terms, renders it with compassion. Audiences know a great film when they see one, because audiences have an uncanny ability to recognize the truth. No matter how powerfully a position is expressed—and one thinks of some masterpieces of early Soviet filmmaking in this regard—its concern must be truthful or it will be merely a technical triumph. That is the only thing the opponents of any of the five following films need fear: not the politics of the men who made them, not even the power of their art, but the truth of what they say.

Vittorio De Sica's The Bicycle Thief 1948

In THE BICYCLE THIEF, Vittoria De Sica and his writer/collaborator Cesare Zavattini are concerned with the poor, the anonymous poor for whom a minor incident becomes a personal tragedy and toward whom society is indifferent. "Look at the story of this ordinary man," they seem to be saying. "There are ten million stories like this happening every day. We must be concerned with this man and his story because we are human and so is he."

THE BICYCLE THIEF is the summit work of Italy's Neo-Realist movement, the school of documentary-style fiction filmmaking that flourished there after the fall of Mussolini. Neo-Realism was characterized by the use of real locations, usually the streets of Italy's war-wrecked cities, of nonactors whose lives resembled the lives of the

214

Preceding pages: Antonio (Lamberto Maggiorani, r.) and son Bruno (Enzo Staiola) drive through streets of Rome in search of stolen bicycle in Vittorio De Sica's Neo-Realistic masterpiece, THE BICYCLE THIEF. Note use of grainy photography to convey documentary "look."

characters they portrayed, and of a certain gritty, documentary look that proclaimed the authenticity of the material. (When one tries to imagine a Neo-Realist film in color, one understands immediately that it is impossible. The drabness of unlit documentary black-and-white photography is essential to the Neo-Realist "look.")

In addition to elements of style, subject matter of a certain type was central to the Neo-Realist film. These pictures told stories about poor people, forgotten people, stories about the passions of the forgotten. They represented an attempt to remove everything that was false, all feelings that were fake. The objective was to peer into the world and find the simple and the true, the unusual that resided, hidden, within the ordinary, and to relate a small, personal story to the problems of society at large. Such an approach may seem naïve from the vantage point of the 1970s, but in the context of more than a quarter century of Fascist rule, in which pompous rhetoric and false emotion were the signature of the head of state, and escapist trash was ground out by the studios, the poignancy of Neo-Realism can be understood. In reaction to the past, amid the ruins of postwar Italy, it was inevitable.

The principal works of the Neo-Realist movement are Rossellini's OPEN CITY (1944) and PAISAN (1946), Zampa's TO LIVE IN PEACE (1946), De Sica's SHOESHINE (1946), De Santis' TRAGIC CHASE (1947), Lattuada's WITHOUT PITY (1947), and Visconti's LA TERRA TREMA (1948). The one authentic masterpiece of the era, the film which represented all that was best in Neo-Realism, and that outlives the movement, is De Sica's THE BICYCLE THIEF, a highly structured, self-consciously simple, deeply concerned, and intensely warm picture that gives the impression of being a social documentary, but which is really, in the best sense of the word, artfully contrived for maximum emotional impact.

The story of THE BICYCLE THIEF develops like a chase, and as a result the audience is kept in suspense. Will Antonio Ricci find his stolen bicycle and keep his job, or will he fall back into unemployment and despair? There is the relationship between Antonio and his son Bruno, slowly, subtly revealed through their day of misery in all of its unspoken tenderness, loving, even in the final moments, when Bruno learns a harsh lesson. In this sense, the film is a story of a boy coming of age. Finally, because of the way the search for the bicycle is structured, the film is a virtual encyclopedia of social comment, revealing the sullen indifference of the police, the tough hypocrisy of the church, and the dehumanization of urban society, illustrated by the way a vast spectrum of people reacts to the problem of a single desperate man. What seems at first to be a simple, linear story is really a story of suspense, a story of relationships, and an exposé of the inadequacy of social institutions, all three interwoven with such skill that audience involvement is total.

De Sica's film reveals certain of the flaws of Neo-Realism. While appearing to be random it is actually contrived, while appearing to be a documentary it is actually theatrical, while appearing to depict the reality of an incident in the life of a poor man, it actually pits him against a stacked deck. THE BICYCLE THIEF also shows the cul-de-sac of Neo-Realism. It is a picture which says, "This is the way things are," and that is as far as it goes. The next step was for a film to say, "This is how things must be changed," to depict class struggle and revolution. Thus, the hard-core Left dislikes THE BICYCLE THIEF, seeing it as a bourgeois film bemoaning the faults in society without showing how they can be cured.

But just as THE BICYCLE THIEF reveals flaws in Neo-Realism, as the ultimate Neo-Realist film it also reveals what was best in the movement: conviction, compassion, humanity, and concern. The performances are rich, radiant, luminous. This apparently was De Sica's special gift: an ability to bring out the nonactors' great authenticity of expression. The relationships between Antonio and Bruno, and Antonio and his wife Maria, are informed by deep and radiant love. No dialogue expresses this—just the looks between these people, the way they act together, their gestures toward one another, their concern. If the long, smooth dolly shots of BICYCLE THIEF look artificial now because *cinéma-vérité* documentaries have reformed our notion of what is truth on film, the truthfulness of these performances nonetheless cancels out any contrivances of production or script.

There is a famous story about THE BICYCLE THIEF. When De Sica was looking for financing, the American producer, David Selznick, offered it on condition that Cary Grant play the role of Antonio Ricci. De Sica refused, and of course he was right on every aesthetic ground. But the story is significant beyond its interest as an amusing anecdote. Great films of the concerned cinema possess an integrity that a commercial producer can never comprehend. One has only to compare THE BICYCLE THIEF to any of the "socially conscious" films of Stanley Kramer, filled with self-congratulation and movie stars (Curtis and Poitier in THE DEFIANT ONES; Peck, Gardner, and Astaire in ON THE BEACH; Tracy and Hepburn in GUESS WHO'S COMING TO DINNER?) to understand the differences between authenticity and fakery, art and product, concern and chic.

215

216

From THE BICYCLE THIEF: Neo-Realist Italian cinema
— a reaction against pomposity of Fascist era — uses
real locations, nonactors, and characters
caught up in social problems. Director De Sica
(fist raised, below r.) was aided by honest and
sympathetic script by Cesare Zavattini.

François Truffaut's **The Four Hundred Blows** 1959

In THE FOUR HUNDRED BLOWS, François Truffaut is concerned with a child and the injustices he endures. The child, Antoine Doinel, is vulnerable, like Antonio Ricci in THE BICYCLE THIEF, and like Antonio Ricci he wages a futile war against the indifference of society. THE FOUR HUNDRED BLOWS is a film about brutalization. Implicit within the picture is a stern indictment of social institutions, but the film is completely different from THE BICYCLE THIEF in aura, mood, and intention. De Sica places Antonio Ricci in a drab, closed, forbidding Rome. The Paris in which Truffaut places Antoine Doinel is also drab, but in addition it is various, open-ended, rich in possibilities. Ricci is a prisoner of his economic situation; Doinel is only a prisoner of his age. De Sica's film is focused on the outside forces that crush an individual; Truffaut's film is about the inner life of a child who resists. The differences between these films are also, in an interesting way, the differences between Italian Neo-Realism and the French New Wave: social comment versus autobiography; broad concern for humanity versus specific concern for the individual; melancholy versus *joie de vivre*; the abstract versus the subjective; the predestined versus the spontaneous; realism versus expressionism.

Along with ANTOINE AND COLETTE, STOLEN KISSES, and BED AND BOARD, THE FOUR HUNDRED BLOWS represents a phenomenon unprecedented in the history of cinema: a series (which might be called *The Life and Times of Antoine Doinel*) of strongly autobiographical pictures by the same director, made over a period of years with the same actor, Jean-Pierre Léaud, enacting various stages in the life of this fictional character while he, the actor, grows up.

In THE FOUR HUNDRED BLOWS, as in the other films of this series, Truffaut creates richly delineated characters who do not represent points of view or philosophies of life, but who simply exist as mysterious and unfathomable human beings. Even the minor characters are revealed as three-dimensional people whom we, through Truffaut's eyes, understand with compassion. Although there are samples of atrocious human behavior in THE FOUR HUNDRED BLOWS, the perpetrators of these atrocious acts are never really villainous. Truffaut shows their good and bad sides without condemnation, and if there is a villain in the picture it is that side of human society that is hard and blind and insensitive, that would crush the spontaneity of youth and destroy the joy of life.

This is the theme of THE FOUR HUNDRED BLOWS, a film about fifteen-year-old Antoine Doinel, free and spontaneous, neither brilliant nor dull-witted, but acutely sensitive to the richness of living. And, too, it is a film about a world of parents, teachers, police, janitors, and psychiatrists who would make him less than a free spirit, who would make him conform to a narrow vision.

THE FOUR HUNDRED BLOWS is permeated by warmth, a love of man even at his worst. It is a film that may have more painful and yet understated moments than any other, and its subject matter—the pain and joy of childhood—is universal.

One thinks particularly of certain scenes: Antoine reciting to himself from Balzac; Antoine taking down the garbage at night, performing the distasteful task with an awareness of the mystery that lies behind every door; Antoine, awake in his bed, listening to his parents' quarrelling; the two occasions when Antoine is slapped, once by his father in front of his fellows at school, and the second time at the reformatory where he has been sent for observation (both times we wince with the pain); and Antoine's disturbing view of the dark streets of Paris as he is hauled away in a police wagon after being caught stealing a typewriter from his father's firm.

There are marvelous scenes in this film which upon first viewing may seem too long. What is one to make of the long series of shots of the boy who keeps smudging the ink in his exercise book? Or of Antoine in the centrifuge staring at the world upside-down? Or of the children reacting to the puppet show? Or of the comic episode of the school gym teacher leading the students on an exercise run through a dingy quarter of Paris and being deserted by them until he is left running alone? These scenes are very much to the point in this sort of filmmaking, for they form the rich tapestry, the humanistic background of the story of Antoine's brutalization.

As we watch this strange boy, this alter ego of Truffaut, stealing a bottle of milk in the cold dawn after he has run from home, breaking the ice in a fountain to find water to wash his face, and, finally, trapped between pursuers and the sea after a long run, turning to us and having his perplexed face suddenly and unexpectedly frozen, our deepest compassion is aroused. A filmmaker has made a work of art out of his own life, has moved us with his concern for the defenseless, the vulnerable,

217

the young, without for a single instant descending into sentimentality.

THE FOUR HUNDRED BLOWS is usually defined as a great autobiographical film, or a great personal film. It is, of course, both of these, but it is also a great film of concern, not in any strict political sense, but in the broad sense that the genre has been defined here. In THE FOUR HUNDRED BLOWS the social comment is implicit, never stated outright. How can one watch this film about the

battering of a child and not read into it an indictment of everything in bourgeois culture, everything that is heavy, routine, heartless, stifling, without compassion? In THE BICYCLE THIEF society has merely deprived Antonio Ricci of his right to the dignity of work. In THE FOUR HUNDRED BLOWS society may have deprived Antoine Doinel of a portion of his soul. Which deprivation constitutes a more serious crime? Which picture, in the end, is more revolutionary?

218

From THE FOUR HUNDRED BLOWS (clockwise from top l.): ''Little Quiz'' (teacher) singles out Antoine Doinel (Jean-Pierre Léaud). Antoine in holding cell at police station. Truffaut with alter ego Léaud. Antoine admonished by parents after his ''homage to Balzac'' starts a fire.

Elia Kazan's **On the Waterfront** 1954

It is difficult to come to grips with ON THE WATERFRONT. On the one hand it has enormous strengths, indisputable elements of greatness, and on the other it is surrounded by ambiguities which cannot be wished away.

The surface concern of ON THE WATERFRONT is gangsterism in the trade-union movement. The film appears to be concerned with the exploitation of working men by the mob, and thus presents itself as a reformist picture, one that demonstrates a social ill and apparently hopes that it will inspire its cure. However, on inspection, this surface concern seems little more than a gloss, covering up a story whose real concern is the problem of whether or not a man should be an informer. The question of informing, of course, is a valid issue, a worthwhile subject for a psychomoral drama. Why, then, surround it with a reformist cocoon? This is one of the ambiguities that tends to blur the greatness of ON THE WATERFRONT.

Terry Malloy (Marlon Brando) agonizes over this problem of informing, but in the end he testifies before the crime commission investigating gangsterism on the waterfront. Everything in his past militates against his becoming a "stool pigeon," a "cheese eater," or a "canary," but he informs nevertheless because events make clear to him that by so doing he will improve conditions on the docks and liberate his fellow longshoremen from the gangster bosses who exploit them. The moral dilemma of Terry Malloy is well drawn in the film. The crucial question of whether or not to "squawk"—which provides the film's suspense—is only resolved after incidents of considerable dramatic intensity: the murder of Kayo Dugan, Terry's terrible confession to the girl he loves that he inadvertently helped kill her brother, the high-pressure moralizing of a very tough priest, the witnessing of various forms of violent and ruthless behavior, and finally the murder of his own brother, Charley, knocked off because he would not betray Terry to the mob. ON THE WATERFRONT not only justifies Terry as an informer, presenting his problem in such a way that his integrity can only be legitimized by his act of betrayal. It elevates it with something close to religious exaltation.

All of this has a curious parallel in the life story of Elia Kazan. Kazan and Arthur Miller, who worked together so successfully on two of Miller's famous plays, *All My Sons* and *Death of A Salesman*, wanted to do a picture together about life on the New York waterfront. But when Kazan testified as a "friendly witness" before the House Un-American Activities Committee, Miller was appalled and collaboration became impossible. Kazan then turned to the writer Budd Schulberg, who had also been a friendly witness, and another friendly witness, Lee J. Cobb, was hired to play Johnny Friendly, the mobster heavy in the story. This triumvirate was involved with a picture that views informing, under certain circumstances, as a noble act, in direct contrast to John Ford's THE INFORMER, where it is viewed as unforgivable, and Arthur Miller's own waterfront play, *View from the Bridge*, which views it as so heinous and ignominious a thing that it can be expunged only by suicide. Although everything was more or less forgiven between Miller and Kazan some years later, it is possible to argue—and many have—that ON THE WATERFRONT is not the film it seems because it is really a self-serving effort used by Kazan to justify his own actions. Whether this interpretation is valid or not, it does provide an explanation of the first of the two areas of ambiguity that surround the picture, the problem of where its concern truly lies.

The second area of ambiguity is an artistic one, known, in some circles, as "the Kazan Problem." Succinctly stated, "the Kazan Problem" revolves around the paradox that Kazan achieves both sublime truthfulness in his films, and moments of mannered hysteria and falseness.

The scene in ON THE WATERFRONT between Rod Steiger and Brando in the taxicab—one of the famous scenes of American film—is an example of Kazan at his best. He himself takes little credit for it, insisting that the special way Brando says "Oh, Charley" is the key to its success. But the conviction of both actors, and the total truthfulness of their performances must be credited to a fine director working at the height of his powers. The same could be said for the scene between Brando and Eva Marie Saint, when Brando confesses his role in her brother's death. It is a love scene of enormous power. Brando's love for Edie Doyle, his anguish at what he must say, and her reactions to both, make it one of the truly exquisite moments in film acting.

On the other hand, Kazan is quite capable of the overblown pretentiousness and total falsity of the scene in the hold of the ship when Karl Malden, as the blue-collar priest, Father Barry, tells the men that Christ is on the waterfront, and the body of Kayo Dugan is then raised as if he were a martyred saint. Suddenly, Kazan and Schulberg seem to be telling us that we are viewing a Catholic

allegory, a sort of Passion Play performed in T-shirts. It is a wretched moment, embarrassing and empty, similar to some of the trashier scenes that ruin Kazan's other concerned film, VIVA ZAPATA. He is also capable of grouping his extras, playing longshoremen, into false, stylized configurations, herding them about, in this supposedly documentary-style film, like the background people in an Italian sword-and-sandals epic.

How can one reconcile this paradox: Kazan the evocator of truth and Kazan the purveyor of phoniness, the artist who controls and the pyrotechnician who supercharges? One cannot, and that is precisely the problem. ON THE WATERFRONT is like a symphony by Mozart with occasional passages by Rimsky-Korsakov thrown in.

As a film of concern, ON THE WATERFRONT is about the best the American cinema has to offer. The classic choice is Ford's THE GRAPES OF WRATH, but this picture is so inferior to the novel, and so dated by its style—lacking the formal contemplation that makes Ford such a master of the western—and suffers from being so tiresomely predictable, that it is best forgotten.

ON THE WATERFRONT offers the required amount of social comment: on the exploitation of the working class, on the toughness of life at the bottom, on the dehumanization of meaningless labor. Whether its overt concern with a specific social ill, gangsterism in the unions, is really its subject, must remain a moot point. One may accept ON THE WATERFRONT at its face value, for, like all great concerned films, its concern is ultimately with the problems of people.

220

From ON THE WATERFRONT: Rod Steiger and Marlon
Brando in famous taxicab scene. Karl Malden as Father Barry.
Brando with Eva Marie Saint. Lee J. Cobb fights
Brando. Far right: Brando as Terry Molloy, one of his great
roles, not equalled until his appearance eighteen years
later in Bernardo Bertolucci's LAST TANGO IN PARIS.

Alain Resnais' **Hiroshima, Mon Amour** 1959

When HIROSHIMA, MON AMOUR opened in New York in 1960, it was received with the hushed reverence reserved by the public and the critics for a "film of the year." Months later backlash developed in certain critical and political circles. Alain Resnais, it was said, had trivialized the horror of Hiroshima by equating it with a banal story about lost love and had made a "woman's picture." He was also accused of palming off staged footage from a Japanese propaganda film as newsreel footage of Hiroshima after the bomb.

Why such reverence and such damnation? Perhaps the controversy proves, in a way, the greatness of this picture, which is audacious in subject matter as well as style, and whose concern is so vast, so all-encompassing, as to be invisible to a viewer looking only for a film committed to a specific program of social justice, or to some particular act of struggle and revolution. HIROSHIMA, MON AMOUR is concerned with man, in the fullest sense, and must be considered among the most powerful films of social commitment ever made.

Alain Resnais, and his writer-collaborator Marguerite Duras, combined a love story with an antibomb story; they made a film that delves both into the horror of Hiroshima and the sorrow of a lost first love. In Resnais' own words: "[in the film] we oppose the immense, fantastically enormous quality of Hiroshima and the little story of Nevers, reflected through Hiroshima as the light of a candle is magnified and reversed by a lens. The explosion of the bomb over Hiroshima is a gigantic event and it cannot be measured in relation to the case of this woman and her love affair. That is the whole point." On another occasion Resnais acknowledges that the Nevers story is a "threepenny romance."

When Resnais was asked to make a feature-length documentary about the atomic bomb, he brooded over the subject and then went to Marguerite Duras with an extraordinary idea: a love story set in Hiroshima, a love story "within a framework of other people's suffering." Duras explains the reasoning when she points out that in dealing with such an enormous subject as Hiroshima, "All one can do is talk about the impossibility of talking about Hiroshima." Hiroshima is a place, she says, where "every gesture, every word, takes on an aura of meaning that transcends its literal meaning."

Thus, a love story in Hiroshima, which might seem at first to be a vulgar and impossible contradiction, becomes instead a brilliant concept for a film. No matter the horror of the exhibitions in the Hiroshima Museum, and of the footage of the city in the days after it was bombed, Hiroshima is a tragedy that numbs us, while the "threepenny" story of love in Nevers makes us cry. But, if the two stories are entwined, allowed to resonate, we can begin to understand the true relationship between our personal tragedies and the tragedy of mankind as revealed in the bombed ruins of Hiroshima, or, for that matter, if Resnais had chosen to set it where he made his famous documentary, NUIT ET BROUILLARD, in the gas chambers at Auschwitz.

The story of Nevers does not trivialize the story of Hiroshima. Rather, on account of this audacious counterpoint, all our emotions are engaged in a most extraordinary and powerful way. We gasp at the tragedy of Hiroshima as we weep over the tragedy at Nevers; we contemplate a cosmic and a personal problem at the same time.

The sheer daring of this film might be enough to justify calling it great, but HIROSHIMA, MON AMOUR is also great on account of the virtuosity of its technique and the invention by its director of a new film language. Its experimental style, which so annoyed those who think a film cannot be socially committed unless it appeals to the stupidest member of the audience, is as audacious as the juxtaposition of subject matter.

Near the end of the first reel we see a closeup of Emmanuèle Riva, who has just glanced at Eiji Okada, asleep. Suddenly there is a brief flash-cut of the body of a wounded young man lying in approximately the same position in another place. Resnais cuts back to Riva's face, and then back to Okada asleep, and in that split second the technique of the subliminal flash cut, used to describe

222

Emmanuèle Riva and Eiji Okada in HIROSHIMA, MON AMOUR. Shots of their lovemaking (opposite) are intercut with images of destruction in famous opening in which Resnais explores the sensuality of death, and counterpoises personal drama and cosmic tragedy.

a character's state of mind, is born.

This cut is the key to the film, for it is the man whom she calls "Hiroshima" who reminds her of her lover at Nevers. It is the tragedy of his race that reminds her of the small tragedy of her life. This identification is carried through in the most neurotic moments of her recitative, when she looks at the Japanese and speaks to him as if he were her German lover of fourteen years before.

The whole Nevers story is told in a mosaic of images, out of sequence if one is concerned with chronology, in sequence in terms of emotional importance to the girl who is remembering. This Proustian technique of examining the past, remembering through triggering events in the present, was a startling and powerful innovation. Unfortunately, it has since been imitated endlessly by lesser directors, used by them to say, in effect, "Look, everybody, I can do it, too!" and has become so familiar as to seem, at times, tawdry.

The interlocking of Riva's narration of her story with fragments from her memory is ingenious. The camera moves flow together. We are drawn from present to past and back to present. The shots are designed to fit together perfectly. The sound track of the present always covers the images from the past, so that we know that

what we are seeing at Nevers is in her mind.

HIROSHIMA, MON AMOUR is not plotted with a beginning-middle-and-end. Rather, it is structured like a piece of music, with themes and variations that entwine, and movements paced at different tempos. It is filled with slow traveling shots, dollies forward, pullbacks, and pans. (Resnais says: "I love the street. I love to walk in streets. That, too, is traveling, and then I often ride my bicycle through the streets. . . .") The sound track and the picture fit together with equality, neither one dominating the other, the two synthesized with classical restraint. The picture, finally, has an unforced flow which is extraordinary when one analyzes its intricate structure. It is a film of complements: image and sound; past and present; the actual and the remembered; Hiroshima (a city of neon) and Nevers (a city of gray stone); the personal and the cosmic; a man and a woman; concern for the individual and concern for mankind.

Gillo Pontecorvo's **Battle of Algiers** 1967

If in the genre of concerned films THE BICYCLE THIEF is concerned with the poor, THE FOUR HUNDRED BLOWS with the brutalization of children, ON THE WATERFRONT with exploitation and the morality of informing, and HIROSHIMA, MON AMOUR with human destiny, BATTLE OF ALGIERS finally gets down to the core subject of socially-oriented filmmaking. It is concerned with the people who make a revolution.

The film has become famous, sort of a cinematic parallel to Frantz Fanon's *The Wretched of the Earth*. There are some people who think it should be banned because they view it as a movie textbook of urban guerrilla warfare. It is the sort of picture that frightens the middle class. They note the parallels between the Algerian Casbah and the black ghettos of America, and comprehend their vulnerability if these ghettos should ever explode. The film z, on the other hand, which is far less compassionate and much more a work of tendentious propaganda, is a picture the middle class can appreciate.

They can enjoy the luxury of feeling a liberal distaste for a distant Greek fascism without having to think about any possible echoes in their own political milieu.

BATTLE OF ALGIERS is frightening—so much so that it was banned in France for years, and when it finally did open the Paris theatre that showed it was threatened with bombing. What is interesting about all this is that the picture was not made by the Algerian government or any other third-world force, but by an Italian director, Gillo Pontecorvo, working in the tradition of Italian Neo-Realism. Though Pontecorvo is clearly sympathetic to the struggle of the Algerian people for independence, he is understanding of French colonialism, too. BATTLE OF ALGIERS does not make torture palatable, but it makes the French use of torture in Algeria explicable. It is a human document, not a propaganda piece, and in this way it can be considered a direct descendant of Rossellini's OPEN CITY, and the two "concerned" warm pictures of De Sica, SHOESHINE and THE BICYCLE THIEF. Its debt to

223

these earlier works can also be seen in its documentary style and its use of nonactors in primary roles. (The only professional actor in the picture is Jean Martin, who plays the French Colonel Mathieu. The FLN leader, Kadar, is played by Yacef Saadi, who actually held a high position in the National Liberation Front apparatus, and who was instrumental in organizing resistance in the Casbah.)

There is a note on the screen at the beginning of BATTLE OF ALGIERS saying that the picture contains "*not one foot* of newsreel or documentary film." This disclaimer is neither boastful nor gratuitous. In some countries the effect of the film was so real that audiences believed they were watching a documentary compilation with some fictional episodes thrown in. Though every single frame has been staged, many scenes look like newsreel coverage. This verisimilitude is the result of a documentary style of camerawork—a simulation of *cinéma-vérité* by using a hand-held camera—and the use of high-contrast, high-grain lab processes. Above all, it is a credit to the expertise of Gillo Pontecorvo, who spent more than a year researching the subject, poring over photographs and newsreels and talking with eyewitnesses, and then five painstaking months shooting the story as accurately as he could. The major strength of BATTLE OF ALGIERS is its overpowering sense of truth.

There is something inexorable about the progress of the story and its punctuation by subtitles representing FLN communiques and news headlines in the Algerian papers. Each act of violence on one side is countered by an act of violence on the other. As the film progresses this violence escalates to crueler and more frantic heights.

It begins with random incidents of terror, FLN assassinations of French police. The French close off the Casbah, which plays into the hands of the FLN by polarizing the two races. FLN terrorism continues and is countered by right-wing French vigilantism. Some Frenchmen bomb the house of an innocent Arab worker,

and the Arabs retaliate by dispatching three women to blow up mobs in the French quarter of the city. Paratroops arrive from France. They use torture and provocation to smoke out the insurgents. The FLN calls a general strike, the paratroops raid the Casbah, the FLN orders even wilder and more random terrorism, and the French engage in more torture and killing. At the end the French seem to win; they succeed in tracking down all the FLN leaders. But revolutionary fervor cannot be stifled. Two years later the Casbah erupts again. The people pour out in an orgy of celebration. French rule in Algeria is doomed.

Pontecorvo sees revolution as something sublime, something like a holy rite. When men are tortured he gives us organ music, and when Ali La Pointe and his friends are blown up we hear it again. The Arabs are not cardboard puppets; they are human, but also obsessed with gaining their liberty. Nothing can stop them because they are prepared to die. The French, for all their cruelty, are human too. Colonel Mathieu, leader of the paratroopers, is a complicated and ambiguous man. He is paid by the French government to do a very dirty job, and there is a harsh logic in the situation, as he points out at a press conference: "If you want France to stay, you must accept the consequences."

The film is Marxist, perhaps even Maoist. It is concerned with people who are colonized and oppressed by foreign masters. It has implications for Vietnam, Rhodesia, South Africa, Latin America. It is a human document about the twentieth century—about throwing off the imperialist yoke—and though committed to revolution it is also tempered with compassion. At the end of the picture when the Arab masses break out of the Casbah and dance wildly in the squares of the French quarter, waving FLN flags they have secreted for years, it is impossible not to be stirred by this image of men coming out of a dark maze of oppression, bursting into sunlit plazas of liberty.

Credits

The Bicycle Thief
(Ladri di Biciclette)
Italy; 1948; 90 minutes;
originally released in the U.S.
by Mayer-Burstyn.

Directed by	Vittorio De Sica.
Produced by	Vittorio De Sica.
Screenplay by	Cesare Zavattini from
	the novel by Luigi Bartolini.
Photographed by	Carlo Montuori.
Edited by	Eraldo da Roma.
Music by	Alessandro Cicognini.
Cast:	Lamberto Maggiorani; Enzo Staiola;
	Lianella Carell; Elena Altieri;
	Gino Saltamerenda.

On the Waterfront
U.S.A.; 1954; 108 minutes;
released by Columbia.

Directed by	Elia Kazan.
Produced by	Sam Spiegel.
Screenplay by	Budd Schulberg,
	based on a story by Schulberg
	suggested by articles by Malcolm Johnson.
Photographed by	Boris Kaufman.
Art direction by	Richard Day.
Edited by	Gene Milford.
Music by	Leonard Bernstein.
Cast:	Marlon Brando; Karl Malden;
	Lee J. Cobb; Rod Steiger; Pat Henning;
	Eva Marie Saint; Leif Erickson;
	James Westerfield; Tony Galento; Tami Mauriello;
	John Hamilton; John Heldabrand; Abe Simon;
	Mike O'Dowd; Martin Balsam; Fred Gwynne.

The Four Hundred Blows
(Les Quatres Cents Coups)
France; 1959; 94 minutes;
released in the U.S. by Janus.

Directed by	François Truffaut.
Produced by	François Truffaut.
Screenplay by	François Truffaut, with dialogue
	by Marcel Moussy,
	based on a story by François Truffaut.
Photographed by	Henri Decae.
Art direction by	Bernard Evein.
Edited by	Marie-Josèphe Yoyotte.
Music by	Jean Constantin.
Cast:	Jean-Pierre Léaud; Claire Maurier;
	Albert Rémy; Guy Decomble; Patrick Auffay.

Hiroshima, Mon Amour
France; 1959; 91 minutes;
originally released in the U.S. by
Zenith International.

Directed by	Alain Resnais.
Produced by	Samy Halfon.
Screenplay by	Marguerite Duras.
Photographed by	Sacha Vierny and Michio Takahashi.
Edited by	Henri Colpi, Jasmine Chasney, Anne Sarraute.
Music by	Georges Delerue and Giovanni Fusco.
Cast:	Emmanuèle Riva; Eiji Okada;
	Bernard Fresson; Stella Dassas; Pierre Barbaud.

Battle of Algiers
Italy; 1967; 118 minutes;
released in the U.S. by
Allied Artists Pictures.

Directed by	Gillo Pontecorvo.
Produced by	Antonio Musu.
Screenplay by	Franco Solinas and Gillo Pontecorvo.
Photographed by	Marcello Gatti.
Art direction by	Sergio Canevari.
Music by	Ennio Morriscone and Gillo Pontecorvo.
Cast:	Yacef Saadi; Jean Martin;
	Brahim Haggiag; Tommaso Neri; Samia Kerbash.

225

Gillo Pontecorvo (l.) in Neo-Realist tradition
works with nonactors during shooting of BATTLE OF
ALGIERS. His skill in simulating newsreel
"look" of mass action, and his sympathy for his characters,
no matter their politics, gives his film an
extraordinary quality rare in the genre.

Period Films

12

The period film—or the historical film, or costume film—is not a genre in the strict sense of the western, the suspense thriller, or the musical. There are no strict criteria that a period film must meet other, of course, than that it be made in period. Many pictures that fall into other genres—westerns, war films, adventure films, etc.—can be produced in period. Furthermore, one can argue that the five pictures discussed here as great period movies could just as easily be placed in other genres. BONNIE AND CLYDE could be classified as a gangster picture, or even as a comedy, THE MAGNIFICENT AMBERSONS as a film of social comment, LES ENFANTS DU PARADIS and GONE WITH THE WIND as romances, and HENRY V either as a war film, or as one of that special breed, a screen adaptation of a famous play. Because of all this overlap and ambiguity, the question arises: Why create a category which is, in some respects, a catchall?

The answer is that although a filmmaker need not fulfill specific requirements when making a period film, there are a certain number of great pictures made in period which have certain elements in common when viewed from the outside. If the period film is not a genre in the commercial sense, in that producers do not sit down and say, "Let's make a film in period to appeal to the segment of the audience that goes for things like that," it is a genre that has been created by critics and moviegoers who have set its standards by deduction.

What, then, are these deduced standards?

First of all, a picture produced in period has in common with other pictures produced in period the problem of historical authenticity, which is not so obvious as it may sound. Anthony Mann's EL CID, for instance, doesn't even try to recapture its period. Its costumes look Venetian, and Charlton Heston, six feet tall and clean-shaven, plays the part of an historical personage who was known for his small stature and enormous beard. In a great period film costumes and decor must be correct, art direction and production design must be informed by authenticity. Richard Sylbert's master set for Sidney Lumet's LONG DAY'S JOURNEY INTO NIGHT is impeccable, but in some early exteriors we see out-of-period motorboats in the background—a minor flaw, not sufficient to destroy the illusion, but indicative of the sort of problem that must be met. There are one hundred thousand pairs of eyes searching the background of period films for just such errors. The connoisseur of period films cannot resist

---

Marcel Carné's Les Enfants Du Paradis 1945

LES ENFANTS DU PARADIS is old-fashioned and this quality may be its greatest strength as a period movie. It is old-fashioned in the sense that it has a complicated plot filled with chance encounters between strong characters whose lives are traced over a period of years. It is old-fashioned, too, in that it is a story with a grand encompassing theme, in this case the Shakespearean idea that "all the world's a stage, and all the men and women merely players." It is a story that makes comparisons between the behavior of people in different social strata, between different forms of theatre, and between different types of love. It is long, complex, and highly structured, very much like a nineteenth-century French novel by Balzac or Dumas père. Since it is set in the Paris of the 1840s, the time and place in which these authors lived and wrote, one can say that it not only recaptures a specific period, but also a specific literary style.

In this sense it is different from the other period films considered here. It does not use its period as a means of distancing the past and then interpreting it through a modern sensibility, like BONNIE AND CLYDE. It does not

attempt to recapture and interpret a poignant historical moment, like THE MAGNIFICENT AMBERSONS. It does not fabricate a lush romantic style for the purpose of creating escapist entertainment, like GONE WITH THE WIND, or poeticize the past to encourage those in the present, like HENRY V. Instead, LES ENFANTS DU PARADIS immerses itself in its period in a deliberate effort to find a cinematic equivalent for a literary style. It does not attempt so much to recreate the reality of the past, as the reality of its fiction.

The story is the sort that is laughed at now, an involved series of encounters between several different men, and the evolution of their relationships with a single dominating female presence. At times LES ENFANTS DU PARADIS approaches the brink of sentimentality; sometimes it even teeters at that brink. But it never falls because of the good taste of its authors, the poet Jacques Prévert and the director Marcel Carné, and a cast of actors as great as has ever been assembled in any French film: Jean-Louis Barrault, who plays the mime-actor Deburau; Pierre Brasseur, certainly the Laurence Olivier

228

Preceding pages: Clark Gable and Vivien
Leigh as Rhett Butler and Scarlett O'Hara in Victor
Fleming's GONE WITH THE WIND. Opposite:
Balconies of a mid-nineteenth century Parisian theater.
At top are the cheap seats where sit "the children
of paradise" in Marcel Carné's film of that title.

rising from his seat and pointing his finger at the television aerial on the house in the picture set during Prohibition, or the 1970 Chevrolet in the picture set in 1964. It is said that Erich von Stroheim carried period realism too far when he insisted that extras playing Austrian cavalrymen had to have Hapsburg double eagles sewn into their underwear. Be that as it may, Stroheim understood the first essential requirement of a great period film: Its period must be authentically reproduced.

Secondly, a great period film must do more than use its period setting as a backdrop for a story. It must also provide an interpretation of the past. When a novel set in the past is to be adapted for the screen, the first question that arises is whether or not the story should be updated. If the answer is no—that the story should be kept in period—it is incumbent on the filmmaker to put that period to some specific use, either to comment on the past, or to evoke nostalgia, or to draw some analogy or contrast with the present, or to provide a sense that the story being told could only have happened in a certain time and place, or even, if necessary, to pervert the past, to alter its sensibility (but not its costumes and decor!) in order to make a point. On this ground alone, most Biblical spec-

tacles, mythological epics, and sword-and-sandal dramas (including Stanley Kubrick's bizarre if interesting SPARTA-CUS) can be dismissed. Not only are such pictures usually abysmally unauthentic, but for all their historical references, they could as easily have been set in the year 2001.

Ultimately, and this is the most important standard that must be met, the director of a great period film must go beyond authenticity. He must convey period by a directorial concept that leads to stylization. It is not sufficient to dress an actor in a suit of armor and then tell him to act like G. I. Joe, because, the director says, "all soldiers act alike." The director of a great period film imposes a sense of period upon his picture by employing a style that conveys a point of view. He may get his ideas from scholarly research, or he may invent them in his own mind; it doesn't matter. In the end the picture must have a sense of itself, a photographic style, a camera style, an acting style that tells us, rightly or wrongly, that this is what this period was like. Two pictures by Ken Russell may illuminate this point: WOMEN IN LOVE has a comprehensive style that conveys a sense of period; THE MUSIC LOVERS employs a dozen styles which make useful dramatic points but destroy the period entirely.

of France, who plays the tragedian Lemaître; Marcel Herrand, who plays the failed playwright and ruthless gangster Lacenaire; Louis Salou, who plays the cold and hypocritical Count de Montray; and finally the actress who calls herself, simply, Arletty, who plays Garance, the mellow, mysterious, self-contained *femme fatale*, with whom the four men, each in his own way, is in love.

Deburau loves Garance with the idealizing passion sometimes known as sacred love; Lemaître loves her carnally, profanely; the selfish and self-hating Lacenaire loves her as much as he is able, with a sort of skeptical friendship; and the Count de Montray loves her in the agonizing, possessive way of a man who owns a woman but suffers because he knows his passion is not returned.

These characters interact, and circle Garance, against a lavishly presented background of the world of show business in mid-nineteenth-century Paris, the carnival atmosphere of the "Boulevard of Crime," and the mobs called by the actors "the children of paradise"— those who sit in the cheap seats in the high balconies of the theatres where they hoot or applaud the performances taking place on the stage. The story and the film are stylized and artificial, and yet also great, in the same way that Balzac and Victor Hugo are great: They are irresistible. The acting and the dialogue are so good, and the camera work and editing so unobtrusive, that the viewer is drawn into and then absorbed by a fictional world. LES ENFANTS DU PARADIS is a splendid theatrical experience, a three-hour immersion in history and art, an archetypal escapist film.

This element of escapism was very much to the point when the picture was made, during the German occupation of France, and under the supervision of Gestapo censors. One can imagine the difficulties, and also the incongruities, of mounting so lavish a production (the Boulevard of Crime set, built in Nice, was more than five hundred feet long, and involved the manipulation of hundreds of costumed extras) in a time of severe shortages and national anguish. Many of the scenes were shot secretly, and several people who worked on the production did so while being hunted by the Nazis. The electricity often failed and it is said that the food provided as props for the banquet scenes was eaten by starving extras before these scenes were filmed. Somehow under these conditions Carné was able to make the picture without ever succumbing to pressures which would unnerve lesser directors. The film does not contain a moment that is not in keeping with its overall design. Its high style is maintained throughout, and there is no evidence of compromise in its many vast and complicated scenes. From the time Deburau encounters a "blind man" (who turns out to be a jewelry estimator for the underworld), goes with him to a crowded dance hall, encounters Garance, dances with her, fights off one of Lacenaire's henchmen, and takes her to his hotel, we are fascinated beyond our expectations. Barrault's mime scenes must rank with the finest mime work ever filmed, and the finale, when he fights his way through the teaming masses on the Boulevard of Crime, searching for Garance, is surely a superb example of personal passion counterpoised against a joyful celebration—a favorite formulation of the Soviet cinema. It is an ending strong enough to make one reel as one walks out of the theatre, onto streets which seem mundane compared to the Boulevard of Crime.

From LES ENFANTS DU PARADIS: The great Pierre Brasseur playing the great nineteenth-century actor Lemaître playing Othello carries out theme of Carné and screenwriter Jacques Prévert that "all the world's a stage." Right: Brasseur with Marcel Herrand as the failed playwright and gangster Lacenaire.

231

Jean-Louis Barrault as the mime Baptiste Deburau
with Arletty as the *femme fatale* Garance (top and middle l.).
Film, a speculation on the interplay of life and art,
was lavishly shot in costume during Nazi occupation of
France, while some of its actors were sought by
Gestapo. Its completion was a triumph of ingenuity.

Victor Fleming's **Gone With the Wind** 1939

A world apart from LES ENFANTS DU PARADIS is GONE WITH THE WIND, a picture that is a masterpiece of mass entertainment and decidedly not a work of art. Here the period is conceived in lush and romantic terms, stylized to serve the purposes of escapism. There is little doubt that the Old South wasn't much like the milieu of GONE WITH THE WIND, but it doesn't make any difference. A concept, derived from the style of Margaret Mitchell's long, complex, best-selling historical novel has been imposed, and the result is a picture that has very much a sense of itself.

At the time of writing, GONE WITH THE WIND has earned more than $75,000,000 in rentals in the domestic market alone and the end is not in sight. This phenomenal success is not difficult to understand. The picture was based on the most popular book of its day, set in the most turbulent and romantic era of American history, the years during and after the Civil War. It was well produced by a top-rank showman, David O. Selznick, stars Clark Gable, the most dashing male actor of his time, and runs three-and-a-half hours, thus providing the viewer with a vast, epic world of fantasy.

But more important, and perhaps the true key to the picture's success, is that its story is built around the adventures of a character named Scarlett O'Hara (played by Vivien Leigh), whose actions, motives, whims, joys, and sufferings make her the perfect centerpiece for a lush, romantic film. Her obsession—to rebuild her plantation, Tara, to "never be hungry again," to restore the majesty and romance of a "land of cavaliers and cotton fields in the Old South"—is calculated to stimulate the audience to heights of sympathy and identification.

GONE WITH THE WIND is not only King, it is also King Corn—King of Soap Opera, King of Schlock, tear-jerker of tear-jerkers—produced on a mighty scale with a sense of itself, a vibrating aliveness, that sets it apart from other screen soap operas. GONE WITH THE WIND is King Corn with a difference, with a certain something that continues to move people, and reap in the millions each time it is released, an artifact of universal fantasy fulfillment that is worthy of serious consideration.

1. Certainly Vivien Leigh must be credited with a good deal of the success of this picture. She was an obscure British actress when introduced to Selznick at MGM the night he supervised the shooting of the Burning of Atlanta sequence—really a conflagration of old movie sets on the back lot. A debate had raged through the nation over who should play Scarlett O'Hara. Something about Miss Leigh appealed to Mr. Selznick. He chose her by instinct and thus performed one of the inspired pieces of casting in movie history. Vivien Leigh is magnificent. She carries the picture, she dominates it, and reproduces the character of Scarlett in all its mercurial complexity.

2. The film is deceptive in a strange and interesting way. Many people who have seen it long ago recall it as an epic of the Civil War. They think they remember seeing many vast scenes containing thousands of extras, and including scenes of battle. In fact, their recollections are faulty. GONE WITH THE WIND is not really a "spectacular" except in terms of its length. It is basically a film of interiors and medium shots. It contains no battles, although it gives an impression, quite powerfully, of the Civil War by its one really grand scene, the thousands of wounded lying about the Atlanta railroad station. As for the famous Burning of Atlanta sequence, there are a couple of shots of collapsing buildings, but the whole flight-through-the-fire sequence is highly stylized, with action taking place against a red sky. In GONE WITH THE WIND we see very little in the way of big scenes, certainly a lot less than in Griffith's INTOLERANCE, and yet we feel as though we have seen a lot. In the obligatory nightrider and KKK sequence, for example, we are shown nothing except a group of women sitting around worrying, while men come in to tell them what has happened outside. The fact that this scene works extremely well, and that we are deceived into recalling the picture as a spectacle, is proof of the power of its technique. In short, GONE WITH THE WIND is good cinema.

3. Rhett Butler is a first-class bastard, Scarlett O'Hara is a first-class scheming bitch, and both characters are fascinating. The goody-goodys on the other hand, Ashley Wilkes and Melanie Hamilton, are bores. Considering the prevailing moral standards at the time this picture was made, this use of a couple of hustlers to give the picture life must be considered a daring stroke, and one that keeps the picture alive today.

4. The bleeding sunsets and the wallowing sentimentality of the picture are good fun. One can enjoy them because GONE WITH THE WIND does not pretend to be anything but an impossible romantic fiction, and, thank God, does not attempt to make an Important Social Statement.

5. When one sees the picture in a theatre today, the Negro characters, Mammy (Hattie MacDaniel), Pork

Clark Gable, leading male star of the era,
was the inevitable choice to play gambler and lady-killer
Rhett Butler, but debate raged over who should get
role of Scarlett. Gable, evidently displeased by George
Cukor's direction, asked Producer David Selznick
to replace him. Victor Fleming got the job.

(Oscar Polk), and Prissy (Butterfly McQueen), produce about as much laughter as they produced when the film was first released. The difference is that in 1939 audiences were laughing at the quaint childishness of these slave characters; today they are laughing at the patronizing sensibility that thought black characters acted that way.

6. The screenplay of GONE WITH THE WIND is extraordinarily fine. It is credited to Sidney Howard, who did the original treatment for Selznick before he died. Selznick hired other writers to produce other drafts, and on one occasion suspended shooting while Ben Hecht completely rewrote the first nine reels in seven days. Hecht's account of this experience in his autobiography, *A Child of the Century*, is hilarious, and most revealing of the outrageous methods by which Hollywood films were then made.

7. The director of GONE WITH THE WIND was Victor Fleming, brought in after George Cukor was fired at Clark Gable's request. The final version of the film contains scenes shot by Cukor, and though we cannot be sure exactly which ones they are, we can be certain that they are among the picture's very best. Cukor was a first-class director, while Fleming was an erratic director-for-hire. The irony is that Fleming ended up directing two of the most entertaining films ever made, GONE WITH THE WIND and THE WIZARD OF OZ, while Cukor, who directed many fine pictures, never made anything quite so popular.

8. Much credit must go to Selznick and the expert production designer William Cameron Menzies. Menzies, who had originally been an illustrator of children's books, was legendary for his sketches, which were not simply drawings of costumes and sets, but also of characters, their entrances, exits, the camera angles from which they should be shot, and instructions on how they should be lit. He drew more than 2,500 sketches for GONE WITH THE WIND, one for each and every camera set-up.

As for Selznick, he never got over the enormous success of GONE WITH THE WIND, which came relatively early in his career. For years afterward he would interrupt a meeting on another picture, or begin the dictation of one of his long and infamous memoranda, with the phrase: "This is how we did it when we shot GONE WITH THE WIND. . . ."

9. As a period film, GONE WITH THE WIND is a perfect example of a case where a specific period has been thoroughly used—in this case milked—for everything it has to offer. A fortune was spent on costumes, props, and decor, and it shows. GONE WITH THE WIND is full of authenticity, even, in some of the period war scenes, resembling the ambience of photographs by Mathew Brady. The people are not authentic. They are fictitious, impossible. Yet placed in this special period, surrounded by authentic props and locales, with a consistent, polished, and highly artificial romantic style imposed upon them, they come to life. The incredible thing about GONE WITH THE WIND is that it is possible to believe in Rhett Butler and Scarlett O'Hara—not only to believe in them but to care about them, to suffer and rejoice with them, to feel that their lives are bound up with one's own.

Laurence Olivier's **Henry V** 1944

The background of HENRY V is well known. During World War II, when England was under siege as never before, Laurence Olivier was persuaded to mount an extravagant and expensive production of Shakespeare's *Henry V.* It was believed that this play, filled with so much heroism and chauvinism, would in the form of a film be helpful in raising British morale. It seemed a brilliant idea: to use the greatest English writer to rouse the English people, to use the past as propaganda, to make an historical film that would serve the same purpose as Winston Churchill's inspiring speeches.

But if this were all there is to HENRY V, the movie would only make an interesting footnote to film history. HENRY V achieves greatness on its own artistic merits, apart from any of the intentions surrounding its production. It is a brilliant transposition of a play to the screen, brilliant in its handling of period reality, and enriched by a brilliant Olivier performance.

The problem that comes up whenever a play is to be filmed is: "How are we going to 'open it up'?" The reasoning goes that since theatre is the art form of writers, and cinema the art form of directors, it is not sufficient to merely photograph a stage play—even if it is only a musical comedy. Something must be added, and that "something," whether the play is *Cyrano de Bergerac* or *Who's Afraid of Virginia Woolf*, is usually the pitfall of the filmmaker concerned.

Shakespeare presents more problems than most

Above: Scarlett and her beloved Tara Hall in "a land
of cavaliers and cotton fields." Actual location was Westchester
County, N.Y. Far left: Ashley, Rhett, and Yankee
captain (Ward Bond) at Melanie's door. Left: Atlanta burns.
Scene was shot on back lot of MGM
even before production of main part of film began.

239

playwrights, since his language is so much more sublime than the vision of even the most talented directors. Orson Welles has stumbled against him several times, his falls barely broken by his high cinematic ambition. Perhaps the one man who has been lucky with Shakespeare has been Laurence Olivier, an outstanding actor and a shrewd and intelligent director, who has brought Shakespeare to the screen successfully three times. His HAMLET is played in a dark, moody Elsinore, shot in black and white and lit with powerful arc lamps, so that the depth of field is immense. His RICHARD III is played almost like a German Expressionist horror film, filled with violence and neurosis. And his HENRY V invents a new way of bringing Shakespeare to the screen by, in effect, spitting in the face of the convention of suspension of disbelief.

Olivier's solution is to begin his film in Elizabethan London, then move his camera to the Globe Theatre, where Shakespeare's *Henry V* is being played. By showing us the audience, and activities backstage, he gives us the impression that we are going to see an historical film set in Shakespeare's own time.

But then, little by little, the play itself begins to take over the film. Somewhere (and we are never precisely certain where) the proscenium arch disappears. Though we are still, clearly, watching a play, the fourth wall has slowly closed. Now we are inside the play, amidst painted sets and theatrical props, but out of the Globe, perhaps in a movie studio. And then, as we become accustomed to this new situation, we are quite suddenly thrust into real exteriors, in the year 1415, when the action of Shakespeare's play (as opposed to its presentation in a sixteenth-century theatre) took place. A great

and realistically bloody battle scene, the Battle of Agincourt, is played as if it were really happening. We have been drawn through the conventions of the theatre into the reality of the cinema, from the stylized world of Shakespearean poetry into a real world without dialogue or artifice. When the battle is over Olivier slowly leads us back from the real exteriors, through the three-dimensional sets, to the Globe Theatre in time for the finale.

The effect is something like a dream, as if we have become so wrapped up in the performance of a play upon the stage that our minds have been stolen into a world where fantasy becomes reality; and then, as the dream recedes, Olivier gently leads us back to our seats. It is an amazing accomplishment, something never quite done before, in which cinematic realism and theatrical illusion are subtly mixed, and three levels of the past are reproduced in period.

HENRY V is an exemplary period film, but something must be added about Laurence Olivier. Even in roles beneath his talent—Max De Winter in REBECCA or Archie Rice in THE ENTERTAINER—he is phenomenal. Playing Shakespeare he has been at his best, and deserves the accolades he has received as the world's superlative living actor. In HENRY V he brings such energy to his heroic role that he makes the swashbuckling of Douglas Fairbanks and Errol Flynn look tame. And as a filmmaker his invention of what the aesthetician Erwin Panofsky called the "oblique close-up"—when we watch his face in repose listening to his own off-stage voice pronouncing a soliloquy—is one of the few startling visual innovations since the days of D. W. Griffith and Sergei Eisenstein.

240

From HENRY V: Laurence Olivier as the king in most successful film yet made from a Shakespearean play. Spectacular Battle of Agincourt. Victorious Henry woos French princess (Renée Asherson). Olivier studies script on wartime set. Grandeur shrinks within confines of Globe Theater's "wooden O." Felix Aylmer between player king and queen, Leslie Banks (Chorus) at left.

Comedy mixes with blood, crime with social comment, romance with death in BONNIE AND CLYDE. Above: Gene Hackman, Warren Beatty, and Faye Dunaway pull a bank caper. Right: Clyde is wounded in gun battle with cops. Film was loosely based on adventures of Barrow gang, whose robberies in Southwest were a brief sensation during the 1930s.

Arthur Penn's **Bonnie and Clyde** 1967

We know from the credit sequence of Arthur Penn's BONNIE AND CLYDE that the film will be in period. The titles are interspersed with sepia photographs of the real Bonnie Parker and Clyde Barrow, and our nostalgia is stimulated by the sound of a pop tune of the 1930s that emerges quietly on the sound track.

Of the several films made about the Barrow gang, none comes close to the level of BONNIE AND CLYDE, whose superiority was barely acknowledged at the time the picture opened. One highbrow critic referred to it as "a bunch of decayed cabbage leaves smeared with catsup"; another called it "clever trash," ending his review with the comment that "slop is slop, even served with a silver ladle." *The New York Times* said the picture was corrupt, accused it of making violence palatable, and a critic for a major newsweekly called it "a squalid shoot-em-up for the moron trade"—a statement he retracted a few weeks later. The tide began to turn, the audience began to swell, and BONNIE AND CLYDE became a *cause célèbre*. It stirred and moved young people, stimulated a trend toward 1930s fashions, and earned more than $22 million in rentals in the domestic market alone.

Speaking of the authenticity to the period of the film, Arthur Penn has said: "We stripped away almost all the extraneous details we could. . . . I didn't think that for a minute we were creating any kind of real world or society. . . . The movie is an abstraction rather than a genuine reportage." Penn created a mood in BONNIE AND CLYDE, an evocation of the 1930s filtered through his 1960s sensibility. Though he says that "the death of Bonnie and Clyde in the film was literally and historically accurate; they did fire a thousand rounds; eighty-seven direct hits were found on their bodies," of course he does not mean that Bonnie Parker and Clyde Barrow died a ritualistic death in slow motion. The sense of period in BONNIE AND CLYDE reflects Penn's vision of how the 1930s seemed, and for all the perfection of the costumes and props, this vision is highly personal.

What is also personal about BONNIE AND CLYDE, and constitutes its unique flavor, is its curious blending of comedy and horror, its romanticization of crime as something that is fun, and that also leads to violent bloody death. BONNIE AND CLYDE is both real and abstract, a gangster movie and a comedy-romance. It is a comedy that turns dark, a romance that ends with death. One could add that the banjo music that covers the interludes are the refrains in Arthur Penn's ballad-like picture.

An alternation between fun and darkness is important to the structure of the film. After their first successful bank stickup, a daring and gay maneuver goes sour when Clyde is forced to shoot a bank guard and real blood gushes from his face—a shot strongly reminiscent of a closeup in the Odessa Steps sequence of POTEMKIN. In the next scene the gang broods in a movie theatre while the gay musical number, "We're in the Money," from a Busby Berkeley picture, plays on the screen.

Bonnie and Clyde take adolescent pleasure posing for photographs with their captive, Texas Ranger Hamer, but when cornered by police in a motel, they turn into vicious outlaws fighting for their lives. C. W. Moss, particularly, evokes Baby Face Nelson, when he blasts at police with a blazing machine gun, his baby face in Cagneyesque repose.

One of the poignant moments in the film occurs when Clyde chases Bonnie through a corn field, while a cloud crosses the sun and slowly shadows the landscape. Here the flavor of the Midwest and the darkening mood of the story are both expressed. The famous reunion scene is distanced and turned into a mood piece with filters, slow motion, and muffled sound. Of this scene Penn has said: "It was supposed to be happening, but in the sense that it was unreclaimable, that it was disappearing like an ancient photograph. That it was there and yet it was all dealing with values that belonged to the past."

This sort of mythic, abstract, nostalgic flavor of the depression is evoked again when C.W. drives his bloodied leaders into an Okie camp and the Okies come around the car to look with awe at the legendary outlaws.

The final "ballet of death," when Bonnie and Clyde are gunned down, has an extraordinary effect upon audiences. (Several cameras were used to shoot this scene, each turning at a different speed; Faye Dunaway's leg was tied to the emergency brake so that she could slump over dead without falling from the car.) Startled birds fly out of trees, we catch a glimpse of weapons shredding shrubbery, and see Bonnie and Clyde grasping for one another in prolonged and exultant agony. There have been premonitions of this throughout, even in the opening titles when their names slowly bled red, but nothing quite prepares us for the reality. Despite the blood they have spilled, our sympathy for them is overwhelming.

Orson Welles´ **The Magnificent Ambersons** 1942

The distancing of BONNIE AND CLYDE, which gives the film its unique dreamlike quality, is partly a result of nostalgia for the 1930s. World War II is a barrier between now and then, sufficiently high to distance those years, making them an appropriate period for the singing of a ballad or the recounting of a myth. Nostalgia: It is key to certain period films, the overriding emotion that makes them work. BONNIE AND CLYDE uses nostalgia, but another film, Orson Welles' THE MAGNIFICENT AMBERSONS, goes even further. It not only plays upon the nostalgia of its audience, but also deals with the nostalgia of its characters. Furthermore, it takes place over a period of years, so that by its end we are nostalgic for its beginning.

In discussing THE MAGNIFICENT AMBERSONS one may take many points of view. Here, briefly, are a few of them:

1. As a *film maudit:* A cursed, a damned film, like Stroheim's GREED, THE MAGNIFICENT AMBERSONS was massacred, dismembered, thrown away. Certain portions were directed by other people and massive cuts were made without Welles' consent. To add insult to injury it was released in combination with a tawdry comedy, in effect dismissed by its studio as a piece of junk. Welles says that forty-five minutes were cut out and that these sections were the heart of the picture. Despite all this, THE MAGNIFICENT AMBERSONS holds up as a magnificent work. Its

245

Opposite: Tim Holt and Agnes Moorehead converse on staircase of Amberson mansion in Orson Welles' THE MAGNIFICENT AMBERSONS. Note lighting here and in railway station above. Stanley Cortez' cinematography was as extraordinary in its way as Gregg Toland's in CITIZEN KANE.

flaws, ellipses, and some abruptness in the second half seem minor compared to its enormous strengths. Since it is impossible to know what it might have been, it is fruitless to sigh over its fate.

2. As the other side of Orson: The famous Welles, the legendary Welles, is the Welles of CITIZEN KANE, *Wunderkind*, boy genius, the screamer for attention, the flamboyant artist, the magnificent show-off, the megalomaniacal sleight-of-hand magician. But he has always had another side and it shows most clearly in THE MAGNIFICENT AMBERSONS: Welles the sensitive artist, tranquil, lyrical, and tender, the decent Welles who would credit his collaborators at the expense of his own ego, the quiet, refined, subtle Welles, more interested in making a fine film than in showing the world he can dance circles around his competitors. In public the first Orson dominates the second, but those who know him personally assure us that the second Orson is the true Orson, revealed in unguarded moments. In THE MAGNIFICENT AMBERSONS we face that second Orson, a young man of twenty-six who has made a picture filled with the wisdom, compassion, and refinement that is only supposed to come to an artist in later years. Is it a pose? Decidedly not. THE MAGNIFICENT AMBERSONS radiates sincerity from every frame. One can speculate endlessly about the contradictions in Welles, and attempt to plumb his complicated psychology, but one fact about THE MAGNIFICENT AMBERSONS may provide an important hint. It is the only film he has directed in which he does not appear. This suggests that when Welles' presence is not on the screen, dominating everything around him, his director's eye gives way to something more subtle; that when he no longer needs to use his camera to love himself, his love for others is able to show through.

3. As a technical tour de force: THE MAGNIFICENT AMBERSONS is filled with technical achievements. It is the supreme example of the famous "Welles sound": overlapping dialogue, volume diminishing as characters recede into backgrounds, sound effects and dialogue muffled by architecture, speeches trailing off, voices subdued and hushed by environment and age. As for the camera work, Stanley Cortez may have achieved a greater tour de force than Gregg Toland in CITIZEN KANE. There are long, slow dolly shots through rows of rooms, each one differently lit, sometimes containing mirrors or polished furniture which, only on account of split-second manipulations by the crew, do not reflect the camera; there are extraordinary crane shots; people framed in architectural elements, reflected in mirrors, passing mysteriously through the backgrounds of scenes; and always there is a dark, brooding low-keyed look to everything—the sort of subdued light one finds in photographs of the period. The acting is superb, splendid ensemble playing that shows the hard work of long rehearsals. Agnes Moorehead as Fanny Minafer deserves particular mention; she creates one of the offbeat characterizations for which Welles is so famous. Neurotic, fierce, at times even loathsome, she rises by the end from a mere object of our compassion into a character whom we know will survive.

4. As a film of great sequences: There are enough sequences in THE MAGNIFICENT AMBERSONS for any great film and any one of them alone would make the picture memorable. The spectacular, lush, rich, party sequence at the Amberson mansion is one; the kitchen scenes, in which the camera barely moves, and the early montages, including the breathtaking camera move down main street, are others. But by far the greatest is the unparalleled sleigh-riding sequence shot by Welles over a period of twelve days in a Los Angeles ice factory. It's hard to believe this scene wasn't shot outdoors. The characters' breath steams in the air, the snow is real, and the mood is sublime—lyrical, gay, sensuous, and ultimately sorrowful.

5. As a brilliant period film: THE MAGNIFICENT AMBERSONS is, of course, a story about the vanishing past, of what happens to a town that becomes a city and a rich family that falls when the nineteenth century closes and the industrial twentieth begins. It is a picture steeped with nostalgia for a graceful way of life that disappears before our eyes as characters die and rooms are closed in the great Amberson mansion. The film is compassionate toward Eugene Morgan, who survives and prospers with the change, and George Minafer, who loses everything on account of it. The automobile is the thing that symbolizes the destruction of the past, that kills off the landed gentry and elevates the bourgeoisie, and even the automobile is treated with compassion.

Strangely enough, THE MAGNIFICENT AMBERSONS may be the only Welles film that has anything to do with his own life. As the child of a proud midwestern family, he has obvious sympathy for the Ambersons and the other people of Indianapolis, as well as understanding of a way of life and a region of the country, which comes through with poignant clarity. In the end, THE MAGNIFICENT AMBERSONS is a film about period, about people growing old, people dying, the fall of one way of life and the rise of another. Unlike the other period films discussed here, it does not merely use a period, it is *about* a period. Its period is its subject, and so is nostalgia, which is also its effect.

Credits

Les Enfants Du Paradis
(The Children of Paradise)
France; 1945; 173 minutes;
originally released in the U.S. by
Tricolore Films, Inc.

Directed by	Marcel Carné.
Produced by	S. N. Pathé Cinéma.
Screenplay by	Jacques Prévert.
Photographed by	Roger Hubert and Marc Fossard.
Art direction by	A. Barsacq, R. Cabutti,
	and Alexandre Trauner.
Edited by	Henry Rust.
Music by	Joseph Kosma, Maurice Thierte,
	and Georges Mouque.
Cast:	Jean Louis Barrault; Arletty;
	Pierre Brasseur; Marcel Herrand; Pierre Renoir;
	Fabien Loris; Louis Salou;
	Maria Cassares; Etienne Decroux; Jeanne Marken;
	Gaston Modot; Pierre Palau;
	Albert Remy; Paul Frankeur.

Henry V
Great Britain; 1944; 134 minutes;
released in the U.S. by United Artists.

Directed by	Laurence Olivier.
Produced by	Laurence Olivier.
Screenplay by	Laurence Olivier and Alan Dent.
	Based on ''Henry V'' by William Shakespeare.
Edited by	Reginald Beck.
Photographed by	Robert Krasker and Jack Hildyard.
Art direction by	Paul Sheriff and Roger Furse.
Music by	William Walton.
Cast:	Laurence Olivier; Leslie Banks;
	Robert Newton; Renée Asherson; Esmond Knight;
	Leo Genn; Felix Aylmer;
	Ralph Truman; Harcourt Williams; Ivy St. Heller;
	Ernest Thesiger; Max Adrian;
	Francis Lister; Valentine Dyall; Russell Thorndike;
	Michael Shepley; Morland Graham;
	Gerald Case; Janet Burnell; Nicholas Hannen;
	Robert Helpmann; Freda Jackson;
	Jimmy Hanley; John Laurie; Niall MacGuinnes;
	George Robey; Roy Emerton;
	Griffith Jones; Arthur Hambling; Frederick Cooper;
	Michael Warre.

Gone With the Wind
U.S.A.; 1939; 220 minutes;
released by MGM.

Directed by	Victor Fleming.
Produced by	David O. Selznick.
Screenplay by	Sidney Howard from
	the novel by Margaret Mitchell.
Photographed by	Ernest Haller.
Production designed by	William Cameron Menzies.
Edited by	Hal C. Kern.
Music by	Max Steiner.
Cast:	Vivien Leigh; Clark Gable;
	Leslie Howard; Olivia de Havilland; Hattie McDaniel;
	Thomas Mitchell; Barbara O'Neil;
	Caroll Nye; Laura Hope Crews; Harry Davenport;
	Rand Brooks; Ona Munson;
	Ann Rutherford; George Reeves; Fred Crane;
	Oscar Polk; Butterfly McQueen;
	Evelyn Keyes; Victor Jory; Isabel Jewell;
	Paul Hurst; Jane Darwell;
	Roscoe Ates; William Bakewell; J. M. Kerrigan;
	Yakima Canutt; Ward Bond;
	Lillian Kemble Cooper.

Bonnie and Clyde
U.S.A.; 1967; 111 minutes;
released by Warner Bros.

Directed by	Arthur Penn.
Produced by	Warren Beatty.
Screenplay by	David Newman and Robert Benton.
Photographed by	Burnett Guffey.
Art direction by	Dean Tavoularis.
Edited by	Dede Allen.
Music by	Charles Strouse.
Cast:	Warren Beatty; Faye Dunaway;
	Michael J. Pollard; Gene Hackman; Estelle Parsons;
	Denver Pyle; Dub Taylor;
	Evans Evans; Gene Wilder.

The Magnificent Ambersons
U.S.A.; 1942; 88 minutes;
released by RKO-Radio Pictures.

Directed by	Orson Welles.
Produced by	Orson Welles (a Mercury Production).
Screenplay by	Orson Welles, from
	the novel by Booth Tarkington.
Photographed by	Stanley Cortez.
Art direction by	Mark Lee Kirk.
Edited by	Robert Wise and Mark Robson.
Music by	Bernard Herrmann.
Cast:	Tim Holt; Joseph Cotten;
	Dolores Costello; Anne Baxter; Agnes Moorehead;
	Ray Collins; Erskine Sanford;
	Richard Bennett; Don Dillaway.

Acknowledgements

The following persons are quoted by the kind permission of their publishers:

Marguerite Duras (page 222), from **Hiroshima, Mon Amour**, copyright 1961 by Grove Press, Inc.; published by Grove Press; reprinted also by permission of Editions Gallimard, and by Calder and Boyars Ltd.

Akira Kurosawa (page 128), from **The Seven Samurai**, copyright 1970 by Lorrimer Publishing Limited; published in the Classic and Modern Film Scripts series by Simon & Schuster, New York, and Lorrimer Publishers, London.

Arthur Penn (page 243), from an interview, copyright 1968 by Robert Edelstein and Martin Rubin, included in **The Director's Event**, copyright 1969 by Eric Sherman and Martin Rubin; published by Atheneum; all rights reserved.

Jean Renoir (page 106), from **Sight and Sound**, vol. 31, no. 2, Spring, 1962. Also (page 104-106), from **Film: Book 2**, copyright 1962 by Robert Hughes; published by Grove Press.

Alain Resnais (page 222 and 223), from **Film: Book 2**, copyright 1962 by Robert Hughes; published by Grove Press.

Andrew Sarris (page 70), from **Interviews With Film Directors**, copyright 1967 by Andrew Sarris; published by the Bobbs-Merrill Company, Inc.

François Truffaut (page 159), from **Cahiers du Cinéma**, no. 138, 1962. Also (page 202), from **Hitchcock**, copyright 1967 by Simon & Schuster, Inc.; published by Simon & Schuster; reprinted also by permission of A. D. Peters and Company for Martin Secker & Warburg Ltd.

Picture Credits

The editors gratefully acknowledge the studios, collectors, and film archives listed below for their courtesy in providing illustrations.

BB — Brown Brothers
CP — Culver Pictures
Col. — Columbia Pictures
GA — Gene Andrewski
KC — Kobal Collection
MGM — Metro-Goldwyn-Mayer
MOMA — Museum of Modern Art / Film Stills Archive
RKO — RKO Pictures
UA — United Artists
UFA — Universum Film Aktien
WB — Warner Brothers

8-9: CP. 10: (top l. and bot. r.) CP, (others) GA. 11: (top, l. to r.) CP, GA, CP; (middle, l. to r.) UA, CP, Universal-International, GA; (bottom) GA. 12: GA. 13: (top) CP, (l.) William K. Everson, (r.) BB. 14: (clockwise from top l.) CP (3), GA (2). 15: CP. 16: (l.) John Allen; (r., from top) BB, BB, William K. Everson. 17: (clockwise from top l.) CP, BB, CP, CP, MGM. 18: (clockwise from top l.) CP, BB, CP, BB, GA, GA. 19: GA. 20: (top l.) CP, (top r.) GA, (bot.) Paramount. 21: (clockwise from top) WB, GA, GA, BB. 22: Douglas Kirkland. 23: (l.) GA, (top r.) GA, (bot. r.) UA.

24-25, 28-29, 30: UA. 31: (top) MOMA, (bottom, l. and r.) CP. 33: CP. 34: WB. 36-37: UA. 39: J. R. Eyerman. 41: WB. 42: (l.) WB. 42-43: James R. Silke. 44: John Bryson. 45: William K. Everson.

46-47: KC. 49: (top) Nero Film, (bot. l.) William K. Everson, (bot. r.) MOMA. 51: Don Ornitz — Globe Photos. 54-55: CP. 57: KC/Universal-International. 58: Universal-International. 59: CP. 60: WB. 61: (top) WB, (bot. l.) MOMA, (bot. r.) CP. 62: WB.

64-65: William K. Everson. 66: CP. 68: (top l.) CP, (top r.) John Allen, (bot.) KC/UA. 69: (top l.) UA, (top r.) CP. (bot.) UA. 71: (top) Cinemabilia, (bot. l.) CP, (bot. r.) MOMA. 72: (top, l. and r.) CP, (bot.) The Bettmann Archive. 74: (clockwise from top) CP (3), Paramount. 77, 78, 79, 80: Col. 82: (top) UA, (frames) Marvin E. Newman.

84-85: RKO. 86, 87, 88: CP. 89: RKO. 90: KC/MGM. 92, 93: MGM. 94: (clockwise from top l.) MGM (4), KC/MGM. 95: KC/MGM. 98-99: UA.

100: (clockwise from top) UA, CP, CP, William K. Everson, UA. 101: MOMA.

102-103: Col. 105, 106: World Films. 107: Col. 109, 110, 112: Bob Willoughby. 113: Col. 114-115: (bottom, from l.) CP (3), UA; (top) UA. 116: UA. 118: (top l., bot. center, bot. r.) Twentieth Century-Fox, (all others) Norman Snyder.

120-121: WB. 123: Col. 125, 126-127, 128: Toho. 130: (left, from top) WB, WB, CP; (top r.) WB; (bot. r.) WB. 131: (top) KC/WB, (bottom, l. and r.) CP. 133: CP. 134: (top and bot.) John Allen, (middle) WB. 135: CP. 138, 139, 140-141: Col.

142-143: Col. 145, 146, 147: World Films. 149: CP. 150-151: CP. 151: (from top) RKO (2), CP. 152: (l.) RKO, (r.) CP. 153: GA. 155: Astor Pictures. 156: (from top) Astor Pictures (2), CP, Astor Pictures. 157: Astor Pictures. 158, 159: Les Films du Carrosse/SEDIF. 162: Col.

164-165, 168, 169: Paramount. 170: CP. 171: Twentieth Century-Fox. 173: MGM. 174: (clockwise from top l.) MGM, UA, MGM, Col., MGM, MGM, Bob Willoughby. 175, 177, 178: Avco Embassy Corp.

180-181, 182: Trans-Lux. 185: Kingsley International. 186-187: (clockwise from top l.) Kingsley International, KC, KC, Kingsley International, KC, KC. 188-189: Lopert Pictures Corp. 191, 192: New Line Cinema. 194: (l. and top r.) MGM, (bot. r.) KC/MGM. 195: MGM.

196-197, 199: UFA. 200: (top) KC/UFA, (bot.) UFA. 201: (top, middle, bot. r.) UFA, (bot. l.) KC/UFA. 202-203: Universal Studios. 204: William K. Everson. 205: CP. 206: Gades Films International. 207, 209, 210: MGM.

212-213, 216: Mayer-Burstyn. 218: Janus Films. 220-221: Col. 222-223: Zenith International. 224-225: Allied Artists.

226-227: MGM. 229, 230, 231: Tricolore Films. 233, 234-235, 236, 238-239: MGM. 240: (l.) The Rank Organisation, (r.) CP. 241: The Rank Organisation. 242: (top) WB, (bottom, l. and r.) Ron Thal — Globe Photos. 244, 245: RKO.

Index

Caption references in italic numbers

A

Agee, James, 70
Air Force, 104, 124
Aldrich, Robert, 27, 172
Alexander Nevsky, 104
Alex in Wonderland, 172, 174
All About Eve, 53, 170-171, *171,
    172,* 179 (credits)
Allen, Woody, 66
All Quiet on the Western Front, 104
Altman, Robert, 117, *118*
American in Paris, An, 87, 173
Andersson, Bibi, *189, 190*
Andrews, Julie, 86
Ann-Margret, 30
Antoine and Collette, 217
Antonioni, Michelangelo, 183, 193-194, *194*
Apache, 26
Arlen, Harold, 86, 91, 92
Arletty, *230, 231*
Arthur, Jean, 39, 40, 122, *122*
Asherson, Renée, *240*
Asphalt, Jungle, The, 53
Astaire, Fred, 86, *86, 87, 88,
    91,* 125
Autry, Gene, 26
Axelrod, George, 204
Aylmer, Felix, *240*

B

Bacall, Lauren, *61, 62,* 87
Bad and the Beautiful, The, 166-167,
    173, 174, 175, 179 (credits)
Baker, Carroll, 172
Ballard, Lucien, 44
Bancroft, George, 26
Banks, Leslie, *240*
Bardot, Brigitte, *174, 175, 176*
Barefoot Contessa, The, 171, *172, 173*
Barkleys of Broadway, The, 88
Barrault, Jean-Louis, *228, 230, 231*
Barthelmess, Richard, *122*
Basehart, Richard, *184*
Battle of Algiers, 104, 223-224,
    225 (credits), *225*
Battleship Potemkin, 214
Baum, L. Frank, *91,* 91
Baum, Vicki, 10
Baxter, Anne, 170, *171, 171*
Beatles, the, 87, 97, 100
Beatty, Warren, *242*
Bed and Board, 217
Bedoya, Alfonso, *130*
Bells Are Ringing, 92
Bergman, Ingmar, 27, 76, 183, 188-190,
    189, 191, 198
Bergman, Ingrid, 52, *134, 136,* 137
Berkeley, Busby, 50, 86, 88
Berlin, Irving, 86, 88
Bertolucci, Bernardo, 220
Best Years of Our Lives, The, 104
Bicycle Thief, The, 214-215, *214, 216*
    223, 225 (credits)
Big Country, The, 26
Big Knife, The, 172
Big Sky, The, 35

Big Sleep, The, 60-62, *61, 62,
    63* (credits)
Blandish, Clara, 92
Blow-Up, 148, 183, 193-194, *194,
    195* (credits)
Bogart, Humphrey, 60, *61, 62, 62,
    87,* 122, 128, *130, 132, 133,
    134,* 136, 171
Bolger, Ray, *91*
Bond, Ward, 40, *238*
Bonnie and Clyde, 38, 228, *242,
    243, 245,* 247 (credits)
Borgnine, Ernest, *42,* 111, 173
Boyd, William, 26
Brackett, Charles, 167
Brady, Mathew, 73
Brando, Marlon, 23, 27, 219, 220
Brasseur, Pierre, *228, 230*
Brats, 20
Brazzi, Rossano, *171*
Brecht, Berthold, 96
Bresson, Robert, 183, *191, 191,* 192
Bridge on the River Kwai, The, 104,
    107, 108, 119 (credits), 137
Bridges, Lloyd, 172
Brief Encounter, 137
Bruckman, Clyde, 66
Brynner, Yul, 124
Bullitt, 62
Buñuel, Luis, 67, 117, *118,* 183,
    185, 187, 188
Burton, Richard, 172
Butch Cassidy and the Sundance Kid,
    26, 27

C

Cabaret, 87, 96, 99, 101 (credits)
Cabinet of Dr. Caligari, The, 199
Cabin in the Sky, 91
Cagney, James, *21*
Calhern, Louis, 74
Capra, Frank, 67
Carefree, 88
Carné, Marcel, *228, 228, 230, 230*
Carpetbaggers, The, 172
Carradine, John, 26
Casablanca, 132-137, *133, 134,*
    141 (credits)
Catch-22, 104, 117
Chandler, Raymond, 62
Chaney, Lon, 198
Chaplin, Charles, 67-70, *68, 69, 73,* 186
Charge of the Light Brigade, The, 125
Charisse, Cyd, 86, *93*
Chase, Borden, 35
Cherrill, Virginia, *68, 69*
Chimes at Midnight, 154
Christian, Susanne, *114*
Churchill, Berton, *31*
Circus, The, 67
Citizen Kane, 30, 148-154, *148,
    151, 152, 155, 161, 163* (credits),
    173, 177, 178, 245, 246
City Lights, 66, 67-70, *68,* 83 (credits)
City Streets, 17
Clarke, Arthur C., 208
Clift, Montgomery, 35, 36, 38,
    52, 111, *111*
Clockwork Orange, A, 92
Cobb, Lee J., 219, 220
Cohn, Harry, *108,* 111, *111,* 172
Colbert, Claudette, *18*
Collins, Ray, *151*

Comden, Betty, 92, 93
Comingore, Dorothy, *151, 152*
Condon, Richard, 204
Contempt, 167, 174,
    175-176, 179 (credits)
Cook, Elisha, Jr., 39, *61*
Cooper, Gary, 17
Coppola, Francis Ford, 166
Cortez, Stanley, 245, 246
Cotten, Joseph, 52, 53, *151*
Covered Wagon, The, 26
Crawford, Joan, *16*
Cromwell, John, 172
Crosby, Bing, 30, 86
Crowther, Bosley, 53
Cukor, George, 86, 87, 166, 172,
    232, 237
Curtis, Tony, 215
Curtiz, Michael, 137

D

Dali, Salvador, 184, 187
Dalio, Marcel, 104, 106, *107,* 145
Daniels, William, 10
Dassin, Jules, 44
Davis, Bette, *14,* 170, *171,* 172
Day, Doris, 52, 86
Death in Venice, 73
Defiant Ones, The, 215
Dekker, Albert, 44
del Rio, Dolores, 88
De Mille, Cecil B., 167, 168, 169
De Santis, Giuseppe, 215
De Sica, Vittorio, 104, 214, *214,
    215, 216,* 217
Destry Rides Again, 26
Devil Is a Woman, The, 17
de Wilde, Brandon, 39, 40
Diamond, I. A. L., 67
Dietrich, Marlene, 17, 53, *59*
Dirty Dozen, The, 104, 124, 172
Disney, Walt, 92
Dmytryk, Edward, 104, 172
Dr. Doolittle, 96
*Dr. Strangelove, or How I Learned
    To Stop Worrying and Love
    the Bomb*, 67, 76-80, *76, 78,
    80, 81,* 83 (credits), 104, 117
Donen, Stanley, 86, 91, 93, 94
Don't Look Back, 97
Douglas, Gordon, 30
Douglas, Kirk, 114, *114, 116,* 173, *173,
    174, 175*
Dreyer, Carl, 183
Dru, Joanne, 35
Duck Soup, 67, 73-76, *74,
    83* (credits), 104
Duel in the Sun, 26
Dullea, Keir, 208, *210*
Dumont, Margaret, *75*
Dunaway, Faye, *242*
Durand, Jacques, 145
Duras, Marguerite, 222
Dylan, Bob, 97

E

Easy Rider, 97, 144, *144,
    160-161, 162,* 163 (credits)
Eclipse, 193
Eddy, Nelson, *14,* 86
8½, 172, 175, 176-178, *176,
    179* (credits), *179,* 183
Eisenstein, Sergei, 104

249

Ekberg, Anita, *156*
El, 185
El Cid, 228
Entertainer, The, 240
Evans, Edith, 81

F

Fairbanks, Douglas, Jr., *17*, 92
Fanon, Frantz, 223
Farewell to Arms, A, 166
Faulkner, William, 62
Fellini, Federico, 67, 154-155,
    154, 172, 175, 176-178,
    176, 179, 182, 183, 184
Ferrer, Jose, 140
Fields, W. C., *20*, 66
Finch, Peter, 173, *174*
Finney, Albert, 81, *82*
Fleming, Victor, 91, 228,
    232, 237
Flying Down to Rio, 88
Flynn, Errol, *15*
Follow the Fleet, 88
Fonda, Peter, *144*, 161
Fontaine, Joan, *52*
Ford, John, 26, *26*, 27, 29, 31, 32,
    34, 35, 38, 40, 41, 44, 67, 91,
    104, 182, 219, 220
Foreign Correspondent, 52
Foreman, Carl, 104
Fort Apache, 30
Fosse, Bob, 96
Four Hundred Blows, The, 217-218,
    218, 223, 225 (credits)
Frankenheimer, John, 204, *204*
Freed, Arthur, 86, 91, 92, 94, 96, 99
Fresnay, Pierre, *104*
Freund, Karl, *198*
Frölich, Gustav, *200*
From Here to Eternity, 108, 111,
    111, *113*, 119 (credits)
Fuller, Samuel, 27, 48

G

Gabin, Jean, *104*, *106*, 107
Gable, Clark, *18*, 91, 228, *232*,
    232, 237
Gaborit, Jean, 145
Garbo, Greta, *10*, *12*
Gardner, Ava, 171, 215
Garland, Judy, 21, 86, 91, *91*, 92, 96,
    172, *174*
Gay Divorcee, The, 88
Gaynor, Janet, *174*
General, The, 66, 70-73, *70*, *73*,
    83 (credits), 104
General Della Rovere, 104
Gershwin, George, 86
Gilliat, Penelope, 161
Gimme Shelter, 97
Godard, Jean-Luc, 167, 175-176, 192,
    198, 206, *206*
Goddess, The, 172, *174*
Godfather, The, 111, 166
Gold Rush, The, 67
Gone With the Wind, 104, 166, 228,
    228, 232-237, *232*, 237, *238*,
    247 (credits)
Gould, Elliott, *118*
Goulding, Edmund, *10*
Gowland, Gibson, *17*
Grable, Betty, *14*
Graduate, The, 97

Grand Hotel, 10
Granger, Farley, 52
Grant, Cary, *14*, 52, 122, *122*, *123*, 215
Grapes of Wrath, The, 30, 220
Grapewin, Charley, 92
Great Expectations, 137
Great Train Robbery, The, 26
Greed, *17*, 124, 132, 245
Green, Adolph, 92, 93
Greene, Graham, 53, 56
Greenstreet, Sidney, 137
Grey, Joel, 96, *99*
Griffith, David Wark, *16*, 166, 183
Griffith, Hugh, 81
Gründgens, Gustaf, *49*
Guess Who's Coming to Dinner?, 215
Guinness, Alec, 67, *104*, *107*, 139, 140
Gunfight at the O.K. Corral, 26

H

Hackman, Gene, 242
Hagen, Jean, 93
Haley, Jack, 91
Hamilton, Margaret, 91
Hamilton, Neil, *16*
Hamlet, 240
Hammett, Dashiell, 62
Hanging Tree, The, 26
Harbou, Thea von, 48, 199
Harburg, E. Y., 91, 92
Hard Day's Night, A, 97, 100,
    101 (credits)
Hardy, Oliver, *20*, 66, 70
Harlow, 172
Harlow, Jean, *18*, 91
Harper, 62
Hart, William S., 26
Harvey, Anthony, 76
Harvey, Laurence, 204
Hathaway, Henry, 27
Hawkins, Jack, 140
Hawks, Howard, 26, 30, 35, 36, 38,
    48, 60, 61, 62, 67, 91, 104,
    122, 124, 182
Hayden, Sterling, *78*, 80
Hayworth, Rita, 122
Head, Edith, 172
Hearst, William Randolph, 148
Hecht, Ben, 237
Heflin, Van, 39
Heisler, Stuart, 172
Hell Is for Heroes, 104
Helm, Brigitte, *200*
Hemmings, David, 194
Henreid, Paul, *134*, 137
Henry V, 104, 228, 237-240, *240*,
    247 (credits)
Hepburn, Katharine, *19*, 87, 88, 215
Hermann, Bernard, 152
Herrand, Marcel, 230, *230*
Hersholt, Jean, *17*
Heston, Charlton, *58*, *58*, 59
Heydt, Louis, *61*
Higham, Charles, 153
High Noon, 26, 111
Hiroshima, Mon Amour, 104, 220,
    222-223, 225 (credits)
Hitchcock, Alfred, 30, 48, 50, *51*,
    52, 53, 55, 56, 58, 67, 161, 182,
    202-203
Holden, William, 41, *41*, 42, 44,
    107, 167, 168, 169
Holt, Tim, *122*, 245

Hopper, Dennis, *144*, 160-161, *162*, 166
Hopper, Hedda, 167, 172
Horse Soldiers, The, 30
Hour of the Wolf, 76
Houseman, John, 173
Howard, Leslie, 237
Howard, Sidney, 237
Howard, Trevor, 53
Hughes, Robert, 104
Hunchback of Notre Dame, The, 198
Hustler, The, 199
Huston, John, 48, 60, 62, *62*,
    104, 122, 128, 130, 132, 166
Huston, Walter, 122, 128, 130, 132

I

Il Bidone, 183
I'm No Angel, 21
Informer, The, 30, 219
Inside Daisy Clover, 172
Intolerance, 183, 199, 232
It Happened One Night, 66
It's Always Fair Weather,
    91, 92, 93
I Vitelloni, 183

J

Jazz Singer, The, 86
Johnny Guitar, 26
Johnston, Julanne, *17*
Jolson, Al, *16*
Jones, James, 111
Jones, L. Q., *41*
Jordan, Dorothy, 40
Joslyn, Allan, 122
Jules and Jim, 159-160, *159*,
    163 (credits)

K

Kael, Pauline, 125
Kaye, Danny, 66, 67
Kazan, Elia, 166, 219-220
Keaton, Buster, 66, 67, 70-73, *70*, *73*,
    167
Kelly, Gene, 86, 91, 93, 94
Kelly, Grace, *51*, 52, 171
Kennedy, Arthur, 140
Kennedy, Edgar, 75
Kern, Jerome, 86
Kerr, Deborah, 111, *113*
Kid, The, 67
Kilian, Victor, 122
King, Henry, 104
Kitses, Jim, 35
Klein-Rogge, Rudolf, *200*
Klossowski, Pierre, 192
Korda, Alexander, 53
Kramer, Stanley, 104, 114, 215
Krasker, Robert, 53
Kubrick, Stanley, 27, 56, 67, 76-80,
    80, 92, 114, 116, *116*, 117, 198,
    206, 208-209, *209*, 210, 229
Kurosawa, Akira, 41, 44, 124, *125*, 126

L

Ladd, Alan, 38, 39, 40
La Dolce Vita, 154-155, *154*, *156*,
    163 (credits), 175, *176*, 183
Lady From Shanghai, The, 154
Lady Vanishes, The, 50
L'Age d'Or, 184, *185*, 187
La Grande Illusion, 104-106, *104*, *107*,
    108, 119 (credits), *144*, 145, 153

Lahr, Bert, 91
Lamarr, Hedy, 14
Lancaster, Burt, 111, 113, 172
Langdon, Harry, 66, 70
Lang, Fritz, 48, 49, 50, 67, 161,
	176, 183, 198-199, 198, 200
La Notte, 193
Lardner, Ring, Jr., 117
Lassally, Walter, 81
La Strada, 182, 183-184, 195 (credits)
Last Tango in Paris, 23, 220
Last Year in Marienbad, 175
La Terra Trema, 215
Lattuada, Alberto, 215
Laughton, Charles, 198
Laurel, Stan, 20, 66, 70
Laurentiis, Dino de, 184
L'Avventura, 193
Lawrence of Arabia, 104, 137,
	139, 140, 140, 141 (credits)
Lawrence, T. E., 139
Lean, David, 108, 137, 140, 140
Léaud, Jean-Pierre, 217, 218
Left-Handed Gun, The, 26
Legend of Lylah Clare, The, 172-173, 174
Leigh, Janet, 52, 58, 59, 202, 203
Leigh, Vivien, 228, 232, 237
Leone, Sergio, 26
Les Enfants du Paradis, 228-230, 228,
	230, 231, 247 (credits)
Lester, Richard, 97, 100, 160
L'Eventail Magique, 198
Levine, Joseph E., 175
Lewis, Jerry, 66, 67
Lifeboat, 50
Life of Crime of Archibald
	de la Cruz, The, 185
Limelight, 70, 73
Little Big Man, 26
Livingston, Margaret, 16
Lloyd, Harold, 66, 70
Lockwood, Gary, 208
Logan, Joshua, 87
Loneliness of the Long-Distance
	Runner, The, 81
Long Day's Journey into Night, 228
Longest Day, The, 104
Look Back in Anger, 81
Loren, Sophia, 23
Lorre, Peter, 48, 49, 50, 55, 137
Los Olvidados, 185
Lubitsch, Ernst, 86
Lumet, Sidney, 228

M

M, 48-50, 49, 62, 63 (credits), 199
MacDaniel, Hattie, 232
MacDonald, Jeanette, 14, 86
Mack, Marian, 73
Macready, George, 114
Maggiorani, Lamberto, 214
Magician, The, 198
Magnificent Ambersons, The, 154, 228,
	245-246, 245, 247 (credits)
Magnificent Seven, The, 124
Malden, Karl, 219, 220
Malone, Dorothy, 62
Maltese Falcon, The, 60, 62, 62
Mamoulian, Rouben, 17, 86
Manchurian Candidate, The, 198
	204, 204, 211 (credits)
Mankiewicz, Herman, 111, 152, 170, 171
Mann, Anthony, 27

Man's Fate, 166
Man Who Knew Too Much, The, 50, 52
Man Who Shot Liberty Valance, The, 30
March, Frederic, 174
Marshman, D. M., Jr., 167
Martin, Chris, 26
Martin, Jean, 223
Martin, Strother, 41
Marx Brothers, 66, 67, 73-76, 74
M*A*S*H, 117, 118, 119 (credits)
Masina, Giulietta, 182, 184
Mason, James, 174
Mastroianni, Marcello, 155, 156, 176
Mayer, Louis B., 152, 172
Maysles, Albert, 183
Mazursky, Paul, 172
McCabe and Mrs. Miller, 27, 117
McQueen, Butterfly, 237
McQueen, Steve, 62
Meek, Donald, 26
Meet Me in St. Louis, 91, 173
Méliès, Georges, 198
Menjou, Adolph, 114
Menzies, William Cameron, 237
Merrill, Gary, 171
Metropolis, 50, 198-199,
	198, 200, 211 (credits)
Mifune, Toshiro, 125, 125, 126, 128
Milestone, Lewis, 104
Miller, Arthur, 219
Minnelli, Liza, 96, 99
Minnelli, Vincente, 86, 88, 91,
	96, 172, 173, 173
Mister Roberts, 117
Mitchell, Margaret, 232
Mitchell, Thomas, 122, 122
Mix, Tom, 26
Modern Times, 67, 69
Monroe, Marilyn, 23, 171, 172
Monsieur Verdoux, 70
Monterey Pop, 97
Montgomery, Robert, 52
Moorehead, Agnes, 245, 246
Moravia, Alberto, 175
Moreau, Jeanne, 159, 160, 187
Morgan, Frank, 91
Moss, C. W., 243
Mulligan, Robert, 172
Murnau, F. W., 16, 183
Music Lovers, The, 229
My Darling Clementine, 30
Myers, Harry, 69
My Fair Lady, 87, 96

N

Navigator, The, 66
Nazarin, 185
Newman, Paul, 52, 62
Nichols, Mike, 172
Nicholson, Jack, 162
Night at the Opera, A, 75, 76
Night of the Hunter, 198
Nights of Cabiria, 183
Nilsson, Anna Q., 167
North by Northwest, 50
No Time for Sergeants, 117
Notorious, 50
Novak, Kim, 52, 173, 174, 203
Nuit et Brouillard, 222

O

Oates, Warren, 42
O'Brien, George, 16

O'Connor, Donald, 93, 94
Odets, Clifford, 172
Okada, Eiji, 222, 222
Oklahoma, 87
Oliver!, 87
Olivier, Laurence, 52, 237, 240, 240
One-Eyed Jacks, 27
Only Angels Have Wings, 35, 91,
	122-124, 122, 141 (credits)
On the Beach, 104, 215
On the Town, 87, 91, 92, 93
On the Waterfront, 171, 219-220,
	220, 223, 225 (credits)
Open City, 215, 223
Ophuls, Max, 116
Osborne, John, 67
Oscar, The, 172
O'Toole, Peter, 139, 140
Our Man in Havana, 56
Ox-Bow Incident, The, 26

P

Paisan, 215
Palance, Jack, 39, 40, 174, 175, 176
Panofsky, Erwin, 240
Passion of Anna, The, 189
Paths of Glory, 114-116, 114,
	116, 117, 119 (credits)
Peck, Gregory, 52, 215
Peckinpah, Sam, 27, 41,44, 44, 166, 183
Penn, Arthur, 27, 243
Perkins, Anthony, 52, 202, 203
Persona, 153, 189-190, 189,
	195 (credits)
Phantom of the Opera, The, 198
Pickens, Slim, 78, 80
Pinal, Silvia, 187
Pitts, ZaSu, 17
Platt, Louise, 26
Poitier, Sidney, 215
Polk, Oscar, 237
Pontecorvo, Gillo, 224, 225
Ponti, Carlo, 183
Porter, Cole, 86
Potemkin, 243
Powell, Dick, 173
Prévert, Jacques, 228, 230
Professionals, The, 124
Psycho, 198, 202-203, 202, 211 (credits)

Q

Quayle, Anthony, 140
Queen Kelly, 167
Quiet Man, The, 35
Quinn, Anthony, 139, 140, 182, 184

R

Raft, George, 21
Rains, Claude, 134, 137, 140
Rancho Notorious, 26
Ray, Aldo, 111
Raymond, Gene, 88
Rear Window, 50-53, 51, 62,
	63 (credits)
Rebecca, 240
Red Badge of Courage, The, 104
Red Desert, 193
Redgrave, Vanessa, 194
Redman, Joyce, 82
Red River, 27, 35-38, 36, 40,
	45 (credits), 124
Reed, Carol, 48, 50, 53, 55, 56, 87
Reed, Donna, 111

Renoir, Jean, 50, 91, 104, *104*,
   106, 114, 144-145, *144, 147*, 154
Resnais, Alain, 222-223, *222*
Rey, Fernando, *187*
Reynolds, Debbie, 93
Richardson, Tony, 67, 81, 82, 125
Richard III, 240
Riefenstahl, Leni, 50, 199, 214
Rio Bravo, 27, 35, 124
Ritter, Thelma, 171
Riva, Emmanuèle, 222, *222*, 223
Robin Hood, 92
Robinson, Edward G., *174, 175*
Robson, Mark, 152
Rogers, Ginger, 86, 87, 88, *88*
Rogers, Roy, 26
Rooney, Mickey, *21*, 86
Rope, 50, 52
Rosemary's Baby, 198
Rossellini, Roberto, 104, 215
Rules of the Game, 91, 144-145, *144, 147*,
   148, 154, 161, 163 (credits)
Russell, Ken, 229
Ryan, Robert, *41, 44*

S

Saadi, Yacef, 224
Saint, Eva Marie, 219, 220
Sakall, S. Z., *133*
Salou, Louis, 230
Sanders, George, 171
Sandrich, Mark, 88
Sarris, Andrew, 67, 70
Sartre, Jean-Paul, 26
Satyricon, 183, 198
Scalphunters, The, 26
Schnee, Charles, 173
Schneider, Maria, 23
Schulberg, Budd, 219
Scott, George C., 76, 78, 80
Searchers, The, 27, 30, 32, 34,
   35, 40, 45 (credits), 153
Sellers, Peter, 66, 67, 76, *76, 78*
Selzer, Milton, 173
Selznick, David O., 215, 232, *232*, 237
Sennett, Mack, 70, 81, 97
Serre, Henri, *159*
Seven Samurai, The, 41, 44, 104,
   124-128, *125, 126, 129*,
   137, 140, 141 (credits)
Seventh Seal, The, 189
Shadow of a Doubt, 50
Shane, 27, 38-40, *39*, 45 (credits)
Sharif, Omar, 140
Shaw, Irwin, 173
She Wore a Yellow Ribbon, 30
Shimura, Takashi, 124, *125*
Shoeshine, 215, 223
Shufton, Eugene, 199
Sidney, Sylvia, *17*
Siegel, Don, 48, 104
Silence, The, 189
Sinatra, Frank, 86, *108*, 111, 172, *204*
Singin' in the Rain, 87, 91,
   92-93, *94*, 101 (credits)
Skolsky, Sidney, 173
Sloane, Everett, *151*
Smiles of a Summer Night, 189
Snow White, 92
Sound of Music, The, 96
Spaak, Charles, 104
Spartacus, 116, 229
Spellbound, 50

Stagecoach, 26, 27-30, *29, 31*,
   45 (credits)
Staiola, Enzo, 214
Stanley, Kim, 172, 174
Stanwyck, Barbara, *18*
Star, The, 172
Star Is Born, A, 91, 172, 174
Steiger, Rod, 172, 219, 220
Stevens, George, 27, 38, 39, 40
Stewart, James, 50, *51*, 52, 203
Stolen Kisses, 217
Story of G.I. Joe, The, 104
Story of Vernon and Irene Castle, The, 88
Strangers on a Train, 50, 52
Streisand, Barbra, 86, 87
Stroheim, Erich von, 104, 106, 132,
   166, 167, 168, 169, 229
Sturges, Preston, 172
Sullivan's Travels, 172
Sunrise, 16
Sunset Boulevard, 53, 73, 166, 167-168,
   169, 170, 171, 172, 179 (credits)
Suspicion, 50
Sutherland, Donald, *118*
Swanson, Gloria, *166, 167, 168*,
   169, 170, 171
Sweet Charity, 96
Sylbert, Richard, 228

T

Tamiroff, Akim, *58, 59*
Taradash, Daniel, 111
Taste of Honey, A, 81
Taylor, Elizabeth, 23
Taylor, Robert, *18*
Temple, Shirley, 86, 91
They Were Expendable, 104
Third Man, The, 50, 53-56, *55*,
   62, 63 (credits), 148
39 Steps, The, 50, 52
Threepenny Opera, The, 96
3:10 to Yuma, 26
Through a Glass Darkly, 189
Time Out for War, A, 104
To Have and Have Not, 61, 124
Toland, Gregg, *151, 152*, 245, 246
To Live in Peace, 215
Tom Jones, 67, 81, 82, 83 (credits)
Top Hat, 86, 88, *88*, 101 (credits)
Touch of Evil, 56-59, *56, 58*, 62,
   63 (credits), 154
Tracy, Spencer, *18*, 87, 88, 215
Tragic Chase, 215
Traven, B., 128
Treasure of the Sierra Madre, The,
   122, 128-129, *130*, 141 (credits)
Trevor, Claire, 27
Trial, The, 198
Triumph of the Will, 199
Trouble with Harry, The, 67
Truffaut, François, 52, 94,
   159-160, *159*, 202-203, 217, *218*
Twelve O'Clock High, 104
2001: A Space Odyssey, 27, 116, 198,
   199, 206, 208-209, *209*,
   210, 211 (credits)
Two Weeks in Another Town,
   173-175, *173, 174*
Two Women, 104
Turner, Lana, 18, 173, *173*

U

Ullmann, Liv, *189, 190*

Un Chien Andalou, 184, *185, 187*
Unforgiven, The, 26

V

Valentino, Rudolph, *13*
Veidt, Conrad, *134, 137*
Vertigo, 50, 52, 203
Victors, The, 104
Vigo, Jean, 183
Virginian, The, 26
Viridiana, 117, *118*, 184-185, *185*,
   187, 195 (credits)
Visconti, Luchino, 73, 215, 220

W

Wagon Master, 30, 35
Walker, Alexander, 114
Wallach, Eli, *108*
Walsh, Raoul, 48
Warner, H. B., 167
Warner, Jack, 132
Warrick, Ruth, *151*
Way Down East, 16
Wayne, John, 26, *26*, 27, 29, 32,
   34, 35, 36, 38, 40
Weekend, 198, 206, *206*, 208,
   211 (credits)
Weill, Kurt, 96
Welles, Orson, 30, 48, 53,
   55, 56, *56*, 58, 59, 67,
   148-154, *148, 151, 152*, 166,
   175, 177, 178, 198, 240, 245
Wellman, William, 172
Werner, Oskar, *159*
Wernicke, Otto, 49
West, Mae, *21*, 66
West Side Story, 96
Wiazemsky, Anne, 192
Wicki, Bernard, 104
Wiene, Robert, 199
Wild Bunch, The, 27, 40-44, *41, 42*,
   44, 45 (credits), 104, 124, 161
Wilder, Billy, 67, 73, 166, 167,
   170, 175
Wild Strawberries, 189
Wilson, Dooley, *134*
Winchester .73, 26
Winter Light, 189
Wise, Robert, 96, 152
Without Pity, 215
Wizard of Oz, The, 87, 91-92,
   91, 92, 96, 101 (credits), 237
Wollen, Peter, 182
Women in Love, 229
Wood, Natalie, 34, 38, 172
Woods, Eddie, 21
Woodstock, 97
Wyler, William, 87, 104
Wynn, Kennan, 78, 80

Y

Yates, Peter, 62
York, Susannah, 81
Young, Freddy, 140
Young Lions, The, 104

Z

Zabriskie Point, 183
Zampa, Luigi, 215
Zanuck, Darryl, 104
Zavattini, Caesare, 214, *216*
Zéro de Conduite, 183
Zinnemann, Fred, 87, 111, *111*, 116

252